The Struggle of the
Shi'is in Indonesia

THE STRUGGLE OF THE SHI'IS IN INDONESIA

by Zulkifli

Australian National University

E PRESS

ANU
E PRESS

Published by ANU E Press
The Australian National University
Canberra ACT 0200, Australia
Email: anuepress@anu.edu.au
This title is also available online at http://epress.anu.edu.au

National Library of Australia Cataloguing-in-Publication entry

Author:	Zulkifli.
Title:	The struggle of the Shi'is in Indonesia / Zulkifli.
ISBN:	9781925021295 (paperback) 9781925021301 (ebook)
Subjects:	Shiites--Indonesia. Shī'ah--Relations--Sunnites. Sunnites--Relations--Shī'ah. Shī'ah--Indonesia--History. Minorities--Indonesia--History.
Dewey Number:	297.8042

Cover design and layout by ANU E Press

Islam in Southeast Asia Series

Theses at The Australian National University are assessed by external examiners and students are expected to take into account the advice of their examiners before they submit to the University Library the final versions of their theses. For this series, this final version of the thesis has been used as the basis for publication, taking into account other changes that the author may have decided to undertake. In some cases, a few minor editorial revisions have made to the work. The acknowledgements in each of these publications provide information on the supervisors of the thesis and those who contributed to its development. For many of the authors in this series, English is a second language and their texts reflect an appropriate fluency.

Contents

Curriculum Vitae

Zulkifli was born on 13th of August 1966 in Bangka, Indonesia. He completed a *doctorandus* (BA Hons) degree in 1990 in the Faculty of Tarbiyah (Education), the State Institute for Islamic Studies (IAIN, Institut Agama Islam Negeri) Raden Fatah in Palembang. In 1991 he was appointed Lecturer in the same faculty and in 1998 he was transferred to the Faculty of Adab (Arts) of the same institute. From 1992 to 1994 he pursued his MA program in the field of Anthropology at The Australian National University, Canberra. From 2001 to 2005 he conducted his PhD program at Leiden University under the Indonesia-Netherlands Cooperation in Islamic Studies (INIS) and was awarded the degree in 2009. In 2007 he was promoted to Provisional Chairman of the State College for Islamic Studies (STAIN, Sekolah Tinggi Agama Islam Negeri) Syaikh Abdurrahman Siddik Bangka Belitung, Indonesia. At present he is Lektor Kapala (Associate Professor) and Head of the Department of Sociology, Faculty of Social and Political Sciences, Syarif Hidayatullah State Islamic University, Jakarta. Zulkifli publishes widely in both English and Indonesian.

Acknowledgements

This publication has grown out of an academic endeavour that has been nourished by the support, suggestions and advice from individuals and institutions to whom I am indebted. I wish I could mention them all. I shall record the great debt to INIS (Indonesia-Netherlands Cooperation in Islamic Studies) for the scholarship and facilities that enabled me to conduct research and academic activities. At INIS, I sincerely thank Prof. W.A.L. Stokhof, Dick van der Meij, Rosemary Robson in Leiden and Prof. Jacob Vredenbregt in Jakarta. My gratitude is also expressed to the International Institute for Asian Studies (IIAS) for its programs and academic atmosphere that enabled me to increase my academic quality and extend my scholarly network.

My sincere gratitude is expressed to all the Shi'i informants and respondents who became the subject of my research. They provided me the chance to interview them, use their collections and even participate in a variety of their activities. Without their permission and cooperation this present work would not have been completed.

My special thanks also go to IAIN Raden Fatah Palembang, particularly the Faculty of Adab, which freed me from academic duties during my PhD program.

I also thank my fellow Indonesian scholars in Leiden. They assisted me in their own ways, which were important for my life in Leiden. Mufti Ali, Anwar Syarifuddin, Didin Nurul Rosidin, Muslih, Euis Nurlaelawati, Jajat Burhanudin, Noorhaidi, Noor Ichwan, Arief Subhan, Dahlan and Suryadi are only some of the names I could mention here.

Last, but not least, I thank my wife, Ai Juariah, my daughter Dhea UZ and my son Azka KZ who gave me the moral support to finish this thesis which is dedicated to them.

Leiden-Sukabumi, 2008

Foreword to *The Struggle of the Shi'is in Indonesia*

James J. Fox

Zulkifli's *The Struggle of the Shi'is in Indonesia* is a pioneering work. It is the first comprehensive scholarly examination in English of the development of Shiism in Indonesia. It focuses primarily on the important period between 1979 and 2004 – a period of nearly a quarter of a century that saw the notable dissemination of Shi'i ideas and a considerable expansion of the number of Shi'i adherents in Indonesia. Since Islam in Indonesia is overwhelmingly Sunni, this development of Shiism in a predominantly Sunni context is a remarkable phenomenon that calls for careful, critical investigation. Zulkifli has provided precisely this much needed investigation. His work offers both a starting point for understanding and a foundation for future research.

This book gives evidence of a depth of engaged, sympathetic research on and among the key figures who were critically involved in the development of Shiism in Indonesia and on their social and intellectual backgrounds. There is also an important examination of the principal ideas underlying the *Madhab Ahl al-Bayt,* the Imamate and Imam Madhi, *Ja'fari* jurisprudence and ritual piety. Appropriately, in his discussion, Zulkifli provides a succinct outline of contrasts with Sunni ideas and practice. He also examines the publishing efforts that underpinned the dissemination of Shi'i ideas and the founding of IJABI (*Ikatan Jamaah Ahlul Bait Indonesia*) in July 2000 for the propagation of *Ahl al-Bayt* teachings. Given the Indonesian context, Zulkifli is also concerned with Sunni reactions to these Shi'i developments – a story that continues to unfold to the present.

It is particularly appropriate that Zulkifli's work appear in this ANU series on Islam. Zulkifli did his MA in Anthropology at ANU for which he wrote a thesis entitled *Sufism in Java: The Role of the Pesantren in the Maintenance of Sufism in Java*. Besides its general discussion, this thesis focused specifically on Pesantren Tarekat Suryalaya in Tasikmalaya in West Java. Zulkifli's thesis formed part of a succession of ANU studies on Indonesia's *pesantren* that began with Zamaksyari Dhofier's study of Tebuireng in 1980.

Scholars at Leiden University, who became aware of Zulkifli's research and eventually succeeded in bringing him to Leiden for his PhD research made an effort, as well, to publish his ANU thesis in the Leiden INIS series in 2002. Now ANU has the opportunity to reciprocate by publishing Zulkifli's Leiden PhD in the ANU E Press series on Islam.

For me personally, it is a special privilege to be able to recommend this work, as I recommended his earlier work, to a wider audience. I regard this book as a work of great value and significance for the continuing understanding of the richness and complexity of Indonesian Islam.

Wendy Mukherjee of the College of Asia and the Pacific, ANU prepared the thesis for ANU E Press publication.

A Note on Transliteration

For Arabic terminology I have used the system of transliteration adopted by the *International Journal of Middle East Studies* but diacritics have been reduced for simplification. For the plural forms of Indonesian words I do not always add 's' and such words as *santri* and *pesantren* may be singular or plural. I maintain the plural forms of certain Arabic words like *'ulama* (singular, *'alim*) and *maraji'* (singular, *marja'*). In the matter of personal names, I follow exactly the way they are written by themselves or as they appear in the sources that I cite. For the translation of Qur'anic verses, I use Abdullah Yusuf Ali's *The Meaning of the Holy Qur'an*, New Edition with Revised Translation and Commentary, 1991.

Glossary

abangan: Javanese nominal Muslims

adat: indigenous tradition, customary law

adhan: the call to prayer

'adl: justice

ahl al-sunnah wa al-jama'ah (*ahlussunnah waljamaah*) Sunnis, distinguished from the Shi'is; refers to traditional orthodox Islam which follows Ash'ari theology, Shafi'i jurisprudence and al-Ghazali's Sufism

ahl al-bayt: literally 'the people of the house'; the Prophet Muhammad's household: himself, 'Ali and Fatimah and their sons Hasan and Husayn, also spelled variously as *ahl ul-bayt* and *ahli bait*.

ajengan: title of *'ulama* in West Java, equivalent to the term *kyai* in Central and East Java

akhlaq: morality, ethics

'alim (singular) / 'ulama (plural): Muslim scholar/s

'aql: reason

Arba'in: literally 'forty'; the commemoration of the fortieth day after the martyrdom of the third Imam, Husayn

'Ashura: anniversary of the martyrdom of Imam Husayn, commemorated on the tenth day of Muharram, the first month of the Muslim calendar

Ayatollah: Ayat Allah, literally 'Sign of God'; honorific title bestowed upon a Shi'i *mujtahid*

Ayatollah Uzma: 'Grand Ayatollah'; honorific title bestowed upon the Shi'i *marja' al-taqlid*

da'wa or *dakwah*: Islamic missionary activity, outreach, predication

da'i: propagandist, evangelist, one who carries out Islamic propagation

DDII: Dewan Dakwah Islam Indonesia [Indonesian Islamic Missionary Council]

DEPAG: Departemen Agama [Indonesian Ministry of Religious Affairs]

dhikr: literally, 'remembrance' of God, Sufi practices

DI/NII: Darul Islam/Negara Islam Indonesia [House of Islam/Islamic State of Indonesia]; Indonesian rebellion and movement for an Islamic state, 1948-1962; nowadays remains active in a largely non-violent form

do'a: supplication, prayer

DPC: Dewan Pimpinan Cabang, Sub-District Leadership Council

DPD: Dewan Pimpinan Daerah, District Leadership Council

DPW: Dewan Pimpinan Wilayah, Provincial Leadership Council

FAJAR: Forum Jamaah Ahlul Bait Jawa Timur [Forum of East Java Ahl al-Bayt Congregations]

faqih: jurist, expert in Islamic jurisprudence

fatwa: religious opinion issued by an authorised Islamic scholar

fiqh: Islamic jurisprudence

Golkar: Golongan Karya, 'Functional Group'; the political party of the New Order government

Hadith: account of the words and deeds of the Prophet Muhammad transmitted through a chain of narrators; with the Qur'an, the basic source of Islamic law

Hawl: the annual commemoration of the death of a saint or a scholar, observed especially among Shi'is

hawzah 'ilmiyya: college of learning in the Shi'i world, notably in Qum, Iran

hikayat: Malay historical tale or account

HMI: Himpunan Mahasiswa Islam [Association of Muslim University Students]

HMI MPO: Himpunan Mahasiswa Islam Majelis Penyelamat Organisasi [Council of Organisation of Saviours of the Association of Islamic University Students]

HPI: Himpunan Pelajar Indonesia [Association of Indonesian Students]

Hujjat al-Islam: literally, 'Proof of Islam'; title of an aspiring Shi'i *mujtahid*

IAIN: Institut Agama Islam Negeri [State Institute for Islamic Studies]

'ibadat: worship; the rituals and religious duties in Islam

ICC: Islamic Cultural Center of al-Huda, Jakarta

ICIS: International Center for Islamic Studies

ICMI: Ikatan Cendekiawan Muslim se-Indonesia [Association of Indonesian Muslim Intellectuals]

'Id al-Ghadir: (celebration of) the Day of the Prophet's designation of 'Ali as his successor at Ghadir Khumm

IJABI: Ikatan Jamaah Ahlul Bait Indonesia [Indonesian Council of Ahl al-Bayt Associations]

ijaza: license, the authority granted by a *mujtahid* to a student to exercise *ijtihad*

ijma': agreement or consensus of expert legal opinions in Islam

ijtihad: independent interpretation of Islamic doctrine or question based on a sufficient knowledge of the Qur'an and Sunnah

Ikhwan al-Muslimin: 'Muslim Brotherhood', reform movement founded in Egypt by Hasan al-Banna in 1928; of influence in Indonesia

IKIP: Institut Keguruan dan Ilmu Pendidikan [Institute of Teacher Training and Pedagogy]

Imam: 'leader' in matters religious, spiritual and political; honorific title for those believed by Shi'is to be the successors of the Prophet Muhammad

imamate: such leadership based on divine appointment, a basic tenet of Shi'ism

IPABI: Ikatan Pemuda Ahlul Bait Indonesia [Indonesian Association of Ahl al-Bayt Youth]

Iqro': literally, 'reading'; a 'modern' method of learning Qur'anic recitation

Al-Irsyad: 'The Guidance', non-Sayyid Arab Sunni reformist organisation and system of schools, founded in 1914

ITB: Institut Teknologi Bandung [Bandung Institute of Technology]

Ithna 'Ashari: Ja'fari or 'Twelver' jusrisprudence followed by Indonesian Shi'is

'itra: progeny, for Shi'is especially the Prophet's descent

JABODEBEK: abbreviation of Jakarta, Bogor, Depok, Bekasi

jahiliyya: 'ignorance'; refers historically to pre-Islamic society in Arabia

jama'a: religious congregation or community

Jami'iat Khair: mainly Sayyid Arab Muslim organisation, founded in 1901

kafa'a: compatibility or equality between partners in marriage, Sayyid practice

Khums: literally 'one-fifth'; religious tax of one-fifth upon certain categories of goods and income paid by Shi'is, originally paid to the Prophet Muhammad and the Imam. Now paid to the *marja' al-taqlid* in his capacity as representative of the Imam

KIBLAT: Komunitas Ahlul Bait Jawa Barat [West Java Ahl al-Bayt Community]

KKM: Kuliah Kader Muballigh [Courses for Preacher Cadres]

LDII: Lembaga Dakwah Islam Indonesia [Institute of Indonesian Islamic Propagation]

LDK: Lembaga Dakwah Kampus [Institute of Campus Mosques and Da'wa]

LPII: Lembaga Pembinaan Ilmu-ilmu Islam [Institute for the Establishment of Islamic Sciences]

LPPI: Lembaga Penelitian dan Pengkajian Islam [Institute of Islamic Studies and Research]

madhhab: school of Islamic jurisprudence

madrasah: literally 'school'; modernized Islamic school offering both religious and general subjects

Mahdi: the expected final Imam, a key concept in Shi'ism

MAHDI: Majlis Ahlulbait di Indonesia [Council of the Ahl al-Bayt in Indonesia]

majlis ta'lim: 'council of learning', religious educational gatherings

maqtal: account of the massacre of Imam Husayn and his followers at Karbala on 9 Muharram 61 AH (680 CE)

Marja' al-taqlid: literally, 'reference for emulation'; in Shi'ism the authoritative source who through his learning and probity is to be followed by the laity in all points of religious practice and law

marja'iya: the position of the source of imitation; also the relationship between *marja'al-taqlid* and the *muqallid* or laity

Masjumi: Madjelis Sjuro Muslimin Indonesia [Consultative Council of Indonesian Muslims]

ma'tam: chest-beating as a sign of mourning in the *'Ashura* ritual

Mawlid: the celebration of the Prophet Muhammad's birthday

MPR: Majelis Permusyawaratan Rakyat [People's Consultative Assembly]

mu'amalat: social transactions and dealings governed by Islamic law

muballigh: Muslim preacher

Muhammadiyah: Indonesia's largest reformist Muslim organization, founded in 1912

MUI: Majelis Ulama Indonesia [Council of Indonesian Muslim Scholars]

muqallid: 'imitator'; an ordinary believer who follows a *mujtahidin* in Shi'ism

mustad'afin: the very poor and oppressed, to be helped by Shi'i social work

mut'a: 'temporary' marriage, a practice specific to Shi'ism

Mutahhari Foundation: Shi'i educational institution in Bandung, best known for its SMU Plus schooling programme combining Islamic studies with the national curriculum

NKK: Normalisasi Kehidupan Kampus [the Normalization of Campus Life]

NU: Nahdlatul Ulama [Revival of Religious Scholars]; Indonesia's largest traditionalist Muslim organization, founded in 1926

PAN: Partai Amanat Nasional [National Mandate Party]

Pancasila: 'Five Pillars'; the ideological and political foundation of the Republic of Indonesia consisting of five principles: belief in one supreme God; a just and civilized humanity; the unity of Indonesia; popular rule through policies formed after representative consensus, and social justice

PDIP: Indonesian Democratic Party of Struggle

pengajian: religious gathering(s)

Persis: Persatuan Islam [Islamic Association]; strict reformist Muslim organization, founded in 1923

pesantren: traditional Islamic boarding school(s), educational institution(s)

PHBI: Perayaan Hari-hari Besar Islam [Commemoration of Islamic Holy Days]

PKB: Partai Kebangkitan Bangsa [National Awakening Party]

PKI: Partai Komunis Indonesia [Indonesian Communist Party]

pondok: hostel(s), dormitory accommodation within the *pesantren* complex

priyayi: Javanese nobility, member of the Javanese official administrative class

Qur'an: God's word revealed to the Prophet Muhammad and absolute authority for Islam

ratib: formulae of *dhikr* and prayers formulated by a Sufi teacher

Ratu Adil: 'Just King'; a millennial expectation in Java

Reformasi: 'Reform'; generally meaning political liberation and economic transparency; also refers to the period following the end of Suharto's New Order

Salafism: or *Wahhabism*, strict and puritanical Sunni movement seeking to return to the example of the earliest generations of Muslims

salawat: praise and invocation of the Prophet Muhammad and his family

santri: student(s) of the *pesantren*

Sayyid: descendant of the Prophet Muhammad through Fatimah and 'Ali, thence through their sons Hasan and Husayn

sekolah: 'school' of the modern Western educational system in Indonesia

Shafi'i jurisprudence: the Sunni Islamic law school of the Indonesian Muslim majority

shariah: Islamic law

SMU Plus: Sekolah Menengah Umum Plus, Senior High School with attribute 'Plus' special training

SLTP: Sekolah Lanjutan Tingkat Pertama, Junior High School

STAIN: Sekolah Tinggi Agama Islam Negeri [State University of Islamic Studies]

Sunnah: established custom and normative precedent based on the example of the life of the Prophet Muhammad

tabaruk: the taking of blessing from the Prophet Muhammad and other pious persons through touching any object related to them

tabligh: religious preaching

ta'lim: religious teaching

Tabut: the annual Shi'i observance in Bengkulu and Pariaman, West Sumatera to commemorate the martyrdom of Imam Husayn

tafsir: exegesis, explanation or interpretation of the text of the Qur'an

tawassul: supplications to God by the uttering of names of persons having a high position at His side

TBC: *Tahayul, Bid'ah, Churafat* [Superstition, Innovation, Myth] the targets of Islamic reform

taqiyya: the dissimulation of religious faith in order to protect one's self, family or property from harm, or for the sake of Islamic fraternity; an accepted practice of Shi'ism

taqlid: 'emulation' or 'imitation'; the following of the dictates of a *mujtahid* in Shi'ism

Thaqalayn: literally 'two weighty matters'; the two safeguards of Shi'i Muslims, the Qur'an and the persons of the Prophet Muhammad's household

TK/TPA: Taman Kanak-kanak/Taman Pendidikan Al-Qur'an [Kindergarten/ Qur'an Kindergarten]

UI: Universitas Indonesia [University of Indonesia]

UII: Universitas Islam Indonesia [Islamic University of Indonesia]

UNPAD: Universitas Padjadjaran [Pajajaran University], West Java

UIN: Universitas Islam Negeri [State Islamic University]

umma: the community of Muslim believers

ustadh: Muslim religious teacher

'ulama: Muslim religious scholars

wali: guardian, helper or defender; Sufi saint

Wali Sanga: the 'Nine Saints' who introduced Islam in Java

Wilayat al-Faqih: literally 'guardian of the jurist'; the Shi'i concept that government belongs by right to those who are learned in Islamic jurisprudence, the persons called *walifaqih*

Wujudiyya: Sufi teaching of the unity of being (of God and His creation)

YAPI: Yayasan Pesantren Islam [Foundation of Islamic Pesantren] a *pesantren* established in 1976 and located in Bangil, East Java; also Yayasan Penyiaran Islam [Foundation of Islamic Propagation] in Jakarta

Ziyara: the visitation of the graves of Muslim saints and eminent teachers

Introduction

This study is concerned with the Shi'is[1] of Indonesia, their position as a minority Muslim group within a population of an overwhelming Sunni majority and the ways in which they act to gain recognition in the country. For the purposes of this study, Shi'ism is confined to the *Ithna 'Ashariyya* (also known as Twelver or *Ja'fari*) form of Shi'ism. This is a *madhhab,* or school of Islamic jurisprudence which venerates the twelve Imams who succeeded the Prophet Muhammad and has adopted a specific set of practices as a consequence of its belief system. Shi'ism is a minority denomination of Islam and the Shi'is, constituting around 10 percent of the world's Muslim population, have frequently been stigmatised by Sunnis. While most Shi'is reside as a minority group in Muslim countries, they form a majority in Iran of around 90 percent, in Iraq of 60 percent and in Bahrain of 60 percent. The Shi'is of Iran came to the world's attention with the Islamic revolution of 1978-79 and the subsequent establishment of the Islamic Republic of Iran. Following the American invasion of Iraq in 2003, the Shi'is there have played an increasingly significant political role and a moderate form of Shi'ism, adhered to by Ayatollah Ali Sistani, has formed a powerful web of networks that is expected to strengthen civil society in the south of the country.

Scholars, not only in the Muslim world but also in the West, have generally focussed their attention on Sunnism. In the Muslim world Shi'ism is often seen as a heterodox schism deviating from the true teachings of Islam with regard to its theology and jurisprudence. Western scholars of Islam, who once relied on Sunni interpretations of Shi'ism, have contributed to misconceptions about its nature. Kohlberg[2] reveals that this lack of appropriate understanding of Shi'ism can easily be found in the writings of the prominent German Islamologist, Goldziher and others. Shi'ism did not become a subject of central research until the Iranian revolution forced scholars to understand its ideological foundation, which is strongly rooted in Shi'i tenets.[3] This led to the association of Shi'ism with radical and revolutionary movements, while creating an impression that Shi'ism is identified with Iranian society and culture. Indeed, as a result of Iran's ambitious attempts to export its version of revolution to other Muslim countries, studies of Shi'ism outside Iran tend to attempt to measure the effects of the Iranian revolution on Shi'i communities in Iraq, the Gulf states, Lebanon, Syria and South Asia,[4] as well as on Sunni communities in Southeast Asia.[5] However,

---

1 In this thesis, I hardly ever use the term 'Shi'a' and when it is used, it refers to the generic meaning, 'partition'. I use the term Shi'ism to denote the denomination as opposed to Sunnism. The term Shi'i is used both as adjective and human noun.
2 Kohlberg (1987).
3 Kohlberg (1987:41).
4 See collection of articles edited by Kramer (1987).
5 Esposito (1990) and Menashri (1990).

more than a quarter of a century on, no revolution following the Iranian model has occurred elsewhere, even in countries such as Iraq and Bahrain, where the Shi'is constitute a clear majority and where Iran has allegedly supported Shi'i movements. What is striking is that in the eight-year war between Iran and Iraq between 1980 and 1988, Iranian Shi'is in battle against Iraqi soldiers were fighting their co-religionists. In this regard, Nakash has shown historical, economic and political features of Iraqi Shi'i society that differ significantly from that of Shi'is in Iran.[6] This clearly indicates that a monolithic perspective on Shi'ism does not aid our understanding of the diverse realities of its adherents. Any study of Shi'ism necessitates a consideration of social, political and cultural aspects unique to a particular society, region and history, for the simple fact that Shi'is have "employed a wide range of strategies in different times and places."[7]

While the Sunnism that predominates in Indonesia has been widely studied by scholars employing a variety of approaches, the reality of Shi'ism in Indonesia and its related historical, sociological, political and religious dimensions is hardly known among scholars or even among the majority of Muslims themselves. This present study attempts to address this imbalance and to understand the reality of the Shi'is in Indonesia. It describes the main aspects of the social and religious life of this minority Muslim group, including the formation of the Shi'i denomination, an examination of its prominent leaders, beliefs and practices, *da'wa,* or missionary outreach, education, publications, organisations and Sunni responses. Furthermore, an understanding of the Shi'is is crucial to our understanding of Indonesian religion and society at large.

Previous Studies on Shi'ism in Indonesia

Despite the fact of their minority in Indonesia, a number of scholars (including Muslim scholars), historians and social scientists have written articles or books concerned with aspects of Shi'ism in this region. In particular, historians and Muslim scholars studying the historical Islamisation of the Indonesian archipelago have dealt with the development of Shi'ism in the country. Here we find two opposing views with regard to whether it was Sunnism or Shi'ism which came first to the area: the first theory, widely accepted among historians, social scientists and Indonesian Muslim scholars such as Hamka[8] and Azra,[9] neglects the existence of Shi'ism and generally affirms that Sunnism was the first branch of Islam to arrive in Indonesia and so continues to predominate

---

6   Nakash (1994).
7   Kramer (1987:2).
8   Hamka (1974).
9   Azra (1992, 1995).

today. In contrast, proponents of the 'Shi'i theory' such as Fatimi,[10] Jamil,[11] Hasymi,[12] Azmi,[13] Atjeh[14] and Sunyoto,[15] believe that the Shi'is have been present in Indonesia since the earliest days of Islamisation and that in fact its adherents have played an important part in this process. Their theory is based on elements of Shi'i tradition maintained by Muslim communities in the Malay-Indonesian archipelago, as well as on Arabic, Chinese and local written sources and on existing material cultures. Proponents of this theory generally admit however that most traces of Shi'ism have vanished over the course of time and as a result of the huge impact that Sunnism has had on the country.

Fatimi, Azmi, and Atjeh establish the view that Shi'ism came to the Malay-Indonesian world prior to Sunni Islam's influence on the region. Like their opponents, the proponents of the Shi'i theory believe the present Province of Aceh to be the first place in Indonesia to experience Islamisation. Aboebakar Atjeh speculates that Arabs, Persians or Indians coming from Gujarat, India - all followers of Shi'ism - were among the first propagators of Islam in the archipelago.[16] Kern shares a similar opinion, arguing that the influence of Shi'ism in Gujarat had not been less than in other areas of India.[17] Fatimi points to the kingdom of Champa, in parts of present day Vietnam and Cambodia, as the place from which the Shi'is came to the Malay-Indonesian areas of Southeast Asia. According to Fatimi, there is a strong possibility that there were "Muslim settlements in the neighbourhood of Champa in the second half of the 8th century" which adhered to Shi'ism.[18] Using a variety of sources, he also tries to show the close, though often neglected, relationship between the Chams and the Malays throughout history from the 7th century onwards.[19] Following Fatimi's viewpoint, Azmi tries to connect Fatimi's description with the development of Muslim kingdoms in Aceh. He goes on to point out that the Shi'is then spread through trading centres in Southeast Asia, including Perlak in Northern Sumatra, which is said to have become the first Muslim Sultanate in the Malay-Indonesian archipelago.[20]

The first Shi'i ruler of the Perlak sultanate is said to be Sultan Alaiddin Sayyid Maulana Abdul Azis Shah, who reigned from 840 until 864. However, during the reign of the third king, Sultan Alaiddin Sayyid Maulana Abbas Shah (888-913),

---

10   Fatimi (1963).
11   Jamil quoted in Hasyimi (1983) and Azra (1995).
12   Hasyimi (1983).
13   Azmi (1981).
14   Atjeh (1977, 1985).
15   Sunyoto (n.d.).
16   Atjeh (1977:31, 1985:21).
17   Kern (2001:85).
18   Fatimi (1963:47-53).
19   Fatimi (1963:53-55).
20   Azmi (1981:198).

Sunnism began to spread and exert influence on the Perlak population.[21] In this regard, writers such as Azmi, Jamil and Hasjmy, who base their theories on local sources, conclude that the Shi'is not only arrived in the early days of Islamisation but held considerable political power in the archipelago. Yet it was at this time that the Shi'is and the Sunnis became embroiled in a long and bitter political struggle. These scholars suggest that around the end of the 10th century, as a result of four years of outright civil war between Shi'is and Sunnis, the Perlak sultanate was divided into two: Shi'i coastal Perlak and Sunni hinterland Perlak. Both territories had their own kings. It is suggested that the two kingdoms were united in the face of an attack from the kingdom of Sriwijaya to the south. During the long war which ensued, the Shi'i king died, marking the end of the Shi'i sultanate in Aceh. Sriwijaya ceased its attack and the Sunni Perlak sultanate continued to exist until its collapse in 1292.[22] Sunyoto, acknowledging the existence of the Shi'i Perlak sultanate for nearly a century, points out that its collapse caused Shi'i followers to migrate to other regions. Some moved to Pasai, an area dominated by the Sunnis, and Sunyoto suggests that the resulting interrelationship between the two branches of Islam led to a specific formulation of Shi'ism and Sunnism. He goes on to claim that while officially the Muslims in Pasai followed the Shafi'i school of Sunni jurisprudence, they also practiced certain Shi'i rituals and ceremonies such as the commemoration of the martyrdom of Husayn, or 'Ashura, the celebration of the fifteenth day of the eighth month in the Muslim calendar, Nisf Sha'ban, the commemoration of the dead on the first, third, seventh, fortieth days and so on after death, and the annual death commemoration known as Hawl.[23]

Sunyoto goes on to apply his theories to the Muslims in Java. He suggests that these Shi'i traditions were also taught in Java by some of the Wali Sanga[24] or Nine Saints, who were known to have propagated Islam among the population of the island. According to Sunyoto, two of them in particular, Sunan Kalijaga and Syaikh Siti Jenar, were responsible for popularising Shi'i traditions. He admits, however, that in contrast to these two saints, the majority of Wali Sanga expounded Sunni Islam. A moderate figure, Sunan Bonang attempted to bridge the two opposing groups. Sunyoto emphasises that this moderate, 'third way' - culturally Shi'i but theologically Sunni - had a great impact on the formulation of Islam in Java.[25] Basing his ideas on a local Javanese source, the Babad Tanah Jawi (History of the Land of Java) Muhaimin points out that Shaykh Siti Jenar,

---

21   Azmi (1981:198).
22   Azmi (1981:199-200), Hasjmi (1983:45-47).
23   Sunyoto (n.d:27-29).
24   The names of the Nine Saints are frequently given as Maulana Malik Ibrahim, Sunan Ampel, Sunan Bonang, Sunan Derajat, Sunan Giri, Sunan Kudus, Sunan Muria, Sunan Kalijaga and Sunan Gunung Jati (Zuhri 1981:247-352). Many studies such as Salam (1960), Sunyoto (n.d.), Fox (1991) and Van Dijk (1998) have been devoted to the role of Wali Sanga in the propagation of Islam in Java.
25   Sunyoto (n.d:105-108).

also known as Lemah Abang, was said to follow Twelver Shi'ism, upholding "a doctrine that claims that the Imam should be the supreme political figure in the state". This doctrine, also adhered to by the Persian Sufi martyr Mansur al-Hallaj (d. 922),[26] is the Sufi *wujudiyya* doctrine of the unity of God and man. Muhaimin suggests that Siti Jenar came to Java from Baghdad and is said to have converted a number of rulers and their subjects on the island.[27] Similarly, Rachman tries to trace Shi'i philosophical and pragmatic elements in Java. He points to the belief in the arrival of the Imam Mahdi, the twelfth Imam of Shi'ism, a belief which has been traditionally and historically significant in Java. Even though Rachman agrees with the rather speculative view that the Islam that first came to the archipelago was Sunni and Sufi Islam, he supports the hypothesis that there was peaceful interaction between Sunnis and Shi'is. This interaction "greatly and equally contributed to the emergence of the unique Islamic community in the region."[28]

Another issue relevant to the study of Shi'ism in Indonesia is the widespread commemoration of *'Ashura*, the anniversary of the martyrdom of Imam Husayn, the Prophet's grandson and the third Shi'i Imam, at the battle of Karbala in Iraq, on 10 October 680 (10 Muharram 61AH).[29] The *'Ashura* ceremony is generally celebrated throughout Indonesia with the cooking of red and white rice porridge (*bubur sura*), while on the west coast of Sumatra, in Bengkulu and Pariaman, a *Tabut* (in Iran, *ta'ziya*)[30] ceremony takes place instead, with the parading of ritual sarcophagi of Imam Husayn. Snouck Hurgronje provides us with an interesting account of the ceremonies related to *'Ashura* festivals held in Aceh, as well as in Bengkulu and Pariaman at the end of the 19th century. He suggests that this celebration originated during one of two waves of Shi'i influence in Indonesia in the late-17th and early 18th centuries, at a time when the British brought in *Sipahis* (Sepoys) from India.[31] Djajadiningrat remarks that widespread ceremonies in Indonesia relating to the martyrdom of Husayn clearly indicate a Shi'i influence on Indonesian Islam.[32] Kartomi[33] and Feener[34] have provided anthropological accounts of the *Tabut* ceremony in Pariaman and Bengkulu respectively. Kartomi uncovered evidence of substantial Shi'i elements in the coastal Sumatran towns, including the annual *Tabut* festival.

---

26   Mansur al-Hallaj was a famous Persian Sufi, teacher and writer who was executed in Baghdad in 922 for famously saying '*Ana al-Haqq*' namely 'I am the Truth' and thus claiming divinity with God.
27   Muhaimin (1995:176).
28   Rachman (1997:56-57).
29   On *'Ashura* commemoration among Shi'is in Indonesia today, see Chapter Three.
30   The *Tabut* or *Tabot* in Bengkulu and Pariaman is the annual observance which takes place from the first to the tenth of the month of Muharram. In the narrow sense, it refers to the decorated portable cenotaphs carried in procession during the observance.
31   Snouck Hurgronje (1906:202-207).
32   Djajadiningrat (1958:380).
33   Kartomi (1986).
34   Feener (1999a).

She observes that there are very few Shi'i families in the towns of Pariaman and Bengkulu and the Shi'i families that are there claim to be descendants of the British Indian soldiers who came to the area at the end of 17th and the early 18th century. Kartomi also suggests that "their beliefs and practices are tolerated, even assisted by local *imams* or prayer leaders, who pray and chant in the Shi'i manner on each occasion that a *Tabut* festival is held."[35] The above scholars maintain that there have been changes to the practice of *'Ashura* commemoration over time. Snouck Hurgronje points out that a wave of Islamic orthodoxy from Mecca in the nineteenth century was to purify Islam in the Dutch East Indies of sundry heresies, including the *'Ashura* ceremonies.[36] Atjeh holds a similar view. "International relations between Indonesia and Muslim countries, especially Mecca and Egypt, made traces of the Shi'i beliefs vanish in the Indonesian Muslim community."[37] Kartomi also points out that since 1974 the *Tabut* ceremony has been diverted towards attracting tourists and this has meant a loss of "the essential element of passion, which is a distinguishing feature of Shi'ism."[38]

Other studies related to Shi'ism in Indonesia are concerned with the literature of the region. In scrutinising the *Hikayat Muhammad Hanafiyyah*,[39] a major Shi'i literary work, which was translated into Malay from the Persian not much later than the 14th century, Brakel reviews remarks on the relationship between the *hikayat* or Malay epics and the Shi'i character of early Islam in Indonesia. He points out that the possibility for such a Shi'i text to be received into the body of Malay literature implies a definite role for Shi'i influences in the formation of early Indonesian Islam.[40] Brakel writes:

> The mere fact that a Shi'a text of the more extreme kind was received into Malay literature at all, to thrive there up till the present day, is already of great significance. It provides strong proof not only of the strong links between Malay and Persian literature, but no less of the heretical character of early Indonesian Islam.[41]

Similar studies were made by Baried. After examining 17 Malay stories said to contain Shi'i elements,[42] Baried concludes that these stories are rough and

---

35 Kartomi (1986:141).
36 Snouck Hurgronje (1906:205).
37 Aceh (1985:33).
38 Kartomi (1986:159).
39 Muhammad bin al-Hanafiyya was a son of Ali by a Hanafi woman and is regarded by Mukhtar bin Abu Ubaid al-Thaqafi, the initiator of the Kaysaniyya sect, as the person said to have taught that the Imamate was transferred from Husayn bin Ali to Muhammad bin al-Hanafiyya. After the death of Muhammad bin al-Hanafiyya, the Kaysaniyya split into a number of groups. On this Shi'i sect, see Momen (1985:47-49).
40 Brakel (1975:58).
41 Brakel (1975:60).
42 The seventeen Malay stories that she studies include *Hikayat Nur Muhammad, Hikayat Bulan Berbelah, Hikayat Raja Khaibar, Hikayat Pendeta Raghib, Hikayat Muhammad Hanafiyah, Hikayat Ali Kawin, Hikayat*

imperfect data, as "they constitute only fragments of stories about Ali and his family."[43] She argues that these 'fragments' fail to indicate real Shi'i elements but that her corpus in fact is representative of all existing Malay documents that clearly indicate Shi'i elements. This very limited study, which is based on synopses from old manuscripts catalogues, can only produce a general statement rather than a definitive conclusion. In order to discover any real elements of Shi'ism in Malay literature, all existing Malay documents would need to be carefully scrutinised to "bring light that Shi'i elements exist in stories other than those of which the contents have bearing on Shi'i narratives."[44]

Wieringa also remarks that through a fairly extensive range of Malay-Indonesian literature one can find Shi'i traces in Indonesian Islam which are not recognised by common readers. He affirms that traces of Shi'ism were gradually purged over time, particularly from the 19th century onwards, due to close contacts with Middle Eastern Islam. With Brakel, Wieringa regards this as "a de-Shi'itization of Malay *hikayat* literature."[45] He concludes that the prominent position of Ali and Fatima in Malay *hikayat* literature has to be understood in the context of early Islamisation in the Malay-Indonesian world: stories were provided to new Muslim converts at a time when Indonesian Islam was still tinged with Shi'ism, but gradually the Shi'i elements of the stories were neutralised to the extent that they became acceptable to Sunni Muslims.[46]

Another topic relevant to the study of Shi'ism in Indonesia is the position and role of the Sayyids, or those who claim to be descendants of the Prophet Muhammad through his daughter Fatima in the Islamisation of the Malay-Indonesian world. Scholars such as Atjeh believe that the Sayyids played a major role in the spread of Shi'ism. They point to the fact that a great number of sultans in Aceh used the title of Sayyid. Atjeh suggests that most of these sultans were Shi'is, or at least sympathetic to this branch of Islam and, consciously or unconsciously, they included a Shi'i doctrine and world-view in their propagation of Islam.[47] Scholars such as al-Baqir[48] and Al-Attas[49] also suggest that the *Wali Sanga* of Java and other leading figures were Sayyids. Al-Baqir cites the Sayyid construction of graves for the Muslim saints in Indonesia, a practice contrary to Sunni tradition but acceptable within Shi'ism. This, according to al-Baqir, indicates that the first propagators of Islam in the archipelago were Sayyids who upheld

---

Fatimah Berkata dengan Pedang Ali, Hikayat Nabi Mengajar Ali, Hikayat Nabi Mengajar Anaknya Fatimah, Cerita Tabut, Hikayat Amirul Mukminin Umar, Hikayat Raja Khandak, Bustanussalatin, Hikayat Nabi Bercukur, Hikayat Nabi Wafat and *Hikayat Abusamah* (Baried 1976:63-65).

43   Baried (1976:65).
44   Baried (1976:65).
45   Wieringa (1996:106).
46   Wieringa (1996:107).
47   Atjeh (1985:35).
48   Al-Baqir (1986).
49   Al-Attas (1999).

Shi'i beliefs, despite the fact that some of them followed Shafi'i jurisprudence.[50] Similarly, Pelras mentions the Shi'i influence of Sayyid Jalaluddin al-Aidid, who brought Islam to South Sulawesi, the areas of Cikoang Laikang and Turatea in particular, at the start of the 17th century. This propagator of Islam was a son of Sayyid Muhammad Wahid of Aceh and Syarifah Halisyah. He left Aceh for Banjarmasin, where by the end of the 16th century he was delivering teachings heavily tinged with Shi'ism. Al-Aidid then travelled to Goa, where he met with opposition from the ruler, so he moved back to Cikoang, where he converted the pagan nobility and population. His arrival is still commemorated every year on the occasion of the *Mawlid* festival which celebrates the birth of the Prophet.[51] Al-Baqir, Al-Attas and Ibrahim[52] have tried to trace the early historical development of Sayyid pre-eminence from the 9th to the 13th centuries. They point to the leading historical figure, Ahmad al-Muhajir, of the 8th generation after Ali and his grandson, Alawi bin Ubaidillah who, after performing the *hajj* in 930, left Basrah for Yemen. The Sayyids in Southeast Asia mainly came from Yemen. Protracted debates still exist between scholars who believe these Sayyid figures were Sunni and those who believe they were Shi'i who practiced *taqiyya*, or the dissimulation of religious faith to practical Shi'i ends.[53]

Azra has strongly criticised those who propound a great influence of Shi'ism in Indonesia prior to the Iranian revolution of 1979. He rejects the existence of a Shi'i sultanate in Aceh, along with the idea of political struggle between the Shi'i and Sunni sultanates there. In his view, the principal weakness of the above writers, particularly Jamil, Hasjmi and Parlindungan[54] is their uncritical and unverified use of local sources and their comparison with other contemporary sources, specifically with regard to historical developments in the wider world of Islam during the period in question. Azra argues that there is no indication of political or ideological conflict between Sunnis and Shi'is in the historical evidence of Islam in the Middle East before the 16th century. He suggests that descriptions of conflict are likely to be based on Sunni-Shi'i conflicts of a later period, which are projected back onto the past, with additional support being sought in local sources. While Azra's criticism on the question of political conflict can be historically justified, I believe there is ample indication that minority Shi'is *were* present in Indonesia's past.

Azra also rejects views that the celebration of *'Ashura* and *Tabut* are irrefutably influenced by Shi'i traditions, saying they are devoid of Shi'i theological or political ideology.[55] He does however recognise a significant Persian influence

---

50 Al-Baqir (1986:51).
51 Pelras (1985:113).
52 Ibrahim (2000).
53 For a full description of this practice, see Chapter Three.
54 Parlindungan (1965).
55 Azra (1995:13).

on Malay-Indonesian Muslim literature. A great number of early texts are translations or adaptations of Persian originals. Even the *Taj al-Salatin* (Crown of the Sultans), one of the earliest historical works in Malay, is a translation of a lost Persian original that may have been brought to the archipelago from India. Similarly, another important Malay history entitled *Sejarah Melayu* (The Malay Annals) includes a great number of Persian verses and contains terminology foreign to Malay-Indonesian. Azra admits that the relatively high degree of Persian influence upon Malay-Indonesian literature has led to lengthy debates among scholars as to whether Shi'i doctrines were also found among Muslims in the archipelago.[56] In this debate, however, Azra takes a negative stance, arguing that Persian influence is not always identifiable with Shi'ism, suggesting that "Shi'i religious thought has hardly ever spread in the archipelago, let alone had a strong influence."[57] Using a variety of written sources to examine the influence of Shi'ism in the field of politics, literature and religion, Azra concludes "It is clear that certain Islamic practices in the Malay-Indonesian archipelago which are associated by some people as Shi'ite, are essentially just similarities, empty of the theological framework and political ideology of Shi'ism."[58] According to Azra, Shi'ism as a school of religious and political thought only attracted followers in Indonesia after the Iranian revolution and through translations of Iranian scholars and thinkers such as Ali Shari'ati, Muthahhari, and Khomeini.[59]

Interest in studying Shi'ism in Indonesia has increased recently. In addition to the above debate concerning the historical arrival and influence of Shi'ism, two studies on its contemporary development have appeared. The first is a preliminary study on Shi'ism and politics conducted by a research team at the Indonesian Institute of Sciences, led by Abdurrahman Zainuddin and published under the title *Syi'ah dan Politik di Indonesia* (Shi'ism and Politics in Indonesia).[60] Zainuddin et al. attempt to explore the impact of contemporary Shi'i thought on the political life of Muslims in Indonesia. They begin by briefly introducing Shi'ism and its development up to the Iranian revolution of 1978-1979 and noting the contemporary Shi'i concept of *wilayat al-faqih* (the guardianship of the jurists). This is followed by a comparison of the political thought of Ayatollah Khomeini, the then leader of the Iranian revolution and of Ali Shari'ati, a prominent intellectual regarded as an ideologue of the revolution, emphasising the unique nature of Shi'i political thought which unites religion and politics. While Khomeini maintains that during the occultation of the twelfth Imam, the jurists, or *faqih* are entitled to rule the Muslim community, Shari'ati proposes that what he calls "the reformed intellectuals" should play a

---

56   Azra (1992:86-87).
57   Azra (1995:12).
58   Azra (1995:17-18).
59   Azra (1995:17-18).
60   Zainuddin et al. (2000).

major role in government. The book then attempts to explore the impact of the revolution on the development of Shi'ism in Indonesia, attempting to explain the implications of this development on the political life of Indonesian Muslims and raising an appeal for dialogue between the two Muslim communities in order to prevent conflict. It also includes Azra's critical article and notes from an interview with Indonesian Shi'i intellectual Jalaluddin Rakhmat, previously published in the journal *Ulumul Qur'an* (The Koranic Sciences). Many criticisms have been directed towards this book, such as those by Nurmansyah[61] who questions the significance of the comparison between the political thought of Khomeini and Shari'ati, while accusing Azra of ignorance of Shi'i history. In my opinion, one of the most noticeable weaknesses of the book is its failure to examine the identity and reality of the Shi'is in Indonesia.

Another study by Syamsuri Ali focuses on intellectual and social relations among the Indonesian alumni of *Hawza 'Ilmiyya*, the College of Learning of Qum, Iran and how they relate to the transmission of Shi'ism in Indonesia.[62] In this pioneering research, Ali provides us with important information on the Indonesian educational institutions and leaders who send students to Qum, biographies of Qum alumni, their discourses on aspects of Shi'ism and their role in establishing Shi'i institutions and local associations in Indonesia. However, Ali's work comes with a caveat: the scope of his account of the Qum alumni is limited, particularly in terms of actors and regions discussed. The same is admitted by Jalaluddin Rakhmat, who was a co-promoter of the thesis as well as the most prominent Shi'i intellectual in Indonesia.[63] Ali's research focus excludes the important role of other *ustadh* and intellectuals who are not Qum alumni. As a result, the true extent of Shi'ism in Indonesia is not revealed in Ali's account. Despite this caveat, however, Ali's study is an important contribution to our topic.

Although there have been a considerable number of studies relevant to Shi'ism in Indonesia, as yet the true nature of the Shi'i denomination in the country - its leading figures, beliefs and practices, institutions and organisations as well as reactions from the majority Muslim community – is still to be fully revealed. This present work will deal with these aspects in order to provide a comprehensive understanding of Shi'ism within the context of the Sunni majority in the country, as well as to shed light on the complex nature of Indonesian religion and society.

---

61   Nurmansyah (2001).
62   Ali (2002). This is a draft PhD thesis examined in *ujian tertutup* (examinations not open to the public) in 2002 by the Graduate Programme, UIN Jakarta, but was not promoted until April 2004, when I received a copy of the thesis. I thank Prof. Azyumardi Azra for informing me of its existence and his attempts to make a copy available to me. I also thank Fuad Jabali and Idzam Fautanu for their assistance.
63   Rakhmat, interview, (2/7/2002).

Theoretical Framework

In analysing the Shi'is in Indonesia as a minority Muslim group this study employs the theory of 'stigma'[64] proposed by the sociologist Erving Goffman.[65] I also follow Devin Stewart's steps in his study of the Twelver Shi'i response to Sunni legal theory. Stewart maintains the applicability of this theory to Shi'is "who have lived as a stigmatised minority dominated by a potentially hostile majority in most areas of the Muslim world and during most periods of Muslim history."[66] According to Goffman's theory, stigmatised groups tend to adopt strategies that fit into a social system dominated by the majority. While Sunnism has become the norm in the Muslim world, Shi'ism is considered 'abnormal' and Shi'is have to implement certain strategies in order to gain recognition and respect from the Sunni majority.

Methodology

This study is based on fieldwork and library research. Two periods of fieldwork, both lasting eight months, were conducted in several cities and towns in Indonesia, including Jakarta and Bandung. Each period lasted eight months: the first, from June 2002 until January 2003 and the second, from October 2003 until May 2004. I interviewed leading Shi'i figures and adherents, observed and participated in a number of religious activities at Shi'i institutions, visited their libraries, engaged in dialogue with them and collected Shi'i and anti-Shi'i books, periodicals, pamphlets, cassettes, DVD's and other materials. I also gathered information from the websites of organisations and institutions. My relationship with the Shi'is was such that I was welcome to participate in their activities and conduct conversations with them in a way that allowed me to collect as 'natural' data as possible. To facilitate my interaction with members, I took a three-month course in Persian at the Islamic Cultural Centre of Jakarta in January-March 2004. To collect data on Sunni responses, I visited the offices of DDII (*Dewan Dakwah Islamiyah Indonesia*, the Indonesian Islamic Missionary Council), LPPI (*Lembaga Pengkajian dan Penelitian Islam*, Institute of Islamic Studies and Research) in Jakarta, centres of Persis (*Persatuan Islam*) in Bandung and Bangil, the library of MUI (*Majlis Ulama Indonesia*, Council of Indonesian Muslim Scholars) in the Istiqlal Mosque in Jakarta, the Office of Research and

---

64 'Stigma' may be defined as "the situation of the individual who is disqualified from full social acceptance" (Goffman 1986:n.p.). Goffman classifies three types of stigma: first, physical deformities; second, blemishes of individual character perceived as weak, unnatural, treacherous or dishonest; third, "the tribal stigma of race, nation, and religion" (Goffman 1986:4). The stigma of Shi'ism is included in the third category.
65 Goffman (1986).
66 Stewart (2000).

Development and Training, Department of Religious Affairs (*Badan Penelitian dan Pengembangan Departemen Agama*) in Jakarta, UIN *Syarif Hidayatullah* in Ciputat, Banten and UIN *Sunan Gunung Djati* in Bandung.

The Structure of the Study

This study is presented in nine chapters, in addition to the introduction. Chapter One describes major elements and factors in the historical formation of the Shi'i community in Indonesia. This is followed in Chapter Two by a description of the types of leaders in the Shi'i community and portraits of Husein al-Habsyi, Husein Shahab and Jalaluddin Rakhmat. Chapter Three examines the characteristics of Shi'ism as a *madhhab* as it is understood and practiced by the Indonesian Shi'is themselves. This includes outlining the concept of *ahl al-bayt* (members of the House of the Prophet), the doctrine of the Imamate and the Mahdi, *Ja'fari* jurisprudence, aspects of Shi'i piety and the teaching and practice of *taqiyya*, or the approved dissimulation of faith.

Chapters Four, Five and Six deal with the efforts of the Shi'is to spread their teachings in Indonesian society and to gain recognition for Shi'ism as a valid interpretation of Islam. These chapters examine institutions founded by the Shi'is and include analysis of the fields of *da'wa*, or missionary outreach, education and publishing. In the chapter on *da'wa* I describe the characteristics of Shi'i institutions and the ways *da'wa* has been conducted. This includes stated ideals, types of *da'wa* activity and *da'wa* training. The chapter on education presents accounts of educational institutions organised by leading Shi'i figures. Another important means of disseminating Shi'ism is by print publishing and this is dealt with in Chapter Six, with a survey of Shi'i publishers and their products - Indonesian translations, works by Indonesian Shi'i figures and periodicals — and the impact of such publications.

Chapter Seven scrutinises IJABI (*Ikatan Jamaah Ahlul Bait Indonesia*, the Indonesian Council of Ahlulbait Associations), the mass organisation established by the Shi'is as a means of gaining legal recognition from state authorities. An historical account of its establishment, its ideological foundations and its development are presented in this chapter.

Finally, a study of Shi'ism in Indonesia will never be complete unless the varied responses of the Sunni Muslim majority are covered. Chapter Eight therefore includes an analysis of the general attitude of large Sunni organisations, both traditionalist and reformist, to Shi'ism and the responses of the Council of Indonesian 'Ulama and the Department of Religious Affairs. It also presents a description of ways in which anti-Shi'i groups propagate the fight against Shi'ism. This is followed by an examination of the moderate attitudes of influential Muslim intellectuals which have paved the way for the further development of Shi'ism in Indonesia. Chapter Nine provides the conclusion to this study.

1. The Formation of the Shiʻi Community

The precise number of adherents to Shiʻism in Indonesia is not known. Many notable Shiʻis have tried to estimate their numbers, even though there are no reliable sources to call upon. Several years ago the Lebanese scholar Muhammad Jawad Mughniyya (d. 1979) mentioned the figure of one million.[1] The same number was cited in 2003 by Andi Muhammad Assegaf, head of the Fatimah Foundation in Jakarta.[2] In 1995 Ahmad Baragbah, who leads *Pesantren Al-Hadi* in Pekalongan, Central Java estimated there to be 20,000 Shiʻis in Indonesia,[3] while in 2000 Dimitri Mahayana, former chairman of the national Shiʻi organisation, IJABI (*Ikatan Jamaah Ahlubait Indonesia*) predicted a figure of 3 million.[4] All of these estimates are without basis and therefore cannot be relied upon. It is almost impossible for researchers to provide the quantitative data necessary to produce reliable statistics. In 2000, the Islamic Cultural Centre of Jakarta, an institution sponsored by Iran, attempted to provide a database of all Shiʻi *ustadhs,* or religious teachers and their folllowers in Indonesia. The project failed, due to many Shiʻis simply not returning the distributed questionnaire. Despite this lack of quantitative data, it is certain that the Shiʻis constitute only a very small proportion of Indonesia's Muslim population. Even though Shiʻism has been evident in Indonesia in the past, the majority of Shiʻis are actually converts from Sunnism following the victory of the Iranian revolution of 1979.

This chapter seeks to identify the elements and factors which have contributed to the formation of the Shiʻi community in Indonesia. I begin by tracing its genesis, that is, the presence of a Shiʻi group among the community of Arab descent, and by examining the way in which the Shiʻis have maintained their existence throughout history. Secondly, I deal with the emergence of the 'Qum alumni' and their promotion of their Islamic education in Qum, Iran. This is followed by a description of the emergence of the Shiʻi campus group. A brief description of the ways of conversion to Shiʻism will conclude the chapter.

A. The Arab Community

The Arabs have been a significant element of the Shiʻi community in Indonesia in terms of both quantity and quality. Quantitatively, the group constitutes a

---

1   Mughniyya (1973:204).

2   *Gatra* (6/12/2003:59).

3   Nurjulianti and Subhan (1995:21).

4   *Pikiran Rakyat* (2/7/2000:9).

large proportion of that community. Qualitatively, the most prominent Shi'i *ustadhs* in Indonesia have been of Arab origin, particularly those of Sayyid lines claiming descent from the Prophet. The Arabs are considered to be the original members of the Shi'i community in Indonesia, despite the exact date of the arrival of Shi'ism remaining unclear.

The Shi'is have existed in strength among the Arab community in the region that is now called Indonesia since at least the late 19th century. Since this period there have been close relations between the Hadramaut, the Yemeni region in the South Arabian Peninsula and the Malay-Indonesian world. Riddell suggests that European visitors to the Hadramaut in the early decades of the 20th century witnessed extensive contacts with the Malay world. He regards this period – one of an intensified increase in Arab emigration due to economic stress and political tensions - as a turning point for Hadramis, both in their country of origin and in Southeast Asia. They left the Hadramaut to become imams and teachers,[5] and it is among Hadrami migrants and Indonesian-born Arabs, particularly the Sayyids, that we can identify adherents to Shi'ism in this region. Muhammad Asad Shahab (1910-2001), a famous Shi'i Sayyid writer and journalist mentions that several prominent Sayyid leaders and scholars belonged to the families of al-Muhdar, Yahya, Shahab, al-Jufri, al-Haddad and al-Saqqaf. There were also Shi'is among other Arab clans in the Dutch East Indies.[6] However, we cannot generalise that all members of the aforementioned Sayyid clans were Shi'is. In fact, the majority of them were, and still are, Sunni. Moreover, as we shall see below, some members of these families actually joined anti-Shi'i groups.

The fact that some Sayyid families belonged to the Shi'i branch of Islam was not widely acknowledged among the Sunni majority. A number of them were even assumed to be Sunni scholars and leaders, since they had considerable knowledge of Sunni teachings and were involved in the religious life of the community at large. This may have been due to the practice of *taqiyya,* the permitted concealment of true faith.[7] Publicly, they practiced the obligatory rituals in accordance with the regulations of Sunni Shafi'i jurisprudence while inwardly holding to the Shi'i fundamentals of belief.[8] Only a few openly observed aspects of worship in accordance with the Shi'i Ja'fari school of jurisprudence.

From the Shi'i minority group in the Arab community there came several prominent *'ulama* and leaders who played major roles in social, religious and

---

5   Riddle (1997:224-225).
6   Shahab (1962:43-54). Abubakar Atjeh, for instance, notes the presence of Sayyid Shi'is from the Bilfaqih family in Kutaraja (Banda Aceh) in the early 20th century (1985:33).
7   On *taqiyya* and other teachings of Shi'ism as understood and practiced in Indonesia, see Chapter Three.
8   This is not an unusual case. In the history of Islam in the Middle East, from the 10th to the 17th century, for instance, Shi'i jurists performing *taqiyya* not only studied with Shafi'i teachers but also participated in the Sunni legal education system. Some were recognised as professors of Sunni law, served as legal authorities in Sunni circles and wrote books within the Sunni tradition (Stewart 1998:109).

political fields. Before the first half of the 20th century, we find three eminent Shi'i leaders in the Dutch East Indies, representing different Sayyid clans. The first and foremost was Sayyid Muhammad bin Ahmad al-Muhdar (1861-1926) of the al-Muhdar clan. Very little is known about the early life of this figure. We are informed that he was born in Qereh, in the Hadramaut, Yemen, around 1861 and received a religious education in his homeland. He came to the Dutch East Indies at the age of 24, living first in Bogor, West Java and later in Bondowoso and Surabaya in East Java. He was engaged in teaching and propagating Islamic teachings in various religious gatherings in Surabaya, Bondowoso and other towns in East Java, in Pekalongan, Central Java and in Bogor and Batavia, now Jakarta. In 1908, he was involved in the establishment of *Jam'iyya al-Khairiyya al-'Arabiyya*, a sister organisation of the pioneering Arab *Jami'at Khair* (Benevolent Society) of Batavia which built Islamic schools, the *Madrasa al-Khairiyya* in Surabaya and Bondowoso. However, these schools were not Shi'i in character.[9] Muhammad al-Muhdar passed away on 4 May 1926 in Surabaya, where he was buried.[10]

During his life Muhammad al-Muhdar was said to have expressed his devotion to Shi'ism through his teaching and preaching. For instance, he was said to have been critical of the *al-Sahih* of Bukhari, the most authoritative Sunni collection of Hadith.[11] Such criticism is common among Shi'is but is rarely found in the Sunni community. Among the Shi'is, both past and present, Muhammad al-Muhdar is regarded as a prominent scholar who contributed to the spread and perpetuation of the faith. Besides his teaching and *da'wa*, he composed a number of literary works which contain principal Shi'i doctrines, such as the doctrinal designation of 'Ali bin Abi Talib as the first Imam to succeed the Prophet Muhammad. These works, however, were never published.[12]

The second prominent Shi'i figure in the Dutch East Indies was Sayyid Ali bin Ahmad Shahab (1865-1944) who greatly contributed to the educational, religious, social and political development of Indonesian society. Born in Batavia to a Sayyid father, Ahmad bin Muhammad bin Shahab and a Sundanese mother,[13] Ali Ahmad Shahab studied basic Islamic knowledge with his father and other Sayyid scholars in the region. Widely known as Ali Menteng, he was one of the leading Arab figures in the Dutch East Indies at the end of the 19th and the first half of the 20th centuries. He was a scholar,[14] activist and successful

---

9   Zainal Abidin al-Muhdar, interview, (27/8/2002).
10   Shahabuddin (2000:114).
11   Zainal Abidin al-Muhdar, interview, (27/8/2002).
12   Shahab (1962:43-45), Hamzah Al-Habsyi, interview, (15/10/2002).
13   Ahmad bin Muhammad bin Shahab (d. 1891) was a wealthy Sayyid who financed the building of a number of mosques in Batavia and the Hadramaut (Shahabuddin 2000:43-44). Ali Ahmad Sahab's mother, Nursatri came from Cianjur, West Java (Salam 1992:17).
14   Ali Ahmad Shahab wrote a number of books, published and unpublished, in Arabic, including *al-Thalatha al-Abtal* (Three Heroes), *Tarbiyyat al-Nisa'* (The Education of Women) and *al-Sa'ada al-Zawjiyya*

merchant. He was also one of the founders of the abovementioned *Jami'at Khair*, the first Muslim organisation in the Dutch East Indies, established in Jakarta in 1901. Ali Ahmad Shahab was elected general chairman of *Jami'at Khair* in 1905 when it gained legal recognition from the Dutch East Indies government.[15] He was one of the most vocal opponents of *Al-Irsyad* (The Guidance), an organisation founded in opposition to *Jami'at Khair* because of long standing conflicts between Sayyids and non-Sayyid Arabs in both the Hadhramaut and the Indies from the second decade of the 20th century.[16] Ali Ahmad Shahab was the chief informant to the British Consul-General in Batavia until the 1920s and he used this position to provoke the British into taking action against the non-Sayyid movement of *Al-Irsyad*. He convinced the British to use their control over the ports of India and Singapore and prohibit the travel of followers of *Al-Irsyad* to the Hadramaut and to intercept their money remittances home.[17] He also influenced the Qu'ayti sultan in the Hadramaut to establish alliances with the British. Apparently he was relatively successful in this regard, as *Al-Irsyad* people had difficulty visiting the Hadramaut when the British government refused to grant them entry. Their relatives in the Hadramaut also faced similar obstacles.[18]

Like other leading Muslim figures in this region, Ali Ahmad Shahab was influenced by the spirit of Pan-Islamism. He established contact with Sultan Abdul Hamid of the Ottoman Empire, visiting Turkey to meet with the Sultan to discuss arrangements for providing education in Istanbul for Sayyid pupils from the Dutch East Indies. As a result of this mission, three Sayyid boys, his own son, Abdulmutallib, Abdurrahman al-Aydrus and Muhammad bin Abdullah al-Attas entered the Galatasary Lyceum, a modern educational establishment in Istanbul.[19]

(the Felicity of Marriage) (Salam 1992:13-20). He contributed to periodicals such as the reformist journal *al-Manar* (The Beacon) and the daily *al-Mu'ayyad* (The Reliable) published in Cairo, *Thamarat al-Funun* (The Fruits of the Arts) in Beirut and *Utusan Hindia* (Indies Messenger). In his contributions to *al-Manar* he suggested that modern schools should be established in the Hadramaut.

15   Assegaf (1993:9).

16   Mobini-Kesheh (1999:60). *Al-Irsyad* was founded in 1914 by mainly non-Sayyid Arabs, including Ahmad Surkati, following his resignation from his position as an inspector of *Jami'at Khair*. The dispute between *Jami'at Khair* and *Al-Irsyad* concerned three issues of Sayyid privilege: *kafa'a* (equality in status between partners in marriage), the kissing of the hands of the Sayyids in greeting and the use of the title 'Sayyid'. Whilst *Jami'at Khair* supported these customs, *Al-Irsyad* strongly opposed them (Mobini-Kesheh 1999:92-107). Other studies regarding the conflict include Noer (1973), Kostiner (1984), Haikal (1986) and De Jonge (1993).

17   Freitag (1997:124-125).

18   Noer (1973:67).

19   Freitag (2003:210-211). From the late-19th century onwards a number of wealthy Sayyids sent their children to Constantinople to pursue their education. Before Ali Ahmad Shahab, Sayyid Abdullah al-Attas sent his four children to Turkey, Egypt and Europe to gain a modern education. In 1898, four Arab boys from Java arrived in Constantinople, which became a cause of consternation among the Dutch colonial authorities. The Dutch, fearing the influence of pan-Islam, urged the Turkish government to discourage people from Java from studying in Constantinople. In response, the Turkish government rejected a request from the Consul-General in Batavia for 30 boys from Batavia and Singapore to be sent to Constantinople (Van Dijk 2002:68-69). In spite of this, the following two years saw the number of boys from Java studying in Constantinople

Ali Ahmad Shahab was not recognised as Shi'i among the Muslim population in the Dutch East Indies. However, his son, Muhammad Asad Shahab affirms that he not only adhered to Shi'ism in terms of belief and practice but also became a famous propagator of this *madhhab*.[20] We do not have information as to whether Ali Ahmad Shahab was a student of Sayyid Abu Bakr Shahab,[21] an influential Shi'i Hadrami teacher in Southeast Asia in the period. Not much is known about the ways in which Ali Ahmad Shahab propagated Shi'i teachings, but it is understood that it was exclusive, limited to his family and close associates. Ali Ahmad Shahab had many disciples to whom he granted the licence to practice and teach certain prayers, including prayers transmitted through the purified Imams. One of the prayers to be recited every morning says, "... grant us the means of subsistence, you are the best who grant it. Grant mercy to the most glad of your creatures, who is our Prophet Muhammad, his household as the ship of salvation and to all propagating Imams."[22] The last phrase clearly indicates the Shi'i character of the prayer.

The third famous Shi'i scholar was Sayyid Aqil bin Zainal Abidin (1870-1952) of the al-Jufri clan. Born in Surabaya in 1870, he first studied Islamic knowledge with his father. When he was seven years old his father sent him to Mecca to study with Shafi'i *'ulama* and he is said to have memorised all chapters of the holy Qur'an by the age of ten, a feat considered to be a great religious and intellectual achievement. Aqil al-Jufri's teachers of the Qur'an were Muhammad al-Sharbini[23] and Yusuf Abu Hajar. He studied Arabic syntax under 'Umar Shatta and 'Abd al-Rahman Babasil. 'Abd al-Rahman al-Hindi al-Haidar and other Shafi'i scholars taught him the Qur'an exegesis of *al-Jalalayn*[24] and Hadith, particularly collections by Muslim (d. 875), Abu Daud (d. 889) and al-Nasa'i (d. 915). In this period, Aqil al-Jufri probably adhered to Sunnism. Then, in 1899, he moved to Singapore, where he studied *al-Durr al-Manthur*[25] and *al-Amali* ('the Dictations') of Shaykh al-Saduq al-Qummi[26] under the renowned

---

increase to 17. However, their studies were not successful because of a lack of preparatory education in the Netherlands-Indies. Moreover, "they were not model students, who could be paraded as paragons" (Van Dijk 2002:69). By 1901, only eight students remained in Constantinople. Four had died, two had returned to Asia, two had travelled to other countries in Europe and one was missing (Van Dijk 2002:69).

20   Shahab (1962:47).

21   Shahabuddin (2000:78).

22   Shahabuddin (2000:155).

23   Muhammad al-Sharbani al-Dimyati (d.1903) was widely considered to be the grandmaster in the field of Qur'anic studies. A number of Indonesian students, including Shaykh Mahfuz al-Tirmisi (d. 1919) studied with him (Rachman 1998:39).

24   *Al-Jalalayn* ('The Two Jalals' after the authors' names) is a concise Qur'an exegesis written by Jalal al-Din al-Mahalli (d. 1459) and his student Jalaluddin al-Suyuti (d. 1505). It is a well-known text in the Sunni Muslim world.

25   *Al-Durr al-Manthur fi al-Tafsir bi al-Ma'thur* (Scattered Pearls in Traditional Exegesis of the Qur'an) is a famous exegesis by al-Suyuthi (d. 1505) frequently cited in Shi'i works.

26   Shaykh al-Saduq Muhammad bin 'Ali Ibn Babawaih al-Qummi (d. 991) was a leading scholar of Shi'i Hadith. His manual, *Man la Yahduruh al-Faqih* (For those not in the Presence of a Jurisprudent), is one of the four authoritative Shi'i Hadith collections.

scholar Abu Bakr bin Shahab (1846-1922). In addition, Muhammad bin Aqil bin Yahya (1863-1931) taught Aqil al-Jufri the *fiqh* book entitled *al-'Urwa al-Wuthqa* (The Indissoluble Bond) by Sayyid Muhammad Kazim Tabataba'i Yazdi[27] and consequently Aqil al-Jufri took this prominent Shi'i legist as his *marja' al-taqlid*, or 'source of imitation'.[28] These Shi'i scholars may well have been influential in Aqil Al-Jufri's conversion to the Shi'i *madhhab*. Three years later, he returned to Mecca where he joined the Shi'i congregation of Ali al-'Amri al-Madani and other Shi'i scholars.[29] He also made contacts with prominent *'ulama* of the world, including Ahmad Zawawi of Mecca.

After several years of living in Mecca, Aqil al-Jufri went to Jambi, Sumatra, where he married a daughter of Sayyid Idrus bin Hasan bin Alwi al-Jufri. Subsequently, he moved to Mecca and stayed there until 1921, at which point he returned to his home town, Surabaya, where he remained until his death in 1952.[30] In Java Aqil Al-Jufri devoted his life to teaching, preaching and writing. He was also known for his charitable concern for the poor.[31] He tended to adopt an open approach to the propagation of Shi'ism. As a result, he became involved in debates with Sunni *'ulama* in Surabaya and one particular debate was cut short following physical threats against him. Like Ali Ahmad Shahab, Aqil al-Jufri was said to have been involved in the struggle for Indonesian independence.[32] He also produced some literary works. These unpublished writings affirm his allegiance to Shi'ism and the validity of its *madhhab*.[33] In 1924, for instance, together with his brother, Ahmad al-Jufri he published one of Muhammad bin Aqil's works, *al-'Atb al-Jamil 'ala Ahl al-Jarh wa al-Ta'dil* (A Beautiful Censure of Men of Sarcasm and Modification).

These three figures maintained connections with two Shi'i Hadrami scholars, Sayyid Abu Bakr bin 'Abd al-Rahman bin Muhammad bin Shahab (1846-1922)[34] and Muhammad bin Aqil bin Yahya (1863-1931). Abu Bakr bin Shahab wrote a large number of books dealing with various branches of knowledge and some collections of poetry.[35] His books on logic are still taught at al-Azhar University in Cairo.[36] The role of Abu Bakr bin Shahab as a travelling merchant, scholar and teacher was important in international Hadrami networks of the

---

27   Muhammad Kazim Tabataba'i Yazdi (1831-1919) was born in Kasnu near Yazd, Iraq, and died in Najaf. He became the sole *marja' al-taqlid* after the death of Akhund Khurasani in 1911 (Momen 1985:323).

28   See below for details on the educational system for Shi'i jurists; on the obligation of laity to follow them, see Chapter Three.

29   Al-Tihrani (1404/1984:1273), Al-Amin (1986:147).

30   Al-Tihrani (1404/1984:1274), Shahab (1962:52).

31   Al-Tihrani (1404/1984:1274).

32   Shahab (1962:52).

33   Shahab (1962:51-52).

34   A lengthy biography is provided by Muhammad Asad Shahab in *Abu al-Murtada* (1996) on which Freitag (2003) relies for her account of the role of Abu Bakr bin Shahab.

35   Al-Amin (1986:394-402).

36   Freitag (2003:187).

second half of the 19th and early 20th centuries. Abu Bakr bin Shahab was "an important propagator of reformist ideas among Hadramis, both at home and in the Diaspora."[37] He travelled to countries in the Middle East, Africa, South Asia and Southeast Asia. He stayed for some time in Surabaya and Singapore for business and to visit relatives, as well as to teach. Our three prominent Shi'i figures probably studied with Abu Bakr bin Shahab when he visited the Southeast Asian region and maintained close connections with him.

Muhammad bin Aqil bin Yahya (1863-1931) was also a student of Abu Bakr bin Shahab. Like his teacher, he was a travelling merchant and scholar. He visited Southeast Asia and stayed for a relatively long period in Singapore. In March 1908, together with Hasan bin Shahab and other Sayyid leaders, he engaged in the reorganisation of the management of *al-Imam*, an influential reformist magazine, and was appointed the managing director of the company.[38] In addition, he devoted himself to teaching and writing. One of his students was Aqil al-Jufri who also printed one of Muhammad bin Aqil's works. However, in Singapore in 1907 he triggered a hostile reaction from the Sunni Muslim community by publishing his controversial book entitled *al-Nasa'ih al-Kafiya liman Yatawalla Mu'awiya* (Ample Admonitions to Whomever Accords Allegiance to Mu'awiya). The book received public acclaim from Abu Bakr bin Shahab.

This book clearly indicates Muhammad bin Aqil's adherence to Shi'ism. Werner Ende[39] provides an important account of Muhammad bin Aqil's Shi'i inclinations, especially with regard to the permissibility of cursing Mu'awiya bin Abi Sufyan,[40] the founder of the Sunni Umayyad dynasty in Baghdad, the dynasty eventually responsible for the death of Husain. However, while Ende is reluctant to affirm that Muhammad bin Aqil was a Shi'i, my reading of the book clearly indicates that he was. The book cites both Sunni and Shi'i sources to prove the enjoinment of the cursing of Mu'awiya. Muhammad bin Aqil points out that both Sunnis and Shi'is have agreed on the historical obligation of killing Mu'awiya when there was an opportunity and that this was an excellent deed rewarded by God.[41] A further indication of bin Aqil's adherence to Shi'ism is that he used the term 'Imam' to address the Shi'i Imams and the words *'alayhi*

---

37 Freitag (2003:187).

38 Hamzah (1991:117), Roff (2002:104).

39 Ende (1973). Another discussion of Muhammad bin Aqil's book is given by Roff (2002:100-103).

40 Mu'awiya bin Abi Sufyan was the governor of Syria during the caliphate of 'Uthman after the death of the Prophet Muhammad. He refused to accept 'Ali's caliphate that was approved of and accepted by the large majority of Muslims, because he accused 'Ali of sheltering the murderers of his cousin. In 657 he led the Battle of Siffin against the Caliph 'Ali, the first Shi'i Imam, but the war ended in a call for arbitration. After the death of 'Ali, he established the Umayyad Dynasty (661-750). Prior to his death, he appointed his son, Yazid, who sent an army to defeat Husayn bin 'Ali and his followers on the plain of Karbala on 10 Muharram 61AH (10 October 680).

41 Muhammad bin Aqil (1907:36).

al-salam (peace be upon him) after the mention of their names. This is a tradition not present in Sunni Islam. In addition, bin Aqil had two criticisms of Sunnism. First, he criticised consensus in the four Sunni schools of jurisprudence under the rule of tyrannical kings.[42] The second criticism was that the Sunnis reject the Shi'i propagation of the infallibility of the twelve Imams, utter cries of denial, disgrace their names and reject the rational and textual evidence of their existence.[43] The following quotation, from the writing of Muhammad bin Aqil, contains further aspects of Shi'i teaching rejected by Sunni scholars

> Astonishingly, a large number of people and even some of the scholars think that whoever wipes his feet instead of washing them in the ablution (before prayer). is a heretic. Similarly, whoever says that good deeds come from God whilst bad deeds come from himself, whoever includes '*hayya 'ala khayr al-'amal*' (come to the best of actions) in the call to prayer, whoever says that 'Ali is more excellent that Abu Bakr, whoever does not approve religious obligations by slyness, [...] all are erroneous heretics in the views of most of our Sunni *'ulama*.[44]

Inevitably, the book provoked fierce reactions from Sunni *'ulama* in the region and particularly from prominent Arab *'ulama*, including the famous Honorary Adviser on Arab Affairs to the colonial government and Mufti of Batavia, Sayyid Uthman bin Abdullah bin Aqil bin Yahya (1822-1914),[45] Muhammad bin Aqil's father in-law and Hasan bin Shahab, Muhammad bin Aqil's friend. Scrutinising the entire contents of the book, Hasan bin Shahab proved that Muhammad bin Aqil's work was heavily tinged with Shi'i ways of understanding Islam.[46]

---

42 Muhammad bin Aqil (1907:37).

43 Muhammad bin Aqil (1907:138).

44 Muhammad bin Aqil (1907:112).

45 In 1911, Sayyid Uthman published his work, *I'anat al-Mustarshidin 'ala Ijtinab al-Bida' fi al-Din* (Guidance for Seekers of Direction in Avoiding Innovations in Religion). Even though Sayyid Uthman himself never mentions Muhammad bin Aqil's work in this treatise, his book was meant to reject Shi'ism and the cursing of the companions of the Prophet Muhammad, and to demonstrate the invalidity of Wahhabism. He pointed out that Muslim scholars have agreed, in terms of textual and rational proofs, that Shi'ism is a most deceitful path and the Muslim leaders know well the Shi'is' clever ability in deceiving. He went on to suggest that Abdullah bin Saba' was its founder and wanted to destroy Islam. He mentioned the unbelievers (*zindiq*) who will destroy Islam by supporting the development of Shi'ism. Additionally, Uthman criticised the fact that Shi'is, who were ignorant in knowledge, never refer to the pious scholars of jurisprudence, Hadith and Sufism but to hypocrite unbelievers (Uthman 1911:22). "Shi'is are hypocrites whose *madhhab* is dissimulation" (Uthman 1911:22). Sayyid Uthman further cited several Sunni views affirming that Shi'is wanted to slander the companions of the Prophet, or even accuse them of being infidels. He regarded the Shi'is as heretics who twisted facts regarding the companions of the Prophet and denied 'Ali's recognition of the validity of the first two caliphates, of Abu Bakr and 'Umar (Uthman 1911:22-25). Studies have been devoted to the role of Sayyid Uthman as a Muslim scholar in the Dutch East Indies; see Kaptein (1998) and Azra (1995a, 1997).

46 Hasan bin Alwi bin Shahab wrote a 153-page treatise, *al-Ruqya al-Shafiya min Nafathat Sumum al-Nasa'ih al-Kafiya* (the Curative Charm against the Poisonous Spittle of 'the Ample Admonitions') that was completed in 1328H/1908. In the first page of the book, Hasan bin Shahab states that Muhammad bin Aqil's book calls upon the Sunnis, particularly among the laymen, to follow the Shi'i teachings. He emphasises that the Shi'is are known to lie when citing references in order to support their stance. The author mentions one of the reasons why he wrote the book, namely the fact that many of his fellow Muslims requested him to write a

The continuity of Shi'ism as a minority *madhhab* in Indonesia in a later period was maintained mainly through informal education within families or private circles. Regarding teacher-student relationships, Muhammad al-Muhdar and Aqil al-Jufri had a close disciple who then became a prominent Shi'i leader, Sayyid Hasyim bin Muhammad Assegaf (d. 1970) who lived in Gresik, near Surabaya. It was said that Aqil al-Jufri had bequeathed him the future role of performing his burial ritual according to Ja'fari jurisprudence. He was known to have applied Ja'fari jurisprudence in private and public, even among the Sunni majority. In addition to his close relationships with Shi'is in Indonesia, Sayyid Hasyim bin Muhammad Assegaf made contact with Shi'i *'ulama* of the world and his fame as a Shi'i figure led to some of these *'ulama* and scholars to visit him. Abubakar Atjeh wrote: "In Gresik we met with a famous man named Sayyid Hasyim Assegaf. With him we talked very much about Shi'ism and its books."[47]

At times when the Shi'i group was without an institutional centre, Hasyim Assegaf provided his house as a place for Shi'i commemorations. With regard to his role, Muhammad Asad Shahab wrote:

> In Gresik, East Java, the great ceremony of 'Id al-Ghadir[48] is celebrated annually in the big houses of Shi'i figures. In the latest years the ceremony has been carried out in the house of Sayyid Hasyim bin Muhammad Assegaf, one of the Imamiyya leaders. Today he has reached the age of eighty but he is still very healthy. The ceremony is attended by a great number of Shi'is who came to the town from various cities and from distant places. The biography of Our Hero, Master of the Faithful, Imam Ali (upon him be peace) and Arabic poems (*qasida*) are read and sermons are delivered. Then a meal is served.[49]

Kinship has played an important role in the continuity of Shi'ism. Most followers are the descendants of the aforementioned figures and their relatives. Some of them have become eminent *'ulama* in a number of cities and towns in Indonesia, where they are active in the fields of Islamic education and *da'wa*. From the al-Muhdar clan we find two children of Muhammad al-Muhdar, who are known as *ustadhs*. Muhdar al-Muhdar was very well known in Bondowoso and other towns in East Java whilst Husein al-Muhdar (d.1982) gave Islamic teachings

---

refutation to *al-Nasa'ih al-Kafiyya* which contains clear errors and deceit regarding the Prophet Muhammad, his companions and followers of the companions, as well as recognised Sunni *'ulama* (Hasan bin Shahab 1908:2-3). He scrutinised the entire contents of Muhammad bin Aqil's work that was heavily tinged with the Shi'i ways of understanding of Islam.

47   Atjeh (1977:33).

48   'Id al-Ghadir is one of Shi'ism's religious commemorations held annually on the 18th of *Dhu al-Hijja*, the last month in the Muslim calendar. It celebrates the Prophet Muhammad's designation of Ali as his successor at Ghadir Khumm.

49   Shahab (1962:26-27).

in religious gatherings in various cities in Java, including Jakarta. These two figures continued to spread the Shi'i teachings among their relatives and small groups of acquaintances.[50] Some newly converted Shi'is, both Arab and non-Arab, in the post-Iranian revolution period had the opportunity to receive Shi'i teachings from Husein al-Muhdar.

The best known figures of the Shahab clan are Muhammad Dhiya Shahab (d.1986) and Muhammad Asad Shahab (d. 2001), both sons of Ali Ahmad Shahab. Muhammad Dhiya Shahab was a teacher, journalist and writer. Like his father, he was a leading figure within the Arab community in Indonesia and had a major role in the development of *Jami'at Khair*, becoming its organisational chief for about ten years (1935-1945). He taught at the schools of *Jami'at Khair* and led *al-Rabita al-Alawiyya* (the Alawi League); in doing so he paid great attention to the social and religious development of the Arabs all over Indonesia. From 1950 to 1960 he worked at the Department of Information.[51] He wrote a number of scholarly works, most published in Arabic in Beirut, including *al-Imam al-Muhajir*,[52] which was written in collaboration with Abdullah bin Nuh (1905-1987).

Muhammad Asad Shahab was also a journalist and prolific writer. He first studied at the schools of *Jami'at Khair* and then moved to the *al-Khairiyya* school in Surabaya, which he completed in 1932. From 1935, he was a correspondent for several newspapers. In 1945, together with his elder brother, he founded a news agency named the *Arabian Press Board* (APB), which in 1950 became the *Asian Press Board*. In 1963 APB merged with the national news agency institute, *Antara* because President Sukarno wanted a single news agency in the country. Muhammad Asad Shahab was also the founder of the magazine *National Press Digest*.[53] Like his elder brother, he then worked at the Muslim World League in Mecca from 1965. It is pertinent to note that Asad Shahab introduced the modernist scholar Hamka to various Iranian scholars who contributed to Hamka's acceptance of Shi'i books on Qur'anic exegesis, including Tabataba'i's *al-Mizan* and Ayatollah Khoei's *al-Bayan fi Tafsir al-Qur'an* which also become important sources of his *tafsir* book, *Al-Azhar*.[54] Muhammad Asad Shahab wrote a large number of Arabic books and treatises, which were published in the Middle East.

In the 1960s the two brothers established an Islamic foundation known as *Lembaga Penyelidikan Islam* (Islamic Research Institute) and along with it a

---

50 Zainal Abidin al-Muhdar, interview, (28/7/2002).
51 Salam (1992:18).
52 The complete title is *al-Imam al-Muhajir Ahmad bin 'Isa bin Muhammad bin 'Ali al-'Uraydi bin Ja'far al-Sadiq, ma lahu wa li naslihi wa li al-A'imma min aslafihi min al-fada'il wa al-ma'athir* published in 1980 by Dar al-Shuruq, Jeddah. It is from this 'emigrant' Imam that the clan of Ba'Alawi Sayyids trace their descent.
53 Salam (1986:90).
54 Hamka (1983:326-327).

periodical, *Pembina* ('The Cultivator'). The general goals of the institute were to build up a relatively representative library to provide books, journals, magazines and other sources on Islamic knowledge in general and Shi'ism in particular, to translate foreign language books - mainly Arabic - into Indonesian, and to distribute books and periodicals to the Muslim community of Indonesia. Its last goal was to send students to pursue an Islamic education in the Middle East.[55]

They also tried to establish close connections with the Shi'i *'ulama* in Middle Eastern countries with a view to realising the propagation of Shi'ism in Indonesia and received the support of a number of *'ulama*. Muhammad Kazim al-Quzwaini in Karbala, Iraq sent books and periodicals, including material on several fields of Islamic knowledge such as Ja'fari jurisprudence, Qur'anic exegesis, Hadith and ethics. Similarly, the Grand Ayatollah Muhsin al-Hakim (d. 1970) of Najaf, Iraq, Muhammad Jawad Mughniyya (d. 1979), Hasan al-Amin and *al-'Irfan* (the first Shi'i publishing house in Lebanon), gifted a large number of books and other printed materials to Shi'i Sayyids in Indonesia.[56] With the collections of works received from these *'ulama* and institutions, the Islamic Research Institute functioned well as a centre for the spread of Shi'ism in Indonesia. As a result of its relatively representative collections of Shi'i works, it proved to be very beneficial for those wanting to learn about Shi'ism. One beneficiary was the late Abubakar Atjeh, who used the institute to publish a series comparing *madhhab*, including *Sji'ah, Rasionalisme dalam Islam* (Shi'ism, Rationalism in Islam). Published in 1965, this was the first sympathetic book on the *madhhab* to be written in Indonesian.[57] The institute also became a publisher of several Islamic books.

Visits to Middle Eastern Shi'i *'ulama* were also made. In 1956 Muhammad Asad Shahab met with 'Abd al-Husain Sharaf al-Din (d. 1957), Ahmad Arif al-Zayn of *al-'Irfan* and Muhammad Jawad Mughniyya in Lebanon.[58] He visited Hibbat al-Din al-Shahrastani in Baghdad, the Grand Ayatollah Muhsin al-Hakim (d. 1970), Muhammad Rida al-Muzaffar (d. 1964) and Muhammad Taqi al-Hakim (d. 2002) in Najaf. He reported that the Shi'i *'ulama* showed concern for the condition and development of Shi'ism in Indonesia and they agreed to accept Indonesian students in their Islamic institutions. However, according to Asad Shahab, a variety of reasons, including strict regulations on visas to go abroad, meant that this opportunity could not be fully utilized at the time.[59]

---

55   Shahab (1986:322).
56   Shahab (1962:55).
57   Siradjuddin Abbas criticised Abubakar Atjeh's sympathetic attitude towards Shi'ism. It was one of his motivations to write his famous book, *I'itiqad Ahlussunnah wal-Djama'ah* (the Doctrine of *ahl al-Sunna wa al-Jama'a*), first published in 1969 by Pustaka Tarbiyah, Jakarta. Abbas dedicates many pages of the book to a discussion of the falsity of Shi'i teachings and its contrast to the true teachings of Sunnism.
58   The visit to Lebanon is mentioned in Mughniyya (1973:205).
59   Shahab (1962:56).

Connections between Indonesian Shi'is and Middle Eastern Shi'i *'ulama* were sustained by visits of the latter, or their representatives, to Indonesia. During such visits information was exchanged and knowledge of Shi'ism was transmitted. Meetings with individual Shi'is and discussions of the principal teachings were held. In 1962, for instance, a learned Shi'i from Iraq, Muhammad Reza Ja'fari visited Indonesia to meet Muslim leaders in the country. His itinerary included a visit to the *al-Khairiyya* school in Bondowoso. Teachers and students at the *madrasa,* as well as leading Shi'i figures in the country, including Muhammad Asad Shahab and Husein Al-Habsyi (1921-1994) engaged in discussions about the principal teachings of Shi'ism. Hamzah Al-Habsyi told me that the discussions lasted for four days. Following this event, some teachers of the school converted to Shi'ism. Hamzah Al-Habsyi himself, currently a prominent Shi'i *ustadh* in Bondowoso, admitted that he converted to Shi'ism around 1969.[60]

With its albeit limited instruments of propagation and its Middle Eastern connections, this small group succeeded in maintaining continuity and attracting new members to Shi'ism in various cities, towns and villages across Indonesia. Three figures are worthy of mention in this regard. The first is Sayyid Abdul Qadir Bafaqih of Bangsri in Jepara, Central Java, who converted to Shi'ism after reading books that he had received from Kuwait in 1974. In the village of Bangsri he set up and headed *Pesantren Al-Khairat* where he imparted the teachings of Shi'ism, recorded his instruction and wrote a number of unpublished books.[61] His teachings attracted students and a number of people from the surrounding *pesantren*, who in turn spread Shi'ism to other areas, such as Bulustalan, South Semarang, in Central Java.[62] His propagation elicited negative reactions from Sunni figures in the region and also attracted the attention of the government and mass media in 1982.[63]

The second figure is Sayyid Ahmad Al-Habsyi (d.1994), the leader of *Pesantren Ar-Riyadh* in Palembang, South Sumatra. He established contacts with an Islamic foundation in Tehran called the Muslim Brotherhood. It was Al-Habsyi who sent his students and renowned Shi'i *ustadhs* Umar Shahab and his brother Husein Shahab, to pursue their studies in Qum in 1974 and 1979 respectively.[64] In this regard it is also worth mentioning an effort made by the *Pesantren Al-Khairat* of Palu, Central Sulawesi — another sister educational institution of the *Jami'at Khair* of Jakarta — that had previously sent students to Qum, as

---

60 Hamzah Al-Habsyi, interview, (15/10/2002).
61 Syafi'i (1983/1984).
62 Hakim and Hadiwiyata (1997/1998:12).
63 For the reaction from the government, see Chapter Seven. Some Indonesian mass media which provided reports on the unusual fact that Abdul Qadir Bafaqih was a Shi'i are daily *Berita Buana* 25/10/1982, *Sinar Pagi Minggu* 1/11/3100/XIII, *Suara Merdeka* 27, 28, 29/10/1982, and *Tempo* 20/11/1982.
64 Umar Shahab, interview, (9/1/2003).

illustrated in the section below. These links in the 1970s between Shi'i Sayyids and Iranian *'ulama* contributed to a new and important development in Shi'ism in Indonesia.

The third figure of note is Sayyid Husein Al-Habsyi, who established YAPI (*Yayasan Pesantren Islam*, Foundation of Islamic Pesantren) in Bangil in 1976. He and his *pesantren* have greatly contributed to the spread of Shi'ism in Indonesia.[65] As we shall see below, he sent a large number of students – most of whom were of Arab descent - to study in Qum after the establishment of the Islamic Republic of Iran. Most have since become renowned Shi'i *ustadhs* in Indonesia.

The triumph of the Iranian revolution in 1979 was a very important historical moment for the foundation of the Shi'i community in Indonesia. The revolution contributed not only to many conversions to the Shi'i branch of Islam but also to "a consciousness and awareness of the Shi'is and their history."[66] After the revolution many Arabs, both Sayyid and non-Sayyid, converted. But aside from the Iranian revolution and a heightened consciousness of neo-colonialism, Al-Attas provides us with two major reasons for conversion to Shi'ism within the Sayyid community in Southeast Asia. The first is a general perception by the Sayyids that the other religious and ethnic communities in the region are somehow 'backward'. Second, Khomeini, the leader of the revolution, is a Sayyid and this genealogical convergence between Shi'ism and the Sayyids has attracted this group to turn to Shi'ism.[67] The position of the Arab group within the Shi'i community continues to be significant as a result of its early experience of the Shi'i educational institutions in Qum, Iran. It should be noted however that while this group pioneered the sending of students to Qum, quantitatively speaking, students from other ethnic groups now outnumber them.

B. The Qum Alumni

A very important contribution to the formation of the Shi'i community in Indonesia was the emergence of Qum graduates, those who had pursued Islamic education in the *hawza 'ilmiyya* (colleges of learning) in Qum, presently the most important centre of Shi'i Islamic education in the world. The majority of renowned Indonesian Shi'i *ustadhs* graduated from these colleges. For this reason, Shi'i *ustadhs* are frequently identified with the Qum alumni, even though a number were actually educated in Egypt or Saudi Arabia. Among the

---

65   The position of Husein Al-Habsyi as a Shi'i leader is dealt with in Chapter Two, while his *pesantren* is described in Chapter Five.

66   Al-Attas (1999:335).

67   Al-Attas (1999:337-338).

Qum alumni are Umar Shahab and his younger brother Husein Shahab, two of the most popular Shi'i figures engaged in educational and *da'wa* activities in Jakarta. They are connected to a number of Shi'i foundations in which *pengajian,* or religious gatherings are held. Another renowned figure, although reluctant to accept his status, is Abdurrahman Bima, who leads the Madina Ilmu College for Islamic Studies, a tertiary educational institution located in Depok, South Jakarta. In Pekalongan, Central Java Ahmad Baragbah leads a famous Shi'i *pesantren* called *Al-Hadi.* Frequently, *ustadhs* who had graduated from Islamic schools in other Middle Eastern countries and even intellectuals from secular universities also went to Qum to take short-term training programmes in order to establish connections with Shi'i leaders and *'ulama.* For example, Hasan Dalil, who finished his undergraduate programme in Riyadh, Saudi Arabia, took a three-month training programme in Qum. Even the most renowned Indonesian Shi'i intellectual, Jalaluddin Rakhmat and his family stayed in Qum for a year so that he could attend learning circles and lectures conducted by ayatollahs. This illustrates the extreme importance of a Shi'i education in Qum to adherents in Indonesia.

It is unclear exactly when Indonesian students began to pursue an Islamic education in Qum, but it is known that some did so several years before the Iranian revolution. They were Arabs living in various parts of the Indonesian archipelago. Ali Ridho Al-Habsyi, son of Muhammad Al-Habsyi and grandson of Habib Ali Kwitang of Jakarta,[68] studied in Qum in 1974. Six graduates of the *Pesantren Al-Khairat* of Palu, Central Sulawesi followed over the next two years. In September 1976, Umar Shahab from Palembang, South Sumatra and today a famous Shi'i *ustadh*, went to Qum and, he says, studied alongside seven other Indonesian students.[69] In his fieldwork in 1975, Fischer also noted the presence of Indonesian students in Qum; among the foreign students, including those from Pakistan, Afghanistan, India, Lebanon, Tanzania, Turkey, Nigeria and Kashmir, Indonesians were however in a minority.[70]

Since the establishment of the Islamic Republic of Iran in 1979, interaction between its government and Indonesian Shi'i *'ulama* has intensified. The victory of the ayatollahs inspired Indonesian intellectuals and *'ulama* to study the ideological foundations of the Iranian revolution. At the same time, an 'export

---

68   Habib Ali Al-Habsyi (1870-1968) known as Ali Kwitang was an *'alim* and leader of the Indonesian Arab community. He was the founder of the famous *Majlis Ta'lim* (Meeting place for Education and *Da'wa*) of Kwitang. He was regarded as a sainted *Wali* (friend of God) and his grave has become an important pilgrimage site for Jakarta's Muslims. After Habib Ali died, the *Majlis Ta'lim* was led by his son Muhammad (1911-1993) who was close to President Suharto and to GOLKAR (*Golongan Karya*) political circles. Today it is under the leadership of Muhammad's son, Abdurrahman (Abaza 2004), Ali Ridho's brother. Ali Ridho's sister, Farida Al-Habsyi is a well-known Shi'i figure who runs a number of Islamic foundations in Jakarta, including *Al-Bathul* (The Virgin, an honorific title of Fatimah, the Prophet's daughter).
69   Umar Shahab, interview, (9/1/2003).
70   Fischer (1980:78).

of revolution' occurred, as Iranian leaders and *'ulama* aimed to spread Shi'ism in Indonesia and to attract Indonesian students to study in Iran. In 1982, the Iranian government sent its representatives Ayatollah Ibrahim Amini, Ayatollah Masduqi and Hujjat al-Islam Mahmudi to Indonesia. Among their activities was a visit to YAPI (*Yayasan Pesantren Islam*, Foundation of Islamic Pesantren) of Bangil, East Java, where they met with its leader, Husein Al-Habsyi, who was to become Indonesia's most important confidant to Iranian leaders and *'ulama*. At the time, Husein Al-Habsyi was probably one of the most prominent Shi'i *'ulama* in Indonesia and played a major role in the development of *da'wa* and education. Following the meeting, Qum's *hawza 'ilmiyya* agreed to accept ten Indonesian students selected by Husein Al-Habsyi. From then until his death in 1994, Husein Al-Habsyi hand-picked candidates for study at *hawza 'ilmiyya* in Qum and other cities in Iran.

As a result, among the Indonesian students who went to Qum in 1982 a number were graduates of YAPI. They have become renowned Shi'i *ustadhs* in Indonesia. Of the original 10 students, almost all of whom were Arabs, six were alumni of YAPI while four were from other educational institutions. The YAPI alumni include Muhsin Labib, Husein Al-Habsyi's step-son and Rusdi Al-Aydrus, who have become Shi'i *ustadhs* in Indonesia, while Husein Al-Habsyi's natural son, Ibrahim Al-Habsyi, continues his studies in Qum today. From outside YAPI, Ahmad Baragbah and Hasan Abu Ammar have become Shi'i *ustadhs*. In the later period, graduates of YAPI and/or those recommended by Husein Al-Habsyi still predominated among the students going to Qum. Between 1985 and 1989, Al-Habsyi sent 10 students to Qum and today most of them have established or are affiliated to Shi'i foundations in Indonesia and have been recognised as important Shi'i *ustadhs*.[71]

Subsequently, graduates of other Islamic educational institutions such as the *Muthahhari* Foundation and *Al-Hadi* were selected to pursue their education in Qum. This corresponds to the growing influence of the Shi'i intellectuals Jalaluddin Rakhmat and Haidar Bagir, whose recommendations are now recognised in Iran. Over the course of time, the educational background of the Indonesian students studying in Qum has become diversified. While most students generally go to Qum to complete their secondary education, of late several graduates of tertiary education have also continued their studies there. Among them are alumni of the *Madina Ilmu* College for Islamic Studies

---

71   They include Musyayya Ba'abud, Zahir Yahya, leader of the *Al-Kautsar* Foundation in Malang, East Java and former head of YAPI; Miqdad, head of *Pesantren Darut Taqrib* in Jepara, Central Java; Fathoni Hadi, founder of the *Al-Hujjah* Foundation in Jember, East Java and currently on the staff at the Islamic College for Advanced Studies in Jakarta; Muhammad Amin Sufyan, head of the *Samudera* Foundation in Surabaya; Abdurrahman Bima; Husein Alkaff, adviser at the *Al-Jawad* Foundation in Bandung; Herman Al-Munthahhar, head of the *Amirul Mukminin* Foundation in Pontianak, West Kalimantan; Muhammad Al-Jufri and Abdul Aziz Al-Hinduan.

in Depok. We also find graduates of secular universities studying in Qum. One example is Mujtahid Hashem, a graduate of the technical faculty of the University of Indonesia (UI). Hashem travelled to Qum in 2001 to engage in the study of religious knowledge. While there, he was elected general secretary of the Association of Indonesian Students in Iran (*Himpunan Pelajar Indonesia*, HPI).[72]

The number of Indonesian students in Qum has increased significantly. By 1990, 50 Indonesian students had reportedly completed their studies or were still studying there. Ten years later the Qum graduates in Indonesia numbered more than a hundred. In 2001, 50 Indonesian students were selected to continue their studies in Qum[73] and in 2004, I am informed, 90 more students were selected.[74]

Meanwhile, the Iranian government, through ICIS, the International Centre for Islamic Studies (*Markaze Jahani-e Ulume Islami*)[75] has stepped up efforts to attract international students. Since 1994 ICIS has been under the supervision of the office of the Leader of the Islamic Revolution headed by the Grand Ayatollah 'Ali Khamene'i, who also appointed its Director. Annually, an ICIS representative conducts a selection process at such Islamic institutions as the Islamic Cultural Centre in Jakarta and the Muthahhari Foundation in Bandung. In addition to academic achievement, the knowledge of Arabic is a requisite, as it is an international language for Islamic learning and the language of instruction at certain *madrasas* in Qum. Upon their arrival in Iran, students are also required to follow a six-month training programme in Persian, which is the language of instruction at most of Qum's Islamic educational institutions.

There are two educational systems at the *hawza 'ilmiyya*: the traditional system, which is the most famous and influential, and the modern system. The traditional system's curriculum includes both transmitted and intellectual religious sciences: *fiqh* (jurisprudence), *usul al-fiqh* (principles of jurisprudence), *'ulum al-Qur'an* (the Qur'an sciences), *'ulum al-Hadith* (sciences of the Traditions), *nahw* (Arabic syntax), *sarf* (Arabic morphology), *balagha* (rhetoric), *mantiq* (logic), *hikma* (philosophy), *kalam* (theology), *tasawuf* and *'irfan* (Sufism and gnosis). Each subject has its own standard texts,[76] which are studied in *halaqat, or* study circles under the supervision of an ayatollah. The educational programme comprises three levels: *muqaddamat* (preliminary), *sutuh* (external) and *dars al-kharij* (graduation class) or *bahth al-kharij* (graduation research).[77] All three

---

72   *Syi'ar* (Muharram 1425/2004:31-32). This student association was established in August 2000 (http://islamalternatif.com/tentang_kami/hpi.html).
73   Ali (2002:201-204).
74   They were classified in terms of financial support; some will receive full scholarship whilst others will receive only monthly stipends excluding airfare ticket.
75   A brief account of ICIS can be read in: http://www.qomicis.com/english/about/history.asp.
76   Nasr (1987:165-182).
77   Momen (1985).

levels must be completed by every *mujtahid* or jurist who has achieved the level of competence necessary to make religious decisions based on reasoning from the principal sources of Islam.

At the preliminary stage, which lasts from three to five years, the emphasis is to provide students with various skills in Arabic. The main subjects taught include *nahw*, *sarf*, *balagha* and *mantiq*. In addition, there are optional subjects including literature, mathematics, astronomy and introductory *fiqh* taken from one of the *risalah 'amaliyya* (tracts on practice) by a contemporary *marja' al-taqlid*, an authoritative source in matters of Islamic law. The teaching method at this level involves groups of students gathered around a teacher who will go through the texts with them. Students are free to choose the teachers to become their instructors, who at this level are usually senior students or assistants of *maraji' al-taqlid*.[78]

At the *sutuh* level, which usually lasts from three to six years, students are introduced to the substance of deductive *fiqh* and *usul al-fiqh* on which their progress to the next and ultimate level depends. The optional subjects provided at this level are *tafsir* (Qur'anis exegesis), Hadith, *kalam* (theology), philosophy, *'irfan*, history and ethics. Generally, courses are a series of lectures based on the main texts of the two main subjects and students are free to select which lectures to attend. The students may also attend lectures in the optional subjects. Usually, teachers at this level are *mujtahids* who have just achieved the authority of *ijtihad* and are establishing a reputation.[79]

Although the subjects at the ultimate level, *dars al-kharij* are *fiqh* and *usul al-fiqh*, the method of learning is different from that of the other two levels. Teaching is conducted by the prominent *mujtahids* who inform students of the schedule and places for their class. Students are free to choose whose class they will attend and it is usual for several hundred participants, including other *mujtahids*, to attend lectures delivered by the most prominent *mujtahids*. The dialectical method is generally implemented in the class; students are free to discuss and are encouraged to argue points with the teacher. At this stage, most students are accomplished in the skill of abstract argumentation and are trained to develop their self-confidence. The culmination of the learning process is the attainment of an *ijaza* (licence) from one of the many recognised *mujtahids*. A student at this level is expected to write a treatise on *fiqh* or *usul al-fiqh* and present it to a *mujtahid*, who will consider the student and the work. Based on

---

78   Momen (1985:200-201), Mallat (1993:39-40).
79   Momen (1985:200-201), Mallat (1993:40).

this evaluation, the *mujtahid* will issue the *ijaza*, which authorises the student to exercise *ijtihad*.[80] In this way, students build their careers based on their relationsip with certain *mujtahid* teachers.

When a student receives the *ijaza* that makes him a *mujtahid*, the honorific title of Ayatollah (*Ayat Allah*, 'sign of God') is usually bestowed upon him. An *ayatollah* recognised as a *marja' al-taqlid* usually receives the title of Ayatollah al-'Uzma, or Grand Ayatollah. The usual term for an aspiring *mujtahid* is *hujjat al-Islam* (proof of Islam). The hierarchy of Shi'i *'ulama* is pyramidal; those of the highest level, the Grand Ayatollahs, are the fewest in number and it is these who have played a major role throughout history.

The *madrasa* system is a transformation of the classical system, adopting a modern system of education in terms of gradation, curriculum, classroom learning and rules. Non-traditional *madrasas* 'are set up to serve needs not supplied by the traditional system.'[81] The curriculum consists of a combination of religious and secular sciences presented through a slightly simplified version of traditional study courses. Unlike the traditional system, the *madrasa* system is not intended to train students to become *mujtahids* but rather to become Islamic scholars and missionaries. This innovative type of education has provided an alternative for students who, for whatever reason, cannot follow the traditional system in the *hawza 'ilmiyya*. Many international students, including Indonesians, undertake this modern programme.

The Islamic Republic of Iran has made educational innovations in Qum's *hawza 'ilmiyya* through ICIS, which coordinates programmes for foreign students, assigns students to *madrasas* and monitors their needs within the framework of disseminating Islamic knowledge and teachings globally. The *Madrasa Imam Khomeini*, for example, offers programmes based on grade systems that include undergraduate and graduate levels equivalent to the tertiary education of the modern educational system. Such innovation makes Qum's *hawza 'ilmiyya* even more the leading institutions of the Islamic world.

Indonesian students have been through both educational systems. The first group of Indonesian students were enrolled at *Dar al-Tabligh al-Islami*, a modern institution founded in 1965 by Ayatollah Muhammad Kazim Shari'atmadari (1904-1987).[82] *Dar al-Tabligh* was known for its acceptance of foreign students and for arranging their visas and residence permits. It ran a five-year programme

---

80 Momen (1985:202), Mallat (1993:41-42).
81 Fischer (1980:81).
82 Ayatollah Muhammad Kazim Shari'atmadari (1904-1987) was known as a moderate clergyman. He was one of the *maraji' al-taqlid* in the Shi'i world in 1975, the other being Ayatollahs Khoei and Khomeini in Najaf, Gulpayegani and Mar'ashi-Najafi in Qum, Khonsari in Tehran and Milani in Mashhad. Conducting his fieldwork in 1975, Fischer noticed mild competition and friendly rivalry among these *maraji' al-taqlid* in setting up schools, hospitals, missions and conducting other activities abroad (Fischer 1980:91).

with a credit system[83] and a curriculum that included both religious knowledge and secular sciences such as psychology, philosophy, sociology, mathematics and English. The language of instruction was Arabic. *Dar al-Tabligh* did not follow the traditional system of learning, even though it was strongly entrenched in the traditional *hawza* system.[84] Accordingly, the first group of Indonesian students in Qum followed the formal modern system of education, even though they were free to attend classes or lectures provided by the traditional *hawza 'ilmiyya* system.

After the dissolution of *Dar al-Tabligh*[85] in 1981, owing to its leader's opposition to the concept of *wilayat al-faqih* ('mandate of the jurist') implemented by Khomeini, *Madrasa Hujjatiyya* took over the provision of the same programme for foreign students. Since 1982 nearly all of the Indonesian students who have gone to Iran attended *Madrasa Hujjatiyya*, including the prominent *ustadh* Husein Shahab, who transferred to this *madrasa* after he had studied for two years at *Dar al-Tabligh*.[86] This *madrasa* was founded in 1946 by Ayatollah Muhammad Hujjat Kuhkamari (1892-1963) who was a student of 'Abd al-Karim Ha'iri (d. 1936), the reformer of the *hawza 'ilmiyya* of Qum.[87] Unlike *Dar al-Tabligh*, the *Hujjatiyya* school follows the traditional system of education generally used in the *hawza 'ilmiyya*. Most Indonesian students who become Shi'i *ustadhs* in Indonesia only complete its preliminary level.[88]

The majority of Indonesian students were registered at *Madrasa Hujjatiyya*, but a small number pursued their learning at *Madrasa Mu'miniyya*, which also provided a programme for foreign students. This *madrasa* was founded in 1701 during the reign of Sultan Husayn of the Safavid dynasty. It was rebuilt by the Grand Ayatollah Shihab al-Din Mar'ashi-Najafi (d. 1991) who was known for his

---

83 Fischer (1980:84).
84 Umar Shahab, interview, (9/1/2003). *Dar al-Tabligh* also carried out a number of *da'wa* programmes such as training for preachers, correspondence courses on Islam and publishing Islamic books and journals. It had four journals, *Maktab-i Islam* (School of Islam), *Payam-i Shadi* (Glad Tidings) and *Nasl-i Naw* (New Generation) in Persian, while *al-Hadi* (the Guide) was in Arabic. Their circulation was extensive; *Maktab-i Islam* reached a circulation of 60,000. With its circulation abroad *al-Hadi* served a link to Muslims and Islamic institutions in other countries (Fischer 1980:84).
85 Besides his school being dissolved, Shari'atmadari himself was also formally demoted from the rank of *marja' al-taqlid* on April 1982 (Momen1985:296).
86 Husein Shahab, interview, (2/4/2004).
87 Stewart (2001:218).
88 An exceptional case is Abdurrahman Al-Aydrus known as Abdurrahman Bima, coming from Bima, Lombok. He spent nine years in Qum. After graduating from YAPI in Bangil, under the recommendation of Husein Al-Habsyi he went to Qum in 1987 and entered the *Hujjatiyya* school. After finishing his *muqaddamat* in 1990, he pursued the *sutuh* level and completed the study of *usul al-fiqh* at the *dars al-kharij*. He was then selected to continue at the Imam Sadiq Institute, founded and headed by Ayatollah Ja'far Subhani. At this institution, he majored in Islamic theology under the supervision of the prominent theologian Ayatollah Ja'far Subhani, with whom he continues to maintain a good relationship. He was required to write a PhD thesis for this institute (Ali 2002:246-249). In 1996, Abdurrahman returned to Indonesia and has been engaged in the fields of *da'wa* and education. His activities include the directorship of Madina Ilmu College for Islamic Studies in Depok, South Jakarta. In 2000, he enrolled in a PhD programme at UIN in Jakarta.

role in the establishment of a large library in Qum which holds a magnificent collection of books and manuscripts.[89] *Madrasa Mu'miniyya* formulated its own particular system and curriculum based on its own materials, rather than on recognised textbooks. In contrast to the *Hujjatiyya*, the *Mu'miniyya* school prohibited its students from attending religious lectures and study circles in the traditional *hawza* system.[90]

More recently, there has been educational reform in Qum and a large number of Indonesian students have registered at the *Madrasa Imam Khomeini*. Since 1996, this *madrasa* has been organised to become the main educational centre for international students. Established after the death of leader of the Iranian revolution, it runs a modern system of education in terms of programmes and curriculum, even though it remains entrenched in the traditional character of the *hawza* system. It organises both undergraduate and graduate programmes in various fields of specialisation within the realm of religious sciences.[91]

Early Qum alumni, such as Umar Shahab, Husein Shahab and Ahmad Baragbah, have become prominent Shi'i figures and have contributed to the development of Islamic *da'wa*, education and culture in Indonesia. Thus the Qum alumni can be seen as an influential element in the formation of the Shi'i community.

C. The Campus Group

Another significant group within the Shi'i community in Indonesia comes from campuses of the universities. Although the emergence of this group is generally seen as a response to the success of the Iranian revolution in 1979, there are a few figures who converted to Shi'ism long before. The first to be mentioned is Ridwan Suhud, a lecturer at ITB[92] and a member of IJABI, the national Shi'i association in Indonesia. Another important figure was K.H. Abdullah bin Nuh (1905-1987), whose adherence to Shi'ism can be seen in the light of his family connections with Ali Ahmad Shahab - he was a maternal relative of the Shahab family. He was also a close friend of Muhammad Dhiya and Muhammad Asad Shahab. Early in his career he worked closely with members of the Hadrami community in the Dutch East Indies. Before studying in Egypt from 1926 to 1928, both he and his brother, Abdurrahman had been teachers at the Hadramaut School in Surabaya. Later, he became a lecturer at UII in Yogyakarta (1945-1950) and at UI in Jakarta (1960-1967). Aside from his teaching, K.H. Abdullah bin

---

89   This is the largest library in Qum and may become an important research site for scholars. Reports on this library may be seen in *Syi'ar* (March 2003:39-40) and http://www.al-shia.com/hatml/eng/lib/lib-najafi_h.htm.
90   Ali (2002:192-194).
91   *Syiar* (Muharram 1425/2004:31).
92   Wisananingrum (2001:74).

Nuh was also a journalist and a writer, working for APB and the magazines, *National Digest Press* and *Pembina*. He led the aforementioned Islamic Research Institute and its periodical, *Pembina* for ten years (1962-1972). In this weekly magazine he provided regular commentary on religion, discussing aspects of Islamic teachings such as jurisprudence, ethics and Sufism. He wrote a number of books, some of which are not published, and has also translated a selection of works by the famous Persian philosopher and Sufi al-Ghazali (1058-1111). After 1972, he devoted his life to teaching at his own Islamic foundations in Bogor, West Java: *Majlis Al-Ghazaly, Majlis Al-Ihya, Majlis Al-Husna and Majlis Nahjus Salam,* which have proved to be influential in the Muslim community in this part of Indonesia.[93]

There has been some controversy about whether Abdullah bin Nuh was actually a Shi'i. Indonesian Sunnis claim him as one of their own, while some Shi'is who came into contact with him regard him as Shi'i.[94] Although Abdullah bin Nuh declared himself to be a follower of *Shafi'i* jurisprudence, he frequently attended Shi'i rituals and commemorations held in the Iranian Embassy in Jakarta. He also participated in the first World Congress of Friday Imams held in Tehran in 1983.[95] Further evidence of his adherence to Shi'ism may be found in his work, *Risalah Asyura: 10 Muharam*, in which he provides a short history of Husayn bin 'Ali, the third Imam and a discussion of the famous Hadith of *thaqalayn* (literally 'two weighty matters', or safeguards, which command the faithful to uphold the Qur'an and the Prophet's Household. Having described several versions of the Hadith from the Sunni collections, he affirms that they are all valid. He goes on to point out that the *Hadith* of *thaqalayn* clearly designates that the faithful should acknowledge the leadership of the Prophet Muhammad. He also cites the famous *hadith* of Ghadir Khumm, in which the Prophet appointed 'Ali bin Abi Talib as his successor. Abdullah bin Nuh argues that one of the philosophical qualities of *thaqalayn* is the guarantee of salvation for Muslims because the members of the *ahl al-bayt,* the Prophet's Household were most knowledgeable about Islamic teaching and practice.[96] He writes: "his [the Prophet Muhammad's] exhortation is not a fabricated matter but it is truly a required necessity, particularly in the period of growth and development of Islam."[97] With regard to the identification of the *ahl al-bayt* in the Qur'an (in the 'purification' verse) Abdullah bin Nuh rejects the widespread Sunni view, which includes the Prophet's wives. Instead he shares the view of the Shi'i

---

93 Salam (1986:85-86).
94 Furqon Bukhari, interview, (10/9/2002).
95 Jamaluddin Asmawi, interview, (2/10/2002).
96 Abdullah bin Nuh (1401/1981:13-19).
97 Abdullah bin Nuh (1401/1981:19).

'ulama that limits the identity of the *ahl al-bayt* to 'Ali, his wife Fatima and their two sons, Hasan and Husayn.[98] This interpretation is completely in accord with the Shi'i understanding of the *ahl al-bayt*, as will be shown in Chapter Three.

The appearance of a number of new converts to Shi'ism on the university campuses of Indonesia during the 1980s was in part a response to the Iranian revolution. This does not mean however that a fascination with Ayatollah Khomeini's victory automatically resulted in wide conversion to Shi'ism. In fact, many Indonesian Muslim scholars who followed the historical events occurring in Iran during 1978-1979, particularly through the mass media,[99] have remained Sunni. This includes Hamka (1908-1981), a prominent modernist *'alim* and the then general chairman of MUI (*Majlis Ulama Indonesia*, Council of Indonesian Ulama)[100] and M. Amien Rais.[101] Among the newly converted were lecturers,

---

98   Abdullah bin Nuh (1401/1981:21).

99   The events of the revolution attracted the attention of the mass media in Indonesia, particularly Muslim magazines and Muslim-led newspapers. "At the beginning, the prestige of the Iranian revolution was high in the eyes of the Muslim leaders of Indonesia, even if they were Sunni, not Shi'i" (Tamara 1986:24).

100   Hamka (pseudonym of Haji Abdul Malik Karim Amrullah) is the only Indonesian *'alim* to write his views of the Iranian revolution. This prominent modernist religious scholar paid great attention to what was happening in Iran at the time. In early 1979, for instance, his weekly magazine, *Panji Masyarakat* (Banner of Society) provided detailed reports, combined with reflective views crediting and supporting the revolution. Hamka regards it as one of the greatest historical events in the world and relates it to the phenomenon of Islamic revival in the 15th century of the Muslim calendar. For Hamka, the Iranian revolution is parallel with other great revolutions in the world, such as the French and Russian revolutions. He believes the most important value of the revolution is the success of the Iranians in fighting secularism.

Initially, Hamka presented his appraisal and admiration of events to Ayatollah Ruhullah Khomeini in his writings published in *Panji Masyarakat*. Under the rubric *"Dari Hati ke Hati"* (From Heart to Heart) of the same magazine (1/3/1979) Hamka wrote an interesting article, "Revolution and Evolution" in which he described the victory of the revolution and gave a profile of Khomeini, emphasising how the power of Islamic faith, or *iman*, strongly upheld by Khomeini, succeeded in overthrowing the Shah of Iran, renowned for his powerful army and sophisticated weapons. In his position as a leading Sunni *'alim*, however, it can be argued that Hamka's sympathetic view concerns the Iranian Islamic political revolution and not Shi'ism itself.

101   In 1979 the Chicago-educated political scientist and modernist Muslim, Amien Rais wrote a column, published in *Panji Masyarakat*, entitled "Avoiding Revolution" (reprinted in Rais 1987) in response to the revolution in Iran. In it he provides a theoretical outline of why a revolution takes place, pinpointing five causal factors: contradictions between the economic and political systems of a society, a widening gap between the haves and the have-nots, a protracted financial crisis, a deepening alienation of intellectuals and the role of arrogant, stubborn and brutal elites. In his conclusion, Rais affirms that in the Qur'an there are examples of elites being shattered by a disaffected population. He suggests that such examples are valuable lessons for every nation, including Indonesia (Rais 1987:143). Even though he barely refers specifically to the Iranian revolution in this article, Rais' theoretical construction is clearly inspired by it.

Seven years later, in April 1987, Rais published "Seven Years of the Iranian revolution" which also appeared in *Panji Masyarakat*. In this long article, Rais (1987:199-218) sympathetically describes the historical processes of the Iranian revolution, beginning with the shoddiness and corruption of the Shah's regime, which was clearly vulnerable to revolution. He then analyses the revolutionary ideas of Iranian leaders and ideologues Khomeini, Ali Shari'ati, Ayatollah Taleqani and Ayatollah Mutahhari. This is followed by an analysis of the social and political problems faced by Iran, including the Iran-Iraq war. Important to note here is Rais's favourable view of prospects for Iran; he predicts the end to the Iran-Iraq war, which would enable Iran to realise its Islamic mission of justice. He is highly critical of negative views suggesting a future disintegration of Iran. The failure of the Islamic Republic of Iran is not an option for Rais, as this would mean a setback for the Muslim *umma* to last half a century or more. Rais does not discuss at length the importance of Shi'i doctrines in the revolution. In another article (1985) however he states that: "the revolution itself was founded on the

some of whom have become prominent intellectuals and have played a major role in the development of Shi'ism in Indonesia. A central figure has been Jalaluddin Rakhmat,[102] lecturer at UNPAD (*Universitas Pajajaran*, Pajajaran University) in Bandung, West Java, who established a Shi'i institution called the *Muthahhari* Foundation in 1988. This foundation has played a significant role in the development of Shi'ism in Indonesia. Another Shi'i figure of note is Muchtar Adam (b. 1939) who also lectured at UNPAD and founded *Pesantren Babus Salam* in Ciburial, North Bandung. Besides lecturing in Islamic educational institutions he has written several scholarly works.

Another important converted figure of the campus groups is Muhammad al-Baqir Al-Habsyi, who became familiar with Shi'i teachings through Shi'i works that he received from the Middle East, long before the Iranian revolution. Born in Solo, 20 December 1930, Muhammad al-Baqir adheres only to certain Shi'i doctrines. He practices an eclectic version of both Sunni and Shi'i jurisprudence.[103] During the early 1980s, al-Baqir introduced several Shi'i works to intellectuals such as Jalaluddin Rakhmat, who became convinced by the principal Shi'i doctrines. Muhammad al-Baqir's most important contribution, however, is his translation of a number of Shi'i works into Indonesian, most of which are put out by the publishing house *Mizan* which is directed by his own son, Haidar Bagir. One of the most famous translations is *Dialog Sunnah Syi'ah* (Sunni-Shi'i Dialogue).[104] Before these three men were banned for propagating Shi'ism during Suharto's New Order, they had been engaged in delivering religious lectures at the Salman Mosque of ITB in Bandung.

During the 1980s, Indonesia's university campuses experienced a rapid 'Islamic revival'[105] which originated in the Salman Mosque. "In Java, Salman-inspired religious activities had become a conspicuous feature of campus life at virtually

---

basis of a revolutionary ideology originating in Shi'ah Islam" (1985:37). With regard to Muslim responses to the USA and the Soviet Union, Rais again praises the Iranian revolution, which has attempted to restore the self-confidence of the Iranians, freeing them from the influence of the superpowers.

102   I will deal specifically with this figure in the following chapter.

103   Rakhmat (1997:440). Haidar Bagir notes that his father, Muhammad al-Baqir never distinguished between Sunnism or Shi'ism in the field of Qur'an exegesis, law or Islamic thought in general (Bagir 2003:73). Al-Baqir's thought on jurisprudence may be found in his two volumes of *Fiqh Praktis* (Practical Jurisprudence) which contain a comparative analysis of the four Sunni schools and of *Ja'fari* jurisprudence. Al-Baqir himself emphasises that although he practices religious rituals in accordance with the majority Shafi'i jurisprudence, he is reluctant to join any particular Islamic group (1999:32-33).

104   For a discussion of Shi'i publications, see Chapter Six.

105   A number of Indonesian Muslim leaders have paid more attention to Islamic revival movements rather than to the Iranian Islamic revolution. Collections of articles written by them can be seen in Rusydi Hamka and Iqbal E.A. Saimima (eds) n.d. In Malaysia Muzaffar (1987) points out that the Iranian revolution has two meanings for the Islamic resurgence there. First, it proves the ability of Islam to establish a state in the modern era while at the same time answering criticism posed by scholars or leaders who reject the idea of an Islamic state. Second, it shows that "an Islamic state has its own identity" and that the Iranian experience can be an example for Malaysia. What Muzaffar singles out is the fact that in Iran the imams and religious elites played a major role in the politics and administration of the state and in implementing Islamic law (Muzaffar 1987:36-37). On the rapid growth of Islamic revival among university students in Malaysia see Anwar (1987).

every major university".[106] The 'Salman movement' is a puritanical movement that teaches the totality of the Islamic worldview, encompassing all aspects of human life. It was developed by Imaduddin Abdulrahim, who was heavily influenced by the ideas of Hasan al-Bana (d. 1949) of *Ikhwan al-Muslimin* (The Muslim Brotherhood) of Egypt and Abul A'la Mawdudi (d. 1979) of the *Jama'at-i Islami* in Pakistan. In Indonesia, a number of individuals, university lecturers and students, who were initially impressed with the ideas of Islamic revolution, used various publications to focus discourse on the Iranian case. (As I will show later, there was a proliferation of Shi'i works in Indonesian by such Iranian *'ulama* and intellectuals as Ali Shari'ati and Murtada Mutahhari.) Some of these Indonesians studied the Shi'i teachings intensively and this contributed to their conversion. In this regard, the influence of such figures as Jalaluddin Rakhmat, Muchtar Adam and Muhammad al-Baqir in the propagation of Shi'ism to the students was undoubtedly significant as well.

Since the 1980s, Shi'ism has become a new brand of Islam, attracting students at Indonesia's renowned universities across the country. Campuses in Bandung, Jakarta and Makassar (renamed Ujung Pandang in the New Order era) in South Sulawesi have become centres of Shi'ism. In Bandung, students (mainly Salman activists) from universities such as ITB and UNPAD converted to Shi'ism. The most famous is Haidar Bagir, son of the aforementioned Muhammad al-Baqir al Habsyi, who was born in Solo, 20 February 1957 to a Sayyid family of Hadrami immigrants. He completed his primary and secondary education at the Diponegoro Islamic School, co-founded by his father. In 1975, Haidar Bagir entered the Department of Industrial Technology at ITB, finishing his studies in 1982. During his time at ITB he became an activist at the Salman Mosque and served on the editorial board of *Pustaka*, an Islamic student journal pioneered by Amar Haryono, an ITB librarian.[107] Impressed by the popularity of Ayatollah Khomeini, he studied and converted to Shi'i Islam. In 1983, he founded Mizan, the largest Islamic publishing house in Indonesia, which puts out a number of Shi'i books. Today, Haidar Bagir plays a major role in the spread and development of Shi'ism in the country.

Subsequent generations of university students in Bandung who converted to Shi'ism were mosque activists with close ties to Jalaluddin Rakhmat, Muchtar Adam, Muhammad al-Baqir and Haidar Bagir. A number of them are prominent Shi'i intellectuals and activists today, such as Dimitri Mahayana (lecturer at ITB and former chairman of IJABI), Hadi Swastio (lecturer at the Communication College and former general secretary of IJABI) and Yusuf Bakhtiar (formerly deputy-chief of Muthahhari Senior High School and currently a political activist in the National Mandate Party founded by M. Amien Rais). These figures have

---

106   Hefner (1993:13).
107   Peeters (1998:217).

played, and continue to play, a very important role in the promotion of Shi'ism not only in Bandung but also in the country as a whole. It is not unreasonable to claim that Bandung has become an important centre for the spread of Shi'ism in Indonesia.

The Shi'i converts from universities in Jakarta followed a similar pattern in the sense that they too were engaged in religious gatherings, lectures and discussions on Shi'i thought and doctrine and campus mosque activities. They are found at major universities such as UI, IKIP (now UNJ, State University of Jakarta), UNAS (National University), UKI (Christian University of Indonesia) and Jayabaya University. One student, Mulhandy from Jayabaya University, admitted to converting to Shi'ism in 1983 after he and his colleagues had studied it intensively.[108] At UI, Agus Abubakar Arsal Al-Habsyi, born in Makassar, South Sulawesi, on 6 August 1960, to a Hadrami immigrant family, a Shi'i student who was well known in the early 1980s, was active at the Arif Rahman Hakim Mosque of UI. In 1979, he was enrolled in the Physics Department. He cites his intensive learning of Shi'i teachings at university, plus a familiarity with Shi'ism before the Iranian revolution, due to the presence of some Shi'is in a close village in South Sulawesi, as factors in his conversion.[109] Agus Abubakar gained a reputation for being a spokesman for Shi'ism following a debate with Prof. Rasjidi (d. 2001), who at that time was the Sunni imam of Arif Rahman Hakim Mosque. As a consequence, Agus Abubakar was forbidden to conduct religious gatherings at the mosque and dismissed from his leadership of student organisations. However, this did not reduce his missionary zeal. Using various approaches, Agus Abubakar continued to promote Shi'i teachings and converted a number of students.[110] He has been the head of the *Baitul Hikmah* Foundation in Depok, South of Jakarta and has been engaged in political activities, becoming a national organiser for the Democratic Party (*Partai Demokrat*), which was co-founded by Susilo Bambang Yudhoyono, the current President of Indonesia. Agus Abubakar is undoubtedly a significant figure in the spreading of Shi'ism in Jakarta.

With the increasing number of Shi'i converts in Jakarta, study groups began to emerge. In 1989, the Shi'i students of UI founded a study group named *Abu Dzar,* coordinated by Haryanto of the Faculty of Mathematics and Science and Yussa Agustian of the faculty of Technology. Agus Abubakar was one of their guides. This study group was founded for the purpose of re-awakening Islamic thought and introducing Shi'i ideas to students. To achieve these goals, the group carried out discussions, training and other activities.[111] A later development

---

108   *Panji Masyarakat* (513/1986:19).
109   *Panji Masyarakat* (513/1986:20).
110   *Syi'ar* (Muharram 1425/2004:35).
111   *Syi'ar* (Muharram 1425/2004:35).

among the Shi'i students at UI was an attempt to make HMI (Muslim Student Association) a vehicle for the dissemination of Shi'i thought. Rudy Suharto of the Faculty of Mathematics and Science, (currently editor-in-chief of *Syi'ar*, a magazine of the Islamic Cultural Centre in Jakarta), together with other student activists including Didi Hardian of the Faculty of Technology, Kukuh Sulastyoko of the Faculty of Mathematics and Science and Syaiful Bahri of Guna Dharma university, guided by their seniors, Furqon Bukhori and Zulvan Lindan, succeeded in establishing an HMI branch in the Depok campus. Through this organisation, the Shi'i students of UI undertook various intellectual and religious activities, until 1995 when HMI split into the pro-Shi'i and the anti-Shi'i group, the latter being legitimated by the national leadership of HMI. In a subsequent development of Shi'ism in Jakarta, the FAHMI (Forum Alumni HMI) was established. This association of UI Shi'i alumni was founded in 1997 by activists such as Rudy Suharto.[112]

From Jakarta, we turn to consider the growth of Shi'ism in Makassar, South Sulawesi, where a relatively large number of Shi'is can be found among the student population. My research suggests that Shi'ism exists at almost all university campuses in Makassar, and the majority of Shi'is in this city are university alumni. This phenomenon has developed since early 1990, when a number of Shi'i activists in Makassar intensified their propagation on university campuses. A leading figure in Makassar is Surachman, who has headed the *Al-Islah* Foundation that provides studies and training in Shi'ism. As in Bandung and Jakarta, the propagation of Shi'ism in Makassar gained a certain amount of sympathy from other students associations, particularly HMI.[113] The relatively rapid developments in Makassar can be put down to the holding of continuous, intensive and systematic study programmes, including the inviting of Shi'i religious teachers and intellectuals from Jakarta and Bandung. Intellectuals like Jalaluddin Rakhmat have given lectures on Shi'i thought, philosophy and Sufism. In addition, teachers (Qum alumni and others) have given instruction on Shi'i jurisprudence. Along with the growth in the numbers of Shi'i converts, several foundations have been established with the purpose of propagating Shi'i teachings. As in other cities, the pioneering propagators of Shi'ism in the area have been campus activists used to studying and discussing Islam, as well as participating in training sessions in university mosques. This means that the Shi'i teachings are easily spread through existing networks.[114]

The Shi'is among university students in other cities in Indonesia like Palembang, Yogyakarta, Surabaya and Malang follow similar patterns in terms of being mosque and/or student organisation activists. In the victorious Iranian

---

112 *Syi'ar* (Muharram 1425/2004:35).
113 *Tiras* (1996:30).
114 See: http://rausyanfikr.tripod.com/divmks.htm.

revolution and the Islamic revivalism which followed, these young activists found Shi'i parallels with their own revolutionary ideals. Their zeal also be related to the fact that the majority of them did not have an Islamic educational background and so had a less developed knowledge of Sunni teachings, making them more open to the ideologically revolutionary teachings of Shi'ism.

In contrast, Shi'ism has not received the same attention among students at Islamic universities like UIN (State Islamic University), IAIN (State Institute for Islamic Studies) or STAIN (State College for Islamic Studies), branches of which are located in most of the provincial capitals throughout Indonesia. The 1990s saw the appearance of the so-called 'Flamboyant Shelter' an organisation which carried out intensive studies into Shi'i thought, established by students at Jakarta IAIN and financed by Haidar Bagir.[115] However, the fact that only a handful of students from Islamic higher learning institutions became Shi'i is pertinent. In contrast to students at 'secular' universities, most students of Islamic universities arrive with a good foundation in Islamic knowledge already gained in *madrasa* or *pesantren*. While Shi'i works are widely read among these students, their educational background means that they are not easily influenced by this brand of Islamic revivalism. In addition, at Islamic institutions of higher learning the students continue to gain comprehensive religious knowledge, regardless of which department they choose to study in. The educational curricula are mainly Sunni. That said, the ideas of Islamic renewal promoted by the late Harun Nasution (1919-1998), Nurcholish Madjid (1939-2005) and others have had some impact. At most, the students take on only certain intellectual or philosophical aspects of Shi'ism, as contained in the works of such Shi'i scholars as Ali Shari'ati, Murtada Mutahhari and Hossein Nasr. In general, there remain very few committed Shi'is among students and lecturers at Islamic institutions of higher learning.

The interest in Shi'ism among university students also corresponds to their rejection of the de-politicisation of Islam carried out by the regime during the New Order period. The Shi'i teaching of the *imamate* offered an alternative solution to this process, and in this respect most of the Shi'i converts opposed the implementation of *Pancasila* as *Azas Tunggal*, the sole official foundation of political action. The Indonesian Muslim Students' Organisation (PII), which was dissolved by the regime in 1987, and HMI MPO (*Himpunan Mahasiswa Islam Majlis Penyelamat Organisasi*, Muslim Student Association and Council to Save the Organisation) were the two bodies which most fiercely rejected the imposition of *Pancasila* as the sole foundation of all organisations in Indonesia. HMI MPO has maintained Islam as its stated ideological foundation.[116] In fact, a number of members and leaders of HMI MPO converted to Shi'ism and are

---

115   M. Deden Ridwan, interview (25/5/2003).
116   For an account of HMI MPO, see Karim (1997).

important Shi'i figures in Indonesia today, such as Zulvan Lindan and Furqon Bukhori, the current chairman of IJABI (2004-2008). These two have played a major role in the spreading of Shi'i teachings among members of HMI. There are two others: Yusuf Bakhtiar was a leader of HMI MPO in Bandung, while Saifuddin Al-Mandari, former national chairman of HMI MPO, is a Shi'i who migrated from Makassar to Jakarta where he has been recently affiliated to the Fitra Foundation.[117] Other leaders of HMI MPO have tried to include the topic of the Shi'i principle of *imamate* in the training activities of the organisation, emphasising the importance of Islamic leadership, which has led some members of the association to study Shi'i teachings and, in turn, to embrace Shi'ism.

D. Conversion to Shi'ism

The existence and growth of the 'traditional' Shi'i group, the Qum alumni, and the university campus group are not entirely unconnected. They have tried to establish contact with one another for a number of reasons, not least that it is natural to seek connection with other members of the same religious denomination. In the process of conversion to Shi'ism, intellectuals and university students have also tried to establish contact with Shi'i figures known to them. Individuals from the university campus group have attempted to study with prominent Shi'i *ustadhs* among the Arab community in the country. This has coincided with the missionary zeal of Shi'i figures to attract new followers, and it is how the close relationship between the late Husein Al-Habsyi and Jalaluddin Rakhmat developed. Rakhmat regards Al-Habsyi as his religious preceptor. Today, most Shi'i *ustadhs,* both Qum alumni and non-Qum alumni, and intellectuals in Indonesia are either Al-Habsyi's students or they have had a close connection with him. The relationship between the Shi'i intellectuals, the university campus group and the *ustadhs* has been a complex one. While all three share a common objective – the propagation of Shi'ism – and they tend to cooperate with each other in this regard, disputes have also coloured their relationship.

While the 'traditional' Shi'is of Arab descent, the Qum alumni and the university campus group can be categorised as forming the main segments of the Shi'i community in Indonesia, within these groups themselves there is diversity in terms of socio-economic status and ethnic origin. In the matter of conversion to Shi'ism, these variables do not appear to be determining factors. Those who convert to Shi'ism may come from economically lower or upper class society and from any ethnic origin. Moreover, we find a very small number of Shi'i

---

117   Al-Mandari provides historical notes on the struggle by members and leaders of HMI MPO against the New Order regime (Al-Mandari 2003), as well as a description of the discourse on social revolution among members of HMI MPO (Al-Mandari 2003a).

converts of non-Muslim background. Also, those converts of a religious-oriented background come from both traditionalist and reformist Muslim streams and from the mainstream community, as well as from minority Muslim sects.

A notable element within the Indonesian Shi'i community is the existence of Shi'i converts from a dissident group background. These are minority Muslims whom the Sunni majority consider to believe and practice heterodox teachings of Islam. The dissident groups, which have spread in almost every region in Indonesia, include *Islam Jama'ah* (Islamic Congregation), now named LDII (*Lembaga Dakwah Islam Indonesia*, Institute of Indonesian Islamic Propagation),[118] *Kelompok Islam Isa Bugis* (Islamic Group of Isa Bugis),[119] *Jama'ah Tabligh* (Congregation of Islamic Preaching)[120] and DI/NII (*Darul Islam/Negara Islam Indonesia*, House of Islam/ Islamic State of Indonesia).[121] Although all of these minority groups are in fact Sunni, they are considered to be heterodox and similar to Shi'ism in status.

Shi'is with an *Islam Jama'ah* background are found in Jakarta, Palembang, Malang, Makassar and other cities. A few of them had been national or regional leaders of that sect, and they used such positions to convert some of their followers to Shi'ism. On the whole, they continue to occupy an important position within their new group of converts, despite having been dismissed from their original sect. Another important element in Indonesia's Shi'i community comes from the DI/NII movement. A large number of Shi'is in the region of West Java today are former members of this movement, particularly from areas within the Regional Command IX led by Abu Toto. They are scattered in cities and towns, including Bandung, Cianjur, Sukabumi, Garut, Serang and Tangerang. Slightly fewer in number are former members of *Jama'ah Tabligh,* who can be

---

118   *Islam Jama'ah* was founded by Nurhasan Al-Ubaidah in Kediri, East Java, in the 1950s and spread to several cities in Java, Sumatra and other islands. Since the Jakarta Council of Indonesian 'Ulama banned it in 1979, it has changed its name to LEMKARI (*Lembaga Karyawan Islam*) or KADIM (*Karyawan Da'wah Islam*), denying that they were simply new associations of *Islam Jama'ah* (Anwar 1989:34-35). It was changed once more into *Lembaga Da'wah Islam Indonesia* (LDII). With regards to political orientation, this group fully supported Golkar, the party of the New Order government. For a description of this group, see Marzani Anwar (1989:21-73).

119   The Islamic Group, *Isa Bugis* first emerged in Sukabumi in the 1960s and has since spread to other areas such as Bandar Harapan in Central Lampung. As its name suggests, it is founded by one Isa Bugis from Aceh. Its major concern is the study of verses of the Qur'an which are said to be based on the view of the Prophet Muhammad, which are are then related to empirical reality (Afif HM 1989:75-140). This group attracted followers from HMI, who called their activity 'Qur'anic studies'.

120   *Jama'ah Tabligh* was founded in India by Mawlana Muhammad Ilyas in 1930 and is thought to have come to Indonesia in 1952. It has spread throughout the country in both urban and rural areas. Azra (2002:42-43) provides a short description of this movement.

121   There are a number of studies on the *Darul Islam* movement, the most comprehensive being van Dijk (1981). The division that has come to most notice recently has been KW IX (Regional Command IX) led by Abu Toto, frequently associated with Syeikh Panji Gumilang, the founder of the luxurious *Pesantren Al-Zaytun* in Indramayu, West Java. One of my Shi'i informants in Sukabumi, a former member of NII, suggests that Abu Toto and Panji Gumilang are one and the same person, so *Al-Zaytun* is the educational centre of NII. This can also be seen in Al-Chaidar (2000) and Umar Abduh (2001).

found in Jakarta, Makassar and other places in Java. The final element consists of, as Syamsuri Ali observes, former members of the *Isa Bugis* group who may be found in Jakarta.[122]

Conversion occurs when a person or group discovers a more reasonable and correct set of religious teachings. The term 'religious conversion' is a complex phenomenon involving both intellectual and emotional dimensions. Based on Rambo's classification,[123] conversion from Sunnism to Shi'ism can, to a certain degree, be classified as 'institutional transition', involving the change of an individual or a group from one community to another within a major tradition. This interdenominational transformation may also be termed 'internal conversion'. It should be noted that there is no external rite of conversion from Sunnism to Shi'ism, unlike the conversion from non-belief to Islam, where the convert must proclaim the confession of faith, "There is no god but God and Muhammad is the apostle of God".

The above description of elements within the Shi'i community in Indonesia pinpoints three interconnected modes of conversion: the first is through education in its broadest sense, namely the transfer of knowledge and values. Second, conversion to Shi'ism may take place through ties of kinship and friendship. The third mode is through the reading of Islamic literature. The conversion to Shi'ism by Indonesian Arabs before the Iranian revolution may be included in the first two modes, but these modes characterise the conversion process among other groups as well. Education has become a very important means of conversion to Shi'ism.

After the Iranian revolution a number of Shi'i *ustadhs* from the Sayyid community have continued to propagate Shi'ism to the broader Muslim population through traditional Islamic educational institutions. While the majority of *pesantren* play a major role in the maintenance of traditional Sunni ideology (Dhofier 1999), a few also exist which promote Shi'i teachings. This results from the fact that the founders and leaders of *pesantren* tend to be relatively autonomous in organising curriculum contents and teaching materials and their autonomy provides an opportunity for Shi'i religious teachers to manage their institutions and to inculcate their own religious ideology. The most notable example is Husein Al-Habsyi, who attracted many followers through his institution, YAPI. In some respects, he was able to connect the 'traditional' Shi'i group with those who had converted after the Iranian revolution. A number of relatives and descendants of 'traditional' Shi'is studied with Husein Al-Habsyi at YAPI, which provided Shi'i books and religious guidance. Many of them converted during their studies, and over the course of time a large number of YAPI alumni have become Shi'i

---

122   Ali (2002:456).
123   Rambo (1993:12-14).

ustadhs, disseminating Shi'i teachings all over Indonesia. As described above, some have pursued Islamic learning in Qum and returned as famous *ustadhs.* This is the mode of conversion to Shi'ism through *pesantren.* Conversion during study in Qum undergone by more advanced students is also included in this mode.

While the conversion to Shi'ism among the university campus group more commonly occurs through non-formal Islamic education and self-study, the mode of conversion in *pesantren* has been heavily dependent on the leader of the *pesantren* who introduces Shi'i teachings, gives instruction and provides reading material to their students. Unlike students at university who spend the majority of their time on the 'secular' sciences, the *pesantren* students dedicate themselves to acquiring Islamic knowledge, and so generally have a more comprehensive knowledge of Islam and Shi'ism. In the residential *pesantren* they not only learn Shi'ism but also put its teachings into practice in daily life. Despite *pesantren* students receiving such stimuli, just as with the university students, their conversion process also requires a reading of Shi'i literature.

Conversion to Shi'ism also frequently occurs through kinship, namely by blood, by marriage and through friendship. It is common for Shi'is to inculcate Shi'i teachings in their children, and where possible, in other relatives and friends. We have previously described how the descendants of Indonesian Arab figures have maintained the continuity of their adherence to Shi'ism. Several kin of Husein Al-Habsyi have also become important Shi'i *ustadhs.* As for marriage, it is often recommended that a young man seek a Sunni woman to marry and to convert for the purpose of increasing Shi'i numbers. This mode of conversion tends to interconnect with the other modes listed above.

Woodberry has identified another two modes of conversion to Shi'ism: individual conversion and collective conversion.[124] Conversion among the intellectuals, university and *pesantren* students tends to be individual while conversion among dissident groups tends to be collective, in the sense that a group of people follow in the steps of their mentor. Regarding individual conversion among university students and intellectuals, important ways are through the reading of Shi'i books and participating in discussions at their educational institutions. Conversion within the dissident groups frequently occurs as a result of debate between Shi'i figures and mentors of the groups on essential doctrines within Islam, such as the *imamate.* Ali writes: "but conceptually, their belief is defeated by arguments of the Shi'i concept of *imamate,* so that their defeat in the conceptual matter has made them change pleasantly from the former *madhhab* to the Shi'i *madhhab.*"[125]

---

124   Woodberry (1992:23).
125   Ali (2002:456).

It is generally agreed that it is the intellectual and philosophical aspects of Shi'ism that first attract the converts in Indonesia. It is even common for some university students and intellectuals only to be interested in the intellectual and doctrinal aspects of Shi'ism, but in the course of time they are labelled as Shi'is, despite their being ignorant of its true teachings. In this regard, Rakhmat writes

> The majority of people sympathetic to Shi'ism came from university. Most of them were also attracted to Shi'ism as an alternative to existing Islamic thought. At the time when many people were interested in, for instance, critical theory, in Neo-Marxist groups, some Muslims found a similar matter in Shi'i thought, such as that of Ali Shari'ati. Concepts of the 'left' such as the plight of the oppressed, pedagogy of the oppressed, or corrupt structure, has a similarity in Islam, with the term *mustad'afin* [the Oppressed] and the mission of the prophets to fight against tyrants. And those who clearly present these matters are Shi'i thinkers.... But later, it was from Ali Shari'ati that they entered into deeper thought.[126]

As previously mentioned, and closely related to this quotation, the Shi'i conception of the *imamate* is the doctrine that has been most responsible for attracting university students, intellectuals and members of dissident groups to Shi'ism. *Imamate* becomes an important topic in discussions and training carried out in *usrah,* or study circles, HMI and dissident groups. The *imamate* within Sunni Islam is not as crucial as it is in Shi'ism,[127] so students and intellectuals must turn to Shi'i books to find comprehensive accounts of this doctrine. It is legitimated by the fact that Ayatollah Khomeini can be regarded as an Islamic leader, representative of the Imam, whose revolution succeeded in overthrowing an oppressive regime. The *Imamate* is also very crucial to and strongly upheld within the teachings of some dissident groups, particularly *Islam Jama'ah* and NII. Converts from these groups admit that a reason for becoming Shi'i is because they found the doctrine of the *imamate* to be more correct and authoritative in Shi'ism than in their former teachings. To give an example, Muhammad Nuh (65 years old), told me that he used to be the regional leader of *Islam Jama'ah* in South Sumatra, Lampung and Bengkulu and was active in the propagation of its teachings in those regions. His conversion to Shi'ism took place after participating in discussions on the *imamate* with Shi'i *ustadhs* in Palembang, including the aforementioned Qum alumnus, Umar Shahab. Muhammad Nuh explained that he accepted the Shi'i view of *imamate* as being in accordance with Bukhari's *al-Sahih,* the most authoritative collection of Sunni Hadith and

---

126   Rakhmat (1997:443).
127   Fuad Amsyari (1993), a lecturer at the Faculty of Medical Science, Air Langga University, chairman of *Al-Falah* Muslim Intellectuals in Surabaya and an influential figure in *usrah* circles, explains the necessity of the *imamate* for Muslims in Indonesia, maintaining that it does not specifically belong to the Shi'i doctrine but that it is strongly based on Sunni sources. According to Amsyari, Muslims who do not comprehend the totality of Islamic teachings (*kaffah*), have neglected the Islamic teaching on *imamate*.

the primary source of the doctrine of the *imamate* in *Islam Jama'ah*. At the same time, Nuh is aware that the teaching of the *imamate* in *Islam Jama'ah* has been intentionally manipulated by the founder of the group for his own personal purposes. Shi'i ex-leaders of *Islam Jama'ah* from other regions share similar views. The same holds true for Shi'is ex-members of NII who also uphold the doctrine of the *imamate* and this corresponds with the fact that the leader of the *Darul Islam* movement is usually considered as the Imam.[128]

Those who are interested in the doctrinal and intellectual aspects of Shi'ism but continue to follow Sunni jurisprudence cannot be characterised as being converts in the true sense. To be considered Shi'i, they need to abide by the code of conduct as outlined in *Ja'fari* jurisprudence. According to Jalaluddin Rakhmat, when converts did make the shift in orientation from intellectual and doctrinal aspects to jurisprudence, it occurred for political reasons and as a reaction to slander and attack from Sunnis, particularly in publications promoted by Saudi Arabia.[129] In Rakhmat's observation, the main motivation of this Shi'i group to study jurisprudence is to prove the invalidity of anti-Shi'i views. I was also told that people who had not previously thought of themselves as Shi'i were motivated to learn every aspect of Shi'ism after having been labelled as Shi'is by anti-Shi'i groups. With some inevitability, these people go on to become true followers of Shi'ism, observing almost all aspects of Shi'i jurisprudence. It is important to note that yet others attempted to understand Shi'i law for religious reasons, for the purpose of practicing Shi'i rituals in daily life according to *Ja'fari* jurisprudence. In this regard, the return to Indonesia of the Qum alumni has been fortuitous, since they are now religious teachers able to give instruction on any particular issue. They have established relations with the university campus groups of Shi'is.

For converts, Shi'i Islam is more reasonable and correct than the Sunni Islam they once adhered to. They tend to perceive positively both Shi'ism as a set of religious doctrines and the Shi'is as a historical reality, united in an integrated religious system. Zainuddin and his colleagues[130] offer their explanations of why they converted to Shi'ism. First, the Shi'i doctrine of justice, which is closely related to the doctrine of the *imamate*, they found appropriate in their struggles against the authoritarian New Order regime and for the establishment of a just government. Second, they believe the position of *'aql,* or intellectual reason, to be much stronger in Shi'ism than in Sunnism. Shi'i traditions are considered to have provided more opportunity and motivation to exercise *'aql* in developing

---

128 According to the constitution of NII's Islamic State of Indonesia, *Qanun Asasi,* (article 12, clause 1), "the head of state was the *Imam,* who must be a native Indonesian, of the Muslim faith, and faithful to God and His Prophet" (van Dijk 1981:93). A comprehensive account of this constitution can be found in van Dijk (1981:93-97).
129 Rakhmat (1997:445).
130 Zainuddin et al. (2000:97-103).

many fields of knowledge. Third, they point to the continued evolution of knowledge, thought and philosophy since the early history of Shi'ism, marked by the emergence of Imams and *'ulama* opposing oppressive regimes; the religious view on the necessity of *ijtihad*, or independent effort to formulate religious law; and the dominant position of a philosophical tradition. Fourth, they highlight the reality of modern Indonesian society and the emergence of unqualified Sunni *'ulama* and religious teachers, in contrast to the Shi'i *'ulama*, particularly in Iran, and those occupying the position of *marja' al-taqlid*, who are selected on the basis both of their moral conduct and intellectual achievement. Fifth, they believe that anti-Shi'i views and judgments on Shi'ism are frequently slanderous and speculative, ignoring the true teachings of Shi'ism and the facts of history.

Viewed from these perspectives and taking into account the social and psychological characteristics of converts in the socio-political context of Indonesian society, conversion to Shi'ism can be seen as a double protest against the political regime and the Sunni religious establishment. Converts accept Shi'ism because they find "the anti-government aspect of Shi'ism and its struggle against oppression and tyranny appealing."[131] Shi'ism is seen as the religion of protest while Sunnism, more often than not, tends to legitimise the political regime of the day. With its lesser emphasis on *'aql* and the emergence of unqualified religious authorities, Sunnism is no longer seen as an ideal *madhhab*, able to provide solutions to social and political problems or to offer guidance in spiritual and intellectual quests. Conversion to Shi'ism continues, albeit at a slow rate. Shi'i institutions have been established and various methods are implemented in order to promote this *madhhab* in Indonesia.

---

131 Nakash (1994:45).

2. The Leaders

Currently, there is no single person who is recognised as leader by all of the Shi'i groups in Indonesia. This lack of a central figure originates, in part, in the divided formation and development of the community as described in Chapter One. The leaders can however be classified into two types: the *ustadhs* and the intellectuals, corresponding to the divide between *'ulama* and intellectuals in the Muslim world in general. The *'ulama,* who are also known by various popular terms such as *kyai* in Central and East Java, *ajengan* in West Java, *tengku* in Aceh and *tuan guru* in parts of Sumatra, Kalimantan and Lombok are on the whole products of traditional Islamic educational institutions. The intellectuals, on the other hand, are graduates from secular universities. The position of both types has been discussed by scholars such as Steenbrink[1]. The divide between the two, or more specifically, attempts to bridge the gap between them in terms of knowledge and leadership, has been of great concern to Indonesian Muslim intellectuals. In this chapter I will examine the general characteristics of both types of leaders. I will then consider the roles of Husein Al-Habsyi and Husein Shahab as *ustadhs* and that of Jalaluddin Rakhmat as the most prominent Shi'i intellectual. The portraits will focus on determinants of leadership: educational background, profession, leadership experience and Islamic scholarship.

A. *Ustadhs* and Intellectuals

Traditionally, the term *ustadh* (*ustadz* in Indonesian) means 'religious teacher'. It commonly denotes those who teach in traditional institutions of Islamic learning, the *pesantren*, in formal Islamic schools, the *madrasa*, and in religious gatherings, the *pengajian*. Within the leadership structure of the *pesantren,* the term *ustadh* usually refers to teachers who are yet to achieve the high position of *'ulama* and become men of religious learning and prestige)[2] or *kyai*, head of the *pesantren*. The position of *ustadh* remains firmly below that of *kyai* in this hierarchy. Among the Shi'is of Indonesia however the term *ustadh* denotes both leaders of Shi'i institutions and religious teachers. In fact, the term has been increasingly used to refer to *'ulama* and leaders of certain groups of Muslim society in Indonesia. A case in point is Husein Al-Habsyi, a Shi'i *ustadh* who has also achieved the status of *'ulama.*

It is quite possible that the growing tendency to use the Arabic term *ustadh* in Indonesia is due to the influence of the community of Arab descent on the

---

1   Steenbrink (1985).
2   Humphrey (1991:187).

religious, educational and cultural aspects of the Shi'i community. This tendency can also be seen in the so-called 'scripturalist' segment of the Indonesian Muslim community at large, which is also experiencing an increasing voluntary 'Arabisation'; for example, in their communications scripturalists prefer to use the term *ustadh* to mean *'ulama* rather than the local term *kyai*. This can be disadvantageous from the perspective of the international Shi'i intellectual tradition, as the term indicates that the education of Indonesian Shi'i leaders and scholars is not to the same standard of other qualified scholars. The term *ustadh* suggests that the teacher has not achieved the position of *mujtahid*, or independent legist, or of the higher rank of *marja' al-taqlid*, 'source of emulation'. In the field of jurisprudence, the *ustadhs* of Indonesia become *muqallid*, followers, of certain *marja' al-taqlid* in Iran or Iraq. Nevertheless, the *ustadhs* enjoy prestigious status in the Shi'i community in the country.

Shi'i *ustadhs* have two general characteristics of note. First, their education usually takes place at institutions where a basic knowledge of the various branches of Islamic knowledge is introduced. Several Shi'i *ustadhs* in Indonesia studied at *pesantren* and then went on to pursue their studies at institutions of Islamic learning, the *hawza 'ilmiyya* in Qum. A small number of Shi'i *ustadhs* - the most prominent of all - pursued their learning at other tertiary institutions in Indonesia or abroad. On the whole, this is because their education in Qum only reached the *muqaddamat*, or introductory level. A number of *ustadhs* have entered the State Islamic University in Jakarta. Among them were Umar Shahab, Abdurrahman Bima, Muhsin Labib and Khalid Al-Walid, who undertook doctorates at this university. We should emphasise that generally the Shi'i *ustadhs* specialise in Islamic studies in the classical meaning of the term. Further education in the field of religious knowledge contributes to establishing and increasing their prestige. It should be kept in mind however that the field of specialisation chosen by this group is different from that taken by the Shi'i intellectuals in Indonesia.

Second, the *ustadhs* devote themselves to the fields of *da'wa* and educational activities at institutions of Islamic learning. Many have set up and led their own institutions. Others have affiliated themselves to Islamic institutions as religious teachers or spiritual guides for the *jama'a* of the institutions. Only the heads of such institutions receive a regular salary, while the *ustadhs* are paid for *da'wa* activities. Most *ustadhs* rely on endowments or payments from the institutions and their *jama'a* for their living. They are well respected and enjoy close relations with the *jama'a* who follow their instruction and guidance.

Like the person of the *ustadh*, the intellectual also has a respected position within the community. In everyday life, the intellectual is also given the title '*ustadh*' as a sign of honour. "The intellectuals are the aggregate of persons in any society who employ in their communication and expression, with a relatively higher frequency than most other members of their society, symbols of general scope and abstract reference, concerning man, society, nature and the cosmos".[3] This general definition of the intellectual corresponds with the characteristics of such Shi'i leaders.

Shi'i intellectuals can be distinguished from the *ustadhs* in a number of ways: first, their educational backgrounds differ. On the whole, intellectuals are graduates of secular universities trained in various fields of the secular sciences. Some prominent intellectuals graduated from renowned universities in Indonesia and in other countries. Jalaluddin Rakhmat completed his tertiary education in Communications at Padjadjaran University and took his Masters in Science (also in Communications) at Iowa State University in the US. He then enrolled at The Australian National University to study political science, without however finishing the course. Haidar Bagir completed a degree in Industrial Technology at the Bandung Institute of Technology (ITB) and a Masters in Philosophy at Harvard University. He is currently writing a PhD thesis on philosophy at UI. Hadi Swastio completed a PhD at a university in the UK. Dimitri Mahayana completed an Engineering degree at ITB, a Masters at Waseda University in Japan and then returned to ITB for a PhD in Electrical Engineering. These intellectuals never received religious education or learned about Shi'ism either at any formal Islamic institution in Indonesia or abroad. On the whole, they studied and converted to Shi'i Islam while still students or upon graduation from university, where they had been active in religious circles and had attended lectures at campus mosques or in other Islamic institutions. Their religious knowledge was gained through non-formal education and training carried out in mosques or *da'wa* institutions and through reading books and periodicals. They are considered less qualified than the *ustadhs* in terms of traditional Islamic knowledge.

Secondly, the intellectuals generally earn their living in fields independent of the Shi'i community; they lecture at universities and educational institutions and/or are engaged with social, cultural and business institutions. For instance, Jalaluddin Rakhmat is Professor of Communications at Universitas Pajajaran (UNPAD) and head of the *Muthahhari* Foundation; Haidar Bagir is director of the Mizan Publishing House and affiliated with several social and educational institutions; Dimitri Mahayana is a lecturer at ITB, while Hadi Swastio is a lecturer at the College of Telecommunication Science. All of these institutions are located in Bandung, West Java. As lecturers or businessmen, the intellectuals, with certain exceptions, never take on the role of religious teacher, preacher or guide to the Shi'i community; nor do they lead or deliver sermons at the Shi'i rituals. For these reasons, their connection with the *jama'a* is not as close

---

3   Shils (1968:399).

as that between the *ustadh* and *jama'a*. Instead, they build their position in the community through strong commitment and contribution in the form of material assistance, strategic insight and critical thought.

That said, we do find a small number of intellectuals who also take part in religious instruction and guidance. A case in point is Jalaluddin Rakhmat. While generally known as an influential Shi'i intellectual in Indonesia, his activities as both an academic and a religious figure mean that he is actually positioned more as a combined intellectual and *ustadh*.

B. *Husein Al-Habsyi* (1921–1994)

Husein Al-Habsyi[4] was the most widely recognised leader in the development of Shi'ism in Indonesia. During his lifetime, his leadership was recognised by all Shi'i groups in the community. Since his death in 1994 however his position has not so far been filled by any current Indonesian *ustadh* or intellectual.

Husein Al-Habsyi, or al-Ustadh al-Habib al-Shaykh Husayn bin Abi Bakr al-Habshi - as his student Muhsin Husein[5] wrote in an article in *Al-Isyraq*, a magazine put out by his educational institution - became one of the most famous Indonesian Shi'i *'ulama* after the Iranian Islamic Revolution of 1978-1979. (He should not be confused with Husein bin Ali Al-Habsyi, the current President of *Ikhwan al-Muslimin* (Muslim Brotherhood) of Indonesia.) Born in Surabaya, 21 April 1921, Husein Al-Habsyi was the second son of a Sayyid Arab family. Very little is known about his parents' life. It is said that his father passed away when he was six years old and Husein went to live with his maternal uncle, Muhammad bin Salim Baraja, a prominent *'alim*, and then President of the Hadramawt School in Surabaya. Baraja had also been editor of the twice-monthly magazine *al-Iqbal* in the same city. He had strong links with the Shi'i figure, Abu Bakr bin Shahab mentioned in Chapter One.[6] In short, Husein Al-Habsyi grew up in a religious environment.

He began his formal education in *Madrasa Al-Khairiyya*, one of the oldest and most famous Islamic schools in Surabaya, East Java, co-founded by the Shi'i *'alim* Muhammad al-Muhdar. We are told that at the age of 10 Husein Al-Habsyi was an active participant in religious gatherings, which provided him with instruction in several branches of Islamic knowledge' including *fiqh* (Islamic jurisprudence), *'aqida* (Islamic doctrine) and *akhlaq* (ethics). At the age of twelve he was said to have been capable of reading such Arabic books as al-Ghazali's

---

4   A study on the biography and role of Husein Al-Habsyi has been published in *Studia Islamika* (Zulkifli 2004).
5   Muhsein Husein (1997).
6   Freitag (2003:264).

Ihya 'Ulum al-Din (The Revival of Religious Sciences), one of the most famous classical texts on ethics and Sufism used in in Indonesia.[7] While there is no complete information about who his teachers were during his time in Surabaya, reports from his sons and students suggest that, besides his maternal uncle, he was influenced by other *'ulama* of Hadrami descent, including Muhammad Baabud, Abdulqadir Bilfaqih and Abubakar Asseggaf of Gresik.[8] He also studied with the Moroccan religious scholars Muhammad Muntasir al-Kattani and the Palestinian teacher Muhammad Raba'a Hasuna at the *Al-Khairiyya* school, which also hired religious teachers from Hadramaut, Yemen.

Husein Al-Habsyi's Islamic knowledge was also garnered from institutions abroad. Together with his brother, Ali Al-Habsyi he went on to further his studies in Johor, Malaysia. One influential teacher there was Habib Alwi bin Tahir al-Haddad, the then Mufti of the Johor Sultanate (1939-1961).[9] In Johor, Husein Al-Habsyi also taught at the *Al-Attas* school for a period of time. His students came from various regions in Malaysia and some of them are said to have later become prominent *'ulama*. It is also reported that he visited the Hadramaut for Islamic education before moving to Saudi Arabia, where he stayed for about two years. He then spent a further year in Najaf, Iraq pursuing Islamic studies with eminent *'ulama,* including Sayyid Muhsin al-Hakim (d.1970).[10] He returned to Malaysia and married his uncle's daughter, Fatima bint Abdurrahman Al-Habsyi, with whom he had several children. After living in Malaysia for several years, Husein Al-Habsyi took his family back to his hometown of Surabaya, where he engaged in missionary and educational activities.[11]

Husein Al-Habsyi's cultural capital (his valuable experience and educational qualifications)[12] enabled him to establish himself as a religious scholar and teacher within the Muslim community. With the knowledge he had acquired in Indonesia, Malaysia and the Middle East, he became an important *ustadh* at Islamic schools. Moreover, he had started teaching at an early age, while still a student: when he was just 15 years old, he spent two years (1936-1938) teaching at his alma mater, the *Al-Khairiyya* school.[13]

There was also a period in Husein Al-Habsyi's life in which he was politically active. In his thirties, he joined Masyumi (*Majelis Syuro Muslimin Indonesia,*

---

7   Bukhori (n.d:10, *Dialog Jumat* 28/5/2004).

8   Muhsein Husein (1997:3).

9   Alwi Tahir al-Haddad (1884-1962) was a Sayyid *'alim* and leader in the Dutch East Indies before he was appointed Mufti of the Johor Sultanate in 1939. He wrote several books on history, jurisprudence and doctrine.

10   Beik (1997:14).

11   Panitia (n.d:1).

12   Bourdieu (1986). "Cultural knowledge (is) a resource of power used by individuals and social groups to improve their position within the social class structure" (Joppke 1986:57).

13   Zamzami (1999:4).

Consultative Council of Indonesian Muslims), the largest Muslim party during the era of Sukarno's Old Order (1945-1965). Through this membership, he became acquainted not only with influential Masyumi leaders such as M. Natsir (d.1993), Kasman Singadimedjo and Sjafruddin Prawiranegara (d. 1989) but also with other political figures in Indonesia. He was selected to be a member of *Konstituante* (Constituent Assembly) at the eighth Masyumi conference in Bandung, 22-29 December 1956 and from within the Constituent Assembly he was appointed head of the Human Rights Commission.[14] Like the majority of Masyumi leaders, he was known to have held a very negative attitude towards the PKI (Indonesian Communist Party). In 1954 he participated in the establishment of *Front Anti-Komunis* (Anti-Communist Front),[15] which was set up to prevent the spread of the communist movement in the Old Order.[16]

Husein Al-Habsyi's involvement in the political arena did not last long, however. There were several reasons for this, the most important being that Masyumi was banned in August 1960 as a result of the party's opposition to Sukarno and Guided Democracy. Masyumi also became involved with the separatist movement of PRRI (Revolutionary Government of the Republic of Indonesia).[17] Disillusioned with political developments after the break-up of Masyumi, Al-Habsyi ceased all political activities, devoting himself instead to Islamic education and *da'wa*. For him the growth of Islam simply could not be achieved through political practice; he believed it could only succeed through education. This sea-change is particularly significant in the context of Indonesia's New Order era, beginning in 1966, which implemented a policy of the de-politicisation of Islam. Programmes promoting cultural Islam, education and *da'wa* then became the way forward. We should bear in mind however that Al-Habsyi's brief political experiences clearly had an impact on his later position as a Shi'i *ustadh*; he gained important social capital by maintaining good connections with retired political leaders such as Natsir.[18]

Husein Al-Habsyi returned to his position of *ustadh* at the *Al-Khairiyya* school in Surabaya, where he engaged in instructing students and developing the school. His career progressed not only because of his commitment to Islamic education but also due to his comprehensive religious knowledge, managerial capabilities and social connections. He became head of the branch of *Al-*

---

14   Panitia (n.d:1).

15   *Front Anti-Komunis* was a radical wing of Masyumi established in September 1954 and supported by leaders of Masyumi in Java, Sumatra and Sulawesi. Its chairman was Isa Anshary, chairman of the Masyumi branch of West Java (Campton 1995:41).

16   Zamzami (1999:6).

17   Ricklefs (2001:325).

18   "Social capital is the aggregate of the actual or potential resources which are linked to possession of a durable network of more or less institutionalised relationships of mutual acquaintance and recognition..." (Bourdieu 1986:248).

Khairiyya located in Bondowoso, East Java and led the school for several years.[19] During this period, his worldview was said to have been strongly influenced by the ideology of the *Ikhwan al-Muslimin* (Muslim Brotherhood) of Egypt, an organisation founded by Hassan al-Banna (d. 1949). The banning of Masyumi and the de-politicisation of Islam under Suharto caused many Masyumi leaders to turn to the ideology of *Ikhwan al-Muslimin*.[20] Al-Habsyi became a follower of this so-called 'fundamentalist' movement and established links with its leaders and other high-ranking *'ulama* in the Middle East, such as Yusuf Qaradawi (b.1926) and Muhammad Ghazali. He travelled to Saudi Arabia, Egypt, Kuwait, Libya, Iraq and Iran to meet with these men and to collect donations from individuals and Islamic organisations for the development of education in *Al-Khairiyya* and the Muslim community at large.[21] He attempted to implement the ideology of *Ikhwan al-Muslimin,* maintaining a negative attitude towards secularism and Western worldviews in the pedagogic system of *Al-Khairiyya*. However, the strict discipline and rules imposed on the students and teachers at the school resulted in the majority of the staff rejecting his fundamentalist approach. Conflict ensued between Al-Habsyi and the *madrasa* teachers, as well as the Sayyid *'ulama* in Bondowoso. He was forced to leave *Al-Khairiyya* and Bondowoso for Bangil but many qualified students, sympathetic to his ideas, followed him.[22]

In 1976, Husein Al-Habsyi founded an Islamic educational institution called YAPI (*Yayasan Pesantren Islam*, Foundation of Islamic Pesantren) in Bangil. This *pesantren* has become an important centre of Islamic learning for Shi'is in Indonesia. As a learned man with a comprehensive grasp of Islamic knowledge, Al-Habsyi himself formulated the educational programme. The YAPI principles and approaches to Islamic education followed the *Ikhwan al-Muslimin* model, which combined strict discipline and rules with the strong anti-Western attitude which Al-Habsyi considered to be the best model for achieving his educational ideals. As the leader of YAPI responsible for its development and progress, he not only managed the institution but also carried out instruction in several fields of Islamic knowledge, particularly Arabic language, *tafsir* (Qur'anic exegesis) and *usul al-fiqh* (principles of Islamic jurisprudence). He was also proactive in the formation of cadres. He believed his framework for establishing and reviving religious zeal among students was essential, so that they would later engage in the struggle for Islam and the Muslim *umma*.[23] Over the course of time, YAPI and its head have become increasingly recognised by *'ulama* not only in Indonesia but also in the Middle East.

---

19 *Dialog Jumat* (28/5/2004).
20 Van Bruinessen (2002:125).
21 Muhsein Husein (1997:5).
22 Muhsein Husein (1997:5).
23 Panitia (n.d:2).

Husein Al-Habsyi's endeavours in the field of religious education were relatively successful. Under his leadership, his *pesantren* has become the most famous Shi'i educational institution in Indonesia. This is evident from the fact that a number of YAPI alumni were able to pursue their education in countries such as Iran, India, Pakistan, Egypt, Saudi Arabia, Syria, and Qatar.[24] This was due to their high standard of proficiency in Arabic and in the various fields of Islamic learning, as well as the links established with *'ulama* in these countries by Al-Habsyi. As mentioned in Chapter One, he was responsible for selecting students to study in Qum, Iran and until his death on the 14th of January 1994, he was the most important confidant of Iranian leaders and *'ulama* with respect to the development of Shi'i education and *da'wa* in Indonesia. A large number of YAPI alumni, after studying in Iran, went on to become *ustadhs* in Islamic institutions and to engage in *da'wa* in various parts of Indonesia, some even returning to work at YAPI itself.

Husein Al-Habsyi was a popular preacher. He regularly delivered religious lectures and sermons in mosques in Bangil, Surabaya, Gresik, Jember and other townsin Java. He was an excellent orator, capable of captivating his audiences with his comprehension of Islam, broad insights into the latest developments in the Muslim world and his ability to use the techniques of modern mass communication in his lectures.[25]

His commitment also extended to undertaking *da'wa* activities and creating educational institutions in Indonesia's remote outer islands, including West Irian, East Timor and Maluku, all places where Islam is less well represented.[26] In these regions his main aims were to preach in mosques and places of prayer and to make contact with teachers to discuss the social and religious problems faced by the small Muslim communities. In some areas he set up *pesantren,* which at first were branches of YAPI but later became independent institutions. A number of YAPI alumni were sent out to teach there. One such institution is *Nurul Tsaqalain* located in Hila, Central Maluku, founded in 1989.

When exactly Husein Al-Habsyi converted to Shi'ism remains unclear. His students and children suggest that it was after the Iranian Revolution, but there is a possibility that he had acquainted himself with Shi'i doctrine before that time. The co-founder of *Al-Khairiyya*, Muhammad al-Muhdar (d.1926) was Shi'i and is known to have taught Shi'i doctrines in Indonesia, so it is quite possible that certain aspects of Shi'ism had spread among teachers and students of the *madrasa*. The *Al-Khairiyya* school was frequently visited by Middle Eastern *'ulama* to discuss Islamic teachings, including the Shi'i doctrine, with

---

24 Muhsin Husein (1997:5).
25 Beik (1997:14-15).
26 Panitia (n.d:2).

the teachers and students. It is also recorded that Husein al-Habsyi engaged in discussions with a Shi'i scholar from Iraq who came to visit *Al-Khairiyya* in the early 1960s,[27] and it is known that he studied for a time with the Grand Ayatollah Sayyid Muhsin al-Hakim, a *marja' al-taqlid* in Najaf, Iraq.

Husein Al-Habsyi's students, however, suggest that his primary interest was in understanding the nature of Iran's Islamic Revolution. According to Muhsin Husein, it was Khomeini's victory over the powerful Shah, and not the Shi'i doctrines, that first attracted him.[28] His interest in that victory sparked his curiosity and desire for a deeper understanding of the ideology behind the revolution, which was strongly rooted in the doctrine of the *imamate*, that fundamental tenet of Shi'ism adhered to by the majority of Iran's population.

According to Muhsin Husein, Al-Habsyi went to great lengths to obtain Shi'i books in order to develop his understanding of Shi'ism. His efforts included making contact with the Iranian embassy in Jakarta and with *'ulama* in Iran. The Iranian embassy in Jakarta distributed books and its magazine, *Yaumul Quds*, free of charge to Islamic foundations and individuals who requested them. Through these printed materials and his personal communication with figures in Iran, Al-Habsyi's knowledge of Shi'i teachings and the development of Shi'ism in the world became extensive. He was frequently invited to participate in meetings with Shi'i *'ulama* in Iran. He was also pushed ever more towards Shi'ism by the hostile attitude and conduct of some Sunni leaders in Indonesia, the Sunni view being that Shi'is were unbelievers. Al-Habsyi attempted to defend Shi'i teachings by emphasising that Shi'ism was a true *madhhab* and that its adherents were genuine Muslims. In fact, as Shi'is are permitted to do under *taqiyya* in a hostile environment, he even declared himself to be a Sunni.[29]

From the early 1980s, Husein Al-Habsyi was known for openly praising the Iranian revolution. He paid great respect to Imam Khomeini in his *da'wa* activities in the mosques of cities such as Surabaya, Malang and Bangil, all with the aim of reviving Islamic religiosity within the Muslim community. In turn he gained the respect of the majority of Muslims in the region, and in particular the youth, who regarded him as an ideal *'alim* and leader. However, he also experienced hostile reactions from anti-Shi'i groups once he became generally acknowledged as a Shi'i *ustadh*.

Husein Al-Habsyi's position as an influential *ustadh* can be seen from his intellectual achievements, which began at an early age. Besides teaching and leading Islamic schools, he wrote books and translated books on Islam into Indonesian. He engaged in polemics with one of the most prominent Sunni

---

27 Hamzah Al-Habsyi, interview, (15/10/2002).
28 Muhsin Husein (1997:6).
29 Muhsin Husein (1997:6).

reformist leaders in Indonesia, Ahmad Hasan (1887-1958) of the organisation Persis (*Persatuan Islam*, Islamic Union),[30] who in April 1956 published a book entitled *Risalah al-Madhhab* (Treatise on the Madhhab) which suggests that slavish adherence to a single school of law like *Shafi'i* jurisprudence is forbidden. Ahmad Hasan also wrote *Halalkah bermadzhab?* (Is Following One School of Islamic Jurisprudence Lawful?). In response to these two books, Al-Habsyi produced a critical treatise with the pithy title, *Lahirnya Madzhab yang Mengharamkan Madzhab* (The Birth of a School of Jurisprudence which Forbids Schools of Jurisprudence). The polemics continued with the publication of Ahmad Hasan's refutation of Al-Habsyi's criticisms in *Pembela Islam* in January 1957. In April of that year, Al-Habsyi wrote yet another critical book, *Haramkah Orang Bermadzhab II* (Is it Unlawful for People to Follow a School of Jurisprudence II), in which he affirmed that following a particular school is strongly determined by the Qur'an and Sunna and the opinions of the *'ulama*. In this long-running and at times heated clash of ideas, both writers accused the other of having insufficient knowledge of Islam and both omitted views that did not support their arguments.[31] Finally, both authors agreed to a public debate on the issue in the hope of achieving a final pronouncement. But the debate never took place. Ahmad Hasan's supporters accused Al-Habsyi of avoiding participating in the debate. Al-Habsyi claimed that Mohammad Natsir, another Persis leader and a close associate from his Masyumi days, had advised him not to engage in the debate, as it would provoke religious conflict and disunity within the Muslim community.[32] This claim is supported by one of his close associates, O. Hashem.[33]

Husein Al-Habsyi was not an *ustadh* who was content to remain quiet. In 1979-1980 he once again engaged in theological polemics with the same reformist group, this time regarding the *mawlid* literature and the concept of *Nur Muhammad* (Light of Muhammad)[34] published in *Al-Muslimun*, an organ of Persis in Bangil. It should be noted that there have been controversies among Muslim scholars concerning the nature of this concept at regular intervals. It is a term central to Sufi and Shi'i speculations, transcending the notion of the Prophet Muhammad as a mere human being. "The historical Muhammad was

---

30 Several studies have been devoted to Persis and its scholars. Federspiel (1970) provides us with a detailed discussion of this organisation. It was founded in 1923 and Ahmad Hasan, born in Singapore of Indian origin, joined in 1924. Persis' views on theology and law are generally similar to that of *Muhammadiyah*, but can on occasion be more extreme. Ahmad Minhaji (2001) provides a detailed account of Ahmad Hassan and his reformist legal thought.

31 Minhaji (2001:242). For a description of Husein Al-Habsyi's response to Ahmad Hassan, see Minhaji (2001:241-246).

32 Minhaji (2001:245-246).

33 O. Hashem (2002:8-9).

34 Al-Samarrai points out that the concept might be an invention of Sufis, influenced by ideas from Judaism, Christianity or perhaps Zoroastrianism. The Light of Muhammad is believed among some Sufis to have been created before all things (Al-Samarrai 1968:147:147).

thus metamorphosed into a transcendent light, like the sun, around which everything created revolves."[35] Suherman Rosjidi wrote an article criticising the concept, which he saw as contrary to Islam, reason and history. Rosjidi also points out that the concept is adopted from Christianity and Hinduism. In reaction to this, Al-Habsyi wrote an article published in *Al-Muslimun*, maintaining that the concept of *Nur Muhammad* has a strong basis in Hadith.[36] These polemics continued. Another reformist writer, Imron A. Manan refuted Al-Habsyi's view, claiming that *Nur Muhammad* is not mentioned in the Qur'an and that the Hadith on it are not sound.[37] Once more, Al-Habsyi responded in the same magazine, stating that *Nur Muhammad* is mentioned in the Qur'anic verse 5:15 and many Hadith and is confirmed by the views of a number of *'ulama*. He also asked Manan to justify his claim that such Hadith are weak.[38] Manan wrote another criticism directed towards Al-Habsyi's article[39] and towards a book written by Abdullah Abdun.[40] *Al-Muslimun* also published an article by Abu Hasyim critical of Manan.[41] Finally, in the same edition, the editorial board of the magazine decided that the debate should be brought to a head. It published conclusions and final notes favouring the Persis/Manan view of *Nur Muhammad,* upholding the claim that the concept is based on unsound Hadith that are contrary to the Qur'an itself.[42]

Husein Al-Habsyi's intellectual activities are also marked by the publication of a number of books of a Shi'i nature. His 34-page booklet on the exegesis of Qur'an, *Surah Abasa: 1-10* became one of the most controversial publications for Sunni-Shi'i relations in Indonesia. Published in 1991 under the title *Benarkah Nabi Bermuka Masam? Tafsir Surah Abasa* ('Did the Prophet Really Frown and Turn Away? Commentary on Surah Abasa), the central idea of this book is that the Prophet Muhammad, who is held to be the most perfect human being and immune from major and minor sins, did not frown and turn away from the blind 'Abdullah bin Ummi Maktum, who asked the Prophet for religious instruction while the latter was in conversation with unbelieving members of the Qurayshi elite. Al-Habsyi maintains that the one at the meeting who did frown and turn away was Al-Walid bin al-Mughira, a tyrannical infidel from Mecca. This opinion is in striking contrast to that of the books of Qur'anic commentary widely read and distributed in Indonesia. It also opposes the views

---

35 Schimmel (1995:23).
36 *Al-Muslimun* (117/1979).
37 *Al-Muslimun* (123/1980).
38 *Al-Muslimun* (125/1980).
39 *Al-Muslimun* (126/1980).
40 The complete title of the book is *Sanggahan atas Tulisan Pengingkar Nur Nabi Besar Muhammad SAW* (A Refutation of the Writings of the Denier of the Light of the Great Prophet Muhammad). Unfortunately I have been unable to obtain a copy.
41 *Al-Muslimun* (127/1980).
42 *Al-Muslimun* (127/1980:75-77).

of the majority of Sunni *'ulama,* who believe that the Prophet himself frowned and turned away. For these reasons, the controversy surrounding the book is not surprising.

There have been intellectual reactions to the book, including an article by Ibnu Mursyid in *Al-Muslimun,* January 1992 and a book by Ja'far Umar Thalib,[43] the former leader of *Lasykar Jihad.* In response to these criticisms, Al-Habsyi wrote another scholarly work reaffirming his point of view on the perfection of the Prophet Muhammad: that he was free from bad moral conduct, which meant that he could not have frowned and turned away from a follower when he requested instruction. The work, entitled *Nabi SAWW*[44] *Bermuka Manis tidak Bermuka Masam* ('The Prophet [God grant him and his Household peace and salvation] Smiled and Did not Frown') appeared in 1992.

Somewhat surprisingly in the light of the above, Husein Al-Habsyi promoted the idea of *ukhuwwa Islamiyya,* Islamic fraternity between Sunnis and Shi'is in a book entitled *Sunnah-Syi'ah dalam Ukhuwah Islamiyah: Menjawab 'Dua Wajah Saling Menentang' Karya Abul Hasan Ali Nadwi* (Sunnah and Shi'ah in Islamic Brotherhood: Responding to 'Two Opposing Faces', the Work of Abu al-Hasan Ali Nadwi).[45] The book has become well known. Al-Habsyi criticises Ali Nadwi's work for distorting Shi'i teachings, but the book is also directed to others who make the same mistake of creating division between the *madhabs.* Al-Habsyi demonstrated weaknesses in the writings about Shi'ism by Sunni *'ulama* and intellectuals, whose works do not reflect an appropriate or deep comprehension of Shi'ism and even contain serious misunderstandings. Such criticisms do not deal accurately with matters that are actually agreed upon by the majority of Shi'i *'ulama.* A second weakness in the writings of Sunni *'ulama* and intellectuals about Shi'ism is that in their use of sources they cite only the parts upon which they agree. A third weakness is their reliance on their own interpretations, without referance to existing interpretations by Shi'i *mujtahid.* Provocatively, Al-Habsyi concludes that the Sunni interpretations of Shi'i teachings are mainly based on passion and hatred.[46]

Husein Al-Habsyi appeals to the Sunni *'ulama* to stop distorting the Shi'i teachings, and to stop slandering and judging the Shi'is as a group deviating

---

43 Thalib (1993).
44 SAWW is an abbreviation of *Salla Allah 'Alayh Wa Alih Wa Sallam,* rather than SAW (*Salla Allah Alayh Wa Sallam,* May God Grant Him Peace and Salvation) which is common in Indonesia. The concept of the Prophet Muhammad's Household is explained in Chapter Three.
45 Abu al-Hasan Ali Nadwi is an Indian scholar whose anti-Shi'i work entitled *Dua Wajah Saling Bertentangan Antara Ahlu Sunnah dan Syi'ah* was published in 1987 by Bina Ilmu, Surabaya.
46 Husein Al-Habsyi (1992a:12-13).

from the true teachings of Islam. He calls on Sunni *'ulama* and intellectuals to hold workshops or conferences in which both Sunni and Shi'i *'ulama* participate, so that there may be opportunities to address various polemical matters:[47]

> There can be no doubt that the Shi'i *'ulama* will always be prepared to participate in all of such meetings to present proof of the validity of their *madhhab* which can satisfy their Sunni fellows. The basic aim (will be) that the Muslim *umma* be united and the relationship among all can become closely and strongly tied. Certainly, we very much hope for the realisation of these approaches and demand the unification of fronts, instead of the breaking up of once united fronts.[48]

Al-Habsyi argues that if these conditions are realised, both Sunnis and Shi'is can live in harmony, tolerance and mutual cooperation. Furthermore, the minority group will have nothing to fear from the majority Sunnis, who will then always protect, not oppress them.[49]

Another published work of Husein Al-Habsyi, *Sunnah Syi'ah dalam Dialog* (Sunnah-Shi'ah in Dialogue, 1991) originates from a recorded dialogue held with students of Universitas Gajah Mada (UGM) and the Indonesian Islamic University (UII). In this book, Al-Habsyi explains a number of the arguments surrounding Shi'ism that are widely spread among the Sunnis, arguments such as the accusation that the Shi'is are infidels and cursers of the Prophet's companions, also the validity of Hadith of Ghadir Khum on the appointment of 'Ali bin Abi Talib as the first Imam to succeed the Prophet.[50] As in other writings, Al-Habsyi practiced *taqiyya*. Not only did he declare himself to be a Sunni but he also cited Sunni sources in support of the validity of Shi'i teachings. This, he states, he did in order that "attacks directed to *Imamiyya* Shi'ism can be terminated, because there are no differences in terms of principal matters between the two *madhhab*."[51] In this work, he also appealed for an end to cursing one another and devoted great attention to the social, economic and cultural problems that are faced by Muslims.

Another aspect of Husein Al-Habsyi's intellectual activities can be seen in his translations. They include a translation of *Pendekatan Sunnah Syi'ah* (Sunnah–Syi'ah Approach) and the Christian Barnabas Gospel[52] published by YAPI (*Yayasan Penyiaran Islam*) in Surabaya. He also provided us with an authoritative Arabic-

---

47   Husein Al-Habsyi (1992a:228-229).
48   Husein Al-Habsyi (1992a:229-230).
49   Husein Al-Habsyi (1992a:229).
50   A text of this *Hadith* can be seen in Chapter Three.
51   Husein Al-Habsyi (1991a:3).
52   Most Muslims consider the Barnabas Gospel to be the most original version of the Christian Gospels.

Indonesian dictionary entitled *Kamus al-Kautsar Lengkap*, first published in 1977 by YAPI of Bangil. This 564-page dictionary has been reprinted several times, including twice by Thinker's Library in Selangor, Malaysia.

These printed works[53] confirm Al-Habsyi's position as a prominent Shi'i *ustadh*. In them we find the religious thought which he directed to his followers. The works also confirm his leading role in the propagation of Shi'i teachings in Indonesia. Arguably though, his greatest contribution to the Indonesian Shi'i community has been YAPI, the organisation that has become synonymous with the name Husein Al-Habsyi, dedicating his knowledge, material assistance and time to its *pesantren*. And his influence has spread beyond YAPI. In the 1980s, when the Shi'i community was beginning to develop, Al-Habsyi was in his sixties. He wore a turban, the outward symbol of a man of religious learning. His *habitus*[54] exerted great influence on the Muslim community. He had accumulated economic, social and cultural capital which was transformed into symbolic capital; that is, the recognition of his position as a renowned *ustadh*, head of a *pesantren* and leader of the Shi'i community in Indonesia.

C. Husein Shahab

In contemporary times, Husein Shahab is one of the most prominent Shi'i *ustadhs* in Indonesia. He was born in Palembang, South Sumatra on 27 December 1961 and as his clan name indicates, he is also a Sayyid. Both his primary and secondary education were completed in his home town. He finished *'aliyyah* (religious senior high school) at *Pesantren Ar-Riyadh,* a well-known Islamic institution run by Arabs in Palembang. During this period, he had a close relationship with the head of the *pesantren* and his teacher, Sayyid Ahmad Al-Habsyi, who also had links with other Sayyid *'ulama*, including Husein Al-Habsyi.

Husein Shahab furthered his education in the *hawza 'ilmiyya* of Qum, Iran. His choice of Qum was determined by his good relations with Ahmad Al-Habsyi, who maintained links with *'ulama* in Iran, and also by information from his brother, Umar Shahab, who was already studying there. Husein Shahab left for Qum in September 1979,[55] with motivations more educational than sectarian.

---

53   Husein Al-Habsyi's other published book is *Agar Tidak Terjadi Fitnah* (In Order That Division Does Not Take Place, 1993). It contains his standpoint on a number of polemical topics and includes his views on the most famous Shi'i Hadith collection, *al-Kafi* (The Sufficient) by Muhammad al-Kulayni (d. 939). Al-Habsyi uses this book to defend the validity of a number of Shi'i teachings based on both Sunni and Shi'i sources. He concludes with an appeal for the scrutiny of any specific *madhhab* based on its own authoritative sources.
54   The notion of *habitus* can be understood as "a system of lasting, transposable dispositions which, integrating past experiences, functions at every moment as a matrix of perceptions, appreciations and actions and makes possible the achievement of infinitely diversified tasks" (Bourdieu 1977:82-83).
55   Husein Shahab, interview, (2/4/2004).

He saw his overseas education first and foremost as a prestigious opportunity, something many students in Indonesia could only dream of. The fact that Qum was a centre for the study of Shi'ism was secondary to him. During his time at *Pesantren Ar-Riyadh,* he had studied books written by Shi'i *'ulama,* such as al-Tabarsi's *Makarim al-Akhlaq*[56] (The Perfection of Morality) but it was his schooling in Qum which converted him to Shi'ism.

Husein Shahab was enrolled at the Islamic educational institution, *Dar al-Tabligh al-Islami,* renowned for its non-Iranian student body. For about two years he followed the modern system of instruction offered by the institution. As previously noted, *Dar al-Tabligh* was dissolved by the Islamic government of Iran. Its leader, the Grand Ayatollah Shari'atmadari was formally demoted from the rank of *marja' al-taqlid* in April 1982.[57] Husein Shahab himself had a bad experience during the raiding of the Islamic school by the Iranian military. His education in Qum ceased and in 1982 he returned to his hometown, Palembang.[58]

After a year in Palembang, Husein Shahab departed once more for Qum. This time he headed for the *Madrasa Hujjatiyya,* another institution offering educational programmes for foreign students, but whilst he was registered at the dormitory of the institution, he did not follow its formal programmes. Instead, he decided to participate in the learning circles, the *halaqat* that were conducted by *'ulama* in Qum. In this educational and spiritual city, a variety of religious subjects are offered via these learning circles, while *fiqh* has dominated the educational system of the *hawza 'ilmiyya.* Husein Shahab started out attending the circles on *fiqh* and then changed his orientation to Islamic philosophy and other intellectual sciences. His participation in the *halaqat* enabled him to study under the guidance of a number of renowned *'ulama* and scholars of Qum. Among his *fiqh* teachers were Ayatollah Hasan Zawakhiri and Ayatollah Shaykh Muhammad al-Nuri. He studied Qur'an exegesis under Ayatollah Javadi Amuli (b. 1930),[59] doctrine under Ayatollah Sayyid Adil al-Alawi and Islamic history under Ayatollah Sayyid Ja'far Murtada al-'Amili (b. 1945).[60] He completed his study in Qum in 1986.[61]

---

56   Al-Fadl bin al-Hasan al-Tabarsi (d.1153) is a renowned Shi'i scholar and theologian whose most important work is in Qur'an exegesis, *Majma' al-Bayan fi Tafsir al-Qur'an.*
57   Momen (1985:296).
58   Ali (2002:218).
59   Ayatollah Javadi Amuli is a leading theologian, philosopher and Qur'an exegete in Qum. He was born in 1933 in Amul, Iran where he completed his primary education and entered the *hawza 'ilmiyya.* In 1950 he moved to Tehran to continue his religious study and then to Qum, where he was guided by renowned scholars including Ayatollah Burujirdi and 'Allama Tabataba'i (d. 1981).
60   Born in South Lebanon, Sayyid Ja'far Murtada studied in Najaf (1962-1968) and Qum and returned to Beirut, where he is a theological historian and directs the Islamic Centre for Learning (Rosiny 2001:208-209). His debates with the liberal Muhammad Husayn Fadlullah are discussed by Rosiny (2001:207-219).
61   Ali (2002:218-220).

Husein Shahab's field of specialisation is Islamic thought. In 1994 he pursued a Masters programme in this field at the International Institute for Islamic Thought and Civilization (ISTAC) in Kuala Lumpur, a tertiary educational institution founded and led by Muhammad Naquib Al-Attas. Here he developed his academic interests by conducting research and following lectures delivered by contemporary Muslim thinkers, including the renowned liberal Iranian intellectual, Abdul Karim Soroush.[62] He did not complete the programme, being forced to leave Malaysia after three years. The Malaysian government prohibits Shi'ism in its country because it is seen as contrary to the Sunnism practiced by the majority of the population.[63] I was informed that during his time in Malaysia, the police pursued Shahab because of his Shi'i beliefs, even though he was not actively promoting his *madhab*. In spite of his untimely departure from Malaysia, many Shi'is in Indonesia believe Husein Shahab actually graduated from ISTAC.

His career as an *ustadh* began about five years after his study in Qum. On his return to Indonesia, he went to Bandung to join Jalaluddin Rakhmat's *Muthahari* Foundation. Between 1991 and 1994, he became an important *ustadh* at that foundation.[64] During this period Jalaluddin Rakhmat and his family spent a year in Qum, leaving Husein Shahab to carry out some of Rakhmat's duties, including leading religious rituals, delivering sermons and lecturing for various *da'wa* and educational programmes. Transcripts of his writings and preaching from this period were distributed through *Al-Tanwir*, a *da'wa* periodical of the *Muthahari* Foundation. Since this time, the popularity of Husein Shahab as a Qum alumnus and *ustadh* has been widely acknowledged by Shi'is in Indonesia.

Since 1999, he has chosen to live in Jakarta, where the largest numbers of Shi'is reside. With the cultural capital gained through his religious education in Qum and Kuala Lumpur, Husein Shahab began to build his career by involving himself in a number of *da'wa* and educational activities. He became a popular preacher and attracted the attention of leaders of Islamic institutions, being appointed a lecturer at several Islamic institutions, both Sunni and Shi'i, including *Paramadina*, *Madina Ilmu* College for Islamic Studies, the IIMaN centre for positive Sufism, *Taqwa Nanjar* Foundation and *Al-Batul*. In addition, he has involved himself with the religious programmes of several national television and radio stations. He is both a popular and a prominent *ustadh* in Indonesia,

---

62   Husein Shahab, interview, (2/4/2004). Born in 1945, Soroush is increasingly recognised as a liberal thinker. One of his books, *Menggugat Otoritas dan Tradisi Agama (To Challenge Religious Authority and Tradition)* was first published in Indonesian by Mizan in 2002. For a review of this book, see *Kompas* (23/11/2002).

63   On the social, political and religious behind the prohibition of Shi'ism in Malaysia, see http://www.e-fatwa.gov.my/fatwa_search_result.asp?keyID=194.

64   Husein Shahab, interview, (2/4/2004).

ever-present in leading national Shi'i activities. He teaches and preaches in more than 20 Islamic institutions. With such an extensive *da'wa* programme, he is one of the *ustadhs* who is able to live very comfortably in Jakarta.[65]

In relation to his position as an *ustadh* and leader in the Shi'i community, Husein Shahab also participates in the establishment of Shi'i institutions. He is a co-founder of the Islamic Cultural Centre of Al-Huda (ICC). The programmes of this Iranian-sponsored institution include publishing, teaching and preaching. Husein Shahab's involvement with organising ICC programmes lasted only a year, however. In 2001 he resigned his post as a result of misunderstandings concerning the organisation of a workshop rejecting IJABI, the national Shi'i organisation founded by Jajaluddin Rakhmat on 8th June 2001.[66] After this episode he established the *Fitrah* Foundation in collaboration with Othman Omar Shihab which has become a teaching centre of Sufism in Jakarta. Husein Shahab also participated in the establishment of Forum *Al-Husainy* in 2004. This forum for *ustadhs* and intellectuals living in Jakarta is a new association, active in *da'wa* activities, including a monthly collective *dhikr* session of Sufi practice and *da'i,* or a *da'wa* leader training programme.

With regard to his intellectual achievements, Husein Shahab has produced several scholarly works. Most deal with his interest in Sufism and Islamic philosophy. However, his first book, published in 1988, was *Jilbab* (The Veil) dealing with what the Qur'an and Traditions of the Prophet say about women's head coverings. This work is based on two texts, both with the same title - *Hijab* - written by Abu al-A'la Maududi and by Murtada Mutahhari. Husein Shahab's book attempts to offer new perspectives on controversies surrounding the wearing of *jilbab* in Suharto's New Order era. He analyses textual evidence, from verses of the Qur'an and Hadith, as well as using rational argument to support the obligation of women to wear a *jilbab*. His other book is a practical manual on observing the pilgrimage to Mecca, a chief pillar of obligatory Islamic ritual. Its title is *Cara Memperoleh Haji Mabrur: Tuntunan Ahli Bayt Nabi* (Methods of Achieving Beneficial Pilgrimage: The Guidance of the Prophet's Family) published in 1995.

Husein Shahab's work on Sufism includes the two volumes of *Dialog-dialog Sufi* (Sufi Dialogues, 1994, 1995) which contain interesting stories about questions raised by disciples and answers given by Sufi teachers. His latest book, published in 2002, is *Seni Menata Hati: Terapi Sufistik* (Arts of Governing the Heart: Sufi Therapy). This book attempts to provide a Sufi model to 'diagnose' and 'cure' bad moral characteristics, referred to as 'heart illnesses' such as miserliness, arrogance and spitefulness, which harm human nature and blunt the believer's

---

65   Abaza (2004:183).
66   My account of this workshop can be seen in Chapter Five.

obedience to God. By following this model, the believer can reach the spiritual stage achieved by Sufis and the *walis,* saints or 'friends of God' in the quest to become an *insan kamil,* a perfect man.

Husein Shahab's writings on Sufism, Islamic philosophy and other aspects of Islamic knowledge are also published in such periodicals as the Mutahhari Foundation's *Al-Tanwir,* Al-Jawad Foundation's *Al-Jawad* and *Al-Huda,* belonging to the ICC of Al-Huda. One of the texts focuses on the life of Fatima, the Prophet Muhammad's daughter, whom Shahab invokes as a role model for female Sufis. According to Shahab's analysis, and as is believed by many, Fatima was able to communicate with the angels. These communications, collected by her husband, Imam 'Ali, are known as *Mushaf Fatima.*[67] Further articles by Husein Shahab can be found in published anthologies like *Kuliah Tasawuf* (Lectures on Sufism) and *Belajar Mudah 'Ulmum Al-Qur'an* (Easy Lessons in the Sciences of the Qur'an', 2002).

Husein Shahab's scholarship also includes the translation of several books into Indonesian from Arabic and Persian. He translated both the *fatwas,* or legal judgments of Ayatollah Abu al-Qasim Khoei (d. 1992) and Ali Akbar Sadeqi's work *Pesan Nabi Terakhir* (The Prophet's Last Message). But his most popular translation is that of Muhammad al-Tijani al-Samawi's *Thumma Ihtadaytu* (Then I Was Guided), first published in 1991 in Malay. Like the Arabic original and English versions, which are widely distributed in the Muslim world, the Indonesian version, *Akhirnya Kutemukan Kebenaran* (Finally I Found the Truth), published in 1993, is widely read in Indonesia. It is interesting to note that this book is one of the forbidden books listed in a *fatwa* of Johor State, Malaysia, issued on 19 November 2002.[68]

Husein Shahab's intellectual attainments are unquestionable. He is the prototype of a successful *da'i.* He transforms the cultural and social capital he has accumulated into the economic capital essential for maintaining his living as an *ustadh.* Although he is affiliated to many institutions of *da'wa* and education, there is no single institution powerful enough to establish him as the paramount leader of the Shi'i community to replace the late Husein Al-Habsyi, who was strongly supported by his own *pesantren.*

---

67   Husein Shahab (http://aljawad.tripod.com/arsipbuletin/tasawufwanita.htm). The use of the term *Mushaf Fatima* is a source of controversy between the Sunnis and the Shi'is. The Shi'is are accused of having made their own alternative Qur'an. This derives from the fact that in Sunnism the term *mushaf* is used only in relation to the Qur'an, with the existing Qur'an being known as *Mushaf Usmani.*
68   http://www.e-fatwa.gov.my/mufti/fatwa_search_result.asp?keyID=327, accessed 18/10/2005.

D. Jalaluddin Rakhmat

The most prominent intellectual by far within the Shi'i community is Jalaluddin Rakhmat, known as 'Kang' Jalal.[69] His followers frequently write his full name as K.H. Jalaluddin Rakhmat. This indicates the recognition, or is possibly an attempt to legitimise Rakhmat's religious prominence, placing him on a par with other leaders who bear title K.H., Kyai Haji. Born on 29 August 1949 in Bojongsalam, Rancaekek, a district of Bandung in West Java, Rakhmat comes from a religious family. His father was a man of learning, as well as a village chief and a Masyumi activist who then joined the separatist movment of *Darul Islam*, forcing him and his family to move to Sumatra for several years. Jalaluddin Rakhmat attended public school and studied religion with a traditionalist teacher named Ajengan Shidik. He learned *nahw* (Arabic syntax) and *sarf* (Arabic morphology) known within the *pesantren* tradition as *ilmu alat,* or the 'instrumental knowledge' for reading advanced texts. Rakhmat acknowledges that this understanding of Arabic allowed him to access the vast Arabic literature that shaped his religious thought and his thorough knowledge of Shi'ism. This made his position distinctive compared to other Indonesian Muslim intellectuals who graduated from secular universities and this particular cultural capital underpins his present position as a renowned Shi'i leader.

Jalaluddin Rakhmat received his formal education at secular schools and universities. After completing Junior High School (SMP Muslimin III) and Senior High School (SMA II) he enrolled in the Faculty of Communication Science at UNPAD in Bandung. In addition, he undertook Teacher Training for Junior High School (PGSLP) in the English Department and used this diploma to teach at several secondary schools in the city to support himself. His academic career in the field of communications began with his appointment as a lecturer at his alma mater. In 1980, he won a Fulbright scholarship for further study in communications at Iowa State University, USA. He finished his Masters in 1982 with a thesis entitled *A Model for the Study of Mass Media Effects on Political Leaders*. Some years later, he enrolled in a PhD programme at UNPAD, without completing. Finally, in 1994 he took Political Science as his PhD topic at The Australian National University, but this study was also not completed. Like Husein Shahab, he is wrongly perceived to have received his PhD, a mistake which is beneficial to his position within the Shi'i community.

Jalaluddin Rakhmat has lectured on communications from the beginning of his academic career. His students report that they eagerly looked forward to his lectures because of his convincing rhetoric and his expertise in the field.[70] But

---

69 'Kang' is a Sundanese term, literally 'elder brother' and a common form of address for elder men.
70 Malik and Ibrahim (1998:143-144).

in 1992 he was dismissed from UNPAD, following tensions with what Rakhmat describes as a certain 'campus bureaucrat'.[71] In the course of his academic career, he has written a number of textbooks on his technical specialisation which have become important references for students. They include *Retorika Modern* (Modern Rhetoric, 1982), *Metode Penelitian Komunikasi* (Methods of Communications Research, 1985) and *Psikologi Komunikasi* (Psychology of Communications, 1985). With these materials circulating among students and scholars alike, Rakhmat is widely recognised as an expert in the field. It is unsurprising then that in 2001, after an absence of almost 10 years, he was asked to return to UNPAD as a lecturer and was subsequently inaugurated as Professor of Communications.[72]

Jalaluddin Rakhmat's life history is infused with *da'wa*. This important aspect distinguishes him from most Shi'i intellectuals in Indonesia. Long before his conversion to Shi'ism, he had been affiliated with the Sunni reformist organisations *Persis* and *Muhammadiyah*, two groups strongly opposed to traditional Islamic beliefs and practices in Indonesia. During his studies at secondary school, he joined the youth branch of *Persis* in Bandung. Later, in 1970, he joined the *Muhammadiyah* training camp *Darul Arqam*, held with the purpose of preparing Muhammadiyah preacher cadres. He became a fanatical cadre of *Muhammadiyah* which, along with *Majlis Tarjih Muhammadiyah*, the institution through which it issued its *fatwas*, actively carried out *da'wa* in various areas of West Java. He energetically promoted the reformist ideology of *Muhammadiyah*, in particular the principle of 'anti-TBC' (*Tahayul, Bid'ah, Churafat*, superstition, innovation and false myth) which was an amusing pun on 'tubercolosis'. This reformist programme provoked strong negative reactions from followers of traditionalist Islam in the region. But Rakhmat always considered himself to have been successful in carrying out his duties as a *Muhammadiyah* preacher. In the 1970s, his achievements in this reformist organisation saw him appointed an executive member of the Council of Education, Instruction and Culture of the Bandung branch of *Muhammadiyah* and of its Council of Preaching in the West Java provincial branch.[73] It should be noted that after turning to Shi'ism however he used his *da'wa* outreach to promote specifically traditionalist ideas and practices such as the importance of *ziyara*, or the visitation of graves, *tawassul*, the invocation of Muslim saints or Imams in supplication and *tabarruk*, 'taking the blessings' of relics or mementoes - all of which are incompatible with his former reformist stance.

Jalaluddin Rakhmat's devotion to *da'wa* is seen in the fact that he maintained these activities during his period of study in America. Together with Imaduddin

---

71   Malik and Ibrahim (1998:144).
72   Rosyidi (2004:29-32).
73   Malik and Ibrahim (1998:143), Rosyidi (2004:43).

Abdulrahim and others, he established *pengajian* circles at the *Dar al-Arqam* mosque in Ames, Iowa. One of his missionary tasks was to give the sermon at the Friday Prayers. These were then compiled and published in *Khutbah-khutbah di Amerika* (Sermons in America, 1988). Rakhmat formed a close relationship with Imaduddin Abdulrahim, co-founder of the Salman Mosque at ITB, Bandung, who encouraged him to become a regular preacher at the mosque upon his return from America. Large numbers attended his religious lectures. On one occasion, Imaduddin Abdulrahim was informed that his influence on the Salman activists was so great that the congregation had become divided into two factions: the followers of Jalaluddin Rakhmat and the followers of Nurcholish Madjid.[74] Rakhmat's expertise in communications is frequently cited as responsible for his successes in *da'wa*. Indeed, Rakhmat is a very popular preacher, with his religious lectures attracting large audiences. His fame as preacher and intellectual has spread rapidly, not only in West Java but throughout the country.

In interviews, Jalaluddin Rakhmat told us that his lectures at the Salman Mosque often turned into interactive discussions with his audience. Following his banning from the Salman Mosque, these lectures were first held in Rakhmat's own home and eventually in the nearby *Al-Munawwarah* Mosque in Bandung. To this day he continues to deliver regular sermons at this mosque. He writes:

> It is said that these *pengajian* caused unrest. I was declared persona non grata from the Salman Mosque. At the request of the *jama'a*, I moved the Sunday dawn lectures to my own small house. The participants were crowded in the narrow rooms. Some overflowed outside. Soon after the Al-Muawwarah Mosque was established, they moved again to a mosque. Then the space was larger. The members of *jama'a* increased; most were university students.[75]

With his background in communications and experience as a preacher, Jalaluddin Rakhmat attempts not only to implement scientific concepts in his *da'wa* activities but also to formulate these activities from a communications perspective. His ideas can be found in essays included in two volumes: *Islam Alternatif* (Alternative Islam, 1986) and *Catatan Kang Jalal* (Kang Jalal's Notes, 1997). Rakhmat defines *da'wa* as "a communication activity aimed to realise Islamic teachings in the individual and in social life."[76] He believes all the components of communication can be found in *da'wa*: *da'i* (the preacher), message, media, object and effect. *Da'i*, the agent of *da'wa*, can be a Muslim individual or a group, while the object of *da'wa* includes Muslims and non-Muslims both. While Rakhmat views the media to be the same for both communications and *da'wa*,

---

74   Abdulrahim (1986:15).
75   Rakhmat (1998:xxx).
76   Rakhmat (1997:51).

the message of *da'wa* is different from that of communications. *Da'wa* should include three elements: *amr ma'ruf, nahi munkar,* or the injunction of enjoining good and prohibiting evil, aspects of Islamic *shari'a* and the empowerment of humankind against tyranny and injustice. He also emphasises that *da'wa* must have an impact on individuals and social structures in the form of progressive change within the domains of knowledge, attitude and behaviour.[77] Whether all aspects of his ideas on communication and *da'wa* have been realised, however, remains questionable.

One may wonder how Jalaluddin Rakhmat converted to Shi'i Islam. It is true that he was one of a group of Muslim intellectuals who were fascinated by the victory of the Iranian Revolution and its ideology. He, Amien Rais, Dawam Rahardjo and others were attracted to the works of revolutionary ideologues such as Ali Shari'ati. These works were considered to offer alternative ideological worldviews. But Rakhmat also admits that he began to engage in intensive self-study of Shi'ism in 1984, the year which appears to be the turning point in his religious, intellectual and spiritual quest. Even though we cannot ascertain the exact time of his conversion, it is safe to surmise that it would have followed this period of intensive study of Shi'i literature, discussion and reflection. A brief account of his awakening interest in Shi'ism goes like this: in 1984, Rakhmat, together with Haidar Bagir and Endang Saefuddin Anshary attended an Islamic conference in Colombo during which they became acquainted with some Shi'i *'ulama*. Rakhmat himself admits that the intellectual and religious performance of these *'ulama* at the conference impressed him greatly. What impressed him even more was that the Shi'i *'ulama* gave him a number of books. (It is interesting to note that before they left Indonesia for Colombo, the late Mohammad Natsir, the then chairman of DDII had warned Rakhmat and his peers not to accept books given out by Shi'i *'ulama*.)

Prior to the conference in Colombo, Jalaluddin Rakhmat had not been open to learning about Shi'ism, despite regular access to Shi'i books. Upon his return from Sri Lanka however he began and enthusiastic programme of reading. He says that it was a Shi'i book that really triggered his doubts about the validity of Abu Huraira (generally held to be reliable) as a communicator of Prophetic Traditions, perhaps a surprising claim when we consider that a large number of Hadith that Rakhmat upheld and practiced were narrated by Abu Huraira. From this time onwards, Rakhmat continued to study the teachings of Shi'ism, particularly through Arabic books, and found his religious truth in this branch of Islam.[78] It is highly likely however that he would have been exposed to the works of Shari'ati and al-Musawi's *Dialog Sunnah Syi'ah* (Sunnah-Shi'ah Dialogue) before 1984, since both of these works were available in Indonesian

---

77   Rakhmat (1997:51-53).
78   Jalaluddin Rakhmat, interview, (2/1/2003).

from 1983. Haidar Bagir is even of the opinion that Jalaluddin Rakhmat began to study Shi'i works when he was in America.[79] Whatever the exact timing, Rakhmat admits that after 1984 he had dealings with with many people wanting to become Shi'is, a factor which contributed to his emergence as a leading Shi'i figure in Indonesia.

Jalaluddin Rakhmat also involved himself in discussions with Indonesian Shi'i *'ulama* such as the aforementioned Husein Al-Habsyi of Bangil. Rakhmat even calls Husein Al-Habsyi his teacher. He also established links with Shi'i *'ulama* in Iran and other parts of the world. To gain a more thorough knowledge of Shi'ism, he spent a year in Qum (1992-1993). Initially, he had intended to pursue a PhD in Theology at Tehran University, but the process of enrolment was so complex that he changed his plans.[80] In Qum, he established connections with prominent ayatollahs and attended religious lectures and *halaqat* in the *hawza 'ilmiyya*. This year also provided his children with the opportunity to gain educational and religious experience in the shrine city of Qum. Some of them were enrolled at *madrasas* in Qum; his first son, Miftah Fauzi Rakhmat is currently an important Shi'i *ustadh* at the *Muttahhari* Foundation in Bandung. Even though Rakhmat is not included in the list of Qum alumni, the links he established with Qum ayatollahs and the knowledge he gained through attending lectures and study circles unquestionably enhanced his religious authority among Indonesian Shi'is.

In addition to such educational and *da'wa* experience, scholarship in the religious sciences is also seen as a crucial aspect of religious leadership. In this regard, Rakhmat provides us with numerous works in the form of books, essays, translations and introductory notes to other people's works on aspects of Islamic scholarship. Collections of his essays written in the 1980s are published in two of his best known books: *Islam Alternatif: Ceramah-Ceramah di Kampus* (Alternative Islam: Campus Lecturers, 1986) and *Islam Aktual: Refleksi Sosial Seorang Cendekiawan Muslim* (Actual Islam: Social Reflections of a Muslim Intellectual, 1991). The former consists of essays presented in seminars and lectures at university campuses. It includes ideas about Islam as a mercy for all creatures (*rahmatan li al-'alamin*), Islam and the liberation of *mustad'afin* (the oppressed), Islam and the right establishment of society and Islam and science. The book concludes with a call for readers to follow Shi'i Islam as an alternative. *Islam Aktual: Refleksi Sosial Seorang Cendekiawan Muslim* contains shorter essays which originally appeared in national publications such as *Tempo, Panji Masyarakat, Kompas, Pikiran Rakyat* and *Jawa Pos*. The essays reflect on various topics such as Islamic fraternity, communications and the mass media, politics, intellectual reform, family, leadership, poverty and social problems

---

79   Bagir (2003:72).
80   Rakhmat (1997:457).

and martyrdom. Notwithstanding its promising sub-title, Rakhmat himself acknowledges that, in general, the essays are not based on deep thinking, something he sees as quite in keeping with the character of the mass media.

Jalaluddin Rakhmat has also written books on more specialised disciplines of Islamic knowledge. He has produced two books on Qur'anic exegesis: *Tafsir Bil Ma'tsur* (Qur'anic Commentary by Narrated Sources, 1994) and *Tafsir Sufi Al-Fatihah* (Sufi Commentary of the Opening Chapter of the Qur'an, 1999). "In this area", writes Feener, "Rakhmat adopts the method of interpreting verses primarily in terms of other related ones from the Qur'an itself with material from the Sunnah used as a further means of clarification."[81] This is more correctly called *tafsir bi al-ma'thur* or *tafsir al-Qur'an bi al-Qur'an*, literally, interpreting Qur'anic verses using other Qur'anic verses, and refers to a method developed by the renowned Shi'i scholar 'Allama Muhammad Husayn Tabataba'i (1903-1981). In his second book of commentary, Rakhmat claims: "For the first time in Indonesian, I will include many Hadith from the Prophet's *ahl al-bayt* (Upon Whom Be Peace)."[82]

Other books by Rakhmat deal with Sufism. Besides the above-mentioned Sufi *tafsir* book, there is *Membuka Tirai Kegaiban: Renungan-Renungan Sufistik* (Parting Mystical Veil: Sufi Reflections, 1994), *Reformasi Sufistik* (Sufi Reform, 1998) and *Meraih Cinta Ilahi: Pencerahan Sufistik* (Achieving Divine Love: Sufi Enlightenment, 1999). They are derived from collections of his sermons, in particular those delivered at the regular Sunday religious gatherings at the Munawwarah Mosque and from essays published in the media. Rakhmat clearly recognises shortcomings in his own works as, more often than not, he offers excuses in their introductions. For instance, despite its promising title, Rakhmat acknowledges that his *Membuka Tirai Kegaiban* does not provide its readers with the same in-depth analysis of Sufi teachings as can be found in the classical books of Suhrawardi or al-Ghazali. Nonetheless, he provides innovative interpretations of certain Sufi teachings by comparing Sufism with psychology. In other articles he suggests that the teachings of Sufism can lead to emotional and spiritual intelligence,[83] the chief key to which is the Sufi teaching of patience.

In the field of Islamic history, Jalaluddin Rakhmat wrote *Al-Mustafa: Pengantar Studi Kritis Tarikh Nabi SAW* (The Chosen: An Introduction to the Critical Study of the History of the Prophet [May God Grant Him Peace and Salvation], 2002), adapted from the transcription of his lectures in the *Muthahhari* Foundation. In

---

81 Feener (1999:183-184).
82 Rakhmat (1999:xvi-xvii).
83 There are three articles by Rakhmat dealing with Sufism and its relation to emotional and spiritual intelligence: "Emotional Intelligence *dalam Perspektif Sufi*", "*Dengan Tasawuf Meningkatkan* Spiritual Intelligence" and "*Sabar; Kunci* Spiritual Intelligence". See Bihar Anwar (2002).

this case, 'critical study' means that criticism should be aimed at Sunni sources, particularly those Hadith narrating occasions or events which Shi'is believe to be contrary to the noble character of Muhammad (he being the most perfect man and the best example for mankind to follow). The spirit of this work is similar to that of Husein Al-Habsyi's exegesis. However, Rakhmat does not actually give readers an historical description of the life of the Prophet, save for providing examples of interpretations of events which he believes are worthy of criticism.

Jalaluddin Rakhmat also writes about the validity of certain religious practices which run contrary to reformist views. In *Rindu Rasul: Meraih Cinta Ilahi Melalui Syafa'at Nabi SAW* (Longing for the Messenger: Achieving Divine Love through Intercessions of the Prophet [May God Grant Him Peace and Salvation], 2001) Rakhmat provides us with various ways of showing love and devotion to the Prophet and vehicles through which to approach God, such as reciting *salawat* (invocations), expecting his *shafa'at* (assistance), *tawassul* (prayer through intermediaries) and *tabarruk* (the taking of blessings). Nota bene that Jalaluddin Rakhmat had strongly opposed all such religious practices in traditionalist Islam in Indonesia before his conversion to Shi'ism. "False intellectual arrogance distanced me from loving of the Prophet (May God Grant Him Peace and Salvation). The modernist ideology penetrating my thought had dried my soul."[84] Through *Rindu Rasul*, Rakhmat aims to demolish the intellectual 'arrogance' of reformist groups which denies these practices and he appeals for more reflective religious views. In the wider context of Indonesian Islam, he may have actually contributed to maintaining practices upheld by traditionalist Muslims in Indonesia.

Jalaluddin Rakhmat also wrote a work on ethics with the provocative title, *Dahulukan Akhlak di atas Fikih* (Prioritise Ethics over Jurisprudence, 2002a). The book is intended to solve the long-running problem in the Muslim *umma*, namely the factions which emerged following the death of the Prophet, by implementing his divine message on the universal necessity of noble ethics: "Indeed, I was designated to perfect noble ethics". Rakhmat presents the differences in legal opinion among the various schools of Islamic law during the course of history and analyses the factions and fanatical attitudes of followers of schools that have created conflicts within the *umma*. He suggests that the believer should renounce his or her strict adherence to a certain school of law for the greater good of establishing Islamic fraternity. This scholarly work contains genuine ideas that have received credit as well as criticism from both Sunnis and Shi'is in Indonesia.

Notwithstanding this call to abandon allegiance to particular schools of law for the sake of Islamic fraternity, Rakhmat wrote several essays on *fiqh*. Based

---

84 Rakhmat (2001:xii).

on these essays, Feener identified him as one of the new Muslim intellectuals who have contributed to the development of Muslim jurisprudence in 20th century Indonesia.[85] Like Munawir Sjadzali, a moderate Muslim intellectual and Minister of Religious Affairs from 1983 to 1993 and Nurcholish Madjid, a moderate Muslim intellectual and founder of the *Paramadina* Foundation, Jalaluddin Rakhmat maintains the necessity for the continuous exercise of *ijtihad,* or independent judgment, so that Muslims can adapt to social and cultural changes in their world. He writes: "*Ijtihad* is difficult but necessary."[86] He hastens to add that certain requirements for *ijtihad* mean that not everyone is authorised to undertake such a difficult task. As a follower of Shi'ism, he upholds the view that in terms of jurisprudence Muslims can be classified as *mujtahid* (legists) and *muqallid* (their followers). In Shi'i Islam, the laity should follow a specific *mujtahid* known as *marja' al-taqlid,* who has the attributes of *faqaha* (comprehension of Islamic knowledge) and *'adala* (noble character, firm conviction and sincerity).[87] Since Rakhmat is not a *mujtahid*, his response to issues of Islamic law is to promote the existing views of some *'ulama,* while emphasising the necessity of individual choice and the importance of Islamic fraternity. This attitude can be seen in his book, *Jalaluddin Rakhmat Menjawab Soal-soal Islam Kontemporer* (Jalaluddin Rakhmat Answers Contemporary Islamic Problems, 1998a) which is derived from his spontaneous responses to questions posed by audiences at his lectures at the Salman and Al-Munawwarah Mosques between 1980 and 1998. By not offering his own legal opinions, Jalaluddin Rakhmat clearly positions himself as a *muqallid* in the field of Islamic law and his answers generally reflect his adherence to the *Ja'fari* school of Islamic jurisprudence.

Besides questions of Islamic law, *Jalaluddin Rakhmat Menjawab Soal-soal Islam Kontemporer* also includes aspects of doctrine, Qur'an exegesis, ethics, history and psychology. It addresses such problems as the imamate as the fundamental doctrine of Shi'ism, family planning and love. In an editorial note, Hernowo points out that the image of Jalaluddin Rakhmat as a Shi'i intellectual may be opposed by certain groups. But Rakhmat is very capable of coping with the various responses directed towards him. Hernowo surmises that his success in playing the roles of expert in Sufism, Qur'an exegesis, jurisprudence and philosophy can be attributed to his intellectual powers of logic.[88]

Jalaluddin Rakhmat's works have contributed significantly to Muslim scholarship and this form of cultural capital is an important determinant of Islamic leadership in the Shi'i community in Indonesia. Nurcholish Madjid

---

85   Feener (1999).
86   Rakhmat (1988:173-201).
87   Rakhmat (1986:240).
88   Hernowo (1998:xxviii).

once described Rakhmat as 'a complete intellectual'.[89] This is true. He produces works not only on his technical field of specialisation and Islamic knowledge but also about psychology, education and so on. Another work, *Rekayasa Sosial: Reformasi atau Revolusi?* (Social Engineering: Reformation or Revolution? 1999a) begins with the explanation of what Rakhmat calls the 'intellectual cul-de-sac', namely intellectual fallacies that have to be overcome before social engineering can begin. "It is impossible for there to be change in the right direction if fallacies of thinking still entrap our minds."[90] With introductory notes presented by Dimitri Mahayana, the book offers political revolution as an alternative to the *reformasi* brought into being since the end of Suharto's New Order regime in 1998. On revolution, Rakhmat writes:

> When the whole nation runs into crisis, all the people demand change. The more unbearable the nation's state is, the more desirable it is that change occur soon. Revolution emerges as the best strategy. Reformation is considered too slow, while the stomach cannot wait. When corruption has been entrenched in the whole body of the nation, we need a total surgical operation, that is, revolution.[91]

He goes on to explain four theories of revolution, based on behavioural, psychological, structural and political schools. Taking several definitions of revolution, he points out three dimensions: first, multi-dimensional, comprehensive and fundamental change; secondly, involvement of the masses that are mobilised and rise in a revolutionary movement; and thirdly, the use of force and coercion. However, he personally rejects the third dimension.[92] Rakhmat also suggests circumstances which encourage certain tactics towards revolution, based on specific theories. For instance, according to behavioural theory, revolutionary circumstances include: impeding the fulfilment of needs of the majority of people and provoking disappointment and anger in the people when they compare their conditions with those of the regime.[93] But Rakhmat notes that revolution can only be explained, never predicted.[94] His ideas on political revolution seem to correspond with his appeals for martyrdom, which he considers to be the peak of Islamic wisdom

> *Shahid* literally means 'one who witnesses', 'one who gives evidence'. You believe in the truth of Islam and you prove the belief with your willingness to die to support Islam. You know that all kinds of oppression

---

89 *Kompas* (31/10/1997:15).
90 Rakhmat (1999a:3).
91 Rakhmat (1999a:177).
92 Rakhmat (1999a:190-191).
93 Rakhmat (1999a:201).
94 Rakhmat (1999a:211).

are acts of destruction of the words of God; therefore, you prove your knowledge with a willingness to sacrifice yourself in fighting oppression. Death-witnessing your belief is martyrdom.[95]

Jalaluddin Rakhmat established the *Muthahhari* Foundation in Bandung in 1988. Co-founders included Haidar Bagir, Ahmad Tafsir, Agus Effendi and Ahmad Muhajir. The foundation, which has the slogan: 'The Enlightenment of Islamic Thought', is engaged in *da'wa*, education and publishing. Since 1992, it has organised the programme of SMU Plus (Senior High School with attribute Plus),[96] which has attracted students from various parts of the country. Aside from participating in religious circles, Rakhmat regularly gives religious lectures at Sunday's *pengajian* at the *Al-Munawwarah* Mosque. As previously mentioned, a number of students who have gone on to become Shi'i intellectuals once studied at these lectures and circles. The recorded sermons from the *pengajian* form the main content of the missionary periodical *Al-Tanwir,* published by the *da'wa* division of the *Muthahhari* Foundation. The foundation has a publishing wing which has produced a number of books, including titles by Jalaluddin Rakhmat and students of SMU Plus. All these activities have made the institution and its leader famous throughout Indonesia.

In 1997, with financial support from Sudharmono, Vice-President of Indonesia during the New Order era and his family, Rakhmat founded *Tazkiya Sejati*, a centre for Sufi studies and training in Jakarta. He was its director until he left the institution in 2003, following conflict with Sudharmono's children, Yanti and Tantyo Sudharmono. From 1997 to 2003, *Tazkiya Sejati* organised more than 20 courses on Sufism, attracting participants from Jakarta's upper-middle class, including businessmen, executives and retired functionaries.

Jalaluddin Rakhmat's status as a leader is supported by the fact that he pioneered the establishment of Indonesia's national Shi'i organisation, IJABI (*Ikatan Jamaah Ahlul Bait Indonesia*, Indonesian Association of *Ahl al-Bayt* Congregations) in 2000. Since then, he has become the chairman of the advisory council and the most influential figure in the development of this organisation. In the beginning, Rakhmat and other intellectuals co-operated with Shi'i *ustadhs* in establishing the organisation, but during the process the groups split. While the Shi'i intellectuals, under Rakhmat's leadership, are generally associated with IJABI (which still claims to be the umbrella organisation for all Shi'is in

---

95   Rakhmat (1991:298).
96   The attribute 'Plus' is used because, aside from its concentration on the establishment of morality, the school teaches a number of subjects from the national curriculum of the Department of National Education. For more information about this school, see Chapter Five or http://smuth.net/Profile/03-sejarah.asp accessed 18/10/2005.

Indonesia), the *ustadhs* have rejected it as a social and religious organisation. However, IJABI has enjoyed a stable position because it is legally recognised by the Indonesian government through the Ministry of Home Affairs.

In the light of all the above, Jalaluddin Rakhmat has accumulated considerable cultural capital within the Shi'i community in Indonesia but he lacks social capital. Although he has unquestioned national standing, he still lacks the support of the majority of the Shi'i *ustadhs* of the Arab community and the Qum alumni. This is not yet powerful enough to promote him to the position of chief leader recognised by all of the Shi'i community.

3. The Madhhab

As a distinct *madhhab,* or denomination within Islam, Shi'ism has a complex set of beliefs and practices that set it apart from Sunnism. This chapter deals with the Shi'i teachings as they are understood and practiced by Shi'is in Indonesia and which constitute the religious aspect of their identity. The chapter opens with an explanation of key concepts such as *ahl al-bayt* and *Shi'a* (*syi'ah*, Indonesian). There follows a description of the principal concepts of belief in the imamate and the *Mahdi*. A further section deals with *Ja'fari* jurisprudence and specific aspects upheld by Indonesian Shi'is. This is then followed by a description of some external aspects of Shi'i devotion. Finally, I examine the Indonesian Shi'i interpretation of *taqiyya* and the circumstances of its implementation.

A. The *Madhhab* of *Ahl al-Bayt*

As a stigmatised minority, the Shi'is of Indonesia have utilised and popularised Islamic terms and concepts common to all Muslim communities, even though their interpretation such terms is strikingly different from wider Sunni understandings. Instead of the term *Shi'a*, *ahl al-bayt* (the community of the House of the Prophet) or more precisely, the *madhhab* of *ahl al-bayt*, is more commonly used by Shi'is in Indonesia when describing their brand of Islam and the Shi'is describe themselves as 'followers' and sometimes 'lovers of *ahl al-bayt*. The term *ahl al-bayt* is also used to distinguish Shi'is and Shi'ism from Sunnis and the Sunni *madhhab*, which are known as *ahl al-sunna wa al-jama'a* (the communitiy of the good practice of the Prophet).[1] The promotion of the term *ahl al-bayt* is important, since the term Shi'a has negative connotations for most Muslims who regard it as a sect that deviates from orthodox teachings. "Shi'ism will become correct if the term is replaced with *ahl al-bayt*", says Jalaluddin Rakhmat.[2] Increasing use of this term is expected to result in Shi'i beliefs and practices gaining recognition, and for Shi'ism to become an accepted Islamic *madhhab,* alongside the *madhab* of the Sunni majority of Indonesia.

Literally, the term *ahl al-bayt* means 'the people of the House', the Household of the Prophet Muhammad. Like their fellow Shi'is in other parts of the world, the Shi'is in Indonesia interpret this concept differently from the Sunnis, who include the Prophet's wives among his *ahl al-bayt*. For Shi'is, the concept of *ahl al-bayt* is one only of blood relations. It comprises the Prophet Muhammad, his daughter Fatima, his cousin and son-in-law 'Ali and his two grandsons, Hasan

---

1   Rakhmat (1999:178).
2   Rakhmat (1998:liv).

and Husayn, as mentioned in *Hadith al-Kisa'* (the Tradition of the Mantle) when the Prophet publicly demonstrated his House by spreading his cloak over them. These figures are also called *ahl al-kisa'* (people of the mantle).[3] In several Indonesian Shi'i works we find verses of the Qur'an and Hadith which are used to defend this Shi'i interpretation of *ahl al-bayt*. The most frequently cited verse is the following: "And Allah only wishes to remove all abomination from you, ye members of the Family, and to make you pure and spotless".[4] This is known as the *Tathir* (Purification) verse. It is said that before this verse was revealed, the Muhammad took Hasan and Husayn, 'Ali and Fatima under his striped cloak and stated: "these are my *ahl al-bayt*". The story goes on to say that Ummu Salama, one of the Prophet's wives, asked if she was included in the *ahl al-bayt*. He replied that she was not.[5] Thus, it is clear that unlike the Sunni interpretation, for Shi'is, the wives of the Prophet Muhammad are not considered to be members of his *ahl al-bayt*.

A second meaning of *ahl al-bayt* is the same as that of the term *'itra*, a concept which encompasses the line of all twelve Imams from Imam 'Ali to the Imam Mahdi.[6] Shi'is base this interpretation on the Hadith in which the Prophet stated that God had given the world two safeguards, *al-thaqalayn*, or 'the two weighty matters': the Qur'an and the Prophet's *'itra* or *ahl a-bayt*. Upholding these safeguards will prevent Muslims from going astray. In the Hadith, the two safeguards are grammatically inseparable. This quotation contradicts the famous Sunni Hadith which cites the Qur'an and the Sunna as guides.[7] Shi'i authorities in Indonesia have provided many versions of the Hadith of *thaqalayn*, including

> Verily, I leave you things, which if you keep hold of them, you will never go astray after me, one of which is greater than the other: The Book of Allah is like a rope hanging from heaven to earth and the other is my *'itra*, my Household. These two will never be separated from each other until they encounter me at *al-Hawd*. Therefore, take care as to how you behave towards my two legacies.[8]

---

3   Husein Al-Habsyi (1991:57).
4   Qur'an, Surah 33:33.
5   Elryco (2002:55-56).
6   Husein Al-Habsyi (1991:58-59).
7   A Sunni version of this Hadith reads: "I leave you two things, so that you will not go astray as long as you uphold them, the Book of God and the Sunna of His Prophet" ('Ali Umar Al-Habsyi 2002:337). Although this Hadith is widely taught and strongly upheld in the Sunni community, it is not narrated in the six authoritative Sunni collections, *al-Sahih* of Bukhari, *al-Sahih* of Muslim, *al-Sunan* of Abu Da'ud, *al-Sunan* of Nasa'i, *al-Jami' al-Sahih* of Tirmidhi and *al-Sunan* of Ibn Majah. In the Sunni tradition, the term *Sunna* is commonly understood to be the way or deeds of the Prophet Muhammad and is used interchangeably with the term Hadith, collections of sayings, conduct and things approved by the Prophet. Both terms are often translated however as the 'Traditions of the Prophet'.
8   'Ali Umar Al-Habsyi (2002:44). *Al-Hawd* is the pool in Paradise where Muhammad will meet his community on the day of Resurrection.

This is considered to be one of the most strongly established Hadiths. It is transmitted through various *isnads,* or chains of transmission and in different versions. 'Ali Umar Al-Habsyi, a Shi'i *ustadh* who teaches at YAPI in Bangil, East Java and grandson-in-law of Husein Al-Habsyi, provides a comprehensive account of the numerous *isnads* and versions of the Hadith of *thaqalayn* and affirms its validity and authenticity. On the rational proof of the obligation to uphold the Qur'an and the Prophet's *ahl al-bayt,* Al-Habsyi writes

> The Qur'an and *'itra* are called *al-thaqalayn,* the two safeguards, because both are the very valuable bequest of the Prophet left by him to his *umma.* Both are stores of religious knowledge, secrets of God and sources of information for *shari'a* law. Therefore, the Prophet (Upon Whom be Peace) frequently ordered his *umma* to take knowledge from them, to uphold the guidance bestowed by them and to make them a mirror in their way of life.[9]

Besides the Hadith of *thaqalayn,* there is other textual evidence considered to constitute commands to follow and love the *ahl al-bayt.* The Hadith of *safina,* the ark, reads: "My Household among you is like Noah's Ark. Whosoever embarks in it will be saved and whoever stays behind will drown."[10] The *ahl al-bayt* provide authoritative interpretations of the Qur'an after the death of the Prophet. For Shi'is, only those who follow their example are the true adherents of Islam and will gain salvation. At times Shi'i figures in Indonesia use the term 'loving devotion to the *ahl al-bayt'* as a strategy to encourage the Sunnis to more readily accept the Shi'i presence. But their meaning remains unchanged: that people should adhere to the teachings of *ahl al-bayt.*[11]

Like fellow believers in other parts of the world, the Shi'is of Indonesia uses the term *Shi'a* in an entirely positive sense. They hold the view that the group called *Shi'a* (Party, of 'Ali) has existed since the days of the Prophet, referring to the Hadith in which he said: "O 'Ali, you and your *Shi'a* will gain victory".[12] On occasions such as at the revelation of the Qur'anic verse which reads "those who have faith and do righteous deeds – they are the best of creatures",[13] Muhammad is said to have stated that 'the best of creatures' in this case are 'Ali and his party who will be victorious on the day of judgement.[14] In early Islamic history, prominent companions of the Prophet such as Salman, Abu Dhar, Miqdad and Ammar were known as 'Ali's *Shi'a.* These four companions are also called *al-Arkan al-Arba'a* (the Four Pillars).[15] Following Muhammad's

---

9   'Ali Umar Al-Habsyi (2002:122).
10   Alwi Husein (1998:38).
11   Rakhmat (1998:240-242).
12   Rakhmat (1986:250).
13   Qur'an Surah 98:7.
14   Alatas (2002:2).
15   Hashem (1994:246).

death, this minority group emerged in response to the historic event in the *Saqifa* (Hall) of Bani Sa'ida in Medina. Abu Bakr was elected first Caliph and successor to the Prophet, without involving any members of his *ahl al-bayt,* who were occupied at the time with the burial rites over the Prophet's body. After being informed about the election of Abu Bakr, 'Ali and his followers protested, since they recognised the Prophet's bequest that 'Ali succeed him as leader of the *umma*. The events at *Saqifa* are held to be the source of the Sunni-Shi'a schism within the Muslim *umma*,[16] the first of the 'great temptations' to destroy Islamic unity.[17] Jalaluddin Rakhmat quotes several historical accounts providing 'Umar's response to 'Abdullah bin 'Abbas' opposition: "By God, I know that 'Ali is the most appropriate of all to become the Caliph, but because of three reasons we sideline him. First, he is too young; second, he is tied with the descendants of 'Abd al-Mutt'Alib ['Ali's and the Prophet's grandfather] and third, people dislike prophethood and caliphate united in a single family".[18] In Islamic history, the followers of 'Ali - the Shi'is - considered the election of Abu Bakr to be the usurpation of 'Ali's right and contrary to Islamic teachings. Such is the religious and political background of the establishment of Shi'ism as a distinct *madhhab*.[19]

By affirming that their adherence to the *ahl al-bayt* and the Imams succeeding the Prophet, the Shi'is of Indonesia reject the Sunni accusation that the origin of their *madhhab* lies with one Abdullah bin Saba',[20] whom they consider to be a fictitious character. They point to sources that declare the existence of this figure to be invalid. Another argument goes even further, that the Shi'is reject the idea of Abdullah bin Saba' as the founder of Shi'ism and even curse him. Logic alone would suggest that it is inconceivable that the cursers of a figure are his followers - adherents of any religion or sect naturally praise and side with their founder.[21] The Shi'i intellectual, M. Hashem writes: "The accusation of the Shi'is as adherents of Abdullah bin Saba' is not at all supported by the history of human experience and is impossible to accept by logical reason."[22]

Shi'is in Indonesia argue that they maintain the true teachings of Islam, as taught and practiced by the Prophet Muhammad and his *ahl al-bayt*. In Shi'i publications, *da'wa* activities and gatherings, they emphasise their role

---

16   Hashem (1994).
17   Rakhmat (1986a:83).
18   Rakhmat (1986:250).
19   Rakhmat (1986:251).
20   Abdullah bin Saba' was the founder of a sect called the *Saba'iyya*. He was said to have converted from Judaism to Islam. He introduced ideas that tend to be considered *ghuluw* (extremism in matters of doctrine) such as the exaltation of 'Ali, the divine character of 'Ali and the denial of 'Ali's death. In anti-Shi'i accounts, he is said to be the founder of Shi'ism, who allegedly ignited the early disputes among companions of the Prophet and later divided the Muslim *umma*.
21   M. Hashem (1989:37-39).
22   M. Hashem (1989:39).

in maintaining the continuity, purity and the eternity of his teachings. For instance, in the commemoration of *'Ashura* in certain cities in Indonesia, they chant slogans about the struggle of Imam Husayn against the corruption of Islamic teachings by Yazid, the second Caliph of the Umayyad dynasty, by the Umayyad regime as a whole and even by several companions of the Prophet. It is believed that when the Prophet lay dying he ordered writing materials to be brought to him, intending to write the confirmation of 'Ali as his successor. But some of the companions, including 'Umar, ignored his command. 'Umar is said to have stated that the Prophet was delirious and that the Qur'an was enough for them. Thus Shi'is believe Sunnism to have been corrupted by most of the Prophet Muhammad's companions from the time of his death.

In addition to this, Indonesian Shi'i figures such as Jalaluddin Rakhmat identify Shi'ism as the *'madhhab* of love', based on a paradigm of love, with Imam 'Ali as its founder. Rakhmat also calls Shi'ism the *'madhhab alawi'*, a term referring to Imam 'Ali, while Rakhmat calls Sunnism the *'madhhab umari'*, attributed to the Caliph 'Umar. Followers of the *madhhab alawi* believe that all traditions of the Prophet Muhammad, with regard to doctrine, worship and social interaction, must be followed without exception. According to this *madhhab*, all of the Prophet's traditions are textual proofs, since the Prophet was totally immune from major and minor sins and mistakes. His life was led wholly in accordance with the will of God. Any stories and interpretations contrary to this principle are rejected in Shi'i Islam. Among the Qur'anic verses that are often cited in support of this position are: "Nor does he [the Prophet Muhammad] say (aught) of (his own) desire. It is no less than inspiration sent down to him."[23] According to Jalaluddin Rakhmat, the *madhhab umari*, by contrast, follows the traditions of the Prophet only in relation to doctrine and worship and not in contingent worldly aspects. The *madhhab umari* argues that on several occasions the Prophet made mistakes, was corrected by his companions and then God sent His injunctions to affirm the opinions of his companions.[24] Based on this fundamental difference, Rakhmat provides three characteristics of the *madhhab alawi*: first, since it accepts all of the traditions of the Prophet, this *madhhab* does not recognise the separation of religion from worldly matters. Second, as shown by the attitude and actions of Imam 'Ali, the *madhhab alawi* emphasises the unity of Muslims. Third, it is the *madhhab* of love, which characteristic can be found in the sayings, attitudes and actions of the Imams, which stress the significance of the Sufi concept of *mahabba* (love). Love is also included in Shi'i supplications.[25] "Supplications in the *madhhab alawi* are filled with love of God. Only in the *madhhab alawi* does love towards God reach its

---

23   Qur'an Surah 53:2-3.
24   Rakhmat (1999:293-294).
25   Rakhmat (1999:294-295).

culmination".[26] Related to this attribute is the principle that Shi'is in Indonesia consider Shi'ism to be the *madhhab* of *'ukhuwwa Islamiyya'* (the brotherhood of Muslims) because of its great concern for Islamic fraternity. Imam 'Ali is believed always to have promoted fraternity. His biography provides a complete picture of the realisation of Islamic fraternity in particular and the paradigm of love in general.[27]

Shi'is also generally consider themselves to be 'the chosen', in contrast to the Sunni majority. According to Enayat,[28] the ethos of refusing to recognise that the majority opinion is necessarily true has become one of the most important distinguishing features of Shi'ism, alongside its differences in doctrine and jurisprudence. The Indonesian statement, *'Alhamdulillah kita sudah Syi'ah'* meaning 'Praise be to God, we are already Shi'i' is an expression of their high religious status. While they acknowledge that Sunnis are Muslims, the Shi'is regard themselves as true believers. This view is partly derived from the aforementioned statement by Muhammad commanding the faithful to follow his *ahl al-bayt*, and also the statement that 'Ali and his followers will be victorious on the day of judgement and will enter paradise. Another argument frequently used by the Shi'i community is that the number of people who uphold the truth is usually small, while the majority of people will follow popular teachings propagated by means of political force, which goes to explain the minority position of the Shi'is in Indonesia and in the wider world.

In short, among the Shi'is in Indonesia, terms such as the *'madhhab of ahl al-bayt'* and the *'madhhab alawi'* have been used to denote their denomination in an entirely positive sense. Shi'ism is also built upon fundamentals of religion (*usul al-din*) and branches of religion (*furu' al-din*) containing specific elements that differ from Sunnism.

B. The Imamate

Like the followers of Shi'ism in Iran and other places in the world, Shi'is in Indonesia believe in five fundamental elements of religion, the *usul al-din*. They do not recognise the concept of *rukun iman*, the six pillars of faith common to Sunnis in Indonesia[29] and which can be found in most Sunni theological works. The basic tenets of Shi'ism are: *tawhid* (the oneness of God), *'adl* (the justice of God), *nubuwwa* (prophethood), *imama* (the imamate) and *ma'ad* (resurrection).

---

26   Rakhmat (1999:295).
27   Rakhmat (1991).
28   Enayat (2005:19).
29   Abu Ammar (2002:37). The six pillars of faith are belief in God, His Angels, His Holy Books, His Messengers and the Day of Judgement, and as well in God's decree known as *al-qada* and *al-qadar* (Indonesian, *takdir*).

Indonesian Shi'is agree with Sunnis on three tenets, namely the unity of God, prophethood and the resurrection of the dead. Shi'is share their belief in the justice of God with the *Mu'tazilis*, a rationalist theological stream within early Muslim history.[30] From a Shi'i perspective, the first three are called the fundamentals of religion, while the imamate and justice are the fundamentals of the *madhhab*. To become Muslim, one must believe in the fundamentals of religion, while to become a Shi'i, one must complement this with a belief in the imamate and justice.[31]

Like the Sunnis, Shi'is believe in the oneness of God and His perfect and good attributes. *Tawhid*, or Divine Unity, is the core of Islamic teachings and for Shi'is it is the basis of their world-view.[32] They also uphold the idea that the prophets were appointed by God and that Muhammad was the Seal and Chief of all prophets. Shi'is believe that he was infallible. They share with Sunnis a belief in the Day of Judgement, a time when each person will be brought to life to receive divine reward or punishment. Unlike the Sunnis, however, Shi'is place great emphasis on one of God's attributes, *'adl*, or justice. God cannot act in an unjust manner because His nature is just. This tenet also maintains the consistency of *'aql, or* reason with Islam, because *'aql* can judge the justness or unjustness of an act; thus it too receives great emphasis in Shi'i Islam.

Shi'is in Indonesia believe that the Qur'an possessed by Muslims today contains all of God's words, as revealed through the Prophet Muhammad and that it is a miracle of God granted to the Prophet. It is believed that God protected the originality of the Qur'an so that there could be neither addition nor subtraction made to it.[33] They also believe in the Hadith as a principal source of Islamic teachings, second only to the Qur'an. Included in the Shi'i interpretation of Hadith are sayings of the Imams. Thus, the Hadith are defined as all the acts and sayings of the fourteen infallibles (the Prophet Muhammad, his daughter Fatima and the twelve Imams) even though the deeds of the Imams are not considered to be independent of the sayings, conduct and agreement of the Prophet.[34] This is a consequence of the fundamental Shi'i belief in the imamate.

---

30 In Indonesia, the greatest contribution to the rational theology of Mu'tazilism was provided by the late Harun Nasution (1919-1998). For an intellectual biography of this figure, see Muzani (1994) and for an examination of his theological thoughts see Martin and Woodward with Atmaja (1997) and Saleh (2001:196-240).

31 Khalid al-Walid, interview, (2/7/2002).

32 Rakhmat (1986:178).

33 Hashem (2002:158), Alatas (2003:5-17).

34 Alatas (2002:11). Corresponding to the six collections of Sunni Hadith, there are four authoritative collections of Shi'i Hadith, namely *al-Kafi fi 'ulum al-din* (The Sufficient in the Knowledge of Religion) by Muhammad bin Ya'qub al-Kulayni (d. 940), *Man la yahduruhu al-faqih* (For him not in the Presence of Jurisprudent) by Shaykh al-Saduq Muhammad bin Babuya al-Qummi (d. 991), *Tahdhib al-ahkam* (Rectification of the Statutes) by Shaykh al-Ta'ifa Muhammad al-Tusi (d. 1068) and *al-Ibtisar fi ma ukhtulif fihi min al-akhbar* (Reflection upon the Disputed Traditions) also by al-Tusi (Chittick 1989:16).

For Shi'is the imamate is the essence of religion, without which belief is never complete. It is the fundamental tenet that distinguishes the Shi'i from the Sunni and is the principal doctrine that divides the Muslim *umma* into Sunnah and Shi'iah. Unlike the Sunnis, Shi'is regard the imamate as a religious matter, which they are obliged to establish. In addition, they believe that the Prophet Muhammad appointed the Imams as his successors:[35] "Imam or leader is the title given to a person who takes the lead in a community in a particular social movement or political ideology or scientific or religious form of thought."[36] In Shi'ism, the title Imam designates a religious, spiritual and political leader who performs the same duties as the prophet. Unlike the Prophet, however, the Imam does not receive divine injunctions, although like prophethood, the imamate is based on divine appointment. Just as the Prophet himself was appointed by God, the Imam must be chosen by God through His Messenger. "Thus, the Prophet is God's messenger and the Imam is the Prophet's messenger."[37]

For Shi'is, the existence of the Imam is a necessary condition of human existence. Human society is in need of constant guidance. The presence of a leader or ruler is very significant for the continuation of a society. Without a leader, individual rights and duties cannot be realised and order will vanish from society. Thus every man requires a leader, or Imam. From a theological perspective, the philosophy of the creation of man by God is based on the goal of perfection. To achieve this goal, human beings need God's guidance through His prophets, but prophethood ended with the death of Muhammad. For this reason, Muslims need the Imam to be the guide and authority in matters such as the religious commandments and to provide commentary and interpretation of the Qur'an.[38]

Within Shi'ism, reason dictates that every Muslim not only needs the Imam but is obliged to recognise the Imam as well. The Shi'i *ustadhs* and intellectuals in Indonesia also provide texts that designate this obligation. The most popular Hadith on the matter is: "Those who die without knowing the Imam of his time, it is as if he dies in the *jahiliyya* [the time of ignorance before the message of the Prophet Muhammad]."[39] Interpreting Qur'anic verses and Hadith, they claim that all worship and obedience to God is useless without the recognition of the Imam.[40] Even though someone might believe in the unity of God, His Prophet, the resurrection, divine justice and observe Islamic teachings, "he remains in *jahiliyya* as long as he does not recognise the Imam of the time."[41]

---

35   Rakhmat (1999:424).
36   Tabataba'i (1995:173).
37   Agus Abubakar Al-Habsyi (1984:7).
38   Al-Kaff (http://aljawad.tripod.com/arsipbuletin/imamah.htm).
39   Rakhmat (1997:427).
40   'Ali Umar Al-Habsyi (2002:165-166).
41   Rakhmat (1998:lvi).

Shi'is in Indonesia believe that the Imam must be the best of all men; indeed, the Imam is a perfect man. There are at least two qualities to being an Imam: first, to be the most pious man, totally surrendering his life to the will of God. Second, the Imam must be the most knowledgeable man. Only with these qualities can the Imam guide others on the way to achieve perfection.[42] In the Shi'i faith, like the Prophet, the Imam must be immune from sins or mistakes. Inerrancy (*isma*) is the power that prevents someone from committing sins or making mistakes.[43] Husein Al-Habsyi explains three aspects of inerrancy: first, inerrancy is the peak of piety because a pious man who always behaves according to the Will of God can protect himself from sins and mistakes. The power of inerrancy can protect him even from the desire to commit sins and mistakes. Second, inerrancy is a product of knowledge. Knowledge, by its nature, has the power to protect man from falling into sin and transgression or from being controlled by passion. Third, inerrancy is a consequence of the perfection gained through *ma'rifa,* gnosis, the direct knowledge of God as the source of perfection, allowing one to be open to the power of truth and love. Al-Habsyi believed that piety in itself may produce a mystical knowledge which can uncover the supernatural aspects of man and creatures:[44]

> Such absolute perfection, when it is gained by an *'arif* [Sufi] will enflame in his soul the spirit of yearning and loving, encouraging him towards the point at which he does not need anything except God alone. He will seek nothing except obedience to all His commands and prohibitions. He becomes abhorrent of what is contrary to His commands and pleasure and what is bad in His view. At that moment, truly a man (with the perfection he has gained) becomes protected from transgressions, so with it he does not give importance to things other than God's pleasure alone.[45]

The Prophet and the Imams possess the quality of inerrancy, which guarantees the validity, truthfulness and perfection of Islamic teachings. Shi'is argue that if the Prophet and Imams were not infallible, people would doubt their mission and guidance.[46] This means that Imams must be followed and obeyed: this obedience is an absolute obligation. Besides human reason, many verses of the Qur'an and Hadith are cited in support of the Shi'i view on the inerrancy of the Imams. The previously mentioned verse of the Qur'an about the purity of *ahl al-bayt* is understood also to designate the infallibility of the Imams, as is the Hadith of al-*thaqalayn*. Shi'is argue that the Qur'an is protected from distortion and error and that there is no question about the Prophet, who received and

42 Al-Kaff (http://aljawad.tripod.com/arsipbuletin/imamah.htm).
43 Husein Al-Habsyi (1992a:175).
44 Husein Al-Habsyi (1992a:175-181).
45 Husein Al-Habsyi (1992a:181).
46 Anis (http://fatimah.org/artikel/masum.htm).

propagated the Holy Book. If the Qur'an is so protected, the *ahl al-bayt* and the Imams are also protected. As the same Hadith also states, neither will ever be separated, until the Day of Judgement.[47]

Shi'is believe that it is inconceivable for humankind to choose the Imam, quite simply because they do not have the authority to do so. Only God has the authority to appoint the Imam, through the Prophet,[48] because only He knows who the most pious and knowledgeable among mankind is. In His justice, God pronounces to mankind about the Imams that he appoints.[49] Shi'i *ustadhs* and intellectuals in Indonesia refer to textual proofs of the appointment of Imams by God; for example, one verse of the Qur'an tells how Abraham was appointed an Imam and how he asked God to choose future Imams from his descendants.[50] In addition, they consider there to be many scriptural texts that, beside obedience to God and His Prophet, command Muslims to obey the Imams. The Qur'an reads: "O ye who believe! Obey Allah, and obey the Messenger, and those charged with authority among you."[51] In the Shi'i interpretation, the term *uli al-amr* (*ulil amri*, Indonesian) "those charged with authority" refers to the Imams.[52]

Shi'i *ustadhs* and intellectuals also point to 'Ali as the Imam to succeed the Prophet Muhammad, which they say is specifically stated in the Qur'an and Hadith. One Qur'anic verse reads: "Your (real) friends are (no less than) Allah, His Messenger, and the (Fellowship of) believers — those who establish regular prayers and regular charity, and bow down humbly (in worship)."[53] In their interpretation, the revelation of this verse indicated 'Ali bin Abi Talib. One source for this interpretation is that Abu Dhar, a companion of the Prophet, told that when he performed the noon-time prayer in the mosque with the Prophet, a person in need entered the mosque asking for help, but no-one gave him anything. 'Ali, who was in a position of genuflection, raised his finger towards the person, who then took his ring and left. God praised 'Ali's conduct and revealed that verse,[54] which is widely known as the verse of *wilaya*, or spiritual investiture. The term *wali* is identical to the term Imam, as the holder of authority and leadership. Both Sunni and Shi'i sources are cited to confirm this interpretation. 'Ali Umar Al-Habsyi even claims: "books of Sunni Qur'anic exegesis and Hadith are sufficient to prove the truth of the event."[55]

---

47   Alatas (2002:76-78).
48   Anis (http://fatimah.org/artikel/masum.htm).
49   Al-Kaff (http://aljawad.tripod.com/arsipbuletin/imamah.htm).
50   Qur'an Surah (2:124).
51   Qur'an Surah (4:59).
52   In Sunnism, the term *ulu al-amr* refers to *'ulama* or temporal leaders. In line with the Sunni understanding of the concept, at a conference in March 1953, a number of NU *'ulama* bestowed on President Soekarno the title *w'Ali al-amri al-daruri bi al-shawka* (the Ruler who at present is in power) who had to be obeyed according to the Qur'an, verse 4:59 (Boland 1971:133).
53   Qur'an Surah 5:55.
54   Rakhmat (1991:v), 'Ali Umar Al-Habsyi (2002:153-154).
55   'Ali Umar Al-Habsyi (2002:154).

It is also pointed out that the Prophet appointed 'Ali as his successor on many occasions, from the early days of his prophethood until his death. This is also congruent with the Shi'i comprehension that the Prophet had great concern for leadership. In each of his military expeditions, he appointed a leader and each time he left the city he appointed a deputy. Thus, Shi'is claim, it is inconceivable that the Prophet passed away without first appointing a successor. This successor would certainly be the most qualified person, with the capability to lead and guide the Muslim community, namely 'Ali bin Abi Talib.[56] Many Hadith affirm the Prophet's appointment of 'Ali, one of them suggesting that the this took place at the launch of the Tabuk expedition. He said to 'Ali: "Are you not satisfied that your position beside me is the same as the position of Aaron beside Moses, except that there will not be another prophet after me?"[57] However, the most famous scriptural text is known as the Hadith of *Ghadir Khumm,* transmitted through numerous *isnads* and in different versions. One version, transmitted by Ahmad from Bara' bin Azib, reads as follows

> We were in the company of the Messenger of God (Upon Him be Peace) on a journey, then we stopped at Ghadir Khumm. Then, we were ordered to gather and a place under two big trees was cleaned, then he performed noontime prayer and afterwards he raised 'Ali's hand while saying: "Haven't you recognised that I indeed have the rightful authority over the faithful more than they themselves do?" They answered: "Yes". He went on to say: "Don't you recognise that I indeed have the rightful authority more than each of the faithful himself does?" They replied: "Yes." Then he said: "Whoever (takes) me as his *mawla* (master), 'Ali will be his *mawla*. Oh God, love whoever takes him master and hinder whoever hinders him." Bara' said: "Afterwards, 'Umar met him and said, 'Congratulations, Oh son of Abi Talib, you have become the master of all the faithful.'"[58]

The Prophet is believed not only to have appointed 'Ali as the Imam to succeed him but also to have mentioned the number and names of all the Imams after him. The number is twelve and they hail from the clan of Quraysh and from the Household of Muhammad. This is mentioned in both Sunni and Shi'i traditions, including the most authoritative Sunni collections of Hadith, *al-Sahih* of Bukhari and *al-Sahih* of Muslim. The Shi'i *ustadhs* and intellectuals in Indonesia use both Sunni and Shi'i collections to cite the number of Imams after the Prophet. They quote a Hadith in *al-Sahih* of Bukhari, transmitted by Jabir bin Samurah, who said that he had listened to the Prophet's saying that there would be twelve *amirs* (leaders), all of whom would be of the Quraysh. There is also a Hadith in

---

56 Rakhmat (1986:243).
57 Alatas (2002:60).
58 'Ali Umar Al-Habsyi (2002:155-156).

al-Sahih of Muslim, which states that the affairs of the believers will run well as long as twelve caliphs lead them.[59] So believing in twelve Imams, they are commonly called 'Twelver *Imamiyya'* Shi'is.

For the Shi'is of Indonesia, there are sound Hadith designating that the Prophet publicly announced the names of the twelve Imams and declared each of them his successor. They begin with 'Ali as the first, followed by his two sons, Hasan and Husayn, followed by the descendants of Husayn until the twelfth Imam Muhammad al-Mahdi, the Awaited One, who went into occultation and remains hidden. The twelve names are: 'Ali bin Abi Talib al-Murtada (d. 40/661), Hasan bin 'Ali al-Zaki (d. 49/669), Husayn bin 'Ali Sayyid al-Shuhada (d. 61/680), 'Ali bin Husayn Zayn al-'Abidin (d. 95/715), Muhammad bin 'Ali al-Baqir (d. 115/734), Ja'far bin Muhammad al-Sadiq (d. 148/766), Musa bin Ja'far al-Kazim (d. 183/800), 'Ali bin Musa al-Rida (d. 203/819), Muhammad bin 'Ali al-Jawad (d. 220/836), 'Ali bin Muhammad al-Hadi (d. 254/869), Hasan bin 'Ali al-'Askari (d. 260/875) and Muhammad bin Hasan al-Mahdi.[60] Today, Shi'is recognise Muhammad al-Mahdi as their last and twelfth Imam. He is the Awaited (*al-Muntazar*) whose his appearance is expected to establish God's justice in the world.

Thus the belief in the imamate is the distinguishing feature of Shi'ism. But besides determining Shi'i interpretations of Hadith, it also contributes to Shi'i interpretations of jurisprudence. The complexity of the Shi'i *madhhab* is apparent in the notion of Imam Mahdi, now to be explained.

C. The Mahdi

Shi'is in Indonesia themselves acknowledge that the belief in the Imam Mahdi is a complicated matter. This belief is shared by all Muslims, both Sunni and Shi'i. Even Judaism and Christianity uphold a belief in the coming Messiah, the saviour of the world. In Indonesia, a similar concept of a *Ratu Adil* (Just King) promotes the idea of the coming of a figure who will bring justice and prosperity to the land of Java. However, it should be noted that Sunnism and Shi'ism have different interpretations of the belief in the Imam Mahdi. One stark difference concerns his birth. While Sunnis believe that he is not yet born, Shi'is maintain that he is already born and is still alive but that he went into occultation. Shi'is also devote more attention to faith in Imam Mahdi than Sunnis, since it forms part of their general belief system of the imamate.[61] The main tenets concerning the Imam Mahdi are in respect of his existence and his attributes; namely, that

---

59   Rakhmat (1997:432), 'Ali Umar Al-Habsyi (2002:205-206).
60   Rakhmat (1986:244), 'Ali Umar Al-Habsyi (2002:210-211).
61   Rakhmat (1998:lvii).

he is the son of the eleventh Imam, Hasan al-'Askari, that he is the last Imam chosen by God, that he is infallible and that he has complete knowledge of the Qur'an and Hadith.[62] Abu Ammar writes: "If in these matters you are still in doubt... you cannot yet be considered as Shi'i."[63]

For Shi'is in Indonesia, the Imam Mahdi's name is synonymous with that of the Prophet Muhammad. It is mentioned in a Hadith which states: "Judgement day will not take place until the time of a man from my Household whose name is the same as mine."[64] Under the famous title *al-Mahdi* (the Rightly Guided) he is mentioned in many Hadiths as the twelfth Imam. He is also mentioned with the titles *Sahib al-Zaman* (the Lord of the Age) and *Imam al-Zaman* (the Imam of This Time). These epithets refer to the interpretation that Imam Mahdi is the Imam of the present period, in whom all true Muslims must believe. It also follows the obligation for believers to have an Imam. His other titles are *al-Khalaf al-Hujja* (the Substitute of God's Proof), *al-Qa'im* (the One who will arise), *al-Muntazar* (the Awaited) and *al-Tali* (the Future).[65]

According to Shi'is, the Imam Mahdi was born in Samarra, Iraq, in 256/871. His father, the eleventh Imam, Hasan al-'Askari, cared for him until his martyrdom in 260/875. Imam Mahdi succeeded his father after his death, being appointed Imam around the age of five. This is one of the complicated issues in the belief in Imam Mahdi. For Shi'is, his appointment was a miracle granted by God. Jalaluddin Rakhmat cites Muhammad Baqir Sadr's view that even though Imam Mahdi was only a boy five years old, the political regime attempted to isolate him from his followers and to kill him. "This is evidence that the Imam was very powerful and bright, so that he should be taken into consideration."[66]

Then, by Divine Command, Imam Mahdi went into occultation (*ghayba*, Arabic; *gaib*, Indonesian). The Indonesian term *gaib* is understood by Shi'is to mean "the absence of the Imam Mahdi among mankind."[67] Shi'is believe in two parts to this occultation: the first is the minor occultation (*ghayba sughra*) and the second, the great occultation (*ghaybakubra*). During the minor occultation, the Imam still made contact with people through his special deputies, for during this occultation, which lasted from 260/875 until 329/942, he is believed to have chosen special deputies through whom he could communicate and provide guidance to the community of believers. There were four deputies, known as *Nawwab al-Imam* (the Deputies of the Imam) or *al-Sufara al-Arba'a* (the Four Ambassadors). The first was 'Uthman bin Sa'id al-'Umari. The second, after

---

62   Abu Ammar (2000:149).
63   Abu Ammar (2000:149).
64   Abu Ammar (2000:86).
65   Rakhmat (2001a:4).
66   Rakhmat (1998:251).
67   Al-Walid (2004:11).

'Uthman's death, was his son, Muhammad bin 'Uthman al-'Umari. On his death, Husayn bin Ruh Nawbakhti was appointed, and finally 'Ali bin Muhammad al-Sammari became the deputy. The minor occultation ended with the death of 'Ali bin Muhammad al-Sammari in 942. Thereafter followed the great occultation, which "begins and continues as long as God wills".[68] The above-mentioned Hadith on the Imam Mahdi is used to support the Shi'i argument for the unknown length of this great occultation. But another popular Hadith, from the Sunni collection of Abu Daud, tells of the long life of Imam Mahdi and his reappearance to fulfil justice in the world: "If there were to remain in the life of the world but one day, God would prolong it until He sends a man from my Household, his name will be the same as mine, he will fill the earth with justice, as it was filled with tyranny."[69]

Logical reasoning is also used by Indonesian Shi'i leaders to support their belief in the occultation of Imam Mahdi and in his longevity. *Gaib* (absence) does not mean non-existence, and this becomes the argument for Imam Mahdi's existence. *Gaib* may be absolute or relative. The absence of Imam Mahdi is relative, in the sense that he is not absent for exceptional persons,[70] namely those who are trustworthy. Shi'is argue that God hides Imam Mahdi from his enemies, who try to execute him, even as his followers long for his appearance. They hide him in order to protect him, because he is the last and will be Imam for a long period of time and so the *imamate* that must exist in all periods continues uninterrupted.[71]

Such a long lifetime of Imam Mahdi is considered to be consistent with ideas of Divine injunction. For Shi'is in Indonesia this is another miracle granted by God to Imam Mahdi. They also cite the Qur'anic verses, which assert stories of longevity in the past. The Prophet Noah was 950 years old[72] and 'the People of the Cape' slept for 309 years.[73] The Qur'an also states that God rejects the claim that Jesus died on the cross.[74] It is believed that he is still alive and will appear after the appearance of Imam Mahdi to ensure justice in the world. Shi'is argue that it is impossible to reconcile a belief in the validity of these verses and the existence of longevity, with a rejection of the belief in the long lifetime of Imam Mahdi.[75] To question this matter is to question God as All-Powerful. Abu Ammar writes

> ...Long life is a matter that is very possible to occur and even has occurred. And the matter is not a problem for God, the Almighty. Allah

---

68 Al-Jufri (2000:72-73), Rahmat (http://aljawad.tripod.com/arsipbuletin/imammahdi.htm).
69 'Ali Umar Al-Habsyi (2002:242).
70 Rakhmat (1998:249-250).
71 Abu Ammar (2000:35-38).
72 Qur'an Surah 29:14.
73 Qur'an Surah 18:25.
74 Qur'an Surah 4:58.
75 Abu Ammar (2000:39-40), Rahmat (http://aljawad.tripod.com/arsipbuletin/imammahdi.htm).

creates all [creatures], certainly He can also look after them. Therefore, whoever doubts this power, he should examine his faith again and see its distance, how far or near it is from the materialists....[76]

Another reason is also given, which is related to the duty of Imam Mahdi to ensure justice and prosperity in the world. He was created to live long, throughout different ages, witnessing and experiencing various events and civilisations. With such a wealth of knowledge and experience, Imam Mahdi can fulfil his duty of solving all the problems of this complex world.[77]

In the matter of Jesus, Shi'is in Indonesia believe that he too is alive, but hidden, and that he will perform prayer under the leadership of Imam Mahdi. This means that Jesus also recognises the imamate of Imam Mahdi. Several Hadiths are used to support their argument, including one, which reads "How do you react when Jesus reappears and his Imam is among you?"[78]

Closely related to belief in the occultation of Imam Mahdi and an unfortunate consequence of it is the emergence of humans claiming to be Imam Mahdi. Shi'i leaders in Indonesia warn their followers about these false Mahdis. One of the latest cases in Jakarta is that of a woman named Lia Aminuddin, the founder of the *Salamullah* sect, who declared herself to be Imam Mahdi. Her claim has been rejected outright by Indonesian Shi'is because Imam Mahdi must be a man, must have the same name as the Prophet and must be one of his descendants.[79] In the history of Muslim society, there have been a number of others who have been alleged to be the Mahdi. Mirza Ghulam Ahmad, the founder of the *Ahmadiyya* sect in Pakistan is regarded as one such false Mahdi. For the Shi'is, aside from the identity of Imam Mahdi, other criteria such as his infallibility, his perfect knowledge of the Qur'an and Hadith and his fulfilment of justice in the world are used to disprove the claims of these false Mahdis.[80]

Another problem related to the occultation of Imam Mahdi is the emergence of a number of Shi'is in Indonesia who claim to have met the Imam or to have been able to communicate with him. This too has become a concern for Shi'i leaders. In the history of Shi'ism, there have been many stories about those who claimed to have met Imam Mahdi. Shi'i figures in Indonesia believe all such claims to be invalid. Khalid Al-Walid, a Shi'i *ustadh* and Qum alumnus, affirms: "those who claimed to have been able to communicate with Imam Mahdi (Upon Him be Peace) are in general liars."[81] He bases this judgment on what is said to be a letter from Imam Mahdi himself commanding people to be careful in this matter. Part

---

76   Abu Ammar (2000:40).
77   Rakhmat (1998:252).
78   Rakhmat (2001a:6).
79   Rakhmat (2001a:6).
80   Abu Ammar (2000:143-145).
81   Al-Walid (2004:15).

of the letter reads: "Among my *Shi'a* there emerged persons who claim to be able to witness me. Be careful, those who claim to be able to witness me before the emergence of al-Sufyani, they indeed are liars." Khalid Al-Walid concludes that matters emerging as a consequence of the occultation of Imam Mahdi, including claims to have met him, are to be considered as tests of faith for Shi'is.[82]

The letter indicates one of the signs of the return of Imam Mahdi, namely the appearance of al-Sufyani, who will be assassinated by the Mahdi.[83] The Shi'is consider there to be a number of signs indicating the imminent appearance of Imam Mahdi. Most of these are based on both Sunni and Shi'i Hadiths. The main sign may be subsumed in the sentence: "the entire world is overwhelmed by tyranny, injustice, disorder, and slaying. The most popular mark proceeding to the appearance of Imam Mahdi is the appearance of the one-eyed *Dajjal* (the Devil, or Anti-Christ)". Imam Mahdi is believed to be the one who will kill the *Dajjal*, as part of his duty to bring justice to the world.[84]

For Shi'is in Indonesia, waiting for the appearance of Imam Mahdi is very important. This means a belief not only in the existence and imamate of Imam Mahdi but also in his monitoring of all human actions.[85] In waiting, believers are obliged to obey all of God's commands and to protect themselves from all He has prohibited. This is called *taqwa*, or piety. Believers must also be convinced that Imam Mahdi sees all their actions, because it said in the Qur'an[86] that God, His messenger and the faithful see all people's behaviour.[87] In waiting for the Mahdi, believers plead to be included under his leadership and guidance, and for God to hasten his reappearance. "Let us pray in order that we are united with our Imam, the Lord of the Age, al-Mahdi. We hope we are among the followers of Imam Mahdi and finally will be assembled by God in the Hereafter, together with him and his ascendant, the Messenger of God", says Rakhmat.[88] On the longing for the appearance of Imam Mahdi, Jaffar Al-Jufri writes: "Our Imam, the Mahdi, is the one we very much await in the situation of this age, truly there is no figure that we trust except him."[89]

Waiting for the return of Imam Mahdi is considered to be an act of obedience, *'ibadat*, to God and is understood as a positive philosophical value. It is not fatalism that makes people simply surrender. If waiting for the return of Imam Mahdi contributes to such a fatalistic attitude, then it is deviating and

---

82   Al-Walid (2004:15).
83   There are different opinions about who al-Sufyani is. One is that he is a descendant of Abu Sufyan (Ma'awiyah's father) who will appear and command armies before the advent of Imam Mahdi.
84   Al-Jufri (2000:82-102), Abu Ammar (2000:137-142).
85   Syuaib (1423:2).
86   Qur'an Surah 9:105.
87   Abu Ammar (2000:150-151).
88   Rakhmat (2001a:7).
89   Al-Jufri (2001:70).

destructive.[90] Pious deeds are also required in order to establish a better life. For Shi'is, Mahdism, along with martyrdom, becomes the philosophical basis for the establishment of the future Muslim *umma*. Anguish experienced during such obedience to God is, in reality, motivated by an idealistic world-view, to be witnessed by Imam Mahdi.[91]

Thus the return of Imam Mahdi is seen as a series of struggles between good and evil. "And the Mahdi is the symbol of victory for the pious and the believers."[92] Shi'is in Indonesia support their argument with a scriptural text that God has promised this victory.[93] The return of Imam Mahdi is understood as a realisation of God's promise and His gift to the oppressed, who will gain authority and leadership in the world.[94]

The recognition of the existence of Imam Mahdi and the belief in his return are essential to the Shi'i *madhhab*. This belief has a great impact on the entire Shi'i *madhhab*, including on Shi'i jurisprudence, to which we now turn.

D. *Ja'fari* Jurisprudence

In addition to *usul al-din,* or the fundamentals of religion which must be believed by every Shi'i, there is the concept of *furu' al-din,* or branches of the religion which form the code of conduct for all Shi'is. This parallels the Sunni concept of *rukun Islam,* the pillars of Islam.[95] Basically, *usul al-din* come under in the realm of Islamic doctrine, *'aqida,* while *furu' al-din* are part of Islamic jurisprudence, *shari'a.* There are seven pillars of *furu' al-din*: prayer, fasting in the month of Ramadan, *zakat* (alms), *khums* (the one-fifth tax), Hajj (the great pilgrimage to Mecca), *jihad* (struggle in the way of God) and *amr ma'ruf nahy munkar* (enjoining to do good and exhortating to desist from evil). These seven pillars are called *'ibadat,* or acts of worship and lead to reward by God. All Shi'is in Indonesia consider these acts of worship to be obligatory.

They also consider themselves to be followers of *Ja'fari* jurisprudence, distinguishing them from the majority of Muslims in the country who follow *Shafi'i* jurisprudence. Indonesia's Shi'i leaders frequently affirm that, in general, *Ja'fari* is very close to *Shafi'i,* stating that the difference between *Ja'fari* jurisprudence, *Shafi'i* and the other three Sunni schools of jurisprudence is

---

90　Abu Batoul (1998:68).
91　Mulyadi (http://aljawad.tripod.com/arsipbuletin/mahdiisme.htm).
92　Abu Batoul (1998:68).
93　Qur'an Surah 24:55.
94　Abu Batoul (1998:68).
95　In Sunnism there are five pillars of Islam: the confession of faith, prayer, fasting in the month of Ramadan, religious tithing and the Hajj to Mecca.

smaller than the difference among the four Sunni schools themselves.[96] There are parallels, in almost all aspects of jurisprudence, between the *Ja'fari* and the four Sunni schools.[97] Although the term *Ja'fari* jurisprudence originates from the name of the sixth Imam, Ja'far al-Sadiq (d. 148/765), it differs in meaning from the four Sunni schools, which contain sets of jurisprudential opinions, or the products of *ijtihad* by their founders. Umar Shahab writes

> The term [Ja'fari] does not totally represent a set of opinions or the product of *ijtihad* of Imam Ja'far al-Sadiq. Because in the Shi'i view, Imam Ja'far al-Sadiq, like the other eleven Imams, namely (from the first Imam until the last) 'Ali bin Abi T'Alib, Hasan bin 'Ali, Husayn bin 'Ali, 'Ali Zain al-'Abidin, Muhammad al-Baqir, Ja'far al-Sadiq, Musa al-Kazim, 'Ali al-Rida, Muhammad al-Jawad, 'Ali al-Hadi, Hasan al-'Askari, and Muhammad al-Mahdi, who was not a *mujtahid*, but an Imam who had authority in establishing or producing law, *tashri' al-hukm*.[98]

What is commonly considered to be the major point of difference between the Ja'fari jurisprudence and the Sunni schools is the fact that in Shi'ism the gate of *ijtihad* is not closed, whilst in Sunnism it has been closed since the 9th century. *Ijtihad* is the scholarly inquiry to formulate legal opinions from the principal sources of Islam, namely the Qur'an and Hadith.[99] Although the gate of *ijtihad* is theoretically open to any Shi'is, the *'ulama* oblige laymen to imitate a chief *mujtahid*, known as *marja'* or *marja' al-taqlid,* a 'source of emulation' who has achieved the authority to serve as a reference for the laity.[100] The act of following the *fatwa* of *mujtahid* is called *taqlid* and the layman who follows the *marja'* is called the *muqallid*. Thus, in *Ja'fari* jurisprudence, Muslims are classified as being either *mujtahid* or *muqallid*. A *mujtahid* worthy of emulation must fulfil certain requirements: he must be male and still alive; his product of *ijtihad* must be authorised; he must be just, pious, ascetic, tenacious and free from committing sins. A *marja' al-taqlid* usually publishes the result of his *ijtihad* - on subjects ranging from acts of worship to political matters - known as *risala 'amaliyya, a* 'tract on practice', which becomes the religious code for his *muqallid*.[101] The relationship between *marja'* and *muqallid* is called *marja'iyya*. Rakhmat explains

> In Ja'fari jurisprudence, we may only perform religious practices by following a living *marja'*, a man of Islamic learning, who publishes his

---

96   Adam (2003:44).
97   Bagir (1995:3). The four Sunni schools of law are Hanafi, Maliki, Shafi'i and Hanbali, after the classical jurists: Abu Hanifa Nu'man bin Thabit (d. 765), Malik bin Anas (d. 792), Muhammad bin Idris (d. 204/820), and Ahmad bin Hanbal (d. 855).
98   Umar Shahab (2001:x).
99   Al-Kaff (http://aljawad.tripod.com/artikel/ijtihad.htm).
100 Umar Shahab (2001:xi).
101 Umar Shahab (2001:xii).

jurisprudence in a book. Then, we read his *fatwa* because in Ja'fari jurisprudence we are obliged to imitate [*taqlid*]. So the layman must seek his man of learning, whom he must follow. Then, he carries out religious practices according to the *fatwa* of the imitated man of Islamic learning. [We may say] Ja'fari jurisprudence is outdated [...] because it maintains *taqlid*, or that Ja'fari jurisprudence is progressive; that is, it relies only on someone who has authority, or has specialisation in his field.[102]

Besides this reasoning, there is scriptural evidence in support of the obligation of *taqlid* for the Shi'i laity. The texts are the same as those used to prescribe the obligation of obedience to the Imams. Another common text runs: "If ye realise this not, ask of those who possess the message."[103] An Indonesian Shi'i writer affirms: "It is very clear that this verse designates the obligation of *taqlid* for the laity who have not achieved the position of *mujtahid*."[104] Although the terms *ulu al-amri* and *ahl al-dhikr*, 'those who possess the message' in the Qur'anic texts principally refer to the Imams, the Shi'i view is that during the great occultation, they designate the *'ulama* possessed of a thorough knowledge of the Qur'an and Hadith, namely the *wali faqih* or *marja' al-taqlid*.[105] It is believed that, during his occultation, Imam Mahdi instructed the faithful to follow *'ulama* or jurists who are devoted to the field of religion and obedient to all of God's commands.[106] Furthermore, there is a well-known Hadith which states "The *'ulama* are the heirs of the prophets", which also justifies the compulsion of *taqlid* upon the laity.

All Shi'is in Indonesia are *muqallids*. Most take the Grand Ayatollah 'Ali Khamene'i, the present *wali faqih* of Iran, to be their *marja'*.[107] A few follow the Grand Ayatollah 'Ali Sistani of Iraq,[108] and yet others emulate the Grand Ayatollah

---

102   Rakhmat (1998:383).
103   QS (16:43).
104   Abu Qurba (2003:15).
105   Abu Qurba (2003:16-17).
106   Shodiq (1998:29).
107   'Ali Khamene'i was born in Mashhad, Iran, on 15 July 1939. He studied at the *hawza 'ilmiyya* of Qum. He was a key figure in the Islamic revolution and close confidant of Khomeini. In 1979 he was appointed to the powerful position of Tehran's Friday Prayer Leader. From 1981 to 1989, he was elected President of Iran and, since Khomeini's death, became the Supreme Leader, elected by the Assembly of Experts on June 1989 (http://en.wikipedia.org/wiki/'Ali_Khamenei). In 1994, he was nominated a *marja' al-taqlid*. For more information visit the website of the office of Supreme Leader (http://www.leader.ir) and his official website (http://www.khamenei.ir).
108   'Ali Husaini Sistani was born on 4 August 1930 in Mashhad, Iran, to a family of religious scholars. After studying in his hometown he moved to Qum, where he studied *fiqh, usul al-fiqh* and other sciences under the guidance of renowned *ayatollahs*, including Hujjat Kuhkamari and Allamah Husayn Tabataba'i. He then moved to Najaf, Iraq, to study under, among others, the Grand Ayatollah Khoei (d. 1992) and Muhsin al-Hakim (d. 1970). He was influenced by the prominent quietist scholar Grand Ayatollah Khoei, who made him a *marja al-taqlid* in the 1960s. Before his death in 1992, Khoei named Sistani as his successor. Since the American invasion of Iraq in 2003, he has played an increasingly political role in Iraq (http://en.wikipedia.org/wiki/'Ali_Sistani). Unlike Khomeini, and his successor Khamene'i, Sistani adheres to a quietist tradition

Bahjat Fumani of Iran.[109] A very small number follow the liberal Muhammad Husayn Fadlallah of Lebanon.[110] Efforts have been made, particularly among the Qum alumni *ustadhs*, to encourage their followers to imitate 'Ali Khamene'i. This is seen as advantageous because it combines *marja'iyya* and *wilaya* (sovereignty) in one person. The Shi'i writer, Maulana praises God because in Khamene'i, Muslims today are blessed with both a *wali faqih* and *marja'* and whose position is *a'lam* (most knowledgeable). Moreover, Maulana states that it is obligatory and customary to follow Khamene'i because of his competence and superiority of knowledge.[111] Ahmad Baragbah points out

> In Indonesia in particular, we actually do not have any sufficient reason to refer to other *maraji'* than 'Ali Khamene'i. This is exactly our strength and our pride because this exemplary figure is complete.... Thus to me it is very odd if there are still persons who question whether there are others more *a'lam* than 'Ali Khamene'i. What are the reasons? The *'ulama* who have obvious commitment in the struggle for Islam and in the interest and benefit of society assert that to choose 'Ali Khamene'i as *marja'* is the most beneficial.... In the meantime, we need legal opinions on actual matters. And this means that we need a *marja'* who masters new developments in society. Others say that we need law regarding international matters. Therefore, it seems that nobody is more reasonable or proper than the Grand Ayatollah 'Ali Khamene'i.[112]

Regardless of the different choices of *marja'*, there is no difference of opinion among *mujtahid* in terms of the basic obligatory ritual practices; generally speaking, the outcomes of *ijtihad* differ only in terms of the details. The central items of Shi'i *'ibadat* (prayers, fasting, *zakat* and the Hajj) do not differ from the *'ibadat* as understood and observed by the Sunni majority in Indonesia. The following description however deals with some aspects of *'ibadat* and *mu'amalat* among the Shi'is of Indonesia which do differ from those of Sunni jurisprudence.

---

of Shi'ism, envisaging the participation of *'ulama'* in public and legal spheres while discouraging their involvement in the state (Rahimi 2004). See his website - www.sistani.org - in a variety of languages, including Indonesian.

109   Muhammad Taqi Bahjat was born in 1915 in Fuman, Iran and began his religious education in his hometown. In 1929 he went to Qum and moved to Karbala and then to Najaf, Iraq to study under renowned *'ulama*. In 1944 he returned to Qum to study under Ayatollah Burujerdi and Hujjat Kuhkamari. See (http://www.alshia.com/html/eng/ser/ulama/ola-behj_h.htm).

110   Muhammad Husayn Fadlallah was born in Iraq in 1935 and studied in Najaf under renowned *'ulama*, including Grand Ayatollah Khoei and Muhsin al-Hakim. He moved to Lebanon in 1966 and is alleged to be the spiritual leader of Hisbullah (*Hisb Allah*, Party of God). Several studies on his ideals and role in Lebanon have been conducted. For his theological thought, see Abu-Rabi (1996:220-247). See http://www.bayynat.org.lb (in Arabic, English, and French) which contains his *fatwas* and thought.

111   Maulana (1998:32).

112   Ahmad Baragbah, interview, *An-Nashr* (14/1998:53-54).

In terms of obligatory prayers, Shi'is in Indonesia share the belief that there are five kinds of Prayers, consisting of 17 *raka'at* (units of prayer) which must be observed every day: Dawn (*Subh*), Noon (*Zuhr*), Afternoon ('*Asr*), Evening (*Maghrib*) and Night ('*Isha*). As for the Sunnis, for Shi'is the obligatory prayers are a very important aspect of '*ibadat* not to be abandoned under any circumstances. For the Shi'is, however, it is permissible to run together the Noon, Afternoon, Evening and Night Prayers, which means that Shi'is may complete obligatory prayers on three separate occasions in a day. The goal of consolidating the prayers is to lessen the burden for Muslims,[113] so that prayers are never missed and are seen as more appropriate within the complex life of modern society. In addition, the observance of daily prayers by Shi'is in Indonesia tends to be individual rather than congregational. This also corresponds to the fact that they do not place great importance on the performance of the congregational Friday Prayers at the mosque. Although these, like the daily prayers, are obligatory, their significance is diminished with the occultation of the twelfth Imam, who is considered to be the true leader of the prayers. Shi'i interpretation allows for a choice between observing either the Friday Prayers or the ordinary Noon Prayers. There are numerous recommended Prayers as well, so that the number in a day can total 51 *raka'at*. Shi'is consider this to be the true teaching of the Prophet on the matter.[114]

The main recitations constituting prayer are similar between Sunnism and Shi'ism, but there are differences in terms of recommended utterances and movements. The most marked difference is the position of straight arms during the standing phase. While Shafi'i jurisprudence recommends standing with folded arms, this is forbidden in the Indonesian Shi'i *madhhab* and is said to invalidate the prayer, except during the practice of *taqiyya*. Another distinctive Shi'i feature is that during the prostration, Shi'is place their forehead on the earth or on paper, but never on carpet, believing that prostration must be upon things which grow out of the earth, such as wood, leaves or stone. Their preference is for a block of baked mud, taken from the earth of Karbala, known as *turba*. In their view "the earth of Imam Husayn (Upon Him be Peace) is sublime earth. Therefore, prostration on the earth of Karbala is more excellent than prostration on common earth."[115]

Another minor difference is found in relation to ablutions, or *wudu'* as a requirement for the validity of prayer. Shi'is wipe the upper part of their feet instead of washing the whole. Furthermore, in the call to prayer, the *adhan*, they include the phrase 'come to the best of actions', as part of the original *adhan*, omitted on the command of the third caliph, 'Umar. Another phrase

---

113   Alatas (2002:114).
114   Syarif Hidayatullah Husein (2001:90).
115   Ba'abud (2002:45).

added to the Shi'i *adhan* is 'I bear witness that 'Ali is the Wali Allah', the Friend of God'. This recommended phrase is follows the declaration 'I bear witness that Muhammad is the Messenger of God.'

A specific kind of *'ibadat* observed by Indonesian Shi'is is *khums*, the tax of one-fifth of wealth, which is based on a Qur'anic text.[116] It is considered to be an individual obligation, because in any material benefits gained by a person there are the rights of others, as prescribed by God.[117] Shi'is pay *khums* as an annual tax at the end of every year, and like *zakat*, or alms to the poor, *khums* is paid to their own *marja' al-taqlid* through his deputies in Indonesia; for example, Jalaluddin Rakhmat and Ahmad Baragbah are representatives of 'Ali Khamene'i. Among the duties of these representatives is the collection and distribution of the *zakat* and *khums*. The *khums* is distributed for Islamic *da'wa* and to orphans, the needy and to Sayyid travellers, who, according to *Ja'fari* law, are not allowed to receive *zakat*. It is pertinent to note that *khums* serves a very important function in the development of the Shi'i community in Indonesia.

In terms of social transactions, the custom of *mut'a*, or temporary marriage is a specific practice in Shi'ism and something which has become a matter of controversy in Sunni-Shi'i relations. Sunnis forbid this kind of marriage, deeming it to be prostitution. For Shi'is in Indonesia, *mut'a* is considered permissible, as it was practiced during the Prophet Muhammad's lifetime. They argue that it was Caliph 'Umar who prohibited this form of marriage. Yet scriptural text is cited in support of the legitimacy of *mut'a*. The Qur'anic verse that most Shi'is in Indonesia memorise in this regard is: "Seeing that ye derive benefit from them (women), give them their dowers (at least) as prescribed."[118] In addition, rational proofs are also provided. For Shi'is, the goal of marriage is to permit sexual relations in accordance with God's commands

> Actually, marriage is no more than the fulfilment of the biological need of a person that, if seen from the side of the living creature (organism), which emerges at a certain age. Islam, as a religion created by the Creator of mankind understands very much that condition and for it Islam establishes quite clear and simple regulations, one of which is *mut'a*. This is established merely in order for man to get married and desist from fornication. The biological need has existed since the creation of mankind, it is a characteristic along with another characteristic, namely the reluctance to carry a heavy burden.[119]

---

116 Qur'an Surah 8:41.
117 Turkan (http://aljawad.tripod.com/arsipbuletin/khumus.htm).
118 Qur'an Surah 4:24.
119 Hidayatullah Husein Al-Habsyi (2002:173).

The legitimacy of *mut'a* is also demonstrated by the significance of its teaching. It is seen as the preservation of the vital interests of humankind because while fornication is strongly forbidden in Islam, in certain circumstances a permanent marriage might not satisfy the sexual desires of men, or a permanent marriage cannot be undertaken by certain segments of society. *Mut'a* then becomes the alternative. Jalaluddin Rakhmat provides five significances of *mut'a*: to protect religion (*hifz al-din*), mind (*hifz al-'aql*), wealth (*hifz al-mal*), soul (*hifz al-nafs*) and progeny (*hifz al-nasl*). Rakhmat argues that *mut'a* serves as an alternative way for numerous people, such as students, allowing them to obey all the commandments of Islam and remain free from fornication. According to Rakhmat, children are protected, because a woman married by way of *mut'a* is a legitimate wife. *Mut'a* also protects mankind from mental and physical illness. On the significance of *mut'a* in guarding wealth, Rakhmat points out that *mut'a* ensures that widows will receive material assistance from rich men, who in return fulfil their sexual desires.[120] This significance is reasonable because marriage for economic motivation is permitted in Shi'i Islam.[121]

Although the procedure of *mut'a* is simple, Shi'is in Indonesia consider that a marriage contract performed between a man and woman, with a certain amount of dowry, is valid even if there is no witness and *wali*, or man responsible for the woman's side in marriage,[122] two things which are required in Sunnism. Due to its permissibility and its simplicity, a number of Shi'is in Indonesia practice this type of marriage alongside their permanent marriage. But the practice is secret because *Mut'a* is not legally recognised by the government or the religious authorities. A few Shi'is criticise those who frequently engage in it for following their sensual impulse while ignoring morality. They argue that while *mut'a* is legitimate, there is no obligation to perform it. It is seen as on a par with divorce, which is also legitimate, but is certainly not obligatory. The legitimising of *mut'a* is claimed as an attempt to preserve the originality of the teachings of the Prophet Muhammad.[123]

Customs around food are another distinctive aspect of *Ja'fari* jurisprudence observed by Shi'is in Indonesia. Even though, in general, Shi'is and Sunnis share similar views on the lawfulness of plentiful food, there are certain foods that are forbidden to Shi'ism. The first instance is that Shi'is do not eat fish without scales, these being unlawful in *Ja'fari* jurisprudence. Secondly, Shi'is in Indonesia do not eat food that has been touched by non-believers. In *Ja'fari* jurisprudence non-believers, *khawarij* (seceders from 'Ali's following) and *nawasib* (those who hate the Prophet's *ahl al-bayt*) are considered to be impure,

---

120   Anam (1998:59-64).
121   Hidayatullah Husein Al-Habsyi (2002:176).
122   Rakhmat (1997:242).
123   Khalid Al-Walid, interview, (3/7/2002). On *mut'a* and its consequences, see Marcus and Feillard (2000).

or *najis* and everything impure is unlawful. Jalaluddin Rakhmat explained that he, like many Shi'is, has experienced difficulties living in non-Muslim countries in respect of food

> At the time I was in Germany. I did not want to eat the cooking touched by the hands of unbelievers. At first, I chose fruits. When I saw the fruits taken by hands without gloves, I looked for bread. I thought that bread was made in factories. And at the edge of the station in Frankfurt I saw an unbeliever making bread. His hands – without gloves – moulded loaves to be baked. That day, I experienced hunger.[124]

The aspects of *Ja'fari* jurisprudence described above indicate features of Shi'i religious life which are different from those of the Sunnis. By and large, Shi'is in Indonesia carry out such practices at home or in their own institutions, but most hide them from the public eye. With the teaching of *taqiyya*, this is permissible.

E. Aspects of Shi'i Piety

In addition to the features of jurisprudence just mentioned, there are aspects of devotion that are distinguishing features of Shi'i religious life. Piety is considered to be more than just the formal and legal dimensions of religion. Aspects of Shi'i devotion are very similar to aspects of devotion in Sunni Sufism. They include daily, weekly and yearly preferred rituals. The daily ritual consists of numerous optional prayers, including those conducted before and after the five sets of obligatory prayers. Other recommended devotions include reciting certain chapters of the Qur'an, uttering *dhikr* (remembrance of God), and *do'a* (supplication). This activity is commonly called *ta'qib* of prayer and is a way of achieving the perfection of obligatory prayer.

Do'a, or supplication is strongly recommended and is a feature of religious life in the Shi'i community of Indonesia. The number of supplicationsn in Shi'i prayer are far greater than those in Sunni prayer, partly because there are specific *do'a* to each of the 'fourteen infallibles' (discussed below). By reciting prayers, the great beauty of Arabic is also emphasised. Also included among numerous Shi'i prayers are *salawat,* invocations to the Prophet Muhammad and his *ahl al-bayt*. In all Shi'i gatherings, the *salawat* reverberate. The most common formula is: "O God, bless Muhammad and the family of Muhammad". Besides being commended in certain scriptural texts, the recitation of *salawat* is considered to be an expression of love for the Prophet and it is believed that the intensive recitation of *salawat* draws the believer closer to him in the hereafter. It is also

---

124   Rakhmat (2002:ix-x).

believed that the Prophet listens to *salawat* being recited and that he is even present among those who recite *salawat,* because his soul is considered ever to be alive.[125]

Another kind of Shi'i prayer is known as the *kumayl* prayer, which is commonly performed on Thursday nights after the Night Prayer. Nearly all Shi'i institutions in Indonesia organise this weekly activity. It is usually performed in congregation, led by an *ustadh* who also delivers a sermon. The gathering is called *majlis kumayl* (the gathering of *kumayl*) and lasts for several hours. It is considered to be one of the best supplications of the first Imam 'Ali bin Abi Talib. The prayer is called *kumayl* because it is believed to have been transmitted by Imam 'Ali's faithful companion, Kumayl bin Ziyad.[126] The importance of the *kumayl* in Shi'ism is indicated in the belief that Imam 'Ali told Kumayl bin Ziyad to recite it at least once in his lifetime. It contains praise to God and supplication for forgiveness, lamentations, remorse and admission of sins. Its message is so deep and intense that all those who recite it cannot remain dry-eyed; during the recitation, participants shed tears and cry out collectively.

In addition, there is a prayer called *tawassul*, which is also well known among traditionalist Sunnis in Indonesia. "The *tawassul* prayer is the prayer of supplication to the Almighty God by uttering the names of purified persons on the side of God, or of persons having high positions on the side of God as intermediaries."[127] *Tawassul* is prayer through these intermediaries. A textual proof that is usually cited in support of performing *tawassul* is: "O ye who believe! Do your duty to Allah, seek the means of approach unto him, and strive with might and main in His cause, that ye may prosper."[128] In addition to this verse, many Hadiths are cited in support of the validity of the teaching and practice of *tawassul,* as upheld by the Prophet's companions. Rakhmat writes

> We perform *tawassul* to him [the Prophet] and to all pious servants of God by imitating the example of the Prophet (May God Bless Him and Grant Him Salvation).[129]

Unlike the Sunni version of *tawassul*, the *tawassul* prayer in Shi'ism is directed to the names of the fourteen infallibles: the Prophet, his daughter, Fatima and the twelve Imams. For Shi'is in Indonesia, making these fourteen infallibles intermediaries in supplication to God is reasonable because no other humans are superior to them in terms of piety, knowledge and in the struggle for the establishment of Islam.[130] The *tawassul* prayer can be performed either on

---

125   Rakhmat (1994:289-304).
126   Al-Muhdhar (1998:1).
127   Al-Muhdhar (1998:42).
128   Qur'an Surah 5:35.
129   Rakhmat (2001:188).
130   Al-Muhdhar (1998:42-43).

Tuesdays, or as a part of other kinds of Shi'i prayers. In the *kumayl* gathering, the *tawassul* prayer is usually uttered before the reciting of the *kumayl* prayer. In the *tawassul* prayer, each name of the infallibles is uttered, from the Prophet Muhammad down to the twelfth Imam. Usually, by the time the name of Husayn is uttered, crying and sobbing will have begun in the gathering.

A practice closely related to *tawassul* is *tabarruk*, which literally means 'the taking of blessings', blessings from the Prophet Muhammad, the Imams and all other pious servants of God. This practice is considered to have a strong basis in Qur'anic texts and Hadiths. One of the Qur'anic verses tells how the Prophet Joseph asked his brothers to cast his shirt over his father's face. His father, the Prophet Jacob who had blind eyes; when the shirt was removed Jacob could see again.[131] In addition, many kinds of *tabarruk* are considered to have been practiced by the Prophet's companions, including *tabarruk* by the taking of water, hairs from the Prophet's head, his dress or the sand of his tomb. In *tabarruk* using water, for instance, the Prophet's companions are said to have competed for the remains of the water used by the Prophet in his ablutions.[132] *Tabarruk* is believed to give benefits both in this world and in the hereafter. Jalaluddin Rakhmat writes: "The blessings of the Prophet (May God Bless Him and Grant Him Salvation) guide us to gain prosperity in the world and in the hereafter. They can cure physical and psychic illnesses and save us in the hereafter."[133] *Tabarruk* is also considered to be a way of expressing loving devotion to the Prophet Muhammad, the Imams and other pious ones. With *tabarruk* in mind, Shi'is of Indonesia have attempted to make physical contact with Shi'i *'ulama* from Iran. When Ayatollah 'Ali Taskhiri finished his religious lecture at the ICC of Al-Huda in Jakarta on 20 February 2004, for example, nearly all those gathered tried to shake hands with him. In addition, I was informed that when Jalaluddin Rakhmat visits the Shi'i group in Makassar, South Sulawesi, his sandals and toothbrush are usually taken by members of the group as a way of acquiring his blessing.

In addition to these practices, there are a number of commemorations conducted by Shi'is in Indonesia. These include commemorations related to important events such as the births and deaths of the fourteen infallibles. In this regard, Shi'is share with Sunnis the annual celebration of *mawlid* (the Prophet's birthday).[134] It is a widely observed celebration, as it is also a national holiday. For the Shi'is, *mawlid* is another way to express their love and devotion to the

---

131   Qur'an Surah 12:93, 96.
132   Rakhmat (2001:209-224).
133   Rakhmat (2001:225-226).
134   For the origins and early development of the celebration of this Muslim festival, see Kaptein (1994). One of his conclusions is that the celebration of *mawlid* was originally a Shi'i tradition, first held in the 11th century by a Fatimid caliph in Egypt (Kaptein 1994:28-29).

Prophet. Similarly, the celebration or commemoration of the births and deaths of the other infallibles are also considered to be a way of expressing devotion to them.

The most significant however is the commemoration of the martyrdom of Imam Husayn. Husayn bin 'Ali, the third Imam, was murdered in battle at Karbala, on 10 Muharram 61 (10 October 680). Its commemoration, known as 'Ashura, is held on every tenth day of Muharram in the Muslim year. It is held in every city and town in Indonesia with a large population of Shi'is, and since political *Reformasi*, the commemoration takes place publicly.

'Ashura is also celebrated among certain Sunni groups throughout Indonesia. However, its pattern differs from the 'Ashura of the Shi'is. The most noticeable difference is the cooking and offering of *bubur sura* ('sura porridge)[135] after fasting, which is recommended in Sunni Islam. Shi'is do not cook *bubur sura*, nor do they fast. For Sunnis, the Prophet Muhammad teaches that 'Ashura fasting is thanksgiving for the victory of several prophets of God.[136] For Shi'is, fasting on 'Ashura is considered to be *bid'a* (unlawful innovation) and forbidden. They argue that this fast is a product of false teachings by the Umayyad regime. When the Shi'is commemorated the martyrdom of Husayn as a day of mourning and a symbol of their struggle against tyrants, the Umayyads are said to have turned it into a day of thanksgiving, and are even said to have produced Hadiths to justify this change. In the eyes of Indonesian Shi'is, the Sunni version of 'Ashura fasting is the product of the Umayyad regime.[137]

'Ashura rituals in Indonesia consist of four main activities: religious lectures, *ma'tam* (chest-beating), the recitation of the *maqtal* (story of the massacre of Husayn and his following) and the recitation of the *ziyara* or visitation prayer. As it is a commemoration of mourning, participants usually wear black clothes. Another attribute is the belief in the firm principle and rightful position of Husayn in his battle for Islam. 'Ashura banners are carried, reading "Indeed Husayn is the light of guidance and the ark of victory." Lectures are held, dealing with the struggle of Imam Husayn and its relevance to contemporary conditions of Muslim society. One of the purposes is to encourage the spirit of martyrdom, as modelled by Imam Husayn. *Ma'tam* is chest-beating in accompaniment

---

135 *Bubur sura* is rice-flour porridge boiled with coconut milk and containing various food-stuffs including vegetables, beans, peanuts, potatoes, corns, fish, meat, and eggs. In Cirebon, West Java, it is distributed to neighbours and close kin (Muhaimin 1999:109).
136 The victorious events upheld in Sunnism include God's granting of His grace to Adam and Eve on requesting repentance after being thrown out of paradise; God's endowing of Enoch (Idris) with noble rank; Moses' receiving revelation in the Sinai desert; Moses' escape from Pharaoh's chase and Pharaoh's drowning in the Red Sea; Noah's arrival on land after the long and severe flood; Abraham's escape from being burned by King Namrud of Babylon; Joseph being freed from prison and clearing his name of the rape of Zulaikha, the Egyptian king's wife; Jacob's recovery from blindness; Jonas' escape from the belly of a sea monster and David and Solomon gaining the positions of kings and apostles of God (Muhaimin 1999:108).
137 Rakhmat (1997:324).

to a mournful hymn, performed by participants under the direction of an *ustadh*. It is an expression of the sense of sorrow, injustice and readiness to sacrifice. (However, *ma'tam* is notably absent in the 'Ashura gatherings held by Jalaluddin Rakhmat and his colleagues.) The recitation of the *maqtal* by an *ustadh* represents the climax of grief, the shedding of tears and weeping. It is a presentation of classical narratives about the brutal massacre, by thousands of Umayyad soldiers, of Imam Husayn, his family and loyal supporters, numbering about 70 people, including women and children. The main themes of the *maqtal* are the brutality and inhumanity of the tyrants, in particular, Caliph Yazid and his soldiers, versus the courage and adherence to the rightful principles and martyrdom by Imam Husayn and his following. The recitation of *maqtal* in sad tones and with full emotional strength produces a very real collective shedding of tears and lamentation. The last part of the 'Ashura commemoration is the recitation of the *ziyara* prayer, led by an *ustadh* and followed by the participants.

Another commemoration of the martyrdom of Imam Husayn widely practiced by Shi'is in Indonesia is called *arba'in*, namely the 40th day after his martyrdom. It is held on the 20 Safar, the second month of Muslim calendar, 40 days after the conclusion of the 'Ashura rituals. *Arba'in* is only commemorated by Shi'is. Its pattern is very similar to that of 'Ashura and includes religious lectures, *ma'tam*, the recitation of *maqtal* and the recitation of *ziyara*. Both rituals clearly have similar aims.

'Ashura and Arba'in are the two most important Shi'i commemorations held in Indonesia. Shi'is consider the martyrdom of Imam Husayn to be the most significant tragedy, not only of the Muslim *umma* but also of mankind at large. The tragedy also teaches firm adherence to principles and strong loyalty to leaders

> As a tragedy, 'Ashura is a witness to us about the climax of human tyranny and cruelty of a regime, which have no comparison in history. A grandson whom the Prophet frequently called his son, his beloved and young master of paradise was murdered cruelly under the heat of the barren plain of Karbala. The martyrdom of Imam Husayn and the loyalty of his followers are symbols of the existence of beloved sons in those days, who strongly opposed a tyrannical regime.[138]

The events of Karbala are seen to contain a noble dimension, namely the struggle to gain a true awareness of the meaning of life. "Struggle for liberating mankind from oppression is the true life, even though the body is buried."[139] In addition, Imam Husayn's sacrifice is considered to be greater than that of the Prophet Abraham's, in so far as Abraham was commanded to slaughter

---

138 *Suara Ummah* (1/3/2004:72).
139 *Suara Ummah* (1/3/2004/72).

his son, whilst Husayn gave his own life in his struggle.[140] To follow Husayn's example of sacrifice for truth and justice is one of the lessons acquired from the commemoration of his martyrdom.[141] The appeal for sacrifice is usually emphasised and is illustrated by the famous Shi'i slogan: "Every day is *'Ashura* and every place is Karbala". It is used to encourage the followers of Shi'ism to contextualise the struggle of Husayn in Indonesia. Jalaluddin Rakhmat has said "Arise, O followers of Husayn, contribute your body and soul to transform the whole archipelago into Karbala and every day into *'Ashura*."[142] Similarly, at the end of another *maqtal*, he stated

> We leave Karbala and return to our present place. They have shed their blood to establish truth and justice. The grandsons of the Messenger of God (Upon Whom be Peace) and the infallibles have sacrificed their life to establish a 'Muhammadist' Islam, *Islam Muhammadi*. Let us resolve to continue their struggle to establish truth and justice. Let us resolve to vow an oath of allegiance to the Messenger of God (Upon Whom be Peace) and his pure House, to establish Islamic teachings based upon the Book of God and the Sunna of His Messenger and transmitted by his infallible House. Let us summon pure tenacity to continue this pure struggle until the last day.[143]

Thus, the martyrdom of Husayn is held to be the heaviest sacrifice in human history and its commemoration becomes a means of maintaining the spirit of *jihad*, or struggle in the path of God, which is an act of worship within the Shi'i tradition. In addition, there is another interesting element to *'Ashura*, which is the establishment and preservation of emotion. The Shi'is' love of Husayn and empathy with his sorrow inevitably leads them to shed tears. Weeping itself has become an important feature of devotion, characterising nearly all Shi'is rituals in Indonesia. Weeping rituals are even publicised. For example, national television has shown a programme of prayer, in the month of Ramadan, in which the participants and their leader - a prominent Shi'i *ustadh* - cry collectively. For these adherents, weeping is something strongly encouraged by the Prophet. "The Messenger of God (May God Bless Him and His Family and Grant Him Salvation) instructed us to make crying customary and to fill our religiosity with lamentations."[144]

The above rituals and commemorations are the main claims on the piety of Shi'is in Indonesia. But in fact, their religious life is filled with a great many smaller

---

140   Mahayana (2003:8).
141   Al-Kaff (http://aljawad.tripod.com/).
142   Rakhmat (2003:3).
143   Rakhmat (1999:322).
144   Rakhmat (1999:363).

rituals and commemorations which are a means of expressing of their loving devotion to the fourteen infallibles. These, along with the practice of *taqiyya*, are unique and identifying features of the Indonesian Shi'i *madhhab*.

F. *Taqiyya*

Taqiyya (Latin, *reservatio mentalis*) literally means "to shield or to guard oneself,"[145] and is one of the most misunderstood teachings of Shi'ism. In general, *taqiyya* is understood to be a "strategy in the dissimulation of faith before enemies to prevent the occurrence of danger."[146] The practice of *taqiyya* is important in Shi'ism and has become a distinguishing feature of the Shi'is in Indonesia. Most Shi'is practice it, while rejecting the widespread perception that it is unique to Shi'ism. They argue that the practice of keeping a precautionary attitude is common among all adherents of religion or *madhhabs* in Islam, particularly when they are under oppression by an authoritarian faction or regime.[147] However, other Muslim denominations refuse to use the term *taqiyya*.

Textual evidence is cited in support of the practice of *taqiyya*. The most common is the Qur'anic text which reads "Let not the believers take for friends or helpers unbelievers rather than believers; if any do that, in nothing will there be help from Allah; except by way of precaution, that ye may guard yourselves from them. But Allah cautions you (to remember) Himself; for the final goal is Allah."[148] It is also argued that the practice of *taqiyya* occurred during the life of the Prophet Muhammad himself. The most famous story is the case of 'Ammar bin Yasir, one of the close companions of the Prophet and 'Ali bin Abi Talib. The story tells how the infidels of Mecca imprisoned some Muslims and tortured them, forcing them to leave their new religion and return to the former idolatry. Among these Muslims were 'Ammar bin Yasir and his father and mother. His parents were killed because of their refusal to obey the infidels. In order to escape from torture, 'Ammar outwardly declared that that he had left Islam and accepted idol worship. After he was freed, he secretly left for Medina. He recounted the story to the Prophet in a state of distress and regret. The Prophet then comforted 'Ammar by reciting a verse of the Qur'an.[149] This story is considered to be the historical background to the revelation of the verse which reads "Anyone who, after accepting faith in Allah, utters unbelief

---

145   Enayat (2005:175). Enayat points out that the standard terms used, 'dissimulation' or 'concealment' are pejorative and not satisfactory translations of *taqiyya* into English (Enayat 2005:175).
146   Alatas (2002:142).
147   Alatas (2002:144).
148   Qur'an Surah 3:28.
149   Alatas (2002:143), Suherman (1998:354).

except under compulsion, his heart remaining firm in faith — but such as open their breast to unbelievers — on them is wrath from Allah, and theirs will be a dreadful penalty."[150]

Shi'is in Indonesia also recognise that the practice of *taqiyya* has its foundations in the history of Muslim society, in which "the Shi'is have been a minority amidst the global Islamic community and have lived mostly under regimes hostile to their creed."[151] The tyranny and cruelty of the great Umayyad and Abbasid dynasties forced the Imams and their followers to dissimulate their real faith in order to save their existence and to ensure the continuity of Shi'ism. *Taqiyya* is the only strategy to be implemented by the Shi'is to avoid the tyranny and cruelty of such regimes.[152]

However, *taqiyya* is implemented by Shi'is in Indonesia not only because of fear, but also for the purpose of establishing Islamic fraternity, or *ukhuwwa Islamiyya*. Regarding this type of *taqiyya*, Jalaluddin Rakhmat cited the *fatwa* of Khomeini "What is meant by *taqiyya mudarat* is the *taqiyya* practised in order to unite Muslims by attracting the love of opponents and gaining their affection…"[153] The most popular of Khomeini's *fatwa* in this respect is his recommendation that Shi'is perform prayers together with Sunnis. When questioned about the validity of prayers with the Sunni congregation, Khomeini responded that it was not only valid but even recommended. He said that the reward for praying with the Sunni congregation, and in accordance with Sunni jurisprudence, is the same as the reward for worship with the Shi'is and in accordance with Shi'i jurisprudence. Thus, Khomeini recommended the abandonment of Shi'i jurisprudence for the sake of Islamic fraternity and this has become a legitimate foundation for the practice of this kind of *taqiyya*.[154]

Taqiyya may be understood to be a strategy for maintaining the secrecy of Shi'i identity for various reasons. However, among the Sunni majority of Indonesia, the term has negative connotations and is equated with lying, hypocrisy or cowardice. For this reason Jalaluddin Rakhmat proposed "we can substitute it with the term 'flexible approach and friendship'.…"[155] The best term is probably diplomacy. As strategy or diplomacy, *taqiyya* is implemented in acts of worship, in *da'wa*, in conversation and dialogue and in writing.

The choice of vocabulary or terms commonly acceptable to the Sunni majority characterises the implementation of *taqiyya* in Indonesia. In certain circumstances, Shi'is will avoid giving the impression of emphasising the contrast between

---

150 Qur'an Surah (16:106).
151 Enayat (2005:175).
152 Alatas (2002:144).
153 Rakhmat (1998a:lix).
154 Rakhmat (1998a:lix).
155 Rakhmat (1998a:lix).

Sunnism and Shi'ism. "I think our concern is not to become a Shi'i or Sunni. Instead, our concern is Islam," said Rakhmat on one occasion.[156] The word 'Islam' is a term accepted by both denominations. On another occasion, in his reply to a question about whether he is a Sunni or Shi'i, Jalaluddin Rakhmat said that "people call me Susyi," namely Sunni-Shi'i.[157] Similarly, when he was asked whether he was a Shi'i, Haidar Bagir (mentioned in Chapter Two) answered: "I am the same as others, one who longs for the unity of the Muslims."[158] In short, simple questions about Shi'i identity are usually responded to with diplomatic answers.

Shi'is in Indonesia also try to suppress or modify information, not only about their own identity and beliefs but also about fellow Shi'is, institutions and their community. For example, with regard to Jalaluddin Rakhmat, Haidar Bagir stated "I do not dare say that he is a Shi'i because he is a person who reads, learns and speaks about both Shi'ism and Sunnism. Jokingly, Pak Jalal once called himself Susyi, meaning Sunni-Shi'i. He is a Muslim open to various ideas, from both Sunnism and Shi'ism."[159] Similarly, when questioned about the places where Shi'is in Indonesia gather, Haidar Bagir replied: "As far as I know there are small institutions. I do not know their precise names."[160]

With regard to the practice of *taqiyya*, it is interesting to note that a translation of a personal letter to someone in Iran (name not disclosed) was published in November 1993 in *Aula*, a magazine of the East Java branch of NU, under the title "a Letter to Someone in Iran". The author of the letter, allegedly Husein Al-Habsyi, used the term "my Master" to address the person in Iran. The central purpose of the letter was to respond to the master's suggestion that the author should abandon the practice of *taqiyya* and declare openly that he was a Shi'i. The letter provides several reasons for the author's maintaining the practice of *taqiyya*

> First, I thank you for your correct suggestion to me, which has become my consideration for a long time, that is, since the victory of Imam [Khomeini] over the Shah. Although I postponed doing so [to stop practicing *taqiyya*] I do not doubt at all the validity of *madhhab* of *ahl al-bayt* and this is not because I fear people, or if I am to leave *taqiyya* it is not to be praised by people. Not at all. However, I now consider my environment. The general Sunni fanaticism is still strong.

---

156 Rakhmat (1998:381).
157 *Tiras* (24/11/1997:67).
158 Bagir, interview, *Forum Keadilan* (4/5/2003:57).
159 Bagir, interview, *Forum Keadilan* (4/5/2003:57).
160 Bagir, interview, *Forum Keadilan* (4/5/2003:56).

To come near to them, I want to appear like a Sunni. Because if I were to show my own belief and respond to attacks from their *nawasib* [anti-Shi'i] *'ulama* they would say: a Shi'i defends Shi'ism. I have succeeded in approaching a significant number of their *'ulama* so that they might understand the virtues of the *madhhab* of *ahl al-bayt* over others. I think it is a step forward in our struggle.[161]

Husein Al-Habsyi was known to have practised *taqiyya* in his *da'wa*, dialogue and writing. He always declared that he was a follower of Sunnism. In a dialogue with a group of students from UGM (Gajah Mada University) and UII (Indonesian Islamic University) in Yogyakarta, which was conducted in Solo, Husein Al-Habsyi consistently used the term 'we, *ahl al-Sunna*'. When asked to explain matters related to Shi'ism during the first meeting, he answered "But what a pity, because I am myself not a Shi'i, so it would be more accurate if you ask these questions to those who declare that they are Shi'i".[162]

However, in contrast to the widespread practice of *taqiyya*, some Shi'is in Indonesia, particularly the Qum graduate *ustadhs*, are more likely to express their religiosity overtly. *Taqiyya* is also infrequent among the students and teachers of *Pesantren Al-Hadi* in Pekalongan, a Shi'i *pesantren* headed by Ahmad Baragbah. Similarly, Shi'is affiliated to the *Al-Jawad* Foundation in Bandung, IPABI in Bogor and the Fatimah Foundation in Jakarta do not resort to *taqiyya*. I observed that when leading the Friday Prayer in the *Nurul Falah* Mosque, the mosque leader, Husein Al-Kaff, performed it in accordance with Ja'fari jurisprudence, whilst nearly all members of the *jama'a* were Sunni and followed Sunni jurisprudence. Husein Al-Kaff points out that it is important for Shi'is to practice all the teachings of Shi'ism openly, in front of Sunnis, in order that Sunnis might come to acknowledge the real teachings of Shi'ism, the followers of Shi'ism and their institutions, as well as their contributions to the country.[163] This does not mean that these people renounce the permissibility of practicing *taqiyya*. They see that misperceptions among the Sunnis will not disappear unless Shi'is show the true expressions of their rituals and practices.

Some Shi'i intellectuals like Jalaluddin Rakhmat, however, are of the opinion that the practice of *taqiyya* should be inspired by the ideals of Islamic fraternity and that strict obedience to Shi'i jurisprudence has more often than not created tensions between Sunnis and Shi'is in Indonesia. He considers the Shi'i *ustadhs* to have implemented a legal paradigm of *fiqh*, as opposed to his own paradigm of *akhlaq*, or ethics. For Rakhmat, piety is not based on obedience to a certain school of jurisprudence but is determined on the basis of noble character. Regarding

---

161 *Aula* (November 1993:60).
162 Husein Al-Habsyi (1991:6).
163 Husein Al-Kaff, interview, (19/5/2004).

taqiyya, he writes "*Taqiyya* is the observance of jurisprudence practised by the majority people or jurisprudence that is established by the authority, in order to avoid disputes and fractions. *Taqiyya* means to leave our school of jurisprudence for the sake of maintaining brotherhood among Muslims."[164]

Thus, *taqiyya* can be seen as a strategic element of the Shi'i *madhhab* with the purpose of defending the existence of the *madhhab* and its adherents, or for maintaining Islamic fraternity. It is not an exaggeration to suggest that the teaching and practice of *taqiyya* is instrumental in the spread and development of Shi'ism in Indonesia.

---

164   Rakhmat (2002:51).

4. Da'Wa

As a proselytising religion, Islam obliges its followers, without exception, to undertake missionary activities. These activities are subsumed under the Arabic term *'da'wa'*, which literally means 'a call' or 'an invitation'. In Indonesia, however, as in many other countries, *da'wa* has become a complex term, directed more internally to the Muslim community than to non-Muslims and encompassing both the specific idea of *tabligh,* or preaching as well as the broader idea of "the propagation of Islam not only by preaching and publications, but also by deeds and activities in all areas of social life ... [or] a comprehensive Islamization of society".[1] Both meanings are employed in this chapter. *Da'wa* is a significant means of struggle by Shi'is in Indonesia for the purpose of gaining recognition as a community and a *madhab*. In a broad sense, the institution of Shi'ism itself can be seen as a *da'wa* institution. This chapter provides a brief description of the general developments of Shi'i *da'wa*, followed by an examination of its ideals. I will then describe the basic elements of the institution and the various kinds of *da'wa* activities undertaken by Shi'is. This also includes details of the educational training for agents of *da'wa*, the *da'i*.

A. General Developments of the Da'wa Institution

In the decade following the Iranian Revolution of 1978-1979, *da'wa* activities undertaken by Shi'is in Indonesia were generally carried out on an individual basis, with one exception: the role played by the famous educational institution of YAPI, founded in Bangil, Java in 1976. Missionary activities in this period were not generally institutionalised; in fact they were often conducted 'underground'. This was partly because of the absence of a known institutional centre for Shi'ism. (The government and religious authorities in Indonesia had been unable to identify the existence of this Muslim minority group in the country until the open establishment of Shi'i institutions).

Since the late 1980s, however, leading Shi'i figures have started to establish Shi'i foundations called *yayasan*. The *yayasan* is a legally recognised institution based on relatively loose conditions: a number of people form the executive board of the foundation, a certain amount of money is designated as basic capital and an address has to be registered. Renowned Shi'i foundations in Java, in chronological order of establishment, include: *Al-Hujjah* (founded in 1987) in

---

1   Boland (1971:193).

Jember, East Java, *Muthahhari* (1988) in Bandung, *Al-Hadi* (1989) in Pekalongan, Central Java, *Al-Jawad* (1991) in Bandung, *Al-Muntazar* (1992) in Jakarta, *Al-Kazim* (1994) in Cirebon, West Java, IPABI (1993) in Bogor, *Rausyanfikr* (1995) in Yogyakarta, *Fatimah* (1997) in Jakarta and the Islamic Cultural Centre (ICC) of Al-Huda (2000) in Jakarta. In addition, there have been a number of Shi'i foundations located in cities and towns in Sumatra, Kalimantan, Sulawesi and other islands.

Since the late 1980s, Indonesian Islam has witnessed the proliferation of these Shi'i institutions. Recent estimates suggest that there are more than 80 scattered across the country, mainly in the cities and towns. Although the exact number is unknown, reliable sources show that there has been a significant development in both their quantity and quality. In 2001, 36 Shi'i foundations and 43 *majlis ta'lim*[2] (educational council or meeting place) were affiliated to the *Yayasan Rausyanfikr* of Yogyakarta.[3] Similarly, some years ago, the ICC of Al-Huda in Jakarta published a list of 79 Shi'i foundations.[4] With a few exceptions, all the organisations on the list are inventoried as *yayasan*. (In 2004, when I was concluding my research, the number of *yayasan* must have been even greater, as I came across a number not included on the ICC list). A small number of these foundations develop into larger multi-functional institutions, carrying out various roles in the community - religious, educational and cultural - but most remain small bodies known only to a limited number of people. The development of these institutions may fluctuate, with some even stopping operation. For these reasons it is difficult to provide an accurate figure of the number of Shi'i foundations in Indonesia.

Yet given the relatively small number of adherents to Shi'ism in Indonesia, the number of their institutions is relatively large. The geographical distribution of these institutions reflects the scattered distribution of Shi'i communities throughout the country. It also illustrates the dynamics of their social, cultural, educational and religious activities. Moreover, since the establishment of *yayasan* is an integral part of the Shi'i missionary process, they can be seen to reflect a great missionary zeal among the Shi'is. They are also evidence of a transformation from individual to institutional agency in the *da'wa* activity. From a historical perspective, the establishment of such a large number of institutions marks an advance in the development of Shi'ism in Indonesia.

---

2   Safwan (http://rausyanfikr.tripod.com/makatul/sosio-agama.htm).
3   Abaza (2004:179).
4   Formerly, a list of Shi'i foundations in Indonesia could be seen at http://www.alhuda.or.id/data-yayasan. htm. However, the current homepage of the Islamic Cultural Centre of Jakarta no longer publishes this information.

Several points can be made about this process. First, there has been a tendency among Shi'i *ustadhs* and intellectuals (with a few notable exceptions)[5] to establish foundations as a means of disseminating their teachings. Almost all of Indonesia's Shi'i religious teachers and intellectuals have been or are currently connected to one or more Shi'i foundations. The motivation to establish foundations is enhanced by the fact that there are relatively simple rules for their establishment. Organisations are required to provide three people, statutes and a certain amount of capital, which must be formally recognised by a notary. Since office premises or a building are not required, it is very common for residential properties to be used as operational centres. There are at least two interconnected motivations among the founders. First, most Shi'i teachers and intellectuals earn a living in the private sector and they need an institutional platform for their religious aspirations. Since their *madhhab* is not the *madhhab* of the majority of Muslims in the country, there is little possibility for them to join existing religious institutions. Theoretically, their involvement in foundations is a way of accumulating economic and symbolic capital, both being interconnected. The second motivation, then, is for the accumulation of this social capital in the development of social relations and networks.[6] By means of the *yayasan,* the *ustadhs* and intellectuals can create more formal communication with international Shi'i institutions or organisations; they can more easily obtain free Shi'i scholarly works - books and periodicals - printed by institutions or associations in Iran, Iraq, Kuwait and other countries. Such works have contributed greatly to the development of Shi'i Islam in Indonesia.

The second point to be made is that with a few exceptions, Shi'i foundations are located in urban areas throughout the country, from Sumatra to West Irian. This underscores the fact of the growth of the Shi'i community in Indonesia as an urban phenomenon. It is also congruent with the fact that most university graduates and Qum alumni who become Shi'i intellectuals, activists or *ustadhs* tend to live in cities or towns. Generally, they establish the centre of the foundation close to, or even in, the founder's own home. This satisfies the demands of the local community for religious instruction and guidance in the teachings of Shi'ism and also provides a base for propagating these ideas to the Muslim community at large. (*Nota bene* Shi'i missionary activities have both internal and external orientations). There is a clear correlation in terms of the greater the number of Shi'is living in a particular city or area, the greater the number of Shi'i foundations established there. Thus, Jakarta, home to Indonesia's largest community, has the largest number of foundations. In 1995, the journal

---

5   Included in this category is the famous Shi'i religious teacher, Husein Syafi'i al-Muhdar of Jember, East Java who accuses those who establish foundations of having social and economic interests, rather than promoting religious teachings to the community (Husein Syafi'i al-Muhdar, interview, 12/10/2002).
6   Bourdieu (1986).

Ulumul Qur'an mentions 25 Shi'i institutions having been set up in Jakarta.[7] This is not to say categorically that there are no Shi'i institutions in rural areas; for instance, the *Al-Hakim* Foundation, a famous Shi'i institution established by the late Zainal Abidin Al-Muhdar (d. 2003) attracts people from the rural areas and villages close to its centre in Pringsewu, Lampung. By and large, however, the establishment of Shi'i institutions remains an urban phenomenon.

The third important point regarding the establishment of Shi'i institutions for *da'wa* is that the growing number of foundations in Indonesia corresponds also to the increasing number of Qum alumni returning home. To name a few, Fathoni Hadi established the *Al-Hujjah* Foundation in Jember in 1987, Ahmad Baragbah established *Al-Hadi* in 1989, Abdullah Assegaf founded the *Al-Wahdah* Foundation in Solo in 1994 and Rusdi al-Aydrus established the *Ath-Thohir* Foundation in Surabaya in 2000. Furthermore, many Qum alumni become leaders or *ustadhs* of existing Shi'i foundations. Among them are Zahir Yahya at the *Al-Kautsar* Foundation in Malang (East Java), Husein Al-Kaf at the *Al-Jawad* Foundation in Bandung, Abdullah Assegaf at IPABI in Bogor, Muhammad Syuaib at the *Al-Mujtaba* Foundation in Purwakarta, West Java and Herman Al-Munthahar at the *Amirul Mukminin* Foundation in Pontianak, West Kalimantan. It is evident that missionary zeal has motivated these Qum alumni to act so that *da'wa* activities may be institutionalised and well organised.

A fourth point of interest is that the Shi'i foundations were all established by, or belong to groups of people with ties of friendship or kin. In this regard, institutions rarely belong to a single person. The *Al-Jawad* Foundation, for example, was established in 1991 by a group of activists who graduated from universities in Bandung, including Ahmad Jubaili, Wawan Tribudi Hermawan, Rivaldi and Yusuf Bachtiar.[8] The same was true of the founders of the *Muthahhari* Foundation three years earlier. In contrast, the founders of the *Fatimah* Foundation are all members of the al-Muhdar family living in Jakarta. The al-Muhdar clan were known as Shi'i adherents in Indonesia long before the Iranian Revolution of 1978-1979. The executive board of their foundation consists of Muhammad Andy Assegaf, Akma Syarif and Imah Az-Zahra, who are all children of Abu Bakar Assegaf and his wife Fatimah Syundus al-Muhdar.[9] Ahmad Muhajir al-Muhdar and Alwi Husein al-Muhdar serve as important religious teachers and advisers to the foundation. *Tazkiya Sejati*, also listed among the Shi'i foundations, was founded in 1997 by the family of Indonesia's ex-Vice President Sudharmono in co-operation with Jalaluddin

---

7   Nurjulianti and Arief Subhan (1995:20).
8   Wisananingrum (2001:84).
9   *Syi'ar* (July 2002:46).

Rakhmat. Due to its adoption of various practices of Sufism, this institution has been instrumental in attracting a number of Jakarta's urban upper-middle class to Shi'ism.

Compared to the above-mentioned institutions, the establishment of the ICC of Al-Huda was unique in the sense that it involved the collaboration of several prominent figures in Indonesia with Iran. Its board includes Jalaluddin Rakhmat, Haidar Bagir and Umar Shahab as the founding council and the Iranian Muhsen Hakimollah as director. The ICC is the largest Shi'i foundation in Indonesia and employs about 30 staff, some of whom are Qum alumni, to run its activities. The foundation is highly dependent on its Iranian director, not only in terms of authority and responsibility, but also for financial resources. Since its establishment this Islamic centre has functioned as a co-ordinating body in organising the celebration of Islamic festivals. It also plays an important mediating role among Shi'i institutions in the country and in relations between Iran and the Shi'i community in Indonesia, a function which was once carried out by the Iranian Embassy in Jakarta.

This description leads us to the fifth point regarding Shi'i institutions: aside from the co-ordinating function of the ICC of Al-Huda, some institutions are closely connected and co-operate with each other in the field of *da'wa,* while there are tensions between others. Both of these situations are due to influential relationships between certain *ustadhs* and intellectuals. A pertinent example is the cooperation between several Shi'i *ustadhs* and institutions in West Java that has contributed to the setting up of the regional association called KIBLAT (*Komunitas Ahlul Bait Jawa Barat*, The *Ahl al-Bayt* Community of West Java). This umbrella organisation encompasses several foundations in the province, including *Al-Jawad* of Bandung, *Al-Kautsar* of Bandung, IPABI of Bogor, *Al-Kazhim* of Cirebon, *Al-Mujtaba* of Purwakarta and *As-Syifa* of Garut. However, KIBLAT excludes the *Muthahhari* Foundation, which is known to harbour tensions with *Al-Jawad* and its associates. Co-operation, competition and tension have all characterised the relationship between Shi'i *ustadhs*, intellectuals and institutions in Indonesia.

Finally, the existence of Shi'i institutions is very important for the Shi'i community as a whole, particularly in terms of their functions. First, since the existing Sunni mosques cannot be used as places to perform Shi'i rituals and ceremonies, the foundations have provided alternative space for religious expression. Second, aside from this religious function, the institutions are also places to hold meetings in which a variety of issues can be discussed, including those of the Shi'i community or of Muslims in general. Religious instruction and guidance, as well as educational programmes, can be provided in or through the institutions. Third, the institutions are platforms for spreading the teachings of Shi'ism to the Muslim community at large. A variety of *da'wa* programmes are carried out in or through the institutions. In addition, through the publication of periodicals and books, the institutions extend this role beyond *da'wa* into the cultural field. Thus the multi-functional Shi'i foundations have become institutional agents in the reproduction and dissemination of the Shi'i tradition in Indonesia.

The religious life of the Shi'i community is heavily dependent on the continued existence and functions of these institutions. However, the above description by itself does not identify such institutions as Shi'i in nature. Below we attempt to examine this matter.

B. The Ideals of the Shi'i Institutions

In order to gain a comprehensive understanding of the nature and identity of the Shi'i institutions, it is worth examining the written ideals that form their philosophical basis and programmes, even though these ideals may not always be fully put into practice. With the exception of IPABI (*Ikatan Pemuda Ahlul Bait Indonesia*, Indonesian League of Ahlul Bait Youth) the names of the foundations never include explicit terms or phrases indicating that they are Shi'i. Yet should we look more closely, these names often reveal Shi'i connections. For example, institutions such as Al-Jawad, Al-Muntazar, Al-Mahdi, Al-Mujtaba, Al-Hadi and Al-Kazim are all named after Shi'i Imams. In addition, some foundations take their names from prominent Shi'i learned men, such as Mulla Sadra or Mutahhari, while others use terms closely associated with the Shi'i tradition, such as the *Babul Ilmi* Foundation (Gate of Knowledge) which is the phrase used to refer to 'Ali bin Abi Talib, the first Imam. However, names such as the Islamic Cultural Centre of Al-Huda in Jakarta or LSII (*Lembaga Studi and Informasi Islam*, Institute for Islamic Studies and Information) in Makassar give no clue to their Shi'i nature.

In this respect, the *Muthahhari* Foundation is the single Shi'i institution that provides us with the rationale for using a specific name. Given the fact that *Mutahhari* is the name of an Iranian Shi'i learned man, it follows that many people can identify the foundation as Shi'i. In its publicity brochure, the founders of the institution explain that the name chosen has philosophical meanings related to the organisation's own goals, as well as to the current historical reality that Muslim society is facing a variety of problems. They describe the establishment of the foundation[10] as an attempt to address one of the most fundamental problems, the lack of *'ulama* able to lead and unite the various segments of Muslim society. The founders see this problem as having

---

10 Yayasan Muthahhari (1993:17-18).

originated from a dichotomy in the comprehension of the religious and secular sciences in the Muslim world, including Indonesia. On the one hand, there exist traditional *'ulama,* qualified in the fields of Islamic knowledge but lacking sufficient knowledge of contemporary life. Their approach to problem-solving becomes irrelevant. On the other hand, there are Muslim scholars who have a strong Islamic spirit and understand contemporary information yet are 'ignorant' in Islamic learning. Their problem-solving tends to be superficial. The desire to bridge this divide formed the rationale behind the establishment of the *Muthahhari* Foundation.

Ayatollah Murtada Mutahhari was a reformist Shi'i *'alim* and professor at Tehran University, who after the victory of the Iranian revolution became a member of its Revolutionary Council. He was assassinated on 2 May 1979. The founders of the *Muthahhari* Foundation saw this Ayatollah as a 20th century intellectual-*'ulama* and a model for all Islamic scholars. He met three requisites: qualification in the fields of traditional Islamic knowledge, a comprehension of the secular sciences and a concern for and activities in the social field.[11] His thought, in more than 50 books comprising almost all aspects relevant to the needs of Muslims – individual human existence, society, nature and history – is considered strategic for the establishment of an Islamic civilisation and the maintenance of an Islamic world-view. Furthermore, in the eyes of the founders of the *Muthahhari* Foundation, he was an open and moderate scholar who promoted freedom of thought and religious belief free from sectarianism. Finally, this learned man was known for his exemplary moral conduct.[12] Jalaluddin Rakhmat writes "From Muthahhari we learned three things: the meeting of traditional Islamic knowledge with modern sciences, openness, as well as combination between intellectualism and activism".[13] In this way, the complex of meanings symbolised by the name Muthahhari also characterises the various roles of the institution, its programmes and its activities.

As institutions legally recognised in Indonesia, the Shi'i foundations have various stated ideals in terms of goal, vision and mission. Their philosophical basis supports their missionary nature and orientation. This is reflected in a comparison of the ideals of four of the country's largest: the *Muthahhari* and *Al-Jawad* foundations in Bandung, and the *Fatimah* Foundation and ICC of Al-Huda, both in Jakarta.[14] Al-Jawad was established "to practice the teachings of *ahl al-bayt* in daily life individually and collectively, as well as to develop and

---

11   Yayasan Muthahhari (1993:19).
12   Yayasan Muthahhari (1993:19-20).
13   Rakhmat (1993:6).
14   With the exception of the goals of the *Muthahhari* Foundation taken from its brochure (1993), my analysis of the ideals of the Shi'i foundations is based on their homepages: http://aljawad.tripod.com/aljawad.htm, http://www.fatimah.org/aboutus.htm and http://www.icc-jakarta.com/statis.php?id=abt (formerly http://www.alhuda.or.id/profile.htm). Profiles of the *Muthahhari, Al-Jawad* and *Fatimah* Foundations can be seen in separate editions of *Syi'ar:* October 2003:59-61; February 2003:51-52; and July 2002:46), respectively.

spread them among society at large". The homepage of the website of the *Al-Jawad* Foundation has the slogan "a deliverer of the pure Islamic message" and tells of how it was established to organise activities directed towards achieving its ideals: first, the creation of skills - intellectual, social, spiritual and professional - among its members in carrying out *da'wa* of the teachings about *ahl al-bayt*; second, the establishment of media for spreading the teachings of *ahl al-bayt* to the community at large and third, the collection of economic sources to support *da'wa* activity.

The *Fatimah* Foundation has goals essentially like those of the Al-Jawad Foundation but it formulates them in a different way, stating "the goal of the *Fatimah* Foundation is to create itself as a means for its *ummah* to develop the teaching of the *ahl al-bayt*". The *Fatimah* Foundation has adopted the slogan "penetrating religious insights" and has the mission to be 'a servant' of the followers of the Prophet Muhammad and his *ahl al-bayt*. It sees its missionary activity as necessary in order that Muslims in Indonesia can accept the teachings and follow them in daily life. The *Fatimah* Foundation formulates its vision around the idea of five kinds of responsibility: responsibility to God, to the Prophet Muhammad and his *ahl al-bayt*, to all followers of Shi'ism and to all members of the Foundation. The fifth states: "finally, we are responsible for making our foundation an open one to those seeking the truth". All of the above clearly shows that the *Fatimah* Foundation was established in order to propagate Shi'ism in Indonesia.

The ideals of both the *Al-Jawad* and the *Fatimah* foundations are narrow, in so far as they aim to propagate the teachings of Shi'ism. The word 'Shi'a' is absent in their statements for the simple reason that the term has generally negative connotations in Sunnism and among the Sunni community in Indonesia in particular. The words "*ahl al-bayt*" or "family of the Prophet" are more commonly used because they are acceptable among both Sunni and Shi'i Muslims (see Chapter One). Both *Al-Jawad* and *Fatimah* emphasise the term "the teachings of *ahl-al-bayt*". This is in contrast to the formal written ideals of both *Muthahhari* and ICC of Al-Huda, where the words *ahl al-bayt* are hardly ever found. In this regard, two important points can be surmised: first, the ideals of the *Al-Jawad* and the *Fatimah* foundations are directed towards a Shi'i mission to the wider society, while the written ideals of both *Muthahhari* and ICC of Al-Huda do not confine them solely to the Shi'i version of Islam. Second, the first two institutions tend to implement a strategy of openness and do not practice *taqiyya,* while the other two, as will be shown below, tend to practice *taqiyya.*

The *Muthahhari* Foundation, with its slogan "for the enlightenment of Islamic thought" was established to organise programmes in the fields of *da'wa*, education and Islamic civilisation for the benefit of Indonesian society at large. As mentioned in its brochure,[15] its general goals are:

1. To receive lessons for the development of Islamic thought and propagation from an intellectual-learned man who has the qualifications required to formulate Islamic alternatives in solving contemporary problems.

2. To create a vehicle for the growth of scientific attitudes - a depth of comprehension of modern knowledge, insight, moderation and tolerance.

3. To contribute to a formulation of an Islamic worldview and social planning for a future Islamic civilisation.

4. To participate in the production of intellectual *'ulama* and *'ulama*-intellectuals by means of an alternative system of education in the fields of Islamic knowledge and other relevant sciences.

5. To contribute to the establishment of unity and Muslim brotherhood (*wahdah and ukhuwwah Islamiyah*) free from sectarianism.

Aimed at implementing a *da'wa* programme in its widest sense, ICC of Al-Huda has formulated a more general vision "to realise Islamic society with a spiritual and intellectual enlightenment based on high integrity". The complete missionary ideals of the foundation are:

1. To reconstruct and promote Islamic values in the life of society.

2. To reconstruct an Islamic culture with spiritual values.

3. To motivate intellectual enthusiasm based on Islamic values and objectivity.

4. To describe and reconstruct Islamic understanding in accordance with the Qur'an and Hadith.

5. To motivate love towards Allah, His messenger, the Prophet's family and all human beings.

6. To plant the seeds of good conduct (*akhlaq al-karima*) in every aspect of the life of the nation and the state.

The stated ideals of both *Muthahhari* and ICC of Al-Huda share broad concepts such as the promotion of 'Islamic values', 'Islamic civilisation' and 'Islamic culture'. Furthermore, even though both use the term 'Islam' in a wider sense

---

15 Yayasan Muthahhari (1993:20).

rather than Shi'ism in particular, their emphasis is different. For example, ICC of Al-Huda stresses the importance of Islamic brotherhood and unity among Muslim groups. A striking contrast between the two is that, as their names suggest, ICC of Al-Huda is focused in the field of culture, while *Muthahhari* concentrates more specifically on education and on the production of intellectual-learned men. Compared to the stated ideals of *Al-Jawad* and *Fatimah*, those of Muthahhari and ICC of Al-Huda are much broader, even though all four have missionary characteristics, and all four share the ultimate goal of realising an Islamic society.

An important point regarding the stated ideals of these four Shi'i institutions in Indonesia is their apparent lack of interest in the field of politics. The only slightly political aspect is the sixth point of the missionary ideals of ICC of Al-Huda, which emphasises the importance of moral values in aspects of life related to the state and nation. This becomes the more interesting because Shi'ism itself does not distinguish religion from politics. Viewed from their stated ideals, the Shi'i institutions are concerned only with religion, education and culture, fields considered appropriate in the propagation of Shi'i teachings as well as in the realisation of an Islamic society in Indonesia. The written ideals suggest there will be no involvement in political practice, even though in reality, their leaders and members may individually take part in politics. This illustrates the fact that these stated ideals are just that — ideals — and whether or not they become reality remains to be seen. We now need to understand the institutional elements which make up the Shi'i institutions.

C. The Institutional Elements

Well-established Shi'i institutions in Indonesia possess the following elements: an *ustadh* or some kind of religious teacher, the *jama'a,* or members, a variety of *da'wa* activities and a centre for these activities. These basic elements maintainn the existence and the functioning of the institution and should be considered as a unified system. In addition, there are also supporting elements, which may influence the organisation of *da'wa* activity. In every institution there is an executive board and staff or activists who organise *da'wa* and manage or assist in the development of the institution. Examples of well-established institutions include *Al-Jawad* in Bandung, IPABI in Bogor, *Al-Muntazar*, *Fatimah* and ICC of Al-Huda, all located in Jakarta. There is also YAPI (*Yayasan Pesantren Islam*) in Bangil, East Java, *Al-Hadi* in Pekalongan and the *Muthahhari* Foundation, whose formal educational programme will be described and analysed in detail in the next chapter. With their own buildings and facilities such as an office, library, bookstore and so on, the physical portrait of these institutions shows the extent of their involvement in various kinds of activities. ICC of Al-Huda is the largest foundation, with a luxurious building, facilities and a large number of staff.

The well-established foundations usually have one or more permanent *ustadhs* whose main duty it is to provide religious instruction and guidance to the *jama'a*. The *ustadh* becomes a *muballigh* (preacher) or *da'i* (propagandist, evangelist) in the broad meaning of these terms. As mentioned before, in some cases, the *ustadh* is a co-founder or owner of the institution. In other cases, while not being a co-founder, the *ustadh* occupies an influential position within the organisational structure of the institution. This concurs with the fact that *ustadhs* have a prestigious status within the Shi'i community. In this respect, the term *pembina* (adviser) - a position usually regarded as being higher than the head of the institution – is sometimes used. The position is comparable to that of the *kyai*, or learned man in the *pesantren* tradition. With this high status, the *ustadh* is an influential agent in the development of the institution. In many cases, the *ustadhs*, particularly prominent ones, such as Othman Omar Shihab, Umar Shahab and Husein Shahab are not affiliated to any specific institution but are hired by a range of institutions throughout the country. As mentioned earlier, as a larger number of Qum alumni become *ustadhs*, they too are gaining influence within the Shi'i institutions in Indonesia.

The position of *ustadh*, as one considered to have thorough religious knowledge and whose guidance and advice are to be followed, is crucial for the existence and development of Shi'i institutions. The *ustadhs* are influential in planning and realising programmes, as well as in establishing connections with other institutions. The main duties of the *ustadh* include: providing religious instruction and guidance, preaching, leading rites and ceremonies and giving advice on the direction of the institution. To carry out these duties, the *ustadh* must possess qualifications such as a thorough religious comprehension and skill in leading religious ritual, as well as in preaching. It is not surprising that the position of *ustadh* in most Shi'i institutions is now filled by a Qum graduate.

The second institutional element is the *jama'a*, the congregation. The *jama'a* commonly consists of adult Muslims, male and female, who are motivated to follow the religious, educational and social programmes provided by the foundation. In return, the programmes themselves may be tailored specifically to the demands and interests of the congregation. Sometimes members of the *jama'a* also serve as executive personnel of the institution and are involved in the organisation of the programmes. To a certain extent, this characteristic of the *jama'a* distinguishes the Shi'i foundations as institutions of *da'wa* from the Shi'i institutions of learning such as *pesantren*. There are no formal rules regarding becoming a member of the *jama'a*, except where some programmes demand specific requirements of participants, such as paying expenses. Shi'i foundations commonly attract people living in areas close by. In Jakarta, for example, the *Fatimah* Foundation has members of *jama'a* from areas of South and East Jakarta while *Al-Muntazar* attracts its members from areas in West Jakarta.

Motivations for members of the *jama'a* to join *da'wa* programmes are complex and various, from religious to secular reasons. A motivation to seek religious instruction and guidance cannot be neglected, especially in view of the fact that most members of the *jama'a* do not have a deep religious educational background. Furthermore, most of the Shi'is in Indonesia today have converted from Sunnism as adults. In this regard, I often heard *ustadhs* claiming that Indonesia's Shi'is are in the process of becoming 'ideal' Shi'is. "The Shi'is in Indonesia are still immature", said Husen Shahab.[16] This suggests that they do not yet understand and practice all of the teachings of Shi'ism and that they still need instruction and guidance. Converts are considered to be influenced by the Sunni teachings and traditions to which they once held. Converted Shi'is who are still 'new' and 'young', who do not follow all Shi'i traditions, are called *tashayyu'*.[17] A second motivation is a religious one, in that most Shi'i rituals must be carried out in Shi'i institutions, spaces which allow members to express their religiosity. This also gives rise to an expression of identity distinct from the majority Sunnis. The social and psychological benefits of being active in a congregation also form a motivation. Abaza's explanation is particularly relevant to female participants

> The importance of time spent collectively in 'social gatherings', exchanging information, along with tangential activities, such as selling and buying, takes prevalence. The more I interviewed *da'is*, the more I found that they rely on repetitive sermons and a stylised *habitus* for performance purposes. Indeed, for many housewives, the *Majlis* could be a pleasant way of spending time. Perhaps they thus found comfort in consulting religious lecturers.[18]

The same social and psychological motivation among women to engage in a religious gathering can be seen in other places in the world such as Hyderabad, India, as shown by Howarth, who observed that Muslim women's gatherings are "important opportunities for women to meet and to form friendships outside their family homes".[19]

All such motivations are interconnected and whatever their individual interests, members of the Shi'i *jama'a* contribute to the realisation of *da'wa* programmes.

---

16 Husein Shahab, interview, (2/4/2004).
17 Husein Al-Kaff (1421/2000:2).
18 Abaza (2004:82).
19 Howarth (2002:262).

Moreover, richer members frequently provide fundamental economic patronage for the activities. In return for their contributions, they are given important positions within the community and the *ustadh* and intellectuals are expected to show them respect. In this way, close relationships among members of the institution and between religious teachers and the *jama'a* are formed. Members of the *jama'a* not only expect to acquire religious knowledge from the teachers but also to make them their spiritual guide and counsellor to provide solutions to a wide range of problems, including family-related problems. Close relationships between certain *ustadhs* and intellectuals with members of *jama'a* are a predictable consequence of the intensive interactions between them. The other side to this is that competition and tension are also inevitable in the relationships between *ustadhs*, intellectuals and the *jama'a*.

The relationships between *ustadhs* as individuals, foundations as institutions and among the members of the *jama'a* is mutually beneficial to all parties. There is an exchange of 'goods' in the field of religion – the one material and the other symbolic. Frequently, *ustadhs* in Indonesia earn their living from the money paid by the *jama'a*, who may be charged for participation in *da'wa* activities, or through endowments given for certain programmes or religious occasions. In some cases, *da'wa* activities depend heavily on the material support of a number of rich members of *jama'a*. These rich *jama'a* usually have a strong religious and missionary zeal. They may even make their houses centres for regular *da'wa* activities or provide yet other houses for *ustadhs* to live in. So competition among the *ustadhs* and intellectuals to establish good connections with rich members of the *jama'a* has been a characteristic of the development of Shi'ism in Indonesia. Bourdieu[20] theorises that it is an attempt to accumulate economic capital, alongside the struggle to maintain or improve cultural and social capital. Most institutions depend on the *jama'a* for their economic resources. In return, the *jama'a* receive religious instruction and guidance, as well as entertainment, cultural goods and the social and psychological benefits of being part of a congregation. This interrelation clearly indicates the important position of the *jama'a*, which tends to be overlooked in *da'wa* studies so far.

The third important element of a Shi'i institution is the programmes and activities it provides. These vary in terms of field, approach and orientation and depend on several factors. Some institutions tend to place emphasis on one kind of programme while others focus on another, contributing to the significant differences found in the main attributes of certain institutions. For instance, although the *Muthahhari* Foundation carries out a wide range of programmes, its image is frequently recognised on the strength of its senior high school.

---

20   Bourdieu (1986).

Religious programmes basically comprise Shi'i religious rituals, both obligatory and recommended, and ceremonies. The most famous weekly prayer, the *kumayl* prayer mentioned in Chapter Three, is held in nearly every Shi'i institution in Indonesia. Other religious rituals take place on an annual basis, including those related to the commemoration of the births or deaths of the Fourteen Infallibles and other prominent religious leaders, as well as other important historical events in Shi'i tradition. Some institutions, such as IPABI in Bogor, also conduct the celebration of the two great Islamic festivals of *'Id al-Fitr* (the close the fasting month) and *'Id al-Adha* (the Day of Sacrifice) separately from the Sunnis. Because of the large number of Shi'i commemorations there has been co-operation and co-ordination among certain larger institutions in the organisation of certain festivals. ICC of Al-Huda, in co-operation with others, usually organises the national commemoration of such great events as *'Ashura* and *Mawlid* in Jakarta. The essential dimension of the Shi'i institution, then, is its function to provide all members of the Shi'i community in Indonesia with the space to express their religiosity.

The field of Shi'i education will be discussed in the following chapter; however, it is important to note here that the establishment of TK/TPA (*Taman Kanak-kanak/Taman Pendidikan Al-Quran*, Qur'an kindergartens) has become a very popular programme of Shi'i institutions. This pre-school education provides very young students with some basic teachings of Islam, including using the so-called *iqro'* method which teaches children to recite the Holy Qur'an in Arabic. The *iqro'* is considered by many in Indonesia to be the easiest way of learning Qur'anic recitation, and with its instruction and material (six volumes of *iqro'* and *tajwid*), the students are able to recite the Qur'an in a short space of time. This 'modern' method has replaced the traditional style, known to Muslims in Indonesia as the *Baghdadi* method. Gade describes that while the *iqro'* method is *lebih cepat* (faster), the '*Baghdadi*' method is *lebih dalam* (deeper) in terms of acquisition. She then writes

> The key practical contrast is that with the 'traditional' method, students learned the names of letters along with their sound qualities and 'spelled out' words with the named letters according to set formulae before vocalising them. With the 'modern' method, students vocalised the letters without first going through the process of parsing the word by spelling. The primary difference Indonesians emphasised between the methods was precisely the practice of 'spelling out' (*ejaan*) within the traditional method, which was judged by many to be too time-consuming.[21]

21　Gade (2004:147).

The popularity of this programme may result from its relatively simple requirements in terms of educational facilities and management. Just two or more teachers, usually female, may establish the pre-school institution and meets with the increasing motivation of Indonesian parents to send their children to Islamic educational institutions. A knowledge of Qur'anic recitation is a crucial basic religious skill in observing the obligatory Islamic rituals. This might be the rationale for the leaders of Shi'i institutions to undertake such programmes.

In cultural fields, a number of Shi'i institutions in Indonesia are engaged in publishing. Some institutions, such as IPABI and the *Fatimah* Foundation, have established a separate publishing arm under a different name, while others including those of *Muthahhari*, *Al-Jawad* and ICC of Al-Huda use the same name as their institution. These institutions organise the publication of periodicals and books, both translated texts and Indonesian originals.[22] In addition, large Shi'i institutions such as *Mutahhari*, *Al-Jawad*, *Fatimah* and ICC of Al-Huda have opened libraries providing books in Indonesian, Arabic and Persian to meet the demands of the Shi'is in the country. Observing these libraries, I found that they hold a large number of Shi'i books, on a variety of subjects, which cannot be found in other libraries in Indonesia, including the libraries of Islamic higher educational institutions. Compared with the existing Sunni institutions, this is a unique trait of Shi'i institutions. It is important to note that all these fields, and in particular education and culture, may be included in the realm of *da'wa* in its most general sense, namely, they are all missionary efforts to achieve the ultimate goal of realising an Islamic society.

The fourth element of a Shi'i institution is the physical centre of activity. The majority of foundations are small and use their founders' residences as centres for their activities. However, the big foundations have their own buildings and facilities. There is usually a specific room at the centre for the activities, commonly called the *husainiyya*, a term derived from the name of the third Imam, Husayn, whose death ritual forms a focus in Shi'ism. *Husainiyya* originally means "forum or courtyard where Muharram passion plays and mourning for Imam Husayn is done".[23] Usually, the *husainiyya*, office, library and other facilities are located in one complex. A few *husainiyyas* are big while others are small, depending upon the size of the *jama'a* attending the activities organised by the institution. It is in the *husainiyya* that Shi'is gather to observe prayers, to perform religious rituals and ceremonies, to study religion or to engage in social activities. In my observation, they seldom practice the obligatory daily prayers collectively at the *husainiyya*. (Shi'is place less emphasis on congregational prayers five times a day than their fellow Sunnis). On the whole, weekly, monthly and yearly *da'wa* activities are carried out in the *husainiyya*. For foundations with their own

---

22   This topic is to be discussed in detail in Chapter Six.
23   Fischer and Abedi (1990:511).

mosque, such as *Muthahhari* and *Al-Jawad*, routine *da'wa* activities are centred around the mosque. By and large, the *husainiyya* functions like a mosque, with the exception that it is not the venue for Friday prayers.

The four basic elements outlined above, combined with the written ideals, make up the characteristics of a Shi'i institution, from which we may uncover certain elements that are similar to or distinct from Sunni institutions of *da'wa*. The dynamic nature of the Shi'i institution can be understood through a discussion of the various types of *da'wa* activity espoused by it.

D. Types of Shi'i *Da'wa* Activity

In order to achieve their ideals, all Shi'i institutions in Indonesia undertake broadly similar patterns of activities, which are nevertheless individually distinguishable in terms of approach and orientation. Since the concept of *da'wa* includes all missionary activities aimed at realising an Islamic society, *da'wa* activities provided by the institutions vary considerably. They can be classified into three types: *tabligh* (preaching), *ta'lim* (teaching, training and courses) and social *da'wa*. All three types of activity are interconnected and they may be directed towards either internal or external orientations. The three types of *da'wa* may take the form of either regular or incidental programmes.

Tabligh activities among the Shi'is in Indonesia, as in the Sunni community, go under the name of *pengajian*, or religious gatherings, sometimes also known as *majlis ta'lim*, or councils for learning. Both terms refer to preaching and learning. Mona Abaza has provided us with an interesting analysis of *da'wa* styles among gentrified urbanites in Jakarta (even though her article contains several factual mistakes). The *majlis ta'lim* is not "a typical urban phenomenon that only exists in Jakarta";[24] instead, it is a phenomenon of both rural and urban settings in Indonesia, although it is clearly flourishing in urban areas.

With respect to religious gatherings, Shi'i institutions hold both regular and irregular gatherings for their *jama'a*. The regular type includes weekly and annual gatherings related to the relevant Shi'i rituals. The best known and most widespread weekly religious gathering within the Shi'i community in Indonesia follows the recommendation for Shi'is to recite the *kumayl* prayer, mentioned in the previous chapter. The *majlis kumayl*, in which the *kumayl* prayer is uttered and a sermon is delivered, is held on Thursday evenings. For those foundations with a mosque, such as *Muthahhari* and *Al-Jawad*, this takes place in the mosque (*Al-Munawwarah* and *Nurul Falah* respectively) while for others the gathering takes place in the *husainiyya* or in the leader's residence.

---

24   Abaza (2004:179).

Other weekly gatherings are based on agreement between the *jama'a*, teacher and foundation, so that the form, time and place can vary. In *Muthahhari* and *Al-Jawad*, for example, the weekly religious gathering is held on Sundays, so it is known as *Pengajian Ahad* (Sunday religious gathering). The core of the *pengajian* is the *ceramah agama*, a sermon or lecture delivered by a teacher and followed by a discussion or a question and answer session. The topic of the sermon varies, and is decided upon by the preacher. It is likely that the selection of topic is related to historical events and rituals prescribed by Islamic, and in particular Shi'i, teachings, or it may be in response to events occurring within the community. Sometimes it is purely a matter of the preference of the preacher. Similar sermons may be delivered on different occasions and in different places. The weekly *pengajian* in Shi'i institutions cover a variety of aspects of Shi'ism, particularly doctrine, morality and thought.

The regular annual religious gatherings are linked to the relatively large number of rites and ceremonies within the Shi'i tradition. They are commonly associated with the so-called PHBI (*Peringatan Hari-hari Besar Islam*, Commemoration of Islamic Holy Days), a well-known programme run by all Shi'i institutions in Indonesia. Besides the Islamic festivals shared by the Sunnis, many other important events are commemorated which are distinctively Shi'i. In most of these congregational rituals, the sermon is an essential element, without which the worship is invalid. Here one can see an aspect of *da'wa* and *tabligh* naturally inherent in Islam. At such great events as the *'Ashura, Arba'in,* and *Mawlid,* which are celebrated on a national level in Jakarta, it is common for a famous *da'i,* or preacher to be invited to deliver a sermon.

In a number of the religious ceremonies, *'ulama* or intellectuals from Iran may be invited to attend. For example, the committee of ICC of Al-Huda invited Ayatollah Ali Taskhiri to deliver a sermon to celebrate the New Year of the Muslim calendar of 1425, on 20 February 2004. At this event, he spoke about the struggle of Imam Husayn in the maintenance of *Islam Muhammadi,* or 'Muhammadist Islam' in the period when it had been corrupted by the tyranny of the Ummayad dynasty. The Ayatollah suggested that in all ages there are tyrants present against whom Muslims are obliged to fight. At this annual religious gathering, for which there is always a large number of participants, every effort is made to maximise the effectiveness of *da'wa*. This includes a book fair, to which Shi'i publishers from all over Indonesia are invited.

Regarding the topic of sermons delivered in the various types of *da'wa,* on the whole, the topic chosen is put into a context with today's Muslim *umma* in mind. For example, sermons delivered on the occasion of *'Ashura* must deal with the sacrifice of Imam Husayn, his family and his loyal followers. In the commemoration of *'Ashura* held in Jakarta on 2 March 2004, Hasan Daliel Al-'Aydrus delivered a sermon about the rising of the oppressed, as exemplified by Imam Husayn and its significance in the current struggle of the Muslim *umma*. Similarly, on the occasion of *Mawlid*, the Prophet's birthday, the sermon usually deals with loving devotion to him. At the Mawlid celebration held in the *Munawwarah* Mosque (every year since the establishment of the *Mutahhari* Foundation) Jalaluddin Rakhmat usually emphasises the importance of reciting the *salawat,* or invocation to Muhammad. On 19 May 2003, Rakhmat provided his *jama'a* with a sermon entitled "The Presence of the Messenger of God among us", affirming that the spirit of the Prophet would be present under two conditions: first, when *salawat* to him is uttered in prayer and second, in any place where orphans and the poor gather in a pleasant atmosphere. Rakhmat relates this topic to his previous preaching among the poor of North Jakarta.[25] Such examples illustrate the close relationship between the topic of sermons, the events commemorated and the preacher's efforts to contextualise them.

Specific religious ideologies are promoted in the sermons delivered by Shi'i preachers at weekly and annual activities, or at other events. Scrutinising various recorded sermons, we find two different tendencies that are congruent with the divide between the *ustadh* and intellectual groups: the political tendencies of the *ustadhs* versus the moral or spiritual tendencies of the intellectuals. These are clearly distinguishable in terms of the topics of the sermons they deliver. More specifically, topics related to *wilayat al-faqih,* the mandate of the jurists, are numerous among the *ustadhs* whilst barely present in sermons given by intellectuals. The *ustadhs* emphasise the necessity for Shi'is in Indonesia to adhere to the doctrine of *wilayat al-faqih* and to make a prominent place for jurists in politics, as well as their preaching and teaching. Thus does *da'wa* become an expression of the religious ideology of the preachers and the institutions that they guide.

In addition to *tabligh, da'wa* activities among the Shi'is include the delivery of courses and training, in which participants receive intensive instruction and guidance in the teachings of Shi'ism. This type of *da'wa* is congruent with the meaning of *ta'lim,* that is, teaching to increase the knowledge of the participants.[26] *Ta'lim* is different from *tabligh* in a number of aspects: first, *ta'lim* may require more than one *ustadh* or intellectual instructor; second, it requires the participants to involve themselves in more intensive learning so that they can understand topics offered in depth by the programme.

The Shi'i institutions in Indonesia have organised a large number of training programmes, commonly called *Paket Kajian,* 'packets of courses'. These consist of a series of courses on a certain subject, organised over a certain number of meetings, either regular or incidental, so that the participants may gain deeper

---

25 *Al-Tanwir* (25/5/2003:4).
26 Nagata (1984:82).

understanding of certain aspects of Islam and Shi'ism in particular. Names given to the programmes generally depend on subject or topic offered. This type of training is familiar to Muslims in Indonesia, particularly those living in the big cities. Large Shi'i institutions such as *Muthahhari, Al-Jawad, Fatimah* and ICC of Al-Huda have been active in holding a variety of courses. Some programmes are offered to both Shi'is and Sunnis, while others are open only to Shi'is.

Many institutions provide courses aimed specifically at strengthening the internal Shi'i community, even though the activity itself may be open to both Muslim denominations. The *Al-Jawad* Foundation, for example, tends to organise courses which are specifically Shi'i in nature and which on the whole are only followed by Shi'is. Their best known programme includes a one-year integrated *Ja'fari* course on aspects of *'aqida* (doctrine), *fiqh* (jurisprudence) and *tafsir* (Qur'an exegesis) within Shi'ism, in addition to courses on logic and the Arabic language. ICC of Al-Huda has also participated in offering such courses as Persian, Arabic, *tafsir* and logic. IPABI has conducted a series of training programmes on the principal aspects of Shi'ism, which are structured in elementary, intermediate and advanced levels, and on special topics like *wilayat al-faqih,* all of which are followed by Shi'is from a number of areas in Indonesia.[27] IPABI has also conducted an important national *da'wa* activity in Puncak, Bogor, known as *Training and Silaturrahmi (Friendship)*. It was held from 24-27 July 1997 for men and from 26-29 November 1999 for women participants. *Ustadhs* such as Ahmad Baragbah and Husein Al-Kaf were invited to participate and these activities were considered instrumental, not only in improving levels of religious knowledge but also in establishing close relations among the Shi'i adherents, as well as the *ustadhs,* within a framework of Islamic brotherhood.[28]

This *ta'lim* type of *da'wa* activity is aimed at meeting the needs of the Shi'i community rather than those of wider Muslim society. Shi'is in Indonesia, who are by and large considered 'immature' in their religion, need education of at least two types: first, a thorough grasp of the basic teachings of Shi'ism and Shi'i traditions. This includes the practical knowledge required to perform the prescribed and recommended prayers, and other religious rituals, in accordance with *Ja'fari* jurisprudence. Second, subjects of Islamic knowledge such as *tafsir*, *Hadith*, logic and Arabic are important for members of the community so that they understand the doctrinal and historical bases of the *madhhab* which they follow.

The *ta'lim* type of *da'wa* activity, which is aimed at attracting both Shi'i and Sunni groups, is also undertaken. Two goals are achieved by *ta'lim*: a deeper and

---

27 *Syi'ar* (Ramadan 1423:47).
28 *An-Nashr* (7/July-August 1997, 14/1999).

stronger understanding of Shi'ism by its followers as a result of its comparison with Sunnism, and the acknowledgement and recognition of Shi'ism by the Sunni. Since the establishment of the *Muthahhari* Foundation, for example, this body has organised a number of programmes directed towards attracting both Muslim denominations. The field of Islamic knowledge on offer includes Arabic language, *'ulum al-Qur'an* (the Qur'anic sciences), *'ulum al-Hadith* (sciences of the Traditions), Islamic history, *usul al-fiqh* (principles of jurisprudence), *'ilm al-Qira'a* (the science of Qur'anic recitation), Sufism, *kalam* (theology) and Islamic philosophy. Other options include logic, Western philosophy, journalism, research methodology, management and organisation, entrepreneurship and communication technology.[29] In accordance with *Muthahhari's* goal of establishing brotherhood between Shi'is and Sunnis, a comparative perspective on both branches of Islam is provided, so that Sunnis may come to acknowledge Shi'i views. Furthermore, during this programme, leading Shi'i figures take the opportunity to explain the correct teachings of Shi'ism to Sunnis, while describing misconceptions about Shi'i teachings and addressing stereotypes widely held by Sunnis. In this way, the real teachings of Shi'ism may be well understood by Sunnis.

Included in the *ta'lim* is *da'wa* through Sufism, which is also aimed at both Sunni and Shi'i groups: "Sufism is the inner and esoteric dimension of Islam".[30] Given an increasing interest in Sufism among upper-middle class urbanites in Indonesia,[31] foundations such as *Tazkiya Sejati* in Jakarta and its branch in Bandung, the IIMaN Centre for Positive Sufism and the *Fitrah* Foundation have organised courses on various aspects of mystical practice. *Tazkiya Sejati* is the most famous. From 1997 to 2003, it organised more than 20 courses on Sufism, attracting participants from the upper-middle class in Jakarta, including businessmen, executives and retired functionaries. The courses were usually conducted during the weekends, to make them more convenient for participants to attend. Since the field of Sufism transcends the borderline between Shi'ism and Sunnism, this course was open to all Muslims and were taught and guided by both Sunni and Shi'i teachers. Besides Jalaluddin Rakhmat, the director of *Tazkiya Sejati* himself, prominent Muslim intellectuals and *ustadhs* such as Haidar Bagir, Zen Al-Hadi,[32] Othman Omar Shihab,[33] Muchtar Adam,[34] Abdul

---

29   Yayasan Muthahhari (1993:24-27).

30   Nasr (1988:121).

31   Two indications of the great interest in Sufism among urbanites are first, courses on Sufism have attracted a large number of participants; second, huge sales of books on Sufism have been recorded.

32   Zen Al-Hadi completed his MA at Al-Azhar University in Cairo. Besides being an *ustadh*, he is known as a spiritual healer in Jakarta.

33   Othman Omar Shihab graduated from Al-Azhar University in Cairo and is currently a famous *da'i* who often appears as a preacher on religious television programmes. He is a descendant of the great learned man Sayyid Uthman bin Yahya (d. 1914).

34   Muchtar Adam is the head of the *Babussalam Pesantren* in Bandung. A more detailed discussion of him can be found in Chapter Seven.

Qadir al-Habsyi[35] and Said Agiel Siradj[36] have been invited to teach. In accordance with the Sufi mission of the purification of soul and the belief in siding with the oppressed, the theoretical aspects of Sufism taught at this institution are those of the teachings contained in the Sufi manuals. However, certain religious rituals, such as the recommended prayers and *do'a,* or supplications, follow the rules and procedures of the Shi'i tradition and as are prescribed in famous Shi'i books such as *Mafatih al-Jinan* (Keys to the Gardens of Paradise).[37] Another interesting and related activity held by the foundation in Puncak near Bogor, West Java has been the practice of *'uzla,* or meditation, in which a number of participants perform Sufi rituals, as well as listening to religious sermons delivered by *ustadhs.* The courses on Sufism are aimed at bringing the participants to a spiritual enlightenment which will maintain the balance between life in the here-and-now and in the hereafter.[38]

The courses offered at *Tazkiya Sejati* differ from the courses on Sufism organised by Nurcholish Madjid's *Paramadina* in terms of topics and contents. The main characteristic of the programme at *Tazkiya Sejati* was that it provided participants not only with the theoretical aspects of Sufism but also with everyday rituals observed under Sufism, such as *dhikr,* or the remembrance of God, and guidance from teachers in the correct performance of the prayers. In this regard, one commentator, Sila considers *Tazkiya Sejati* to be the most significant institution of Sufism for upper segments of Indonesian society, because in his experience, he found that many participants at *Tazkiya Sejati* had earlier followed courses at other institutions like *Paramadina.* Sila argues that they moved to *Tazkiya Sejati* because the previous institutions had only dealt with the intellectual aspects of Sufism and not its spiritual dimension. In *Tazkiya Sejati,* he says, "besides receiving contemporary topics of Sufism from Islamic scholars through discussions and seminars, they were taught ways of practicing certain *wirid* and acts of worship".[39] Further research by Zubaidah shows that most *jama'a* responded positively to the courses on Sufism held at *Tazkiya Sejati* and felt that they had transformed them, sending them into a positive direction in terms of knowledge and religiosity.[40]

An increased interest in Sufism among urbanites in Indonesia has been the reason for other Shi'i institutions to offer the same kinds of courses. When, in 2003, because of conflict between Jalaluddin Rakhmat and the children of the co-founder Sudharmono, *Tazkiya Sejati* stopped operating, other institutions such as the *Fitrah* Foundation, run by prominent Shi'i *ustadhs* in Jakarta, continued

---

35 Sayyid Abdul Qadir al-Habsyi is a lecturer at the State Islamic University in Jakarta.
36 Said Agiel Siradj is a Nahdlatul Ulama leader.
37 This is a standard collection of Shi'i prayers compiled by Abbas Muhammad Rida al-Qummi (1877-1941).
38 *Syi'ar* (October/2002:50-51).
39 Sila (2002:7).
40 Zubaidah, cited in Rosyidi (2004:122-123).

to offer courses on Sufism. (The *Fitrah* Islamic Spiritual Centre was established by Husein Shahab and Othman Omar Shihab.) Popular Shi'i *ustadhs* such as Othman Omar Shihab and Zen al-Hadi, who used to teach at *Tazkiya Sejati* are now active with the Fitrah Foundation and are involved in the instruction of Sufism. Similarly, IiMaN, led by Haidar Bagir, continues to organise a number of activities connected with the teaching of Sufism. Apart from motivating numerous debates on the relationship between Sufism and Shi'ism,[41] Sufism seems to have united Sunnis and Shi'is because participants tend to set aside their differences. With respect to the propagation of Shi'ism in Indonesia, this approach seems to have been effective in introducing certain aspects of Shi'ism to the Sunnis.

Another important type of *da'wa* organised by the Shi'is through their institutions are social work activities, or social *da'wa*. This is an implementation of the Shi'i teaching promoting the necessity to side with the *Mustad'afin* ('the Oppressed'), a famous concept frequently found in religious sermons and Shi'i sources. In Indonesia, this type of *da'wa* falls within the concept of *da'wa bi al-hal,* or mission by deeds, in which emphasis is put on the noble moral character, *akhlaq* of preachers to give an example to the community by showing good behaviour, *amal salih*. This is frequently considered to be more important than preaching and teaching, or *da'wa bi al-lisan* ('propagation by the tongue'). Rakhmat, for instance, emphasises that *da'wa* through *tabligh* and *ta'lim,* as taught in the Qur'an and Traditions of the Prophet, is insufficient in terms of the realisation of the Muslim *umma*.[42] In practice, however, the activities of social *da'wa* necessarily also involve *tabligh* as well.

Several Shi'i institutions have participated in the organisation of various social activities for the lower classes in Indonesian society. Since the very beginning, the *Muthahhari* Foundation has devoted great attention to the empowerment of the Oppressed through programmes structurally organised under a division called *Imdad Mustad'afin,* which means 'to give assistance and pay attention to the dispossessed and oppressed'.[43] In practice, this provides educational, social and economic assistance to orphans and the poor. It is done by the Foundation for two reasons: first, it aims to generate and improve the self-respect of the poor and other segments of the lower classes. Second, it is intended to provide guidance to children of the oppressed, in order that they may compete in education.[44] To realise these programmes, *Imdad Mustad'afin* collects and distributes donations to its members, which in 2000 numbered at least 200 children. An interesting creative project of this division has been the establishment of the Islamic music

---

41   Azra (1995).
42   Rakhmat (1986:65-66).
43   Yayasan Muthahhari (1993:39).
44   Yayasan Muthahhari (1993:39-43).

group known as *Cinta Rasul*, 'Love of the Prophet'. Under the leadership of Abu Ali, who also heads the division of *Imdad Mustad'afin*, the group's 20 members have produced their own albums. With a variety of musical *salawat*, or invocations to the Prophet Muhammad as expressions of loving devotion, the group has performed in public, including in religious programmes broadcast on national television.[45]

Within the same category of *da'wa*, important contributions made by the Indonesian Shi'i women's institution, OASE (Organisation of *Ahlulbayt* for Social Support and Education) are worthy of mention. Aside from this organisation's involvement in religious education for the poor, by providing so-called '*kelas akhlaq*', 'classes in morality' in several schools in Jakarta, the institution has also awarded scholarships to the children of poor families. It has also provided other forms of training for the poor in Jakarta and other places, in West, Central and East Java. With its logo 'an eye and tear' OASE aims to assist the lower classes, regardless of their *madhhab*.[46]

Social *da'wa* is also undertaken today by the *Lembaga Dakwah Ukhuwah Al-Husainy* (Da'wa Institute of the Al-Husainy Brotherhood), an institution newly formed by the alumni of KKM (*Kuliah Kader Muballigh*, Course for Preacher Cadres). This new institution focuses on *da'wa* among the lower classes in urban and rural areas and provides not only religious instruction but also various programmes of social and economic aid. For example, through its monthly programme of *Jumpa Mustad'afin* (Meetings with the Oppressed) it has extended financial assistance to poor families in some slum areas in Jakarta, as well as giving religious instruction and guidance. This type of *da'wa* activity is intended to bring Shi'i *ustadhs* and activists closer to the community. It is also considered to be a manifestation of social responsibility and a way of solving the social and economic problems of the Muslim *umma*.[47]

The social *da'wa* activities described above are regularly undertaken by Shi'i institutions. However, there are others which are conducted alongside the organisation of important religious rituals and ceremonies, such as the annual *'Ashura* and *Mawlid*, through which the Shi'is demonstrate social responsibility towards the wider Indonesian community. The commemoration of *'Ashura* in Jakarta on 2 March 2004, for instance, incorporated the organisation of blood donation in co-operation with the Indonesian Red Cross. It was reported that some thousand people participated. OASE have also organised similar humanitarian activity under *da'wa*. In its brochure, this women's association urges Shi'is to side with the oppressed, particularly during *'Ashura*. It invites

---

45 *Syi'ar* (Ramadan 2004:52-53).
46 *Syi'ar* (October 2003:54-56).
47 *Suara Ummah* (4/1/2004:60-70).

participants on the occasion to 'implement their tears of *'Ashura* in an action to help the Oppressed who are suffering and dying'. Again, this activity is inspired by the struggle of Imam Husayn and his followers at Karbala.[48] Similarly, social work activities, including *khitanan massal* (mass circumcision) of poor children - appreciated in Indonesia - are carried out along with the *Mawlid* celebration of the Prophet Muhammad's birthday. It is no exaggeration to say that Shi'i institutions in Indonesia attempt to give a social significance to their religious rituals. Social *da'wa* is significant in relation to the socio-economic condition of the poor in Indonesian society, which is often lower than the minimum standard of living.

By and large, Shi'i social *da'wa* is directed towards all people, regardless of *madhhab*. Nevertheless, there is no doubt that it is hoped that the recipients of *da'wa* will be converted to Shi'ism. The minimum benefit gained through this type of *da'wa* is that the recipients will not discredit Shi'ism and Shi'is. Recognition of their contribution to the development of Indonesian society creates important symbolic capital. Equally, the close relationship between Shi'is and society can in turn become the social capital needed to maintain their existence. The sermons and writings of Jalaluddin Rakhmat promote the necessity of having good morality and conduct, for such virtues form the basis by which Shi'is may be judged. Simple adherence to a specific *madhhab* does not form any basis for judgement among Muslims.

From the three types of *da'wa* activities conducted by Shi'i institutions, the most popular and frequently observed type is *tabligh,* in the narrowest meaning of the term. Shi'i institutions and associations give special attention to producing *da'i* cadres through training, which will now be considered.

E. *Da'wa* Training

Although this study did not intend to examine the effectiveness of *da'wa* activity in promoting Shi'ism and in realising an Islamic society in Indonesia, we do suggest that the continued recognition of the Shi'is by the majority Sunni community is due in large part to *da'wa*. Shi'i institutions and organisations have made attempts to provide training for *da'i,* or cadres capable of carrying out appropriate and effective *da'wa* activities. Basing his analysis on Muslim theorists of *da'wa*, Poston names the training of evangelists as the third phase within the *da'wa* 'realm', coming after the phase of conversion and the phase of

---

48   *Suara Ummah* (4/1/2004/:70).

reinforcing Islam in individuals,[49] while in Nagata's observations, the training of new missionaries is included in all *ta'lim* activities.[50] The training of *da'i* cadres is central to the realisation of all *da'wa* goals.

At least three programmes of Shi'i *da'i* training have been conducted. The first was KKM (*Kuliah Kader Muballigh*, Courses for Preacher Cadres), organised by Forum *Al-Husainy*, a Jakarta-based forum of *ustadhs* and activists founded in 2003. Structured in eight sessions, KKM provided its participants (both Sunni and Shi'i) with training on various *da'wa* topics, including the Management and Methodology of *Da'wa*, *Da'wa* Strategy and Challenge, The Sufi Approach to *Da'wa*, Developing *Da'wa* Paradigm and Empowerment, Psychology, *Da'wa* and Communication, the Role of Preachers in Social Change in Indonesia and topics on Islamic doctrine, history, and current movements in Islam. On the surface, this curriculum does not appear to reflect a Shi'i character to the training, but all lectures were conducted by prominent Shi'i intellectuals and *ustadhs* such as Haidar Bagir, Umar Shahab, Husein Shahab, Othman Omar Shihab, Zen Al-Hadi, Abdurrahman Al-'Aydrus, Agus Abubakar, Muhsin Labieb, and Hasan Daliel. The participants were expected to follow not only theoretical and practical aspects of *da'wa* but also Islamic theology, history and the development of Muslim society. The programme emphasised the importance of Islamic brotherhood, especially between Sunni and Shi'i preachers. The training attracted great interest from *da'wa* activists and university students in Jakarta and the courses were oversubscribed.[51]

The KKM course did not provide either a specific strategy or a manual for missionary activists carrying out *da'wa* activity; however, the participants of KKM have since established the aforementioned *Lembaga Dakwah Ukhuwah*, which has implemented various types of *da'wa* activities and has been involved in social *da'wa*, *tabligh* and *ta'lim*.

The second training activity was organised by the *Muthahhari* Foundation. In fact, this foundation might have been the first Shi'i institution to pay significant attention to the training of *da'i*. Until 1993, the foundation conducted a series of four *Kuliah Muballighin* (Lectures for Preachers)[52] which were attended by numerous participants. The training curriculum included such topics as Principles of *Da'wa*, Rhetoric of *Da'wa*, the Psychology of *Da'wa*, Morality and *Da'wa* Strategy, Islam in Indonesia in a Historical Perspective, Development of Islamic Theological Schools, the Development of Islamic Jurisprudential Schools and a Sufi Approach to Islam. The course instructors were drawn from prominent religious teachers in Bandung including K.H. Muchtar Adam,

---

49 Poston (1992:132).
50 Nagata (1984:82).
51 *Suara Ummah* (1/1/2004:55-56).
52 *Al-Tanwir* (29/3/1993:8).

K.H. A.F. Ghazali,[53] Afif Muhammad,[54] K.H. Abdullah Gymnastiar,[55] Dedy Djamaluddin Malik,[56] Husein Shahab, Agus Effendi[57] and A. Hajar Sanusi.[58] Like KKM, *Kuliah Muballighin* was open to both Sunnis and Shi'is, with a view to promoting the recognition of Shi'ism among the Sunnis.

The third *da'i* training was organised by the national Shi'i organisation, IJABI. In terms of goal, subjects and methods, this training was totally different from those of the *Muthahhari* Foundation and *Al-Husainy*. It was confined to members and executives of IJABI. The elementary *Pengkaderan Muballigh* (Establishing Preacher Cadres) that was conducted over four days (24-27 December 2003) in Bandung warrants special attention here. With about 60 participants from all over Indonesia, from the central board as well as provincial and district branches of IJABI, this programme represented an important step in the development of the organisation. The activities were held in a hostel in Bandung, where all the participants were housed. The goal was to generate a cadre corps of IJABI who, with their knowledge and skill, would: one, be capable of defending the *madhhab* of *ahl al-bayt*; two, be capable of enlightening the Muslim *umma*, and three, be capable of defending Islam in relation to global political developments.

To achieve these goals the participants were instructed in the doctrine of Shi'ism, *'ulum al-Qur'an*, *'ulum al-Hadith*, rhetoric and techniques of argumentation. All the subjects were at an introductory level and presented in lectures. The lectures were given by Jalaluddin Rakhmat and each was followed by a discussion. The main messages of the lectures were as follows: first, that the participants should gain an understanding of the principal teachings of Shi'ism, based on the widespread Sunni material sources and methodology considered authoritative within the Sunni tradition. Second, the participants should apply critical analysis to these Sunni sources, with the purpose of defending and supporting the originality and validity of the Shi'i teachings. By critical study, they should be able to find weaknesses and inconsistencies in the Sunni teachings. Third, they should acquire skills in rhetoric and techniques of argumentation for the times when they discuss or enter into dialogue with Sunni figures. It was emphasised

---

53   K.H. Abdul Fatah Ghazali was a prominent learned man in Bandung and close friend of Jalaluddin Rakhmat. Rakhmat delivered special sermon at the Munawwarah Mosque in memoriam of this scholar, who passed away on 6 May 2001.

54   Dr. Afif Muhammad is a lecturer at Gunung Djati State Institute for Islamic Studies (now State Islamic University) in Bandung. He has written several articles and translated numerous books from Arabic.

55   K.H. Abdullah Gymnastiar, popularly known as Aa Gym, is a famous *da'i* in Indonesia today and the head of *Pesantren Daarut Tauhid* in Bandung.

56   Dedy Djamaluddin Malik is currently a member of parliament of PAN. He was an activist at and secretary of the *Muthahhari* Foundation and a former member of the executive board of IJABI. He completed his Masters in Communications at UNPAD with a thesis on the Islamic thought of Abdurrahman Wahid, Nurcholish Madjid, Amien Rais and Jalaluddin Rakhmat.

57   Agus Effendi is an alumnus of *Pesantren Gontor*. He is a former teacher and executive of the *Muthahhari* Foundation.

58   A. Hajar Sanusi was an activist and executive of the *Muthahhari* Foundation.

that the lack of accurate techniques of rhetoric and argumentation would not only contribute to the failure of achieving the goal of *da'wa,* but would also destroy the originality and holiness of Shi'i Islam. These introductory lectures were very significant in the *da'i* training programme.

In addition to the lectures, all participants were required to join an entire programme outlined by the committee. Included in the programme was a working group and library study, for which participants were divided into several groups. Each group was given a certain topic, including the sources of polemics between Sunnis and Shi'is. In the subject of doctrine, for instance, the topics included 'why do I choose Shi'ism (from both Shi'i and Sunni sources)', *tawhid* (the unity of God), al-Mahdi (the Guided One), *al-raj'a* (return), *al-bada'* (alteration in God's will), *tabarruk* (seeking blessings through persons or things) and *tawassul* (prayers through mediators). Each group studied the topic in the *Muthahhari* library, wrote a paper on it and presented it to the class. All the topics were then discussed and debated, and all the papers were digitalised and submitted to the committee.

The atmosphere of this activity was interesting to observe. In general, the training was academic and intellectual. It was free from indoctrination. It provided a space for open and liberal thought, and for discussion and debate. The participants were free to question and criticise aspects of Shi'i teachings. This atmosphere suggested that the organisers were prepared to defend the originality and validity of Shi'ism as a branch of Islam, based on both Sunni and Shi'i sources, and yet to engage in various forms of dialogue with their Sunni brothers.

Interestingly, there was a final examination for all the participants. However, participants' success in this *da'i* training schedule was based not on the examination results alone but also on the implementation of a *da'wa* programme upon their return home. They were obliged to formulate their own programme in the community where they lived, to implement it and to report back to the committee on its results.

The three *da'i* trainings are very important in the development of Shi'i *da'wa* in Indonesia, even though their impact on the realisation of goals of *da'wa* remains unknown. Not only have the three training courses provided important knowledge and skills for the participants, but they have also motivated and affirmed their missionary zeal. This in turn contributes to the strengthening of the position of the Shi'is and the image of their faith within the community. The aim of all the above activities is to achieve recognition from the Sunni majority.

This recognition is an evolving process that takes time, and the *da'wa* process continues. The organisation of *da'i* trainings reflects a strong missionary zeal among the organisers, the Shi'i *ustadhs*, intellectuals and institutions. In this regard, Shi'ism, as much as Sunnism, is a missionary brand of Islam.

5. Education

At a very fundamental level, the growth of Shi'ism in Indonesia can be attributed to the key role of Shi'i religious scholars, teachers and intellectuals who have established *yayasan,* or foundations and other bodies active in the fields of *da'wa*, education and socio-cultural programmes. While the previous chapter described the nature and characteristics of most of the Shi'i *da'wa* institutions, this chapter focuses on a relatively small number of entities established specifically to serve Shi'i educational aims. Education is generally understood to be the transfer of knowledge and values from one generation to another. In Indonesia, education can be divided into modern institutions of education, that is, the school system and traditional institutions of Islamic learning, commonly known as *pesantren*. In this chapter I will describe examples of both types of institutions established and run by prominent Indonesian Shi'i personalities.

A. Pesantren

Traditionally, the *pesantren* have become "the best means of creating unity of the *ahl al-sunna wa al-jama'a*"[1] in the hands of learned Sunni men in Indonesia. The same institutions have become vehicles to teach and propagate Shi'ism. There are at least five *pesantren* imparting Shi'i teachings to the Indonesian Muslim community: YAPI in Bangil, *Al-Hadi* in Pekalongan, *Dar al-Taqrib* in Bangsri Jepara, *Al-Mukarramah* in Bandung and *Nurul Tsaqalain* in Leihitu, Central Maluku. The two most famous of these, YAPI and *Al-Hadi* will be examined in the first section of this chapter. It is of interest to describe and analyse YAPI and to compare it with *Pesantren Al-Hadi*, as well as to examine both institutions from the perspective of the *pesantren* tradition. Elements of both of these institutions will be revealed, not only in terms of the general characteristics of the *pesantren* tradition, but also as characteristics unique to Shi'i institutions of learning in Indonesia. In turn this will shed light on the dynamics of institutions of Islamic learning in Indonesia as a whole.

YAPI, an abbreviation of *Yayasan Pesantren Islam,* and formally in Arabic, *Muassasat al-Ma'had al-Islami* is located in Bangil, a small town in the district of Pasuruan, East Java. Bangil's Muslims adhere to different denominations. Scholars of Islam in Indonesia are familiar with the strict reformist organisation, *Persis* (*Persatuan Islam,* Islamic Union) and with its chief figure, Ahmad Hasan, who spent most of his life in Bangil, even though the majority of the town's population follow the traditionalist Sunni *Nahdatul Ulama* (NU) or the

---

1 Dhofier (1999:173).

moderate modernist organisation *Muhammadiyah*. The existence YAPI, as a Shi'i institution of learning contributes to the religious complexity of Bangil. It was established in 1971 in Bondowoso, another district in East Java, by Husein Al-Habsyi (1921-1994), who also taught at and led a branch of the *Al-Khairiyya* school in the town. Five years later, on 18 June 1976, YAPI moved to its current location where it has grown and developed rapidly[2] to become an important centre of learning for the Shi'is in Indonesia, although its head and its teachers frequently publicly deny its association with Shi'ism.

Its name resembles the previously mentioned *Yayasan Penyiaran Islam* (Islamic Propagation Foundation) - also abbreviated as YAPI - which was established in Surabaya in 1961. Husein Al-Habsyi, one of the sponsors of YAPI in Bangil, says that the 'original' YAPI, which is devoted to organising social, religious and intellectual activities, inspired him to use the same abbreviation, even though the two institutions have different aims and focus. The Islamic Propagation Foundation moved to Lampung, in South Sumatra and then later to Jakarta, where its primary programme has been to publish translated and original Shi'i writings. Bangil's YAPI became Al-Habsyi's primary concern and was a serious attempt to realise his ideals in Islamic education and missionary activity. He believes that the only way that Islamic educational concepts will be implemented is through *pesantren* like YAPI, in which students can be educated in Islamic teachings, practice them in their daily life and be free from the influences of Westernisation.[3]

Thanks to Al-Habsyi's efforts, experience and considerable social capital (refer to Chapter Two) YAPI has become the most important teaching centre for Shi'is in Indonesia. Al-Habsyi used his Middle Eastern connections to raise financial assistance. Endowed with a sum of money and a plot of land in Bangil, Husein Al-Habsyi was able to construct a relatively large building, which served as both a dormitory and a classroom. With this first adequate facility, YAPI of Bangil housed students from all over Indonesia and provided them with a good quality of Islamic education. Al-Habsyi also maintained contact with eminent *kyai* inside the country in order to garner moral support for his project; for instance, a well-known learned man from Langitan entrusted several of his disciples to assist with the teaching in the *pesantren*.

As a scholar himself, with a comprehensive grasp of various branches of Islamic knowledge, Husein Al-Habsyi was well qualified to formulate the educational programme of his institution. The approaches and principles in YAPI follow the Egyptian *Ikhwan al-Muslimin* model, which emphasises strict discipline and a strongly anti-Western attitude. This Al-Habsyi considered to be the best model

---

2   Bukhori (n.d:17).
3   Zamzami (n.d:102-103).

for achieving his educational ideals. He agreed that an Islamic institution of learning should be free from Western worldviews and secularism. All students are required to obey the rules of the institution as outlined by its head. As the leader responsible for its development and progress, Al-Habsyi not only managed the institution but also taught in several fields of Islamic knowledge, including Arabic, *tafsir* (Qur'anic exegesis) and *usul al-fiqh* (principles of jurisprudence). In addition, he took on the specific role of forming cadres and consciousness among his students in order to revive their spirit for the struggle for Islam and the Muslim Community.[4] Today, YAPI and its founder are well known among the learned, of not only Indonesia but also in the Middle East.

Husein Al-Habsyi's struggle in religious education was relatively successful, as is evidenced by the fact that a number of YAPI alumni were able to pursue their education in countries such as India, Pakistan, Egypt, Saudi Arabia, Syria and Qatar.[5] After the Iranian revolution, many pursued their religious learning in Qum, Iran, possible due to their high levels of competence in Arabic and Islamic knowledge, as well as to the fact that Iranian scholars were willing to accept students recommended by Al-Habsyi. After several years of study in Qum they went on to become teachers in Islamic schools and foundations in various parts of Indonesia, some even returning to teach in YAPI itself.

YAPI aims to produce students who are capable of becoming pioneering human resources, able to face with wisdom a variety of challenges and problems arising in Indonesia.[6] With this goal in mind, the institution organises its programmes, formulates appropriate curriculum contents, provides the necessary facilities and equipment and implements various teaching strategies, methods and techniques.[7] Today, YAPI has three separate complexes. The biggest is for male students and is situated in the village of Kenep, Beji Sub-District, about three kilometres South of Bangil. The second centre is for female students and is located in Jl. Lumba-lumba, Kersikan, close to the town centre of Bangil. (Like the majority of pesantren in Java, YAPI separates its male and female students.) The third complex, also on the Jl. Lumba-lumba site, is the *Al-Abrar* kindergarten. Each complex has its own facilities, such as a *pondok*, or hostel, a mosque or place for prayer, classrooms, library, laboratories and sports centre. With their own facilities, the three centres can organise educational programmes to meet their specific goals.

YAPI attempts "to participate in producing intelligent persons, having a correct and firm faith, a wise and critical attitude in order to face a future full of

---

4   Panitia (n.d:2).
5   Muhsin Husein (1997:5).
6   *Al-Isyraq* (1/1/1417).
7   *Al-Isyraq* (1/1/1417).

challenge."[8] It shares the same basic elements as other *pesantren*: *pondok*, mosque, *santris* (student body), instruction in Islamic texts and a *kyai*, or leader).[9] The *pondok*, where students live together, protects them from unwanted external influences. Both the Kenep and Jl. Lumba-lumba complexes have a *pondok* with adequate rooms and facilities in which all the students, with the exception of those at the kindergarten, are expected to live. In the academic year 2002/2003 there were about 300 students.[10] The *santri* at YAPI come from all over the country: from Java, Sumatra, Kalimantan and Sulawesi to Nusa Tenggara and Maluku, reflecting the diverse ethnic groups of Indonesian society.[11] However, in my personal observation, the majority of students at YAPI are Indonesian Arabs and most students and teachers wear a white *jubah* (Arab robe). In line with the principles outlined by its founder, all students at YAPI are obliged to obey strict rules and regulations; for instance, students may not leave the *pesantren* complex without permission; all electronic and printed media deemed to be pornographic are forbidden; students may not watch Western films or listen to Western songs and they are not allowed to smoke. These rules are believed to keep the students focused on their study and protected from the harmful influences of Western culture.[12]

YAPI has a large mosque in its male complex and a prayer room, called a *musalla*, in its female complex. As integral elements of the institution, these two sites function as centres for training students in such things as the practice of daily prayers, recitation of the Qur'an, recitation of the *ratib*,[13] *tawassul, kumayl* and other prayers and also for public preaching. The mosque serves a number of other functions: first, it is a place for the performance of the obligatory daily prayers - communal as well as individual - for the students, teachers and staff of the *pesantren* and for Friday prayers for the *pesantren* and the wider community. Second, it is a centre for the conducting of recommended rituals, such as the recitation of the Qur'an, *ratib, tawassul*, and other prayers. Third, it is a place for the students to join in extra-curriculum programmes, such as public preaching and *qasidah*, which are Arabic songs performed by female singers. Fourth, it is the centre for the practice of rituals and ceremonies relating to Muslim holy days, such as the birthday of the Prophet, of Fatima, his daughter and of the twelve Imams, 'Ashura and others, including the *Haul*, or the commemoration of the death of the *pesantren's* founder, Husein Al-Habsyi. In another ritual

---

8   Pamphlet (2002/2003).

9   Dhofier (1999:25).

10   Dhofier mentions two types of students in the *pesantren* tradition: the *santri mukim*, who live in the dormitory complex and the *santri kalong*, non-resident students coming from the surrounding villages (1999:31).

11   *Dialog Jumat* (28/5/2004).

12   Zamzami (n.d: 112-113).

13   *Ratib* covers certain formulae of *dhikr* (remembrance) and prayers composed by Sufi teachers. YAPI, since many teachers and students are Indonesian Arabs, practices that formulated by a famous Hadrami Sufi, Abdullah al-Haddad, commonly called *Ratib Haddad*.

related to the late Al-Habsyi, the students are urged to perform *ziyara,* the act of visitation to his grave after the dawn prayers on Fridays. The grave itself is located behind the mosque. Thus, with the exception of those secular and religious lessons conducted in the classroom, all other educational and religious activities of the institution are centred in the mosque, which is called *Ats-Tsaqolain* (*al-Thaqalayn*). These activities are very important for the students of the *pesantren* in terms of their becoming accustomed to Islamic practice and developing a religious spirit to accompany their mastery of various branches of Islamic knowledge.[14]

In relation to the position of the learned men and the leadership of the *pesantren*, there has been a transformation at YAPI from a charismatic to a rationalistic leadership. As stated, YAPI originally came under the authority of Husein Al-Habsyi, who as its scholar, founder and leader was the central element of the *pesantren* and directly responsible for its development. Today, there is no single person able to match Al-Habsyi's qualifications and charisma or to take over his position. While his third son, Ali Ridho Al-Habsyi, was formally appointed leader of YAPI, its programmes and the Islamic foundation supporting it are governed by a formal organisational structure, comprising a chief, a secretary and a treasurer. The organisation is split into several divisions, including education and *da'wa*, which are responsible for the three educational centres at YAPI. Such is the rationalistic leadership of YAPI.

The chief figures at present responsible for the development of the educational programmes in particular, and the foundation in general are - aside from the aforementioned Ali Ridho Al-Habsyi - Muhammad bin Alwi BSA, Ali Umar Al-Habsyi and Muhammad Alwi Al-Habsyi, all of whom are YAPI alumni and students of Husein Al-Habsyi. A number of other Qum alumni also have important teaching roles at the institution.

In the past, the most important figure at YAPI, following the death of Husein Al-Habsyi, was Zahir Yahya, Al-Habsyi's student, son-in-law and Qum alumnus. However, a conflict, most probably originating from struggles over the accumulation of symbolic and economic capital among certain individuals of Husein Al-Habsyi's clan, led Zahir Yahya and his party to leave the *pesantren*. At one point, Iran became involved in the conflict and was said to have sided with Zahir Yahya. Subsequently, the institution's current leadership visited Iran for clarification of their position. Today, it is the abovementioned figures who collectively attempt to maintain the continuity of Islamic learning in the institution and to implement strategies to preserve its existence and to continue its development.

---

14   Zamzami (n.d: 112).

Examined from the perspective of its current educational system, YAPI is a modern institution. Until 1997, it only organised programmes of religious education at the levels of *i'dadiyya* (preparatory), *ibtida'iyya* (elementary), *thanawiyya* (secondary, corresponding to Islamic Junior High School) and *'aliyya* (secondary, corresponding to Islamic Senior High School). The curriculum of the first three levels gives priority to the study of Arabic, including *nahwu* (syntax) and *saraf* (morphology) and to several branches of Islamic knowledge such as *Hadith, tafsir, fiqh* (jurisprudence), *'aqida* (doctrine) and logic. At the *'aliyya* level, the students are introduced to branches of Islamic knowledge from comparative perspectives, such as *kalam* (theology), philosophy, *'ulum al-Qur'an* (the Qur'anic sciences), *usul al-fiqh* (principles of jurisprudence) and comparative Islamic jurisprudence. Additionally, at this level there are lessons in translation and *tahqiq* (editing) instructing students on how to read, translate and edit Arabic materials.[15]

Since 1997, YAPI has transformed its educational programme by incorporating both the national curriculum and traditional religious education, "so as to provide the best solution in the field of education sought by the people of high spirituality and intellectuality."[16] This transformation has involved the integration of religious education at the *ibtidaiyya* and *thanawiyya* levels into the programme of Indonesian Junior High School (SLTP) and Senior High School (SMU). The *'aliyya* level was converted into a special programme for religious education called *takhassus* (specialisation) and was structurally separated from both schools.[17] Following these changes, YAPI now offers a general school, a religious school and *takhassus*. With regard to the first system, YAPI offers a programme of secondary education, providing SLTP (Junior High School) and SMU (Senior High School), both of which teach general secular subjects of the curriculum regulated by the Department of National Education. In order to be formally recognised by the Department, the institution must follow specific guidelines and meet required standards. YAPI also offers a programme combining the national system with its *pesantren* system in the form of a religious school, the curriculum for which comprises 60% general subjects and 40% religious subjects. Now, graduates of YAPI are expected to possess both basic general and religious knowledge and to be capable of successfully pursuing tertiary education at general secular or religious universities. Like the schools belonging to the *Muthahhari* Foundation in Bandung (to be described below) YAPI adds the title 'Plus' to both its SLTP and SMU programmes.

YAPI's religious education programme, also termed the 'mixed' programme, is compulsory for students at both the secondary levels. It consists of three

---

15 *Al-Isyraq* (1/1/1417).
16 *Pamphlet* (2002/2003).
17 *Al-Isyraq* (7/2/1418:42).

stages. The first is known as the *mutawassit* (intermediate) level and is offered to graduates of primary education who, on the whole, do not yet possess the basics of religious knowledge and Arabic language. The programme begins from the first to the sixth semester during the Junior High School period and students are taught the basics of religious knowledge, as well as skills in reading, speaking, listening and writing in Arabic. Arabic is also the language of instruction for the third-year students. As well, the programme provides first year students with courses in Qur'anic recitation, *tajwid* (science of the pronunciation of the Qur'an) and the memorisation of certain chapters of the Qur'an. The primary textbooks for Arabic language instruction are *Al-'Arabiyya li al-Nashi'in* (6 Volumes) and *Al-Amthilah al-Tasrifiyya* on Arabic morphology by Maksum Ali.[18] These resources illustrate YAPI's focus on the students' comprehension of Arabic and its importance for Muslims because — as stated in an institute pamphlet for the admission of new students - about 90% of religious and intellectual sources for Islamic teachings are written in Arabic. It is interesting to note that *Al-'Arabiyya li al-Nasi'in* has recently begun to be used to teach Arabic to the students at the State Institute for Islamic Studies (IAIN) and the State College for Islamic Studies (STAIN).

Students of YAPI's Senior High School also receive religious instruction, thus combining both general and religious components to form a single system of education. Those who finish the intermediate level of religious education go on to the *thanawiyya* level, which provides a much deeper and more extensive programme of religious knowledge and Arabic. Having followed both general (SMU) and religious education (*thanawiyya*) the students are considered to have received the skills to be well-rounded members of society, regardless of whether they go on to pursue tertiary education or not.

The religious curriculum comprises five subjects: Arabic, the Qur'an or specific chapters of the Qur'an, *tatbiq* (reading Arabic texts without diacritical signs), *'aqida* and *fiqh*. Here the primary source for Arabic instruction is *Durus fi al-'Arabiyya* (Lessons in Arabic) and is the next step up from *Al-'Arabiyya li al-Nashi'in*. The main sources for *'aqida* and *fiqh* are those by prominent Shi'i scholars and legists, including Ayatollah Nasir Makarim Shirazi's *'Aqa'id wa Mazahib* and Ayatollah Ruhullah Khomeini's *Zubdat al-Ahkam* respectively.[19] This training gives the students the ability to disseminate this knowledge to their own communities; furthermore, they are prepared to continue their religious learning at higher institutions in the Middle East.

In addition to these two programmes, YAPI offers one that is called *tamhidiyya* (preparatory), designed for students of SMU who have graduated from other

---

18 *Sekilas* (n.d:6-7).
19 *Sekilas* (n.d:7).

SLTPs with a basic religious knowledge. Its curriculum is similar to that of the *thanawiyya* level, with the exception that the main source for the instruction of Arabic is *Al-'Arabiyya li al-Nashi'in*. The goals of this programme are generally the same as those mentioned above. Because *tamhidiyya* students generally join the programme without a prior knowledge of Arabic, twelve out of eighteen hours a week are set aside for practice in spoken Arabic, plus four hours for syntax and morphology.[20]

A unique characteristic of the educational system at YAPI also lies in its exclusively religious programme, the *takhassus*, or specialisation in Islamic knowledge, which is offered to male students intending to concentrate on this field. Since the programme covers only Islamic subjects, to a large extent it resembles the *pesantren salafi* within the *pesantren* tradition.[21] *Takhassus* aims at producing students fully capable of developing Islamic views using comparative and critical methods.[22] The programme, which is organised in three levels, can be considered to be a continuation of the above-mentioned *thanawiyya* programme and many graduates of the *thanawiyya* programme do in fact enrol in the *takhassus* programme. The institution also provides an *i'dadiyya* (preparatory) programme for students who have not come via the *thanawiyya* programme, or for those who lack the necessary knowledge required for undertaking the *takhassus* level. The preparatory programme usually takes four semesters and emphasises proficiency in Arabic language and introductory Islamic doctrine and jurisprudence.[23] In the academic year 2002/2003, 23 students were enrolled in YAPI's *takhassus* programme.

The curriculum of the *takhassus* programme includes nearly all of the subjects from the body of Islamic knowledge, namely Arabic, *tafsir*, *kalam*, *fiqh*, *usul al-fiqh*, Arabic syntax, *balagha* (rhetoric), *Sira* (biographies of the Prophet and his household), *mantiq* (logic) and Islamic philosophy. It differs from Sunni institutions of learning in Indonesia in that not only does YAPI provide instruction in Islamic philosophy, but it also offers an intensive study of general philosophy. Two scientific activities organised at YAPI illustrate the importance given to the study of philosophy and logic at the institution: first, the establishment of the Study Group for the Study of Religion and Philosophy (KSAF) and second, a large number of articles on philosophical topics are published in the journals of YAPI, including the now defunct *Al-Isyraq* (9 numbers, (1417-1418/1997-1998) and *Islamuna* (1424/2003-the present). This is in stark contrast to scholarly findings on the books used in *pesantren* milieus in Indonesia during the 19th and 20th centuries conducted by van den Berg (1888) and van Bruinessen (1990),

---

20 *Sekilas* (n.d:7-8), Ali Umar Al-Habsyi, interview, (5/10/2002).
21 Dhofier (1999:22).
22 *Pamphlet* (2002/2003).
23 *Sekilas* (n.d:8).

which report an absence of the subject. The factors for this are historical: for centuries Sunni learned men and institutions of learning forbade the instruction of philosophy, possibly in consequence of the great influence of al-Ghazali's Sufi teachings in the Sunni world. This prohibition of the study of logic and philosophy in the traditions of Islamic learning in most Muslim countries has been criticised by scholars such as Abu Ali (a pseudonym), who suggests that institutions of Islamic learning should in fact emphasise the instruction of both these sciences. Ali believes they are essential in order for students to be able to discuss, analyse and study Islamic teachings correctly.[24]

Another special characteristic of the *takhassus* programme can be seen in the primary sources used for instruction. While, like the majority of *pesantren* in Java, the *takhassus* programme uses the authoritative texts, Muhammad bin Malik's *Alfiya* on Arabic syntax and *Al-Balagha al-Wadiha* on rhetoric, other teaching resources include books written by prominent Shi'i learned men from Iran or Iraq. Examples are Ayatollah Muhammad Taqi Misbah Yazdi's *Al-'Aqida al-Islamiyya* (3 Volumes) for the study of doctrine, Muhammad Javad Mughniyya's *Al-Fiqh 'ala al-Mazahib al-Khamsa* for the comparative study of Islamic law, Muhammad Baqir Sadr's *Al-Halaqat al-Thalath* for principles of jurisprudence, Ayatollah Rida Muzaffar's *'Ilm al-Mantiq* for logic and Muhammad Husayn Tabataba'i's *Bidayat al-Hikma* for the study of Islamic philosophy.[25] The Shi'i character of the programme is clear and is in striking contrast to the majority of *pesantren* in Indonesia.

As a *pesantren* offering an integrated system of education, YAPI maintains an extra programme to supplement the intra-curricular programme in Arabic and religious subjects and the educational system of the institution at large. Given the fact that all of the teaching texts in the religious subjects are in Arabic, it is imperative that students possess these language skills. Besides formal instruction in the classroom - developing vocabulary, writing essays, speaking in formal activities and in daily life, mastering syntax and morphology - other learning techniques are used. Islamic and Arabic films or other such materials are also presented. Each semester, extra-curricular courses are provided in religious subjects such as *fiqh*, *'aqida*, *akhlaq* (ethics) and *sira* for the students of *mutawassit*, *thanawiyya* and *tamhidiyya,* and in logic, *usul al-fiqh*, and *'ulum al-Qur'an* for the students of *thanawiyya* and *tamhidiyya*. In addition, there is an optional programme for those students wanting to deepen their knowledge of Shi'ism. Other important extra-curricular programmes offered are various kinds of arts, sports and other skills; e.g. the use of computers, English language and journalism. These are provided for the male and female students in segregated groups.

---

24 Abu Ali (1417:18).
25 *Sekilas* (n.d:8).

Thus YAPI is a modern institution of Islamic learning, integrating the general schooling of national education, the classical religious *madrasa* system, elements of *pesantren salafi* in its use of standard texts for Arabic syntax and morphology and the *takhassus* programme. Not to be forgotten is the strong element of Shi'ism in the curriculum and instructional materials, and in the religious rituals and ceremonies conducted at the institution. And like most modern *pesantren*, YAPI requires that all students and teachers use Arabic in their daily life; the mastery of Arabic has been a continuing priority since its foundation.

With regard to its Shi'i orientation, as previously mentioned, the leaders and teachers at YAPI are reluctant to publicly name it a Shi'i institution (in contrast to the view of scholars, such as Zainuddin et al., who wrote: "in Bangil (East Java) *Yayasan Pesantren Islam* (YAPI) was established and openly displays the Shi'i banner".[26] The current leadership's rejection of the Shi'i label is not entirely without justification, since admission to YAPI is not confined to Shi'i students but is open to all Muslims, regardless of denomination. There is also no obligation for students to adhere to the Shi'i school of thought. As its curriculum demonstrates, certain programmes teach comparative theology and jurisprudence with the specific aim of fostering a tolerant attitude in the students. The ideals of openness and freedom within Islam, as promoted by Husein Al-Habsyi, are the foundation of the *pesantren:*

> What forms the basis of all activities and programmes of the Foundation is a reflection of Al-Ustadh Husein Al-Habsyi's open-mindedness and universal worldview, seeing the world of Islam as a (single) system and every Muslim from any religious orientation as a part of the body of Islam. Therefore, YAPI is always proud of its openness and integrates all streams and Islamic organisations.[27]

YAPI's strategy of openness and pluralism can be seen as a reaction to the schism in Islam between the Sunni majority and the Shi'i minority.[28] The same divide is, of course, reflected within Indonesia's Muslim population. For YAPI, openness and pluralism should be encouraged, not only as true teachings of Islam but also to protect the existence of the educational institution and of the Shi'is themselves. There are two benefits to be gained by promoting these ideals: the recognition of Shi'ism as a valid branch of Islamic orthodoxy and a tolerant attitude toward the Shi'is in a framework of Islamic unity. YAPI's stance may also be seen as the strategy of practicing *taqiyya*, a valid teaching in Shi'ism.

Valuable comparisons and contrasts can be made between the educational system of YAPI and that of *Pesantren Al-Hadi*. This latter institution, located in

---

26   Zainuddin et al. (2000:33).
27   *Al-Isyraq* (1/1/1417).
28   Zamzami (n.d:113).

Pekalongan, Central Java, was founded in 1989 by Ahmad Baragbah, who had spent five years studying in Qum. Baragbah, an Indonesian Arab of non-*Sayyid* extraction forged good connections with the late Husein Al-Habsyi, who had recommended him for his study in Qum and supported him in the establishment of his *pesantren*. Although Baraghbah had never studied at YAPI, his relationship with Husein Al-Habsyi is considered to have been one of student and teacher. Both were supportive of each other's institution, especially when faced with internal or external problems.

Al-Hadi is smaller than YAPI in terms of students and teacher numbers, educational facilities and educational programmes. In October 2002, for instance, Al-Hadi had approximately 70 students (male and female) trained and educated by six teachers, all Qum alumni. (This is smaller than a report by *Ulumul Qur'an* in 1995, which gave the number of students as about 112 and teachers as nine).[29] Unlike YAPI, which is open to all comers, *Al-Hadi* tends to attract students only from the Shi'i community. The students live in a hostel on the *pesantren* complex. The complex itself, situated in the residential part of the densely populated city, comprises two houses and two two-storeyed buildings. One large house is for all the activities of the female students – the hostel as well as classrooms - while the second smaller house accommodates Ahmad Baragbah and his family. The first building houses a mosque on the ground floor, while the first floor contains an office and a hostel for teachers and classrooms and a hostel for male students. Unlike YAPI or most other schools in the country, *Al-Hadi* students study sitting on the floor. In short, compared to the educational facilities of YAPI, those of *Al-Hadi* are limited.

Yet this relatively small Shi'i institution has all the basic elements of the *pesantren* tradition: *pondok*, mosque, a student body of *santri*, the instruction of Islamic texts and a *kyai*. Students are drawn from all over Indonesia, including Java, Sumatra, Kalimantan and Sulawesi. They live in the *pondok* and follow all the activities of the institution. Since there is no entry examination, some of the students arrive not having completed their primary education. They can attend a primary school located next to the *pesantren* every morning if necessary, but this is optional. Compared to YAPI, the rules and regulations of this institution are more lenient.

Al-Hadi's small mosque is multi-functional, even though its use is confined to the students and teachers of the *pesantren*. With the exception of the Friday afternoon prayers – which students have the choice of attending at other mosques outside the *pesantren* – the mosque is the hub of education and training activities and for the conducting of obligatory and recommended religious rituals and ceremonies. However, the rituals and ceremonies are limited to those

---

29   Nurjulianti and Subhan (1995:24).

recommended within the Shi'i tradition, unlike YAPI which still carries out the *ratib* recitation, a practice from Sufi traditions. Indeed, the *Al-Hadi* mosque provides a model for the practice of Shi'i teachings, as understood by its leaders and teachers. It is for this reason that parents choose to send their children to this institution. I even heard reports that a few had moved their children from YAPI to *Al-Hadi* because of its direct focus on the instruction and application of Shi'i teachings.

Unlike YAPI, *Al-Hadi* only provides students with a religious education which, to a great extent, follows the educational system of the *hawza 'ilmiyya* in Qum, where its founders and teachers have been trained. This is particularly true in terms of subjects and instructional materials. The educational programme is organised into six stages. The subjects offered are similar to those of the religious education programme at YAPI and include Arabic, *'aqida, fiqh, tafsir, hadith* and Islamic history. All instructional materials are the standard books used in the institutions of Islamic learning in Qum. The basic tenets of Shi'ism, specifically *'aqida* and *fiqh*, are taught at the first stage and the students are expected to follow them in daily life. Guidance and training are provided regarding the Shi'i daily obligatory rituals and ceremonies of the *pesantren*. All instruction, training and guidance given in *Al-Hadi* are directed towards the institution's main goal, which is to provide its students with the basic knowledge and skills to become Shi'i teachers in Indonesia. Furthermore, with the knowledge its graduates possess, they are able to pursue higher Islamic education in Qum itself.

Pesantren Al-Hadi and its head, Ahmad Baragbah, as he himself has admitted, have connections with Iran via the office of *wilayat al-faqih* and a number of individual learned men. The *pesantren* is said to send regular reports of its educational progress to Iran via a representative. Today, the Islamic Cultural Centre of Jakarta also observes the *pesantren's* development, including the curriculum and the activities of students and teachers, in order to ensure progress. Important events occurring in the *pesantren* are all reported to the office of *wilayat al-faqih* in Qum.[30] The *pesantren* also receives financial assistance from Iran, as well as educational aids, particularly books and periodicals.[31] The relationship with Iran is also indicated by the fact that a number of *Al-Hadi* graduates continue their Islamic education in Qum. Some have finished their study and returned to Indonesia: Muhammad in Purwakarta, Ali Al-'Aydrus in Bandung and Salman Daruddin in Jakarta, to name but a few. In addition, representatives of the Supreme Iranian Leader (*wali faqih*) and individual Shi'i scholars frequently take the opportunity to visit the *pesantren* during trips to Indonesia. At the same time, Ahmad Baragbah, with his experience in Qum, has

---

30   Ahmad Baragbah, interview, (21/10/2002).
31   *Tiras* (3/2/1996:29).

been recognised by Iran as an important Shi'i figure in Indonesia and is expected to play a major role in the spread of Shi'ism. Along with other prominent figures such as Jalaluddin Rakhmat and Zahir Yahya, he is an appointed representative of the *wali faqih* in the collection and distribution of the one-fifth tax, *khums,* in Indonesia and together with Umar Shahab, this group were also expected to prepare for the establishment of Shi'i organisations in Indonesia.[32]

The strategies implemented by *Al-Hadi* in the promotion of Shi'ism reveal striking contrasts to those of YAPI. The founder of *Al-Hadi* openly admits that his institution is Shi'i.[33] Its establishment was motivated by "Ahmad Baragbah's anxiety over the emergence of misconceptions in the Muslim community in Indonesia about the Shi'i school – especially after the outbreak of the Iranian Islamic revolution."[34] Baragbah maintains that the institution is not intended to create religious conflict in multi-religious Indonesia, instead, its purpose is to invite fellow Muslims to recognise the existence of Shi'ism as an equal religious stream within Islam.[35] The hope is that by openly expressing all Shi'i doctrinal beliefs and observing Shi'i religious practices in all situations, including those aspects different from Sunni Islam, they and the Shi'i community will be recognised. Consequently, all anti-Shi'i bias and libel will disappear, the goal shared by YAPI and *Al-Hadi.*

Although reactions to its chosen strategy of openness are very negative – as will be discussed in Chapter Eight - *Al-Hadi* continues to maintain this course in its struggle for recognition. The *habitus*[36] of Ahmad Baragbah as a graduate of Qum is integral to the exercise. It seems that this *habitus* was acquired during the 1980s, when he was young and full of missionary zeal. Jalaluddin Rakhmat has described Ahmad Baragbah and other *ustadh* of the Qum alumni as young graduates strong in spirit, determined to save the world by applying a *fiqh*-oriented approach, and according to Rakhmat, their orientation in *fiqh* is exactly what the Shi'is in Indonesia need.[37] To put it more accurately, returning with the knowledge and experience gained at the heart of Shi'i learning, they attempted to provide an exemplary model for the total practice of Shi'i teachings. Baragbah once stated that, in general, his fellow Shi'is had not yet fully implemented Islamic doctrines in real life[38] and thus there had been no attempt by the existing Shi'i figures to outwardly express the Shi'i teachings in all their forms.

---

32   Ahmad Baragbah, interview, (21/10/2002).
33   *Tiras* (3/2/1996:29).
34   Nurjulianti and Subhan (1995:29).
35   Nurjulianti and Subhan (1995:24).
36   See for the notion of *habitus* Chapter Two, n. 54.
37   Rakhmat (1997:446-447).
38   Statement made in Baragbah's speech to the *Al-Jawad* Foundation in Bandung, later published in *Buletin Al-Jawad*. The article is entitled "Menanamkan Sikap Persaudaraan Kaum Muslim (To plant the spirit of brotherhood among Muslims)" (http://aljawad.tripod.com/arsipbuletin/muslim.htm).

Unlike Husein Al-Habsyi, who had already occupied a position of learned man in the wider Muslim community, as a young graduate in religious education, Ahmad Baragbah was still in the process of building up his status. In Bourdieu's terms, he did this by implementing strategies to accumulate symbolic capital that could easily be converted into economic capital. In doing so, he used very different strategies from those of Husein Al-Habsyi, who needed only to maintain the various kinds of capital he had already gained. Even though the two men shared the same goal – to bring about the recognition of Shi'ism and the Shi'i community in the Sunni-dominated country - Ahmad Baragbah is clearly still struggling to accumulate the same kind of capital as Al-Habsyi.

B. Schools

Alongside Shi'i foundations such as YAPI and *Al-Hadi* with their *pesantren*, there are others that have set up school programmes. The first and most famous is the *Muthahhari* Foundation, founded on 3 October 1988 in Bandung by Muslim intellectuals. According to the legal founding document, the first executive board included Jalaluddin Rakhmat (Head), Agus Effendi (Vice Head), Haidar Bagir (Secretary) and Ahmad Muhajir (Treasurer). As with YAPI, the *Muthahhari* founders, and in particular Jalaluddin Rakhmat, frequently rejected the notion that the institution was Shi'i; however, it is still considered to be an important centre for the spread of Shi'ism in Indonesia. An historical account tells that the foundation was born of the good relationship between Rakhmat and Husein Al-Habsyi, who also provided financial capital to the institution.[39] It is not by accident therefore that both Husein Al-Habsyi and Jalaluddin Rakhmat shared similar strategies in their promotion of Shi'ism.

The *Muthahhari* Foundation, with its slogan "for the enlightenment of Islamic thought" was established to organise programmes in the fields of research, education and information to Indonesian society at large. Its brochure[40] states that the general goals are to develop Islamic thought, to formulate an Islamic world-view, to participate in the fields of education and *da'wa* and to contribute to the promotion of Islamic unity, just as all of these were demonstrated in the life of the Iranian intellectual and activist, Murtada Mutahhari.[41] The *Muthahhari* Foundation has organised programmes which are classified into three categories: a specific programme promoting critical studies and the advancement of

---

39   Wisananingrum (2001:81-82).
40   Yayasan Muthahhari (1993:20).
41   For information on the ideals of the Muthahhari Foundation and a brief biography of Murtada Muthahhari, see Chapter Two, pp.126-127.

Muthahhari's thought; a general programme comprising all efforts to develop Islamic thought and education and an additional programme which serves as a link between the foundation and the community at large.[42]

In order to implement its educational programmes, the foundation established the *Lembaga Pembinaan Ilmu-Ilmu Islam* (Institute for the Establishment of Islamic Knowledge), abbreviated as LPII and headed by Jalaluddin Rakhmat. As a division within the structure of the foundation, LPII runs a number of programmes with the purpose of overcoming the dichotomy between religious scholars, the *'ulama* and the intellectuals (as discussed in Chapter One). Besides providing the opportunity for intellectuals to study fields of Islamic knowledge and for *'ulama* to acquaint themselves with the secular sciences and modern information, the institute provides a forum in which *'ulama* and intellectuals can collectively find solutions to problems in Muslim society. LPII sees its role as advancing a modern curriculum of Islamic knowledge in accordance with the current needs of Muslim society.[43]

In the beginning, LPII organised courses on both Islamic and secular sciences for university students in the form of a *Pesantren Mahasiswa*. The university *santri* were divided into two groups, regular and non-regular. Regular students joined a two-year programme. Like the *santri mukim* of the classical *pesantren* tradition, the regular *santri* were university students or graduates of non-Islamic universities and were treated as having no prior Islamic knowledge. The curriculum included Arabic, *tafsir*, Hadith, Islamic history, ethics, comparative Islamic jurisprudence, Islamic philosophy and Western philosophy. Resembling the *santrikalong* of the *pesantren* tradition, the non-regular *santri* only enrolled in a specific lecture series held on a certain day or week. They were offered courses in the Islamic and secular sciences, from which they chose their subjects according to their interest. Diverse subjects were offered, including, in the field of Islamic knowledge: Arabic, *'ulum al-Qur'an*, *'ulum al-Hadith*, Islamic history, *usul al-fiqh*, *'ilm al-Qira'at* (Qur'anic recitation), Sufism, theology and Islamic philosophy. The secular science course included logic, Western philosophy, journalism, research methodology, management and organisation, entrepreneurship and communication technology.[44] During a sermon delivered at *Darut Tauhid* (an institution founded and headed by Abdullah Gymnastiar) in September 1992, Jalaluddin Rakhmat said that his *pesantren* was established in order to provide traditional Islamic knowledge to the educated who attended campuses within a Western system of education, such as students of ITB, UNPAD and IKIP. At the same time, he was teaching the *santri* of traditional

---

42 Yayasan Muthahhari (1993:21-22).
43 Yayasan Muthahhari (1993:23-24).
44 Yayasan Muthahhari (1993:24-27), *Kompas* (29/3/1992), *Editor* (49/4/1991).

pesantren certain modern sciences. He then stated: "Overall, we would like to become a bridge for intellectual and *pesantren* groups, as well as to develop a non-sectarian attitude."[45]

However, the *pesantren* programme for the regular *santri* did not run as well as was expected. According to an internal report, it only managed to recruit 30 students and was maintained for less than a year.[46] In contrast, the series of courses for the non-regular students, with its diverse curriculum, was more successful and continued to develop. Forced to re-assess their plans, in 1992 Jalaluddin Rakhmat and his associates established a new school, which has since become the main project of the *Muthahhari* Foundation. This school, SMU Plus (Senior High School Plus) is now one of the most desired in Bandung, if not in all of Indonesia. As we saw above, the attribute 'Plus' is used because the programme combines a number of subjects from the national curriculum with Islamic instruction and a focus on fostering good moral conduct.[47] The school has attracted an enthusiastic response from people throughout Indonesia, and parents - both Sunni and Shi'i - from Java, Sumatra, Kalimantan and other islands send their children to study there. While the *Muthahhari* Foundation provides accommodation for first year students from outside Bandung who need it, unlike the traditional *pesantren* system, SMU Plus is not a boarding school. This transformation has enhanced the popularity of the *Muthahhari* Foundation and its leaders, including Jalaluddin Rakhmat, who is now the chief of the foundation and head of the school.

SMU Plus can be regarded as an alternative model for secondary education in Indonesia. It is also an attempt to bridge the gap between the *'ulama* and intellectuals, as explained above. It also has unique characteristics in comparison to other senior high schools (SMU) in the country. Its curriculum integrates the SMU curriculum set by the Department of National education with basic computer science, intensive Arabic and English and fields of Islamic knowledge (*dirasa Islamiyya*) such as *'ulum al-Qur'an, 'ulum al-Hadith, usul al-fiqh* and comparative *fiqh*. Unlike regular high schools, which teach for about five and a half hours a day, SMU Plus requires students to attend eight and a half hours a day, from 7.00 am to 3.30 pm, six days a week, in order for them to complete all their educational requirements. The school also has a library containing a significant number of collections in Indonesian, Arabic, Persian and English and other facilities, such as laboratories.

Various extra-curricula activities are also offered, so that the students may further improve their skills. One example is the so-called 'X-day' (usually Wednesdays)

---

45   *Al-Tanwir* (19/1992:3).
46   Yayasan Muthahhari (1993:27).
47   http://smuth.net/Profile/03-sejarah.asp accessed 18/10/2005.

when students are expected to take part in an extra-curricular programme following their own interests. Activities on offer include Achievement Motivation Training (AMT), various study clubs (computer, English, Arabic), photography, advertising, calligraphy, theatrical arts, graphic design and various kinds of sports. There are also comparative studies and a spiritual camp. The spiritual camp deserves special attention here. In it the students are required to observe the life of 'oppressed' people located in a certain area, interview them and write reports. Spiritual camp also requires certain Islamic rituals and prayers to be performed. The aim is for the students to incorporate the spiritual aspects of religion in their daily life. These activities are seen as an integral element of the educational system of the school.

Four philosophical principles form the basis of SMU Plus's intensive educational programme. These are formulated from the so-called 'quantum learning', an accelerated programme invented by Bobbi DePorter and Mike Hernacki.[48] The first principle is that since human potential is unlimited, education - which is a process towards perfection - should be able to maximise this potential. Second, the relationship between teacher and student should be considered a partnership rather than a one-way 'subject-object' relationship. The third principle is that since humankind is progressing towards God throughout life, both teacher and student attempt to realise within themselves God's qualities, as expressed in his 99 beautiful names. Fourth, education is a process in which physical and psychological dimensions influence each other and so both aspects need to be incorporated in teaching methods. On this basis, the institutional objectives of SMU Plus are: first, to develop the students' intellects by implementing critical methods based on the philosophical principle that humans possess unlimited potential; second, to develop creativity by implementing exercises based on the belief that education attempts to maximise students' potential; and finally, to develop moral conduct by implementing *riyada* (a Sufi ritual) on the basis of the philosophical principle that humans possess the spiritual capability to approach God.[49]

Jalaluddin Rakhmat emphasises that these methods entail maximising the effect of the physique on the psyche, maximising the effect of the psyche on the physique, and guidance towards mystical experience. To maximise the effect on the physique, students are provided with a pleasant physical and social environment, which increases their self-esteem. They carry out physical exercise and also undertake exercises in critical thinking, listening to music, and so on. A so-called 'modelling' method involves presenting examples of figures who have achieved excellence in a certain field as role models. These have a

---

48   *Quantum Learning* by DePorter and Hernacki was translated into Indonesian and published in 1999 by Kaifa, an Offshoot of Mizan.
49   Rakhmat (1997:351-359), *Bandung Pos* (24/5/1994).

psychological influence on students who, when they find their appropriate model, will imitate them in their own behaviour. These and other techniques used at the school are designed to generate self-reliance and positive thinking in the students. In respect of the *riyada*, the students are guided on how to practice religious rituals such as *dhikr* (the remembrance of God's names) and prayers which impress on them the idea that their teachers resemble *murshid,* or teachers in the Sufi tradition.[50]

Another characteristic of the educational method implemented by SMU Plus which sets it apart from other schools in Indonesia is its emphasis on reward rather than punishment. The teachers at SMU Plus do not criticise their students because it is seen as a destructive influence on the learning process. Instead, the students are shown appreciation and rewarded for achievements in order that their potential is maximised.[51] In this regard, the school has developed various types of rewards for achievements in certain subjects and skills; for example, the Quarterly Award for the best score in each class, the Grade Award for the best score at each level, the Annual Award for the best in all levels and the Achievement Award for achievements in academic, moral and extra-curricular activities.[52] With this goal of maximising the students' potential in mind, the school continues to implement new findings in the field of education, such as the principles of multiple intelligences[53] and accelerated learning.

The implementation of the above methods and the unique curriculum, supported by teachers who are graduates from ITB, UNPAD, IKIP, IAIN and Middle Eastern schools, combined with excellent educational facilities, are all factors that make the educational programme of SMU Plus successful. Since its foundation, its students have won prizes in various kinds of educational competitions and a large number of its graduates have gone on to enrol at well-known state universities in Indonesia. For its achievements the school has received praise and credit from the government, particularly the Department of National Education and from other sections of Indonesian society. In 2001 the Department declared SMU Plus to be a model for the development of personality and moral conduct (*akhlaq*) in students in Indonesia.[54] Rakhmat himself admits that a number of senior bureaucrats and eminent leaders of religious organisations send their children to

---

50   Rakhmat (1997:359-365), Rakhmat (1999:33-35).
51   Rakhmat (1999:35).
52   Yulina (1997:44).
53   Howard Gardner has defined eight kinds of intelligences that may be possessed by individuals: linguistic, logic-mathematic, spatial, musical, kinetic, interpersonal, intrapersonal and naturalistic (Hernowo 2001:160-162).
54   *Al-Tanwir* (4/11/2001).

the school.[55] A large number of heads and teachers from educational institutions throughout the country - from primary, secondary and tertiary levels, state as well as private - have made visits to the school owing to its high reputation.[56]

The *Muthahhari* Foundation's success has led it to set up another branch of the school in Jakarta, in order to attract the interest of the population there, with a particular eye on upper middle-class Jakartans. However, while the original school in Bandung attracted significant numbers, the Jakarta branch has proved less successful. For various reasons (the most significant being an internal quarrel) the Jakarta branch of SMU Plus closed in the middle of 2004. Some of its students were transferred to a new school called *Lazuardi* which belongs to Haidar Bagir, a co-founder of the *Muthahhari* Foundation.

In addition to the establishment of the Jakarta branch, in 2000 the Foundation also set up a Junior High School Plus (SLTP Plus) in Rancaekek, a district of Bandung. This branch resembles the *pesantren* system, providing a dormitory for its students. Syamsuri Ali observes that, unlike the SMU Plus, students at SLTP Plus are only instructed on Shi'i teachings within the subject of Islamic jurisprudence.[57] In most other aspects of the school – its philosophy, principles of curriculum and methods, the SLTP Plus attempts to follow the path of SMU Plus. However, as a relatively new school, it is yet to attain the same level of achievement as its sister institution. The development of these institutions reveals the dynamic nature of the *Muthahhari* Foundation and its participation in education in Indonesia, a field that still deserves more attention, not only from the government but also from such private institutions.

The *Muthahhari* Foundation has not only been concerned with education - although its success in this field seems to have overshadowed other influential activities. It is also involved in cultural and social activities; for example, between 1990 and 1997 the foundation published 17 issues of *Al-Hikmah*, a journal of Islamic studies and the bulletin *Al-Tanwir*.[58] In addition, the foundation has produced studies of the life and scholarly works of Murtada Mutahhari, including translations and a biography written by Haidar Bagir, both produced in collaboration with the Islamic publisher Mizan.[59] The foundation is considered to be one of the most active organisations for the spread and promotion of Muthahhari's thought to the people of Indonesia. Like YAPI, the foundation has also expanded its role as a publisher of Islamic works,

---

55   *Al-Tanwir* (4/11/2001).

56   *Al-Tanwir* has continuously reported all the visits and comparative studies by educational institutions throughout the country.

57   Ali (2002:176).

58   A description of this journal appears in Chapter Six.

59   Its title is *Muthahhari: Sang Mujtahid Sang Mujahid* (Bagir 1988).

producing at least twelve books including biographies, prayers and Islamic thought written by Ali Shari'ati, Mutahhari, Jalaluddin Rakhmat and even two by a student team from SMU Plus.[60]

Another important contribution by the Foundation is its work in the social field and specifically its social programme for the poor and orphans, the group called by Shi'is 'the Oppressed'. Since its inception the *Muthahhari* Foundation appears to have paid attention to the education of this unfortunate group for two reasons: first, the foundation's aims include generating and improving the self-respect of the poor and other segments of the lower classes; second, it is intended to guide children of the Oppressed so that they may compete in the field of education, from primary to tertiary levels.[61] As a Shi'i institution, the *Muthahhari* Foundation also organises public religious rituals. Every Thursday evening the *kumayl* supplication is performed collectively at the *Al-Munawwarah* Mosque. Other rituals and ceremonies to celebrate important Shi'i historical events, particularly 'Ashura have involved the participation of not only members of the Foundation and its students but also of participants from outside Bandung. Seen from this perspective, the foundation is, without doubt, Shi'i and aims to preserve Shi'i traditions in Indonesia.

This portrait of the *Muthahhari* Foundation reveals its role in the spread of Shi'ism in the country. Its strategies are similar to those adopted by YAPI, and both institutions embrace the mission to promote Shi'ism as a legitimate school within Islam to the rest of the Muslim community. At SMU Plus, religious subjects are comparative and the students - children of both Sunni and Shi'i parents - are taught the skills of critical thinking and how to utilise critical analysis with regard to religious thought and practice. The students are taught to exercise intellectual freedom and to believe in the principle of plurality, in particular with respect to the Sunni-Shi'i divide. That said, the religious rituals and prayers followed by the teachers are generally Shi'i, although the students are free to continue to perform rituals, particularly the daily obligatory prayers, in accordance with their own beliefs. In this regard, there are maximum and minimum targets set by the *Muthahhari* Foundation: the maximum is the conversion of the students to Shi'ism, whilst the minimum is an acknowledgement of Shi'ism by the students and a tolerance of its followers.

---

60 The full name of the publisher is *Muthahhari Press, Warisan Intelektual untuk Kesucian and Pencerahan Pemikiran* (Muthahhari Press: Intellectual Legacy for Purity and Enlightenment of Thought) and is headed by Jalaluddin Rakhmat's second child, Miftah F. Rakhmat. Its publication of two works by a student team of the SMU Plus shows the creative activity of its students. The first is *Pintu Ilmu: 1001 Filsafat Hidup Pencinta Ilmu* (The Gate of Knowledge: 1001 Philosophies of Life of Knowledge Lovers) and the other is a translation entitled *Mukhtasar Shahifah Husainiyyah: Nasihat, Kisah and Doa Imam Husein as* (the Abridged *Husayniyya* Psalm: Advice, Story and Prayers of Imam Husayn).

61 Yayasan Muthahhari (1993:39-43).

Jalaluddin Rakhmat, the central figure of the Foundation, uses strategies similar to those of Husein Al-Habsyi in promoting Shi'ism. He continues to stress the importance of Islamic brotherhood between Sunnis and Shi'is, stating in an interview in 1995 that the dichotomy between the two is no longer relevant. He maintains that the establishment of the Foundation is not only a bridge between the intellectuals and the *pesantren* but also a means of promoting Islamic brotherhood and the principle that personal achievements, rather than *madhhab*, should become a basis for the judgement of others.[62] Regarding the importance of actions, Rakhmat's response to a letter written by one student's parents questioning the position of the *Muthahhari* Foundation in relation to Shi'ism warrants direct quotation

> If I am questioned whether I am a Shi'i or a Sunni, I will only answer that I am a Muslim. I do not want Muslim society to be divided into *madhhab* and streams, only into knowledge. Everyone has status according to his/her deeds, God says in the Qur'an. Not according to *madhhab*, nor group. That is what we also teach to the children studying at our school.[63]

Another institution of learning that shares many similarities with both *Mutahhari* and YAPI is *Lazuardi*, recently established in Jakarta. The founders of the *Lazuardi Hayati* Foundation are Haidar Bagir, Lubna Assagaf, Alwi Shihab, Nizar Shihab and Abdurrahman Mulakhela. Haidar Bagir heads the foundation, which began in 1994 as a kindergarten led by his wife. Today, *Lazuardi* comprises a playgroup, kindergarten, primary school and Senior High School. The philosophical basis, curriculum and methods implemented in Lazuardi's schools are similar to those of the *Muthahhari* SMU Plus. With the exception of the playgroup and the kindergarten, which have proved very popular, these relatively new schools are yet to establish a reputation in the country.

Shi'is in Indonesia have been active in tertiary education as well. *Madina Ilmu* Islamic College, located in Sawangan, Depok in South Jakarta (on a site next to Lazuardi's SMU) was set up to produce scholars with the skills and capabilities to advance knowledge, as well as to implement this knowledge in Indonesian society. At first the college planned to offer a programme in economics; however, it could only organise a department of Islamic education and *da'wa*, based on the core curriculum of Islamic higher learning as outlined by the Department of Religious Affairs and a curriculum of its own formulation.[64] Like the aforementioned schools, this college, under the leadership of Abdurrahman al-'Aydrus, has adopted the principles of openness and pluralism. It is open to students regardless of *madhhab*. Since its establishment in 1997, *Madina Ilmu*

---

62   *Al-Tanwir* (19/1992:4).
63   *Al-Tanwir* (200/2001:6).
64   *Selayang Pandang* (n.d:5).

has produced a number of graduates, some now working in Shi'i foundations or schools in Indonesia while others have pursued further study in Qum. However, for several reasons – not least a difference of opinion regarding whether or not it should openly present itself as a Shi'i college - its development has fluctuated.

At the graduate level there exists ICAS (Islamic College for Advanced Studies) in Jakarta, established in co-operation with the University of Paramadina, belonging to the late prominent Muslim intellectual Murcholish Madjid. Since it is a branch of a London-based institute, it uses English as the medium of instruction. Reflecting the great interest among Shi'is in the subject of philosophy, ICAS offers a Masters programme in Islamic philosophy and in Sufism. It is interesting to note that most of ICAS's Indonesian staff are Shi'is. Its director, Muhsin Mirri, is Iranian. Even though ICAS is open to students from all schools of thought or religious conviction, most of its students are Shi'i. This newly established school has not yet produced graduates.

In sum, despite their small numbers, Shi'is in Indonesia have participated widely in the field of education from pre-school to the tertiary level. The institutions of learning that they have founded reveal that this religious group views education as an important field for participation and development. In general, their institutions either take the form of the traditional *pesantren* or belong to the modern school system. In some cases there have been attempts to adopt elements of both systems and to integrate them into a single system - a creative idea in the educational domain. With respect to their connections with Iran, the Shi'i institutions (perhaps with the exception of the Lazuardi schools) have, or used to have, good connections with the Iranian government or with Iranian learned men. With the exception of *Al-Hadi*, they attempt to provide all Indonesian Muslims, regardless of *madhhab,* with educational programmes designed for their children to develop their full potential. With regard to religious orientation - again with the exception of *Al-Hadi* - these institutions have adopted open strategies in order to promulgate Shi'i teachings. They are educating their students to recognise that Shi'ism is a valid and legitimate *madhhab* within Islam. Recognition among the Sunni in the country is without question a crucial issue for Indonesia's Shi'is, and they consider education to be a key to achieving this goal.

6. Publishing

Publishing has been another important means for Indonesian Shi'is to spread their teachings, and has gone hand in hand with the development of the *madhhab* in Indonesia. The publication of books and periodicals can, to a certain extent, be considered to be a form of *da'wa,* but it is also a contribution to the intellectual and cultural life of the country. The discussion in this chapter is divided into five parts: first, I give a brief description of the general characteristics of Shi'i publishers in Indonesia. The second and third parts deal with translations of Shi'i books and books written by local Shi'i figures. Fourth, I describe Islamic periodicals published by Shi'i institutions of learning and *da'wa* and finally, I explain the internal impact of publishing on the Shi'i community and the relationship with religious authorities in Indonesia.

A. The Shi'is Publishers

Over the past two decades, in congruence with the increasing number of followers of Shi'ism in Indonesia, there have been more than sixty publishers[1] producing hundreds of Shi'i titles and publications. Shi'i books, in a broad sense, are any books written by Shi'i *'ulama* or intellectuals containing the teachings of Shi'ism and Shi'i thought. This steady growth in the number of publishers and of Shi'i literature is a new and striking phenomenon in the history of Islam in Sunni-dominated Indonesia, and it has to some extent taken Muslim scholars and the country's religious and political authorities unaware. In response to the proliferation of Islamic literature and the Muslim population's thirst for this material, the late liberal Muslim thinker, Harun Nasution (1919-1998) wrote an article for *Tempo,* possibly the best-known Indonesian magazine, on its 60th anniversary in 1987 with a discussion of Islamic literature. Nasution's essay deals with the origins, doctrines and development of Shi'ism, and its inclusion in this special edition of *Tempo* indicates the significance of Shi'i publications. Similarly, about a decade later, Azra noted the growth of Shi'i publishers and literature as an unusual phenomenon in Islamic discourse in Indonesia.[2]

That said, the vast majority of these Shi'is' publishers are little or even completely unknown to the community of mainstream publishers, IKAPI (*Ikatan Penerbit Indonesia,* the Association of Indonesian Publishers).[3] Most small publishing

---

1   This figure is derived from catalogues of the libraries of the *Muthahhari* Foundation, the *Fatimah* Foundation, the *RausyanFikr* Foundation, the *Al-Jawad* Foundation, and the ICC of Al-Huda.

2   Azra (1999).

3   Iwan Setiawan, the deputy head of IKAPI, quoted in *Republika* (28/3/2004:5) gives the total number of Islamic publishers as 50. Watson (2005:179) shows that this is an underestimation and the total number is in fact much greater.

houses are not registered with this professional organisation and they do not take part in the book fairs attended by the mainstream publishers. It is also the case that many of these Shi'i' publishers appear on the market with a number of books and then disappear, usually because their businesses cannot compete and survive in the open market.

There are two types of Shi'i publishers in Indonesia. The first is purely commercial, publishers whose core activity since establishment has been publishing and marketing. This category includes Shi'i-owned firms which produce both Shi'i and non- Shi'i books. The three most important in this category are Mizan, Pustaka Hidayah and Lentera. All have become well-established publishing houses and are registered members of IKAPI. There are numerous others in this category, some of them no longer active. The second type includes Shi'i institutions that undertake publishing as part of their wider activities, including *da'wa* and education. Several big institutions such as ICC of Al-Huda, Muthahhari, Al-Jawad, YAPI (*Yayasan Penyiaran Islam*), YAPI (*Yayasan Pesantren Islam*) of Bangil and Al-Baqir of Bangil fall into this category. Other Shi'i institutions have set up separate publishing houses, such as Pustaka Zahra, belonging to the Fatimah Foundation and Cahaya, belonging to IPABI.

Quantitative data illustrates the popularity of the established Shi'i publishing houses. In terms of quantity, figures provided by *RaushanFikr*, a Shi'i foundation based in Yogyakarta, show that until 2001 the top four publishers were Pustaka Hidayah with 60 titles, Mizan with 56 titles, Lentera with 50 titles and YAPI (*Yayasan Penyiaran Islam*) of Jakarta with 31 titles.[4] It is interesting to note that although Mizan is one of the largest and even enjoys the reputation of being the most popular Shi'i publisher, its output is below that of Pustaka Hidayah. These rankings may change with the appearance of new firms such as Pustaka Zahra and Cahaya, which have been very active in recent years: figures up to March 2004 show that Pustaka Zahra produced more than 50 titles and Cahaya more than 40.

The most active Shi'i institution engaged in producing cultural material is the Iranian-sponsored Islamic Cultural Centre of Al-Huda (ICC). Figures up to March 2004 show that ICC of Al-Huda has published more than 30 books, including an imprint of the Qur'an. This act of publishing the Holy Book may have been an attempt to deny the accusation made in many Sunni polemical writings that the Shi'is have their own Qur'an and that it is very different to that used by Sunni Muslims. (In fact, the contents do not differ at all from the copies printed by other publishers in Indonesia.) Other Shi'i institutions also engaged in publishing but on a smaller scale are the Muthahhari Press, Al-Jawad, YAPI of Bangil, Al-Baqir of Bangil and Al-Kautsar of Jakarta, producing

---

4   Shafwan (http://rausyanfikr.tripod.com/makatul/sosio-agama.htm).

fewer than 20 titles each. These numbers illustrate the limitations of the Shi'i institutions in the field of publishing, which is not altogether surprising when one considers that for most of them publishing serves as an adjunct to their missionary activity.

There is a stark contrast between the two types of publishers in terms of their orientation and management. The firms we have classified as purely commercial have a strong business orientation, while those which fall into the second category can be said to be *da'wa* oriented, only interested in undertaking publishing as a part of their *da'wa* programmes. The management of the 'commercial' publishers tends to be rational and modern, while that of those in the second group can be described as traditional. Both categories are distinguished by the types of books they publish. While the commercial firms produce only a small proportion of Shi'ite literature compared to their total number of publications, the Shi'i *da'wa* institutions tend to confine themselves to the production of Shi'i works alone. Furthermore, the books put out by the commercial publishing houses tend to be directed towards attracting a wider readership than those of the Shi'i *da'wa* foundations. The latter are only likely to publish Shi'i work of interest to the Shi'i community in Indonesia, or works relevant to their current *da'wa* programmes. This also corresponds to the non-profit purpose of *da'wa*.

In order that we may fully understand the two categories of publishers, profiles of Mizan and YAPI (*Yayasan Penyiaran Islam*) now follow. Mizan is one of the biggest and most dynamic publishers of Islamic books in Indonesia today and it has played a great role in the development of Islamic intellectual life in the country. In 1982, Haidar Bagir, together with his friends Zainal Abidin and Ali Abdullah graduated from the Industrial Arts Department of ITB. With financial support from Bagir's maternal uncle, Abdillah Toha and Toha's associate, Anis Hadi the three established a publishing business in Bandung. Mizan has emerged with a distinctive product range, in striking contrast to the great Islamic publishers such as Al-Ma'arif of Bandung. Its distinctiveness is the Shi'i identity of its books, something that has both popularised and stigmatised it. The popularity of Mizan goes hand in hand with the popularity of its co-founder and chief director, Haidar Bagir.

Though Mizan cannot be formally classified as a Shi'i publisher, since its foundation it has been closely associated with Shi'ism and is regarded as having made a significant contribution to its development in Indonesia on several counts: first, Mizan has published a number of Shi'i works, although these are only a fraction of the Sunni works it has produced. Second, Mizan has published works written by Shi'i *'ulama* and scholars, providing a platform for the teachings of Shi'ism in Indonesia. This was a controversial step given that to the majority Muslim population, the name 'Shi'ism' had - and still has - negative connotations and is regarded as heterodoxy. Such brave efforts were clearly counter to the long-running tradition of Sunni Islam in the country. What is more, Mizan's first book and one of its bestsellers, *Dialog Sunni Syi'ah* (A Sunni-Shi'i Dialogue), translated from *al-Muraja'at* "summed up the purpose of Mizan [...] and intended to present a more 'balanced' view of Shi'ism".[5] Haidar Bagir admits that one rationale for publishing this book was the fact that his *madhhab* is so often misunderstood by large numbers of Muslims in Indonesia.[6] Mizan went on to publish numerous works by Shi'i scholars, including Ali Shari'ati, Mutahhari, Khomeini and Husayn Tabataba'i. Today, Mizan is still regarded by many Indonesian Muslims as a Shi'i publisher and in fact some Islamic *da'wa* and educational institutions, such as *Pondok Gontor* in Ponoroga, East Java actually forbid their students to read its publications, despite the fact that it has become a well-developed publishing house whose leaders are determined to promote its inclusive philosophical principles.

The stated goal of Mizan is very broad, to provide information on Islamic thought and the Islamic world in a balanced way and from a variety of standpoints. Haidar Bagir explains that books published by this firm have to fulfil at least two criteria: first, the research contained within the book has to be both scientific and verifiable; second, it has to contribute to developing the role of Muslims as *rahmatan li al-'alamin* ('a mercy to all inhabitants of the world'). Mizan's writers are not all Muslim and include authors from various religious backgrounds, even Western scholars. Bagir bases this principle on the Traditions of the Prophet Muhammad and Imam 'Ali that urge man to take *hikma* (wisdom) from any source available. Bagir quotes the saying of the Prophet Muhammad "Wisdom is a loose thing belonging to Muslims. Collect it, wherever you find it". He quotes Imam 'Ali: "Look at what is said, not who says it"[7] and goes on

> Because for us Islam is a universal religion, but its universality can only be obtained if it is seen to be an inclusive, open religion. On the other hand, we believe that openness can be embraced wholeheartedly without the obligation to sacrifice Islam on the surface. Universality should certainly mean that the teachings of Islam must be understood coherently, so that they do not lose their basic principles. Well, if there is something that is said to be authenticity in a religion, what is meant is coherency. Of course, included here is the coherency in the literal meanings of the Islamic texts. For us, this means that the openness should be 'guarded' — a term which, because I fail to find a substitute, I

---

5   Peeters (1998:218).
6   Bagir (2003:71).
7   Bagir (2003:34-35).

am forced to use with a heavy heart – by our belief in a responsible and reliable interpretation of the principles of the Islamic teachings of the Qur'an and Sunna of the Prophet.[8]

On the strength of this principle, Mizan can be seen as promoting religious pluralism in Indonesia. Its publications reflect its vision of religion and human civilisation. It is a publishing house that produces not only the scholarly works of non-Muslim writers but also those of thinkers from different Islamic orientations. As Haidar Bagir suggests, all civilisations and religions in world history interact with one another and they develop in historical contexts, within which certain elements are adopted. Mizan rejects 'exclusivity' on the grounds that it is "the same as an ahistorical and unrealistic attitude".[9] These ideas form the basis of Islamic thought that might be called 'the *Madhhab* of Mizan', a '*mazhab tengah*' (*madhhab* of the middle way) always open to development and revision.

With this inclusive and realistic religious attitude, the last twenty years have seen Mizan develop enormously in terms of both quality and quantity. It publishes titles in nearly all fields of knowledge and has established several offshoot subsidiaries as a way of attracting a wider readership. Each of the subsidiaries specialises in a particular genre. The subsidiary Hikmah, for example, publishes books on religiosity and Sufism, Misykat on supplications and Harakah on Islamic movements; Kaifa publishes 'how-to' books; Arasy offers titles on *fiqh*; Qanita is for women's issues and Teraju publishes academic books. In addition, Mizan has pioneered the e-book and direct selling through ekuator.com. Hernowo, who has worked for Mizan since 1984 attests to the rapid development of the publishing house, which he believes is the result of attempts to apply a *Hadith* commanding Muslims to seek wisdom everywhere.[10] This also corresponds with Haidar Bagir's statement above.

I now turn to YAPI, which is the oldest of all the Indonesian publishers mentioned. YAPI, a Shi'i foundation established in Surabaya in 1962, long before the Iranian revolution, is first and foremost a publishing house.[11] Its goals include the organisation of intellectual and religious activities and the publication and distribution of Islamic works. YAPI's co-founders, who still lead the foundation today, are two brothers from a Sayyid family, Omar Hashem (b. 1935) and his elder brother, Muhammad Hashem. Husein Al-Habsyi, who later established *Yayasan Pesantren Islam* (also abbreviated YAPI – refer to Chapter Five) was also one of the sponsors. The Hashem brothers are renowned translators and writers. M. Hashem, who formerly worked at the Iranian Embassy in Jakarta

---

8   Bagir (2003:35).
9   Bagir (2003:46).
10   Hernowo (2003:15).
11   O. Hashem (2002:12).

is a prominent translator of a large number of English originals. His younger brother, O. Hashem, is probably the most famous polemical Shi'i writer in Indonesia today. For many years, YAPI had its centre in Bandar Lampung where O. Hashem, a medical doctor worked for a local government clinic. Currently the institution and its leaders' residence are located in Jakarta.

In terms of YAPI's Shi'i character, there is a clear distinction between its products of the pre-Iranian revolution era and those produced afterwards. No Shi'i work appeared from YAPI during the pre-Iranian revolution period. (However, YAPI had established connections with Muslim world leaders and scholars, including the Grand Ayatollah Muhsin al-Hakim, who sent the institution a printing machine in 1970). Figures up to 1970 put the intellectual products of YAPI at more than 43 books and brochures, including translations and original writings.[12] During the pre-revolutionary period, YAPI was known for a series of polemical pamphlets against Christianity written by the institution's founders, O. Hashem and Muhammad Hashem.[13] This series included titles such as M. Hashem's *Tantangan dari Gua Qumran* (The Challenge from the Cave of Qumran, 1965), *Darah dan Penebusan Dosa* (Blood and Absolution, 1965), *Jesus dan Paulus* (Jesus and Paul) and O. Hashem's *Keesaan Tuhan: Sebuah Pembahasan Ilmiah* (The Oneness of God, A Scientific Discussion, 1962) and *Djawaban Lengkap kepada Pendeta Dr. J. Verkuyl* (Complete Answers to the Priest Dr. J. Verkuyl). Closely related to these works was the publication of the translation of the *Gospel of Barnabas* by Husein Al-Habsyi. Both M. and O. Hashem wrote and translated works on other topics for YAPI, including O. Hashem's *Marxisme dan Agama* (Marxism and Religion, 1963) and *Menaklukkan Dunia Islam* (Conquering the Islamic World, 1968) and M. Hashem's translation of the words of 'Ali bin Abi Talib entitled *Pedoman Pemimpin* (Guidance for Leaders, 1968). Aside from the fact that YAPI tended only to publish the works of its owners, since its earliest days it has proved itself to be a dynamic institution in the field of cultural production.

The shift in the character of YAPI's publications after 1979 reveals not only the individual conversion of both M. Hashem and O. Hashem to Shi'ism but the conversion of YAPI as an institution as well. Most of the Shi'i works published by YAPI are translations from English, beside several original books written by the brothers. Their close relationship (and that of the foundation) with the Iranian Embassy in Jakarta gave them access to Shi'i materials requiring translation into the vernacular. Like the cultural products of Mizan, some of the Shi'i books published by YAPI have caused controversy. O. Hashem's *Saqifah*, for instance,

---

12   *Pembina* (16/1/1970).
13   Boland (1971:227-228). On polemics against Christianity by Muslim apologetics including O. Hashem, see Ropi (1999).

received bitter criticism from anti-Shi'i groups.[14] Since YAPI is a non-profit institution with limited material and human resources, its products are less attractive in presentation and style compared to those of Mizan. In addition, in contrast to Mizan's professional modern management, YAPI is a family-run business. It is not surprising that a number of its titles were republished by the established Shi'i publishing houses in the hope of gaining wider circulation and to increase the chances of cultural and economic success. That said, YAPI has made an enormous contribution to the development of the religious life of the Shi'i community in Indonesia.

It is an important point to note that all the publishers and individuals involved in this field of cultural production are connected and it is through these networks of individuals and institutions that their products have been able to reach members of Indonesia's Muslim society. Included in this process is the circulation of books and periodicals through the network of existing Shi'i institutions scattered throughout the country, even more significant due to the fact that many of the cultural products of Shi'i institutions cannot be found in the mainstream bookstores. The larger Shi'i institutions such as ICC of Al-Huda, Fatimah, Muthahhari and Al-Jawad have opened their own bookstores, located within their complexes, to distribute and sell Shi'i works. Another channel for reaching readers is through the libraries which most of the big Shi'i institutions provide for the public. These are filled with collections of books and periodicals put out by the aforementioned publishers, in addition imported books in English, Arabic and Persian.

It is clear that both types of publishers profit from networking for their existence and development. With regard to the publication of Shi'i works, an international network - through which material can be produced and distributed - is a necessary element, given that many Shi'i works are translations of foreign originals. This international network is vital for accessing foreign books to be translated into Indonesian. The Iranian connection, through which foreign Shi'i books are imported, is a necessary part of this international network. In the content, message and style of the cultural products produced by the Indonesian publishers their overseas provenance remains clear.

B. The Translation of Shi'i Books

The translation of Shi'i literature into the Indonesian language has become an important dimension in the intellectual and missionary development of Shi'is in the country. Tamara has observed the proliferation of translations of works

---

14   Further on this matter, see Chapter Eight.

by Middle Eastern authors. This is a new phenomenon in Indonesian Islam, first seen in the 1980s as a consequence of the Iranian revolution.[15] What is obvious is the Shi'i nature of the content and message of these translations. Scholars such as Von der Mehden and Meuleman also note the increase in translations of Shi'i texts in the country.[16] Azra describes the phenomenon as a dramatic development, because it "has never taken place in Islamic discourse in Indonesia before".[17] Most books published by the Shi'i publishing houses in Indonesia have been translated from English, Arabic or Persian originals, with English books constituting the greatest number (even though originally these books were written in Arabic or Persian). In general, the authoritative Shi'i texts are still written in foreign languages inaccessible to most Indonesians, so translation is the most effective way for the publishing houses to produce Shi'i works.

It is impossible to recount all the translated books produced by Shi'i publishing houses in Indonesia, but in order to demonstrate the unique characteristics of the Shi'i works it is necessary to pay attention to their authors. On the whole, the authors whose works are translated are modern Shi'i 'ulama or intellectuals of Iran or other Middle Eastern countries. Most are 'ulama who hold the title Ayatollah (*Ayat Allah*, 'Sign of God'), or Grand Ayatollah, educated in the traditional *hawza* system. These authors include 'Abd al-Husayn Sharaf al-Din al-Musawi (1873-1957), Ruhullah Khomeini (1902-1989), 'Allama Muhammad Husayn Tabataba'i (1903-1981), Murtada Mutahhari (1920-1979), Muhammad Baqir Sadr (1935-1980), 'Ali Khamene'i, Nasir Makarim Shirazi (b. 1924), Ja'far Subhani (b. 1922) and Ibrahim Amini (b. 1925). All of these men are authoritative 'ulama whose devotion to their *madhhab* and to religious scholarship are recognised throughout the Shi'i world. There are also authors who are scholars with both a traditional and a modern education, the most popular being 'Ali Shari'ati (1933-1977) who gained a PhD in France and Seyyed Hossein Nasr (b. 1933) who earned his doctorate in the United States. This group of authors is known as 'the intellectuals'.

The author with the most works translated into Indonesian is Mutahhari, with no less than 50 titles, followed by Shari'ati, with 25 titles. Then we find the works of Ruhullah Khomeini, 'Allama Tabataba'i, Muhammad Baqir Sadr and Hossein Nasr, each of whom have between 10 and 15 titles. As for other Shi'i scholars, their works are still limited in number but are likely to increase.[18] It should also be noted that in many cases there is more than one translation of a certain work in circulation. The six most popular authors, in a quantitative sense, represent

---

15   Tamara (1986:24).
16   Von der Mehden (1993); Meuleman (n.d).
17   Azra (1999:223).
18   This is based on catalogues from the publishers Mizan and Lentera and the libraries of the Muthahhari Foundation, Fatimah Foundation, RausyanFikr Foundation, Al-Jawad Foundation and ICC of Al-Huda.

not only the rank of the *'ulama* and intellectuals but also the importance of their revolutionary or moderate religious and political thought. The works of Khomeini, Sadr, Shari'ati and Mutahhari, for example, are revolutionary, while the works of Tabataba'i and Nasr can be classified as moderate and sober. With the exception of Sadr, all the abovementioned scholars are Iranian. Other Shi'i *'ulama*, including the Lebanese 'Abd al-Husayn Sharaf al-Din and the Tunisian Muhammad Tijani al-Samawi have produced works that have been significant in the dissemination of Shi'ism in Indonesia.

Taking into consideration the above estimates, it is clear that Mutahhari and Shari'ati - who were said to have worked together in the establishment of the *Husainiyya-yi Irshad*, a religious institution set up to attract educated Iranian youth,[19] have been very influential in Indonesia. (Both of these men, together with the abovementioned Iraqi, Muhammad Baqir Sadr, are considered to be martyrs.) It appears that the position of Mutahhari is more important to Shi'is in Indonesia than that of Shari'ati, in all likelihood because Mutahhari was an Ayatollah and a model for the *'ulama'*-intellectual in combination. Shari'ati, however, is considered to be an intellectual, but he is a special case, namely a *rawshanfikr, or* 'reformed intellectual'. Muthahhari's status is also indicated by the fact that a Shi'i institution in Indonesia was established under his name, and one of the reasons for establishing *Yayasan Muthahhari* was to publish a series of his works via the institution's journal *al-Hikmah*. This has contributed to increasing Mutahhari's popularity in Indonesia. Nearly all of his works, which reach more than 50 titles, have been translated into Indonesian. These cover most fields of Islamic knowledge: doctrine, Qur'an exegesis, morality, jurisprudence, history, Sufism and philosophy (in which there are the most titles). A circle of Shi'i intellectuals is responsible for introducing Mutahhari's thoughts to an Indonesian audience; for instance, Haidar Bagir has provided us with a short intellectual biography of Mutahhari[20] and Jalaluddin Rakhmat, in lengthy introductory notes to a translation of one of Mutahhari's works, supplies a short biography and details his principal thought.[21] These intellectuals consider Mutahhari to be a model *'ulama*.[22]

However, it is Shari'ati who seems to have had the greater impact on Muslims in Indonesia, both Sunni and Shi'i. Mutahhari's thought simply has not gained

---

19   Mutahhari was one of the founding members of this institution in 1965 and invited Shari'ati to join in 1968. By 1969-70, Shari'ati's lectures were becoming increasingly revolutionary and attracting unfavourable attention from *'ulama* and the state. Mutahhari accused Shari'ati of being a Wahhabi and tried to persuade him to moderate his position. In 1971 Mutahhari withdrew from the *Husainiyya-yi Irshad* and even after the death of Shari'ati in 1977 he wrote to Khomeini about him, "complaining of his dishonesty, slander of the clergy and deviation, and requesting a ban on his works until they have been revised or corrected" (Martin 2000:79).

20   Bagir (1988).

21   Rakhmat (1984).

22   Rakhmat (1991, 1993).

the same level of appreciation as Shari'ati's. As Madrid has shown, Shari'ati occupies the second position after Nurcholish Madjid as most cited author among students in the Central Javanese university city of Yogyakarta.[23] "I was surprised that Shari'ati would be more frequently cited and with more fervour than Mawdudi", says Madrid.[24] The broad influence of Shari'ati's books is also illustrated by the fact that, unlike Mutahhari, Shari'ati has attracted the interest of Muslim intellectuals in Indonesia, both Sunni and Shi'i. Amien Rais, Dawam Rahardjo, Jalaluddin Rakhmat, Muchtar Probotinggi, Hadimulyo and Haidar Bagir have made appreciative and critical analyses of Shari'ati's thought.[25] Aspects of his thought have also been thoroughly analysed by Azyumardi Azra.[26] Mutahhari's writings have yet to attract the same level of interest. Von der Mehden attributes the influence of Shari'ati on the circle of intellectuals to "Shari'ati's views of an egalitarian Muslim society and attacks on corrupt religious leadership".[27] Furthermore, Shari'ati provides his readers with a self-portrait and puts himself in the role of a *rawshanfikr*, the very role that Indonesian Muslims intellectuals wish to imitate in their own Indonesian social, political and religious contexts.

Iran's Ruhullah Khomeini and Iraq's Muhammad Baqir Sadr, whose intellectual works have been translated into Indonesian, were *maraji' al-taqlid* ('sources of emulation'), philosophers and leaders of Islamic movements. Whilst Khomeini succeeded in his revolution, Sadr's brief rise in 1979-1980 resulted in his execution in April 1980. Books by Khomeini translated into Indonesian include work in the field of Qur'an exegesis and Hadith, including the four volumes of *40 Hadis Nabi SAW* (Forty Prophetic Traditions), published by Mizan and *Rahasia Basmallah dan Hamdallah* (Secrets of Basmallah [the first verse of the first chapter of the Qur'an] and Hamdallah [the second verse of the first chapter of the Qur'an]) also published by Mizan in 1994. In relation to his position as a *marja' al-taqlid* to Indonesian Shi'is, several jurisprudential texts by Khomeini are available in Indonesian, including the two volumes, *Mi'raj Ruhani* (The Spiritual Journey) and *Puasa dan Zakat Fitrah* (Fasting and the Fitra Alms[28]) and *Fiqih Praktis Menurut Mazhab Ahlul Bayt* (Practical Jurisprudence According to the *Madhhab* of *Ahl al-Bayt*) in three volumes, published by the Al-Jawad Foundation in Bandung and Al-Huda in Pekalongan respectively. The last two books also incorporate some *fatwas* of 'Ali Khamene'i, who is currently a *marja' al-taqlid* to many of Indonesia's Shi'is. 'Ali Khamene'i's book entitled *Fatwa-fatwa Ayatullah Al-Uzhma Imam Ali Khamenei* (Fatwas of the Grand Ayatollah 'Ali Khamene'i) was published in Indonesian by Al-Huda in Jakarta at the end of

---

23   Madrid (2001:64).
24   Madrid (2001:65).
25   Rais (1991), Rahardjo (1983), Rakhmat (1988), Probotinggi (1986), Hadimulyo (1985), Bagir (1989).
26   Ridwan (1999).
27   Von der Mehden (1993:89).
28   *Fitra* alms are the obligatory alms paid at the end of the fasting month of Ramadan.

2004. The translations of these books are instrumental in the religious practice of Indonesian Shi'is because they help them fulfil the obligation to follow a living *mujtahid*. Khomeini's political thought, which has made a contribution to the political history of Islam, was later translated into Indonesian under the title *Sistem Pemerintahan Islam* (The System of Islamic Government) and published in 2002 by Pustaka Zahra. This significant work was originally a series of lectures delivered by Khomeini in Najaf in 1969-1970. It was published in Persian in the autumn of 1970 and then in Arabic in 1976 in Beirut as part of a five-volume *fiqh* book entitled *Kitab al-Ba'i* (The Book of Purchases).[29] Khomeini argues that Islam is capable of establishing laws for the government and administration of a just society and that since the occultation of the Imam Mahdi, a cleric is responsible for justice and ruling over an Islamic society, based on the *shari'a*. Khomeini's political concept of *wilayat al-faqih,* as set out in this book, has become the main ideological foundation of the Islamic Republic of Iran. Despite the fact that Khomeini, as a scholar and Islamic leader, was - and still is - the ideal figure for Shi'is in Indonesia, there has so far been no fully comprehensive study of him in Indonesian, nor of his religious and political thought. To fill this gap, as previously described, Haidar Bagir - under the pseudonym of Yamani - has written two books, the first on Sufi aspects of Khomeini's thought[30] and the second on Khomeini's political philosophy, in a comparison with that of al-Farabi.[31] In addition, Sihbudi has written a political biography of Khomeini.[32]

Khomeini's political thought is paralleled by Sadr's similarly titled *Sistem Politik Islam* (The Political System of Islam) published in Indonesian in 2001 by Lentera in Jakarta. The subjects covered in Sadr's work are broader than Khomeini's since they include doctrine, Qur'an exegesis, economy, philosophy and jurisprudence as well as politics. Furthermore, Sadr's works, particularly those on philosophy and economics seem to have attracted a wide readership in Indonesia, both Sunni and Shi'i. Unlike Khomeini, who was renowned as a Shi'i leader, not all Indonesian Muslims recognise Sadr as a Shi'i thinker. To date, no serious study of Sadr has been conducted in Indonesian, in spite of the fact that he was a prominent scholar, influential among both Sunni and Shi'i Muslims throughout the world.

From these four radical and revolutionary figures we move to the 'perennial' traditional philosopher,[33] Seyyed Hossein Nasr, who migrated to America in 1979, where he served as professor of Islamic studies at Temple University in

---

29   Martin (2000:115). An English translation of this book is available at http://www.wandea.org.pl/ khomeini-pdf/hukumati-i-islami.pdf.
30   Yamani (2001).
31   Yamani (2002).
32   Sihbudi (1996).
33   'Perennial' philosophy (Latin, *philosophia perennis*) can be understood as knowledge based on universal principles and gained through tradition. It exists at the heart of all religions. It aims to return the human being to its genuine nature - the primordial self (Nasr 1992).

Philadelphia until 1984 and today holds the same position at George Washington University. Nasr's works attract a wide readership among Muslims in Indonesia. With his focus on Sufism and Islamic philosophy, he appears to have had more influence within the Sunni community of the country. His perennialist and universalist ideas are particularly influential among the circle of Indonesian Muslim neo-modernist intellectuals, who discuss his ideas in their meetings and writings. In June 1993 Nasr was invited to Indonesia to participate in a series of seminars, which were reported in the national media, including *Republika*,[34] *Tempo*[35] and *Panji Masyarakat*[36] and reviewed by Azra.[37] Several articles and theses on aspects of Nasr's thought have been published. It should be noted that many of Nasr's books are published by Sunni-owned publishing houses,[38] something which can perhaps be explained by his close relations with the Shah of Iran before the outbreak of revolution. However, this does not mean that appreciation of Nasr's scholarly works is absent in Shi'i circles. In fact, several Indonesian translations of his works are published by the Shi'i publishing house Mizan and can be found in the journal *Al-Hikmah* of the Mutahhari Foundation. Sunni appreciation and acceptance of Nasr's ideas can be explained by the fact that in most of his works he adopts a 'perennial' approach to Islam - and to its philosophical and spiritual aspects in particular - accounting for his appeal to readers interested in Islamic philosophy and Sufism. This approach also reveals a striking contrast between Nasr and Iranian revolutionary thinkers such as Khomeini, Shari'ati and Mutahhari. Given this information, we can conclude that there is little connection between the publication of Nasr's works and the spread of Shi'ism in Indonesia, even though his philosophical thought belongs to the Shi'i intellectual tradition.

It is noteworthy that Nasr's teacher of Islamic philosophy was 'Allama Muhammad Husayn Tabataba'i, one of the foremost philosophers and scholars among the 20th century Shi'i *'ulama*, some of whose works (including aspects of doctrine and Qur'an exegesis) have been translated into Indonesian. Tabataba'i's comprehensive introduction to Shi'i Islam entitled *Islam Syi'ah* (Shi'i Islam) was translated into Indonesian from an English version, which had been translated from the original by Nasr himself. It was published by Grafiti Press in 1989; however, this translation was not done by a Shi'i scholar nor produced by a

---

34 Two reports were titled "Prof. Seyyed Hossein Nasr: *Agama Masa Depan Peduli Lingkungan*" (Prof. Seyyed Hossein Nasr: the Religion of the Future, Caring about the Environment) (*Republika* 29/6/1993) and "Seyyed Hossein Nasr: *Juru Bicara Islam di Barat*" (Seyyed Hossein Nasr: A Spokesman of Islam in the West) (*Republika* 20/8/1993).

35 *Tempo* presented an interview with Nasr in "*Kembali ke Tradisi yang Utuh*" (Return to the Complete Tradition) (*Tempo* 10/7/1993).

36 "*Nasr Menegur Manusia Modern*" (Nasr Admonishes Modern Man) (*Panji Masyarakat* 761/1993).

37 Azra (1993:106).

38 The first translation of Nasr's books into Indonesian was done by the prominent Muslim intellectual, Abdurrahman Wahid and his brother Hasyim Wahid under the title *Islam dalam Cita dan Fakta* (*Ideals and Realities of Islam*) published by *Lembaga Penunjang Pembangunan Nasional* (LEPPENAS), Jakarta (1981).

Shi'i publishing house.[39] In my opinion, Tabataba'i's greatest contribution to the development of Islamic discourse in Indonesia has been in the field of Qur'an exegesis. In addition to several related books and articles, his single most important work is the monumental commentary on the Qur'an, *al-Mizan* (The Balance). However, only certain aspects of the Shi'i teachings contained in the exegesis have been translated into Indonesian. This commentary has become an important source for the most prominent Indonesian exegete, Quraish Shihab and his *tafsir* books, including his magnum opus, *al-Mishbah* (The Light, 2000). The publication of this work led anti-Shi'i groups in Indonesia to declare Quraish Shihab, at the time Suharto's Minister for Religious Affairs, a Shi'i and to castigate him.[40] Tabataba'i's influence can also be found in Jalaluddin Rakhmat's books. In the introduction to his *Tafsir Sufi Al-Fatihah* (Sufi Commentary of the First Chapter of the Qur'an) Rakhmat - who had studied in Qum with Tabataba'i's student, Muhammad Taqi Misbah Yazdi - writes of his admiration for Tabataba'i "In the Islamic world today, particularly among lovers of the *ahl al-Bayt*, no one studies *tafsir* without being influenced by his writings."[41] Yet although Tabataba'i' was a great philosopher, there is no Indonesian translation of his philosophical works, with the exception of a popular booklet on philosophy and Sufism, *Hikmah Islam* (Islamic Philosophy) published by Mizan in 1984.

From the works of the six most prolific Shi'i authors, we discover that they have written about all fields of Islamic knowledge, including Qur'anic exegesis, Hadith, jurisprudence, doctrine, history, philosophy, ethics, Sufism, politics and economics. The conception of Shi'ism as a distinct *madhhab* is affirmed in Indonesia by the distribution of the translated works, which are read, cited and discussed by Sunni and Shi'i scholars alike. Such works, then, are effective instruments for the dissemination of Shi'i Islam in the country.

The transmission of Shi'i doctrine and thought via publications becomes a much more complex matter when the translation of books from the wider range of Arabic, Persian or English originals is taken into account. In order to explain the book as a means of disseminating ideas and its benefits to Shi'is in Indonesia we can classify existing Shi'i books into three categories: doctrinal, intellectual and spiritual. These categories are not distinct from each other but are integrated. The first category, the 'doctrinal' books, is the most important. These concern the Shi'i *madhhab* and are intended to provide readers with a correct understanding of its teachings. Anti-Shi'i groups often consider these books to be tools for converting Indonesian Sunnis to Shi'ism. They recognise a missionary motive in their publication. The 'doctrinal' category ranges from books giving a general introduction to Shi'i Islam to deep analysis of doctrines

---

39 Translated into Indonesian by Djohan Effendi.
40 This can be seen in notes, Chapter Nine.
41 Rakhmat (1999:xii).

and teachings. In addition to the aforementioned *Islam Syiah* (Shi'i Islam) and *Inilah Islam* (This is Islam), both written by Tabataba'i, this category includes the work of the late Lebanese scholar 'Abd al-Husayn Sharaf al-Din al-Musawi, *Shi'i-Sunni Dialogue* which proved so popular in Indonesia that by 2001 it had been reprinted nine times.

It is important to restate that this work was the first book published by Mizan and led to its stigmatisation as a Shi'i publishing house. Its translation into Indonesian was only undertaken nearly half a century after the publication of the original, *al-Muraja'at* in 1936 by al-'Irfan of Beirut, the oldest Islamic publishing house in Lebanon. The original, however, had already circulated widely among a number of Indonesian Muslims, particularly the Hadhrami Sayyids, who had been sent free copies by Shi'i institutions in the Middle East. Islamic institutions, such as the Islamic Research Institute in Jakarta also kept the book in their libraries. In fact, it was the Islamic Research Institute's copy which Abubakar Aceh borrowed when he wrote his sympathetic work, *Sjiah, Rasionalisme dalam Islam* (Shi'ism, Rationalism in Islam), first published in 1965, in which he acknowledged Shi'ism as a valid *madhhab* in Islam.[42] Muhammad al-Baqir, the translator of *al-Muraja'at*, received his original copy directly from the Middle East.[43]

The translation into Indonesian of al-Musawi's title *al-Muraja'at* ('Consultations')[44] as *Shi'i-Sunni Dialogue* is not entirely correct. The book merely uses the literary frame of a dialogue between two *'ulama* to instruct on Shi'i Islam. The first *'ulama* - the author, al-Muzawi - takes the role of Shi'i teacher while the second - the then Shaykh al-Azhar Salim al-Bisri - is a Sunni and takes the role of the student. The 'consultations' between the Sunni scholar and the Shi'i *marja' al-taqlid* which follow are about Shi'i Islam, in which al-Bisri tends to accept all of al-Musawi's arguments. So the dialogue affirms the validity of Shi'ism through a Sunni religious authority. The image conveyed and the contents of the book were of course viewed as provocative by much of the Sunni world. In the published Indonesian translation, Muhammad al-Baqir (Haidar Bagir's father) provides us with a long and interesting introductory note, which also became the subject of criticism by anti-Shi'i figures in Indonesia.[45] For al-Baqir, the translation was intended to provide Indonesian readers with an 'insider's' perspective on Shi'ism.[46] The publication of the Indonesian edition became a

---

42   The book was published by Islamic Research Institute of Jakarta and then republished in 1972 and 1980 by Ramadhani of Solo.
43   Bagir (2003:73).
44   Brunner (2004:51).
45   For example, in a series of texts by Haidar Ali (*Al-Muslimun* 225/12/1988, 227/2/1989, 228/3/1989). An Indonesian translation of Mahmud al-Zu'bi's criticism of al-Musawi entitled *Sunni yang Sunni: Tinjauan Dialog Sunnah Syiah-nya al-Musawi* (Sunni Sunnism: A Review of al-Musawi's Sunni Shi'i Dialogue) was also published by Ganesha Publisher in Bandung in 1989.
46   Al-Baqir (1983:xxiii).

best seller, in turn contributing to the success of Mizan as a newly-established Islamic publishing house. At least two sympathetic reviews of the book have been written, one by the moderate Muslim intellectual Djohan Effendi, the other by the journalist Syu'bah Asa, who 24 years after the book's publication felt the need to demonstrate a strongly pro-Shi'i stance.[47] Controversial as this book may be in some quarters, it is clearly one of the most important works on Shi'i Islam available in Indonesian.

Most books in the 'doctrinal' category deal with the teachings that constitute the core of Shi'i Islam. A distinct characteristic of these books is that many of them include both doctrinal and philosophical reasoning, which distinguishes them from Sunni books on the same topics, Shi'ism paying much greater attention to the use of *'aql* (reason) than Sunnism. As an example, each of the five principles of Shi'i faith - *tawhid* (divine unity), *nubuwwa* (prophecy), *ma'ad* (resurrection), the imamate and *'adl* (divine justice) - for instance, have been analysed in this way by prominent Shi'i figures, including Murtada Mutahhari, Ja'far Subhani, Nasir Makarim Shirazi and Mujtaba Musawi Lari, translations of which are freely available in Indonesia. Some works by these scholars deal with the fundamentals of Shi'ism and constitute the most important tenets of the *madhhab*. Other aspects of Shi'i teachings and tradition are closely related to the central religious dogma of *tawhid*, or the essential oneness of God. Mention should also be made of Shi'i books approving of practices such as *ziyara* (the visitation of graves), *tawassul* (uttering the names of Sufi saints or Imams in supplication) and the celebration of the Prophet's birthday. Such practices have also been the province of traditionalist Sunni Muslims and are strongly opposed by the Wahhabis and reformist groups.[48] Subhani's *Tauhid and Syirik* (Divine Unity and Polytheism), published in 1987 by Mizan affirms that such practices have sound religious foundations; he is highly critical of the challenges of Wahhabism.

We now turn to the second category of Shi'i translations, the intellectual books. Such books are designed to meet the intellectual demands of both Sunni and Shi'i Muslims in Indonesia. This category includes books that are not directly connected to specific Shi'i beliefs and practices, so we cannot consider the

---

47   The writings are *"Dialog Sunnah Syi'ah"* (*Panji Masyarakat* 11/7/1983 and *"Syi'ah: Bayangan Sebuah Jembatan"* (Shi'ism: Shadow of a Dialogue) (*Tempo* 11/6/1983). For Syu'bah Asa's attitude see Chapter Eight and his writings (1998).

48   The most significant of these books are Ja'far Subhani's *Studi Kritis Faham Wahabi: Tauhid dan Syirik* (Critical Study of Wahhabism: Tauhid and Polytheism, 1987), *Tawassul, Tabarruk, Ziarah Kubur, Karamah Wali Termasuk Ajaran Islam: Kritik Atas Faham Wahabi* (Solicitation, Taking of Blessings, Visitation of Tombs, Miracles of the Saints are Included in Islamic Teachings: A Criticism of Wahhabism, 1989) and his *Tentang Dibenarkannya Syafaat dalam Islam Menurut al-Qur'an dan Sunnah* (About the Recommendation of Intercessions in Islam According to the Qur'an and Sunna, 1992), and Ja'far Murtada al-'Amili's *Perayaan Maulid, Khaul dan Hari-Hari Besar Islam Bukan Sesuatu Yang Haram* (The Celebration of the Prophet's Birthday, The Commemoration of Dates of Death and Great Islamic Festivals is not Forbidden, 1990).

translation and publication of this genre as a specific vehicle for the spread of Shi'i Islam. The publications in this category reflect the interest among Shi'is in Indonesia in Islamic philosophy. They generally deal with aspects of philosophy and Islamic thought that might influence the *Weltanschauung* of their readers. Most of the works by the scholars mentioned earlier in this chapter, some being critical of Western philosophies pertaining to society and history, can be included in this group. They tend to promote Islam as a distinct worldview - the adverse of all other worldviews – and a blueprint for humanity, capable of solving the problems facing mankind. This is demonstrated in works such as Sadr's *Falsafatuna* (Our Philosophy) published in 1991 by Mizan; Mutahhari's *Masyarakat dan Sejarah* (Society and History) published by Mizan in 1986 and Shari'ati's *Kritik Islam atas Marxisme dan Sesat-Pikir Barat Lainnya* (Islamic Criticism of Marxism and Other Western Fallacies), also published by Mizan in 1983. In addition, great Shi'i thinkers such as 'Allama Tabataba'i have made their contribution to the field of traditional Islamic philosophy. An example of note is the book *Ilmu Hudhuri* (Knowledge by Presence) by the contemporary Iranian philosopher, Mehdi Hairi Yazdi, published in 1994 by Mizan. Yazdi, the son of the reformer of the *hawza 'ilmiyya* of Qum, Abd al-Karim Ha'iri, studied Islamic philosophy with Tabataba'i. Such works can be categorised as both intellectual and influential in terms of the religious life of Indonesian Muslims.

Books within the third category, the spiritual, deal with the spiritual life of the Shi'i community. Most of them contain the sayings attributed to the Imams (as well as their hagiographies) whose words and deeds are considered within the Shi'i tradition to be part of Hadith, and therefore extremely important to the *madhhab*. These works are principal sources of Shi'i Islam after the Qur'an and are used as a reference for understanding all fields of Islamic knowledge. The most important book in this category has been *Nahj al-Balagha* (The Summit of Eloquence) various versions of which are available in Indonesian. It contains collections of sermons, sayings and letters attributed to Imam 'Ali bin Abi Talib, the first Imam. It was assembled and systematised by the 10th century Shi'i scholar Sayyid Sharif al-Radi.[49] Among the Indonesian versions available are a 1990 edition by O. Hashem and M. Hashem, translated from an English version and published under the title, *Nahjul Balaghah* by YAPI; *Puncak Kepasihan* (The Peak of Eloquence) published in 1997 by Lentera and Muhammad al-Baqir's selective translation from Arabic of Abduh's explanation, *Mutiara Nahjul Balaghah* (Pearls of the *Nahj al-Balagha*), published in 1990 by Mizan. In addition, there are translations of studies of the *Nahj al-Balagha*, including Arif Mulyadi's translation from English of Mutahhari's commentary, *Tema-tema Pokok Nahj al-Balaghah* (Major Themes of the *Nahj al-Balagha*) which was published in 2002 by Al-Huda and a translation of Muhammad

---

49   Nasr (1989:8).

Muhammadi's work, *Kisah-kisah Bertabur Hikmah Nahjul Balaghah* (Stories Scattered with Wisdom of *Nahj al-Balagha*) published by Cahaya in Bogor. There are also translations of *Sahifa* (The Scroll) containing the sayings, supplications, stories and even poems attributed to Fatima and the other Imams. Examples are *Sahifa Fatimiyya, Sahifa Husayniyya, Sahifa Sajjadiyya* and *Sahifa Sadiqiyya,* attributed to Fatima, Husayn (the third Imam), 'Ali Zayn al-'Abidin al-Sajjad (the fourth Imam) and Ja'far al-Sadiq (the sixth Imam) respectively.[50] The most famous of these is *al-Sahifa al-Sajjadiyya,* which is "the oldest prayer manual in Islamic sources and one of the most seminal works of Islamic spirituality of the early period."[51] Aside from being important reference works, these books are functional instruments in the religious and spiritual life of the Shi'is in Indonesia, particularly in the expression of loving devotion to the Prophet's *ahl al-bayt* and the Imams. It should be noted that these works are specifically Shi'i in nature and that there is nothing comparable in the Sunni intellectual heritage.

Also related to the religious and spiritual life is the publication of large numbers of books on *do'a,* or supplications, frequently compiled from Shi'i works. The most famous of these is *Mafatih al-Jinan* (Keys to the Gardens of Paradise) by Abbas al-Qummi (d. 1941). They are usually selective supplications, followed by their Indonesian translation, and the explanations of certain religious rituals and occasions. There is a great demand for this type of book, a demand well met by the Shi'i publishing houses and Shi'i foundations. Some of the books have become best sellers.[52] One, *Doa Kumail, Doa Thaif, Doa Keselamatan, Doa Tawassul, Doa Ziarah* published by the Fatimah Foundation, was reprinted six times between 1998 and 2002. The growth in demand for such books is directly related to the regular performance of religious rituals and the growing number of *pengajian* and other *da'wa* activities carried out by Shi'i institutions and Shi'i communities throughout Indonesia. It is common for leaders of *pengajian* meetings and managers of foundations to order large numbers of these books for individual members or for the institutions' collections.

---

50 The first book, *Shahifah Fathimiyyah: Doa-doa Suci Putri Nabi* (The Scroll of Fatima: Pure Supplications of Prophet's Daughter) was translated by Jalaluddin Rakhmat and M. Taufik Yahya (2001). The second, *Mukhtasar Shahifah Husainiyyah: Nasihat, Kisah dan Doa Imam Husain* as (Abridgements of the Scroll of Husayn: Advice, Story and Supplications of Imam Husayn [upon whom be peace]) was translated by the translation team at SMU Muthahhari (2003). The third, *Shahifah Sajjadiyyah: Gita Suci Keluarga Nabi* (the Scroll of Imam al-Sajjad: Pure Hymn of the Prophet's Household) was translated by Jalaluddin Rakhmat (1998). All three books contain introductory notes by Jalaluddin Rakhmat and were published by the Muthahhari Press. The fourth book, *Shahifah Shadiqiyyah: Pelita Cinta dan Renungan Doa Imam Ja'far Ash-Shadiq* (Scroll of Imam al-Sadiq: Light of Love and Prayer Contemplation of Imam Ja'far al-Sadiqh) was compiled and translated by a team of Qum alumni and published by Morteza of Bandung (2004).
51 Jafri (http://al-islam.org/sahifa/intro.html accessed 13/9/2005).
52 For instance, Mizan has a branch called *Penerbit Misykat* for publishing books on *do'a,* whilst *Pustaka Zahra* has published *Seri Doa Mustajab,* containing not less than ten books, three of which are best sellers. Some of the supplications are supplemented with cassettes of recordings of supplications provided by Ahmad Muhajir al-Muhdar.

The above descriptions reveal the general characteristics of the translated works, in particular those written by the most prolific Shi'i authors. They generally encompass all fields of Islamic knowledge, as well as all aspects of Shi'ism. We can deduce that they have been an effective vehicle for the transmission of Shi'i Islam into Indonesia from Iran, Iraq and other Middle Eastern countries. This migration of Shi'ism and Shi'i thought underscores Coser's statement: "Books are the carriers and disseminators of ideas".[53]

C. Works by Indonesian Shi'is

Shi'i figures within Indonesia have also concentrated their attention and energies on the production and dissemination of religious thought through original works, although thus far I have not found any truly systematic work presenting Shi'ism as a distinct Islamic *madhhab*. It is clear that the translated works continue to dominate in meeting the religious and intellectual demands of the Shi'i individual, group and community. We can identify a number of Indonesian Shi'i intellectuals and *ustadhs* who have published essays and articles in periodicals; however, I intend to focus on those who have written books dealing with the main body of the Shi'i *madhhab*. To mention but a few, the late Husein Al-Habsyi, Jalaluddin Rakhmat, Haidar Bagir, Muhammad Hashem and Omar Hashem have disseminated their religious ideas through their books. Quantitatively, Rakhmat is the most prolific, with more than 20 books (including textbooks), followed by Al-Habsyi with about ten titles (including his *Al-Kaustar* Arabic-Indonesian dictionary) and then the brothers, M. Hashem and O. Hashem, also with around ten. Other writers have produced less than ten titles. It should be kept in mind, however, that while some *ustadhs* have begun to produce scholarly works, most Indonesian Shi'i scholarship remains the product of the Shi'i intellectuals.

The books written by the Indonesian Shi'i *ustadhs* and intellectuals, taken together, cover aspects of doctrine, *fiqh*, *tafsir*, history and Sufism. In relation to doctrine, we can mention several books dealing with the central concept of the *ahl al-bayt* (referring to the twelve Imams. There are at least three works which urge Muslim believers to uphold the Qur'an and the *ahl al-bayt* of the Prophet Muhammad: Ali Umar Al-Habsyi's *Dua Pusaka Nabi, al-Qur'an dan Ahlulbait* (Two Prophetic Heritages: the Qur'an and Ahl al-Bayt. 2002. Pustaka Zahra); Heru Elryco's *Ahlul Bait dan al-Qur'an, Peninggalan Yang Terlupakan* (Ahl al-Bayt and the Qur'an: the Forgotten Inheritance. 2002. Rosda) and Alwi Husen's *Keluarga Yang Disucikan Allah* (The Family Purified by God. 1998. Lentera). Following Shi'i *'ulama*, the authors affirm that this obligation is based

---

53   Coser (1982:362).

on the Qur'an and the sayings of the Prophet that are recognised in both Sunni and Shi'i collections of Hadith. At the same time, this can be seen as a Shi'i rejection of a number of Sunni sayings which are considered to be the Prophet's Hadith, commanding Muslims to follow the Qur'an and his *Sunna*, or exemplary practice. According to Shi'i beliefs, both the transmitters and contents of these Hadith are unreliable.[54]

The most important book on Shi'i doctrine is Hasan Abu Amar's *Akidah Syi'ah* (The Doctrine of Shi'ism). Its full title is *Akidah Syi'ah, Seri Tauhid: Rasionalisme dan Alam Pemikiran Filsafat dalam Islam* (Shi'i Doctrine, Series on *Tawhid*: Rationalism and the Nature of Philosophical Thought in Islam) published by *Yayasan Mulla Shadra*, Jakarta, in 1992 and reprinted in 2002. The book consists of three parts - *usul al-din* (the fundamentals of religion), doctrine and the unity of God – and its writer, a Qum alumnus, known among Shi'i adherents in Indonesia as a literalist *ustadh*, uses logic rather than Qur'anic verses to prove the existence, unity, attributes and actions of God. Abu Amar emphasises the significance of reason in the Shi'i belief system, stating that in Shi'i Islam, the fundamentals of religion must be understood by every Shi'i through logical evidence. Even textual proofs are secondary to logical proofs. In his words, "*al-Qur'an* and *Hadith* occupy a position only to support or endorse the logical proofs."[55] Abu Amar's book contains several references to Qur'anic verses and Hadith; however, with the exception of *Bidayat al-Hikma* (The Beginnings of Philosophy) and *Nihayat al-Hikma* (The Results of Philosophy) - two famous philosophical works by Tabataba'i not yet translated into Indonesian - he refers to no other authoritative Shi'i books on this most essential aspect of religion.

Abu Amar's book on Imam Mahdi, the twelfth Shi'i Imam, published by the Mulla Shadra Foundation in 2000 should also be included in the field of doctrine, because it deals with aspects of the imamate, one of the five fundamentals of Shi'ism. However, it should be noted that the belief in the Mahdi is complex matter and worthy of a separate study. In his *Imam Mahdi MenurutAhlussunnah waljama'ah* (Imam Mahdi According to the Followers of the Sunna and the Community) Amar admits he relies purely on Sunni sources, namely the Sunni Hadith collections and the views of Sunni *'ulama*. Another book which deals with Imam Mahdi as a bringer of justice, *Imam Mahdi: FigurKeadilan* (Imam Mahdi, Figure of Justice) was written by Jaffar Al-Jufri and published in 2001 by Lentera. Both these books emphasise the importance of belief in the existence of Imam Mahdi and his invincibility; yet one author claims the belief has a valid religious foundation in Shi'i sources, while the other claims that the belief is validated by the Sunnis.

---

54 Ali Umar Al-Habsyi (2002:335-349).
55 Abu Amar (2002:57).

While every Shi'i is required to understand the logical and textual proofs of the fundamentals of religion in which *taqlid,* or unquestioning emulation is prohibited in the field of jurisprudence, lay Shi'is are required to follow the *fatwa* of a *marja' al-taqlid* who assumes the authority of reinterpreting it. So the aforementioned translations of books on *fiqh* are important manuals for performing religious duties. Alongside these translations, Indonesian Shi'i figures have also authored several books on aspects of jurisprudence in order to meet local demands of the Shi'i community. Worthy of mention is a booklet entitled *Taqlid dalam Ajaran Syiah Imamiah* (Emulation in the Teachings of Imamiyya Shi'ism. Fathu Makkah. 2003) by Abu Qurba (possibly a pseudonym). In this booklet the author deals with the obligation of *taqlid* for the laity and supports his arguments with logical and textual proofs. Abu Qurba, who lives in Qum, also includes proof of the validity of those who take 'Ali Khamene'i as *marja' al-taqlid*. That evidence involves the declarations of Iranian *'ulama* of Khamene'i's *'alamiyyat* (superiority in religious knowledge) which is a requirement for assuming the position of *marja' al-taqlid*.

In terms of ritual observance, most jurisprudential books deal with prayers and the *hajj*. There have been two books about prayers: first, Abu Zahra's *Shalat Nabi saw Menurut Ahlul Bait* (Prayers of the Prophet According to the Ahl al-Bayt), published in 2001 by Kota Ilmu in Bandung; and second, Hidayatullah Husein's *Shalat dalam Madzhab Ahlul Bait* (Prayers in the *Madhhab* of *Ahl al-Bayt*), published by the Abna' Al-Husayn Foundation in Solo. In addition, a manual on ablutions and prayers, supplemented by a VCD, has been produced by *Yayasan Muhibbin* in Probolinggo, East Java. These works illustrate a number of minor differences between Shi'ism and Sunnism with regard to certain bodily movements and verbal incantations in the prayers. In respect of the *hajj*, we find several books written by Indonesian Shi'i figures, including O. Hashem's *Berhaji Mengikuti Jalur Para Nabi* (Performing Hajj Following the Line of Prophets, 2001), Muchtar Adam's *Tafsir Ayat-ayat Haji* (Commentary on Qur'anic Verses on the Hajj, 1993), *Cara Mudah Naik Haji* (An Easy Way to Perform the Hajj, 1993) and Husein Shahab's *Cara Memperoleh Haji Mabrur* (Methods of Achieving A Beneficent Pilgrimage, 1995). With the exception of Husein Shahab's book published by Pustaka Pelita, the others were published by Mizan. All these works illustrate the distinctive aspects of Shi'i teachings on specific ritual observance. Some writers may use their works to make statements about Sunni-Shi'i relations. Hidayatullah Husein, for instance, appeals for respect and tolerance among Muslims in cases of difference of opinion. The introduction to Al-Habsyi's book was motivated by the fact that some people regard the Shi'is as infidels; the book sets out to explain that Shi'i jurisprudence is based on authoritative religious arguments.[56]

---

56   Hidayatullah Husein (2001:79).

On the matter of *mu'amalat*, or social transactions in Islam, there is a Shi'i book about *mut'a (temporary marriage)*, a controversial issue used by anti-Shi'i groups to attack the *madhhab*. This book was written by Ibnu Mustafa, who used Tabataba'i's *al-Mizan* and Mutahhari's *Hak-hak Wanita Dalam Islam* (The Rights of Women in Islam) as its sources.[57] There is also an Indonesian version of Ja'far Murtada al-'Amili's *Nikah Mut'ah dalam Islam* (Temporary Marriage in Islam) translated by Hidayatullah Al-Habsyi, son of the late Husein Al-Habsyi. Interestingly, Hidayatullah Al-Habsyi, supplements this work with a long chapter of his own on '*Sakralisasi Sebuah Perkawinan*' (Making a Marriage Sacred).[58] These books are intended to explain the permissibility of *mut'a* in Shi'i Islam as an alternative to fornication and prostitution, a point dealt with in Chapter Three of this thesis.

Some Shi'i figures have also authored books in the field of *tafsir*, although these are somewhat limited in quantity and quality. In addition to Husein Al-Habsyi's two polemical works on the commentary of *Surah 'Abasa*, Jalaluddin Rakhmat supplies two books in this field, *Tafsir Bil Ma'tsur* (Qur'anic Commentary by Narrated Sources) and *Tafsir Surah Al-Fatihah* (Commentary of the First Chapter of the Qur'an, 1999), both published by Rosda in Bandung. Ali Umar Al-Habsyi, an *ustadh* at YAPI in Bangil and Husein Al-Habsyi's grandson-in-law also wrote two books: *Tafsir Nuur Tsaqalain* (Commentary on The Light of Thaqalayn Al-Baqir Foundation, Bangil. 1994) and *Nabi Tersihir?* (Was The Prophet Bewitched? As-Sajjad, Jakarta, 1998). A large number of Shi'i sources, particularly books of *tafsir* and Hadith are referred to in these works. Ali Umar Al-Habsyi's *Nabi Tersihir?* for instance, criticises the Sunni commentary that the Prophet Muhammad was bewitched.[59] For Shi'is like Ali Umar Al-Habsyi, the idea that the Prophet Muhammad came under any spell is inconceivable, because he is held to be the most perfect human being, immune to harm or the danger of evil-doing. This is a widely held view contained in the works of Shi'i scholars.

Also related to the issue of sources cited, Rakhmat is correct in his statement that Shi'i authors in this particular field - he includes himself - cannot neglect the influence of Tabataba'i and his work *al-Mizan* in particular, in the implementation of *tafsir bi al-ma'thur* or the *tafsir al-Qur'an bi al-Qur'an*, literally, using the Qur'an to interpret itself. These *tafsir* works by Indonesian authors only deal with a selection of verses, so they cannot be compared with Quraish Shihab's grand masterpiece, *al-Misbah*. Mention should also be made of the collaborative work on the sciences of the Qur'an, *Belajar Mudah 'Ulum*

---

57 Mustafa (1999).
58 Hidayatullah Al-Habsyi (2002:169-217).
59 A widely held view among Sunnis, based on the revelation in Qur'an - namely QS: 113 and 114 - that the Prophet Muhammad was put under a spell by a sorcerer called Labid bin al-A'sam (Ali Umar al-Habsyi 1998: 21).

al-Qur'an (Easy Learning of the Sciences of the Qur'an) edited by Sukardi, a librarian at SMU Muthahhari in Bandung. It is a collection of articles by Middle Eastern *'ulama* and Indonesian intellectuals and *ustadhs*, including Jalaluddin Rakhmat, Muchtar Adam, Haidar Bagir and Husein Shahab. Its editor says that it should be seen as an introduction for those interested in the meanings and commentaries of verses of the Qur'an.[60] All of these works illustrate attempts by Shi'i figures in Indonesia to produce and disseminate literature on Qur'anic exegesis and its sciences.

The field of Sufism is dominated by the work of Jalaluddin Rakhmat. As described in a previous chapter, Husein Shahab and Haidar Bagir also provide works on Sufism. The many works on Sufism available to Indonesian Muslims reflect the great interest in it, particularly among the urbanites and upper-middle class. Such an interest goes hand-in-hand with the Sufi approach to *da'wa* activities undertaken by Shi'is in the country. They hope that books on Sufism will contribute not only to the enrichment of the Sufi tradition but also to the recognition of Shi'i teachings and traditions among the wider Indonesian Muslim population.

In the field of Islamic history, we have previously described an introduction to the critical study of the history of the Prophet Muhammad by Jalaluddin Rakhmat. Controversial works in the field have included O. Hashem's *Saqifah: Awal Perselisihan Umat* (Saqifa: the Origin of Conflict in the Umma, 1987) and M. Hashem's *Abdullah bin Saba: Benih Fitnah* (Abdullah bin Saba: the Seeds of Trouble, 1987), both published by YAPI. Criticising the Sunni interpretation of the election of Abu Bakr as the first caliph to succeed the Prophet Muhammad in the *Saqifa* (Hall) of Bani Sa'ida, O. Hashem suggests that the election was a conspiracy among Abu Bakr, 'Umar and Abu Ubayda, and as a result is the original source of division within the Muslim *umma*. This conspiracy went against the Prophet Muhammad's dying designation of Ali as his immediate successor.[61] In *Abdullah bin Saba: Benih fitnah,* M. Hashem bases his defence of Shi'ism against Murtada al-Askari's belief that Abdullah bin Saba - considered by Sunnis to be the figure responsible for the founding of Shi'ism - was a fictional character.[62] These two books have provoked bitter reactions from anti-Shi'i groups. M. Hashem answers his critics[63] in his book, *Abdullah bin Saba dalam Polemik* (Abdullah bin Saba in Polemics) by simply reiterating the validity of the Shi'i version of the history of Abdullah bin Saba'.[64] O. Hashem's

---

60   Sukardi (2002).
61   O. Hashem (1987).
62   M. Hashem (1987).
63   Criticism of M. Hashem's history of Abdullah bin Saba was included in *Al-Muslimun* (217/4/1988) and republished by *Suara Masjid*. A slightly different version of the text was republished in the form of a leaflet by *Ma'had Ad-Dirasatil Islamiyah* of Jakarta.
64   M. Hashem (1989).

response[65] can be found in his provocative work, *Syi'ah Ditolak Syi'ah Dicari* (Shi'ism Rejected, Shi'ism Sought, 2002). All these historical works provide a common Shi'i interpretation of early Islamic history and are fundamental to the legitimation of Shi'ism as a *madhhab* of Islam. Included in the category of historical books are biographies of the imams, such as Imam Husayn, which recount his martyrdom at Karbala. In this theme, O. Hashem writes *Darah dan Air Mata* (Blood and Tears) which re-iterates the historical evidence for this event, namely the testimony of figures who witnessed the tragedy. Muhsin Labib, Husein Al-Habsyi's stepson and Qum alumnus, has also supplied a series of works on this subject, the latest being *Husain Sang Ksatria Langit* (Husayn, Knight of Heaven, 2004, Lentera.) in the form of an historical novel. In view of the fact that the history of the murder of Husayn in Karbala is deliberately downplayed in Sunni literature, Labib maintains that the historical reality should be highlighted, even though it might undermine the foundation of a certain *madhhab*. Labib claims that his book portrays the reality of Husayn's martyrdom. "In this novel, there is dripping of tears, there is also squirting of blood. There is a big party, there is also a moan tearing one's inner self. Once more, this is a real history!"[66] The writing of this story can be seen as a vehicle for transmitting what Fischer calls the 'Karbala paradigm', the most emotionally intense episode in Shi'i history.[67] Along with the yearly commemoration of *'Ashura*, these texts can be seen as maintaining this deeply embedded emotional paradigm within the heart of Indonesia's Shi'i community.

All the abovementioned works follow the interpretations and arguments of Islamic teachings and history provided in the works of Shi'i *'ulama*. Unlike translations, original works clearly represent the most obvious interpretation of Shi'i tenets by Indonesian Shi'i intellectuals and *ustadhs*. However, as far as the content of these works is understood, we do not find significantly differing views between the religious elites of the Shi'i community with regard to the principal aspects of Shi'i teachings. Suffice it to say that the attention, energy and creativity of Shi'i figures in the field of religio-intellectual life play an important role in the dissemination of Shi'i teachings in the country.

D. Shi'i Periodicals

In the framework of the dissemination of the teachings of Shi'ism to the Shi'i community in particular, and Indonesian Muslims in general, a number of

---

65 In addition to Abu Hanifah's article "*Koreksi atas Buku Saqifah*" (Correction to the *Saqifah* Book) serialised in *Al-Muslimun* (monthly from 213/12/1987 to 221/8/1988), Saleh Nahdi wrote *Saqifah, Awal Persatuan Ummat* (Saqifa: the Beginning of Unity of Umma) that strongly rejects Hashem's interpretation.
66 Labib (2004:11).
67 Fischer (1980:13).

periodicals are put out by Shi'i institutions. In these publications translated articles by Shi'i scholars and by Indonesian *ustadhs* and intellectuals can be found. Cultural production of this kind comprises various journals, bulletins and magazines.[68] Two important scientific journals should be mentioned, the contents of which are serious articles dealing with various aspects of Islamic studies. The first periodical was *Al-Hikmah* (Wisdom), subtitled *Jurnal Studi-Studi Islam* (Journal of Islamic Studies) 17 issues of which were published by the Muthahhari Foundation between 1990 and 1997. In accordance with the foundation's mission, this journal was meant to present scholarly works within the fields of traditional Islamic knowledge, including the Qur'an, Hadith, *fiqh*, philosophy and knowledge. It also featured translated works by Mutahhari and studies of his works, in order to help readers comprehend his ideas. Such content reflected the journal's stated aim "to combine all meanings of wisdom given by Qur'an commentators and Islamic thinkers: the Qur'an, Hadith, philosophy, Sufism, science and other Islamic thought".[69] The mission of *Al-Hikmah* was similar to that of the publisher Mizan. As one reviewer[70] suggests, *Al-Hikmah* contributed to enriching the development of Islamic thought in Indonesia. Its existence seems to have inspired Rakhmat's statement "…we want it to stir you".[71] The reviewer goes on to emphasise the connection between Jalaluddin Rakhmat and the Muthahhari foundation with Shi'ism and Shi'i thought, suggesting, "AH [Al-Hikmah] is issued to distribute Islamic aspirations from a background of Shi'i thought".[72] But as a matter of fact, analysis of all the issues of the journal suggests that it provided readers with the thought of both Shi'i and Sunni scholars.

The second important scientific journal is *Al-Huda* (The Guidance) which began in 2000 and is published by ICC of Al-Huda. As its title suggests, this journal expects to provide "guidance for readers entering the gate of religious consciousness and religiosity through the discourse of the *ahl al-bayt* discourse, in order to be able to distinguish which is true or false".[73] Unlike *Al-Hikmah*, this journal is quite open about its Shi'i nature. "The Journal of Islamic Studies, in the hands of readers and in accordance with its title *Al-Huda*, makes the Prophet Muhammad (May God Grant Him Peace and Salvation) and the *ahl al-bayt* (Upon Whom be Peace) their reference because they are the key holders of the original Guidance".[74] The style of presentation and theme of *Al-Huda* very

---

68 In Indonesia, particularly among Shi'is, the term 'journal' is used to refer to scientific periodicals containing serious articles, while the term 'bulletin' is used for periodicals which are limited in page and rubric. Magazines contain various rubrics.

69 Rakhmat (1990:4).

70 The review was published in the daily *Pikiran Rakyat* (27/5/1990) and then included in a brochure of the foundation (Yayasan Muthahhari 1993).

71 Rakhmat (1990:4).

72 Yayasan Muthahhari (1993:64).

73 Hidayat (2000:n.p).

74 Hidayat (2000:n.p).

much resemble those of *Al-Hikmah,* except that *Al-Hikmah* also contained the specific rubric of Muthahhari. The similarities between these publications can be attributed to the fact that Jalaluddin Rakhmat and Haidar Bagir were the co-founders of both the institutions producing the journals. In terms of content, both journals contain relatively serious articles (translations and originals) covering various aspects of Islamic knowledge, including Qur'an exegesis, Hadith, history, philosophy, Sufism and morality. However, unlike *Al-Hikmah*, *Al-Huda* also provides a number of essays written by Indonesian *ustadhs.*

It is generally accepted that magazines and bulletins are significant means of disseminating the teachings of Shi'ism. Many Shi'i institutions publish some form of periodical. Two other publications of note are *Yaumul Quds,* which at the time of my fieldwork in 2004 had ceased to exist and *Waris* (abbreviation of *Warta Republik Islam* (News of the Islamic Republic) published by the Iranian Embassy in Jakarta and widely read by Shi'is in Indonesia. Notwithstanding the fact that they have a limited circulation, these two publications are instrumental in providing Indonesia's Shi'is with knowledge and information on Shi'ism and the Shi'i world. It is unsurprising then, that in its examination of *Yaumul Quds,* the Body of Research and Development of the Department of Religious Affairs (DEPAG) warned of the potential dangers of these publications to the state, citing the possibility of the embassy using them to spread Shi'i teachings and Iranian revolutionary ideas in Indonesia.[75]

The most regular Islamic bulletin owned by a Shi'i institution has been *Al-Tanwir* (The Enlightenment) published by the Muthahhari Foundation. This bi-weekly bulletin, which has been issued since January 1991, is seen not only as a way for the foundation to communicate with its members but also as a conduit for *da'wa* between the Muthahhari Foundation and Muslim society at large. Its full title is the *Da'wa* Bulletin of Al-Munawwarah Mosque and its offices are located behind Jalaluddin Rakhmat's house. It is issued in cooperation with the Muthahhari Foundation. In fact, most of the articles in the bulletin are derived from transcriptions of Jalaluddin Rakhmat's sermons, delivered at the mosque every Sunday morning. The bulletin also includes articles considered important for Muslim society and reports on the activities of the foundation. In step with the philosophical values of the Muthahhari Foundation, the bulletin provides a moderate view of various aspects of Islam, and in particular regarding the differences between Shi'ism and Sunnism. *Al-Tanwir* is widely distributed and to date boasts more than 250 editions; consequently, it can be seen as instrumental in the spread of the teachings of Shi'ism in Indonesia.

Bahtera (The Ark) is another publication created by Jalaluddin Rakhmat's circle as a collaborative product of the Muthahhari Foundation and the Shi'i

---

75 *Pusat Penelitian dan Pengembangan Kehidupan Beragama* (1985/1986:81-82).

organisation IJABI. The magazine, which published its first issue in December 2003, is designed to be a vehicle of communication for the array of leaders and members of IJABI. *Bahtera* communicates and explains the ideas of the organisation's intellectuals to its members, although it is also of interest to a wider readership. Its contents include topics in religious knowledge, as well as social and educational problems. As its subtitle suggests - *Pencerahan dan Pemberdayaan* (Enlightenment and Empowerment) - this periodical represents the ideology of IJABI.

In Bandung a monthly bulletin, *Al-Jawad* is produced by the Al-Jawad Foundation. It is a combination of three bulletins that the institution once used to publish: *Al-Jawad,* dealing with spiritual guidance, *Risalatuna* (Our Message) dealing with themes related to the unity of God and *Al-Ghadir,* dealing with information about Shi'ism. Historically, *Al-Ghadir* was the first bulletin produced by the institution, published between 1994 and 1997, and carried the writings of Indonesian students in Qum. *Risalatuna* was briefly published in 1997.[76] Now the eight-page *Al-Jawad* attempts to cover all three themes. In practice, like *Al-Tanwir*, each edition usually contains an article derived from a sermon recorded at the Nurul Falah Mosque. It also includes information from the *wali faqihRahbar* (Supreme Leader) 'Ali Khamene'i, or an exhortation from other Shi'i Imams, plus certain aspects of jurisprudence and prayers. *Al-Jawad's* content is distinct from that of *Al-Tanwir* in that it is committed to follow the instructions and advice of Khamene'i, Iran's foremost Shi'i leader. It also pays attention to aspects of jurisprudence, an issue not covered by *Al-Tanwir*. Despite a limited circulation, *Al-Jawad* has clearly participated in the dissemination of the teachings of Shi'ism in Indonesia.

In the same vein as *Al-Jawad* there is a magazine (a genre of generally more than 50 pages) entitled *An-Nashr* (the Victory) published by IPABI of Bogor. This magazine provides several rubrics including doctrine, politics, history, morality and reports on the work of the foundation. Some articles are original, while others are translations. Like *Al-Tanwir* and *Al-Jawad*, *An-Nashr* provides a large number of articles based on sermons, in this case by its leader, Abdullah Assegaff, an *ustadh* and Qum graduate who sometimes uses the pseudonym Abu Sukainah. In several respects, the contents of *An-Nashr* resemble that of *Al-Jawad*, reflecting the similar religious orientation, ideology, *da'wa* strategy and close connection between the two institutions, as well as on a broader level, among members of the *ustadh* group in Indonesia.

Several periodicals have also emerged from YAPI of Bangil. The first was *Al-Isyraq* (The Sunrise) which issued only nine editions from 1996 to 1998 and was then succeeded by *Islamuna* (Our Islam) from 1424/2003 to date. YAPI also produced

---

76   Ali (2002:293).

one edition of *KSAF*, a journal of a study group for religion and philosophy which was meant to include scientific and popular writings on aspects of Islamic knowledge. The goal of *Al-Isyraq* was "to invite all Muslims to enlighten their thought with original and argumentative Islamic views".[77] Compared to the abovementioned bulletins and magazines, these magazines featured more varied topics, albeit in less detail, including articles on doctrine, the Qur'an, history, philosophy, morality, education, contemporary development of Islamic world and a report on the institution's activities. Aside from being a platform for the strategy of the institution and an outlet for articles from the Shi'i perspective, which constituted the largest proportion of their content, both *Al-Isyraq* and *Islamuna* also published the thought of a number of Sunni leaders in the country.

The Friday bulletin of *Al-Huda* and the magazine *Syi'ar* (Magnificence) are both produced by ICC of Al-Huda. *Al-Huda*'s weekly four-page bulletin presents an article, mainly dealing with aspects of Sufism. Most of its articles were later republished in two volumes of a book entitled *Renungan Jum'at* (Friday Reflectiona) by Suharto in 2002. Appearing monthly, the glossy *Syi'ar* carries articles on diverse topics of Islamic interest, making it by far the most varied among the existing Shi'i periodicals. Although it mostly deals with Shi'i thought, both translations and originals, each edition also publishes interviews with Sunni scholars or leaders in Indonesia. However, a noticeable absence from *Syi'ar* are articles on political issues, including political developments in Iran. Despite requests by some readers to include politics, the editorial board remains reluctant to do so. This reflects the stated philosophical basis of ICC as an apolitical organisation. Of note is that *Syi'ar* is well-known for providing opportunities for young Shi'i writers to get into print.

The latest magazine to emerge is *Suara Ummah* (the Voice of the Ummat) published by Forum Al-Husainy of Jakarta. The first edition of this monthly came out in February 2004. According to the editorial board, the publication was the product of a series of meetings and discussions among *ustadhs* and intellectuals. Their aim was to demonstrate the great potential of Muslim society and to encourage its resurgence. "Unity is the key word for resurgence because in it God's mercy awaits".[78] Under the slogan 'Assemble brotherhood, Side with the Oppressed', the magazine presents events, thoughts and aspects of Islamic teachings within a framework of Islamic brotherhood. Unlike other Shi'i periodicals, *Suara Ummah* hopes to attract a wider readership in the country, and it is sold at a number of street kiosks in Jakarta. To reflect its vision of inclusiveness, the opinions of both Sunni scholars and Shi'i intellectuals and *ustadhs* are given space in the magazine, although the Shi'i inclinations of the publication cannot be disguised. For example, one reader named Nurhidayah

---

77   *Al-Isyraq* (1/1/1417).
78   *Suara Ummah* (1/1/2004:4).

wrote to the editorial board asking whether *Suara Ummah* was in fact a Shi'i publication.[79] In response to her letter, the editorial board did not deny the Shi'i nature of the magazine, but emphasised the importance of its contribution to the community, rather than asking questions about *madhhab*

> Miss Nurhidayah, history will show that in the future issues of *khilafiya* [disputed matters] and conflicts of *aliran* [streams] in Islam will be considered out-of-date. Muslims will become more enlightened so that they will be more interested in talking about movements beneficial to empowerment, education and the support of the Muslims based on the principle of justice. One day Muslim society will see the contribution of a movement or the contribution given by a group to the Muslim community and mankind in general, without noticing its *madhhab*. As for *madhhab*, let it be our own business before God. A Muslim has to be able to understand and respect others. Then, he will make efforts to become the supporter of others. Dialogue is still needed and in the end, the freedom to choose the *madhhab* which one believes to be true is needed, without necessarily regarding others infidels. It is then valid if there is group thinking towards excellence, as long as it can be explained with rational arguments or can be proved intellectually.[80]

We may glean several points from the above survey: first, the periodicals produced by Shi'i institutions are of various kinds. Second, these publications are designed to be a means of *da'wa*, communication and education for members of the institutions and organisations and of the Shi'i community. Third, the content, style and presentation of the periodicals reflect the religious ideology of the parent institutions or associations.

E. The Impact of Shi'i Publishing

Without question, Shi'i publishing has had a considerable impact on the lives of Shi'is in Indonesia. Atiyeh has made the observation that "People's lives are definitely influenced by this old and basic vehicle of communication".[81] By exploiting the community's various networks, Shi'i works are readily available to followers. This corresponds to the fact that the majority of Shi'is in Indonesia are literate. Given what we have learned, we can conclude that there are three functions of publishing in the Shi'i context: religious change, education and communication. One of the most remarkable influences of publishing has been in conversion to the *madhhab*. There is no doubt that publishing functions

---

79   *Suara Ummah* (3/1/2004:2).
80   *Suara Ummah* (3/1/2004: 2).
81   Atiyeh (1995:xiii).

as conduit for religious change. Most Shi'i converts in Indonesia admit the significance of books in their conversion process (although it will be appreciated that religious conversion is always a complex psychological and sociological process). It frequently happens that certain Shi'i books are cited as the catalyst for readers to delve more deeply into the Shi'i teachings. A notable example is Jalaluddin Rakhmat's conversion to Shi'ism, which was greatly influenced by the Shi'i works that he read. Rakhmat admitted that his understanding of the imamate, for instance, was a direct result of his intensive reading of Shi'i books on the subject.[82] By the same token, an event which occurred during my observations at the Al-Jawad Foundation on 19 May 2004 underscores the importance of books in the conversion process:

> A man came to the Al-Jawad Foundation in Bandung. In its office he met with Husein Al-Kaff and other staff. In response to a question about his conversion to Shi'ism, the man explained that about four months earlier he had read a book about Imam Ali's excellent words entitled *Mereka Bertanya Ali Menjawab,* (They Question, Ali Answers) published by Al-Jawad [1998]. Reading the book reminded him of his father's advice emphasising the excellence of Ali, something he did not find in his instruction at school. He told how he continued to read Shi'i works in order to understand the teachings. He then converted to Shi'ism, but only through books, since he has not found teachers and had not joined the Shi'i community.

In this example writ large, most people convert from Sunnism to Shi'ism as a consequence of independent study through books, rather than as a result of sermons delivered by Shi'i preachers. While we cannot deduce which book or books are the most influential, we can suggest that it is the category of doctrinal books which attract readers most because they validate the Shi'i teachings with sound proofs. It appears that the more philosophical works, by and large, have very little impact on the conversion process. Many converts have mentioned the influence of al-Musawi's *Dialog Sunnah Syi'ah,* while others point to Muhammad Tijani al-Samawi's works, one of which describes al-Samawi's own experience of conversion. One interesting point is that the writings of al-Samawi have also had a remarkable impact on the conversion of Sunnis to Shi'ism in the United States, and in particular among the Muslim population of US prisons.[83] In Indonesia, al-Samawi's books are read widely. A graduate of the Darussalam Institute for Islamic Studies at Gontor in Ponorogo, East Java, told how his Shi'i beliefs and practices still follow those set out in the works

---

82 Jalaluddin Rakhmat, interview, (2/1/2003).
83 Takim (2000:474).

of Tijani al-Samawi. Al-Samawi's first book, *Akhirnya Kutemukan Kebenaran*[84] (Finally, I Found the Truth) published in Malay in 1991 and in Indonesian in 1993 by Pustaka Pelita, Bandung, has been incredibly influential in conversions to Shi'ism. In this book, al-Samawi, who is a prominent Shi'i figure in Tunisia writes of a journey from Cairo to Alexandria and his subsequent meetings with Ayatollah Khu'i (then a prominent *marja' al-taqlid* in Iraq) and Muhammad Baqir Sadr in Najaf. Following these meetings, al-Samawi begins to question his faith and undertakes intensive study of the Shi'i doctrines and teachings, from both Sunni and Shi'i sources, for a period of three years. At the end of this, he converts to Shi'ism. The book deals not merely with al-Samawi's spiritual quest but also his reflections on and interpretations of Shi'i teachings. On his conversion, Al-Samawi writes:

> Praise be to God, I have found the alternative. After the Messenger of God, I follow the Master of the faithful ... [and other Imams after him]. I have also exchanged the *'ulama* of my people, who discouraged us from thinking, and the majority of whom always obeyed their rulers, for the devoted Shi'i *'ulama* who never closed the gate of *ijtihad*, neither submitted to nor sought mercy from the oppressive rulers.

> Yes, I have exchanged narrow thoughts and beliefs, full of superstition and contradiction, for new enlightened, open and liberal ones based on logical deduction and reasoning.[85]

It is important to note that as a direct result of the impact of this book, on 19 November 2002, the mufti of Johor, Malaysia, issued a *fatwa* declaring it to be a forbidden book. (Books are generally forbidden because they are deemed to be contrary to the true teachings of Islam.)[86] Yet despite its status in Malaysia, this book is still read and openly distributed among Muslims in Indonesia.

The most significant influence of Shi'i publishing is in the process of education, in the broadest sense of the word. For members of the Shi'i community in Indonesia, publishing, along with preaching, education and training activities, has functioned and continues to function as way to deepen and broaden their religious knowledge. While books and periodicals will never surpass the importance of encounters with religious teachers in the educational and *da'wa* process, they are instrumental in increasing comprehension and influencing

---

84 As mentioned in Chapter Two, the Indonesian translation of this work from Arabic (*Thumma Ihtadaytu*) was made by Husein Shahab, a prominent Shi'i *ustadh*. The English version is entitled *Then I was Guided*. Both Arabic and English versions are available online (http://www.al-islam.org/guided/21.html).

85 Al-Samawi (1993:183).

86 (http://islam.gov.my/e-fatwa/mufti/fatwa-warta-view.asp?keyID=327, accessed 18/10/2005). Other forbidden Shi'i works in Indonesian include Tabataba'i's *Tafsir Al-Mizan Mengupas Ayat-ayat Roh dalam Al-Quran* (Tafsir al-Mizan Analysing the Verses of Spirit in the Qur'an) and Shari'ati's *Wanita Dimata dan Hati Rasulullah* (Women in the Eyes and Heart of Muhammad).

the beliefs and practices of the community. Shi'i publications serve not only as sources of knowledge but also as patterns of behaviour. The fact that the majority of Indonesian Shi'is are converts from Sunnism only confirms the influential value of these publications.

Shi'i publishing also plays an important role in sustaining the Shi'i community as a minority Muslim group in Indonesia. Living as a minority requires ways of maintaining identity and continuity, in particular in interaction with the Sunni majority. Shi'i publications are essential tools in the daily struggle within the dominant religious system and culture, providing the community (including new converts) with the religious knowledge to respond to anti-Shi'i attacks and challenges.

As a vehicle of communication, publishing has served not only to connect the Shi'i community in Indonesia with other Shi'i communities in other parts of the world but also to integrate it into the Shi'i world. The importance of being part of this world is of great concern to Shi'i *ustadhs* such as Husein Al-Kaff, who points out that the Shi'is in Indonesia should practice their traditions in order to avoid isolation from other Shi'i communities in the world.[87] Together with the increasing numbers of Indonesian students studying in Iran, Shi'i publishing, and in particular the translations of works by *mujtahid,* has brought the community closer to Iran and increased Indonesia's status as a centre of Shi'ism. Most Indonesian Shi'is regard 'Ali Khamene'i, the *wali faqih,* as their *marja' al-taqlid*. This is a result of efforts by teachers, institutions and publications to promote the *'alamiyyat* (superiority in religious knowledge) and leadership of this figure. (Bestowing the ranks of *wilayat al-faqih* and *marja' al-taqlid* on a single person can be seen as an attempt by Iran to attract as many Shi'is as possible under its leadership). Shi'i publishing has been instrumental in forming and sustaining the intense emotional relationship between the Indonesian Shi'i community and others throughout the world, but in particular with Iran.

The impact of Shi'i publishing can be seen beyond the boundaries of the Indonesian community. Without doubt, translations and works by Indonesian Shi'is have been influential on Sunnis in Indonesia, while works of Shi'i philosophy and thought have exerted an intellectual influence on Indonesian Muslims. Ali Shari'ati's socio-philosophical works are widely read, cited and discussed, as are Hussayn Nasr's works on Islamic thought and Sufism. These works are considered to offer a strong critique of Western philosophy, worldview and modernity in general. Evidence for the impact of this is the fact that many famous Muslim intellectuals and students are influenced by certain Shi'i teachings and thoughts. Indonesia's Shi'is see it as a huge step in their

---

87   *Al-Jawad* (Sha'ban 1421/2000:2).

struggle for the recognition of their *madhhab* when Muslim intellectuals in Indonesia express a positive appreciation of the intellectual and philosophical strengths of Shi'ism.

Shi'i doctrinal works have also contributed to the maintenance of traditionalist Islamic practices, which have come under fire from Sunni reformist groups in Indonesia. (The Sunni traditionalist group rarely produces scholarly works to counter reformist criticism.) As a result, there has been an emergence of translations of traditionalist books and in fact Shi'i leaders, such as Jalaluddin Rakhmat suggest that such works serve as an effective tool for defeating reformist arguments. Rakhmat also claims that traditionalist Sunni groups in Indonesia, such as NU directly benefit from the Shi'i works.[88]

So the impact of books cannot be underestimated. Despite the fact that many anti-Shi'i groups have attempted to fight against the *madhhab*, Shi'i works have become an integral part of the intellectual and cultural life of Muslims in Indonesia. Books and articles published on the internet have further enhanced the impact of Shi'i publishing. A number of Shi'i foundations in Indonesia now provide websites carrying numerous works on various aspects of Shi'ism. Another result of the emergence and development of Shi'i publishing can be seen to have contributed to the fragmentation of religious authority in Indonesia. On the impact of the media on the Muslim world at large, Eickelman and Anderson point out that the transmission and circulation of Islamic texts through a variety of media "… mark a fragmentation of authority. 'Islamic' books set aside the long tradition of authoritative discourse by religious scholars in favour of a direct understanding of texts….".[89] Abdullah also observes that the circulation of religious texts among members of the Indonesian community has expanded the number and scope of its audience. He goes on to suggest that "the spread of literacy and the translation of formerly esoteric texts have terminated the monopoly of the *'ulama* in any religious discourse. Literacy and the growing importance of the print culture have expanded the number of people who can directly conduct a dialogue with the text."[90]

This fragmentation of religious authority in Indonesia takes different forms: first, in the context of the development of the Shi'is, fragmentation has meant the emergence of a religious group distinctive from the majority Sunni community in terms of interpretation of certain tenets of Islam. Second, the rise of a large literate cohort is the product of secular education within the Sunni community, who have the same opportunities to engage in religious interpretation as those religious scholars at the traditional centres of Islamic learning. Unsurprisingly,

---

88   Rakhmat (1997:488).
89   Eickelman and Anderson (1997:49).
90   Abdullah (1996:75).

this has prompted attacks from militant groups who claim to represent legitimate religious authority. We can conclude that the proliferation of Shi'i publishing, together with other Islamic publications, has been an undermining force against the sway of traditional religious authorities in Indonesia.

However, Indonesia is a Muslim country that has no single religious authority and it recognises various forms of Islamic tradition, two factors which encourage religious pluralism.[91] Although there is the Sunni MUI (*Majlis Ulama Indonesia*, the Indonesian Council of Ulama') created by former President Suharto, different Muslim groups tend to follow the understanding and *fatwas* of their own organisations, for example NU, Muhammadiyah or Persis. Such conditions benefit the existence of Shi'is in Indonesia. They have even gained recognition in the eyes of moderate Muslim figures of national standing.

The Indonesian Shi'i organisation, IJABI has also gained official legal recognition from the government. That said, Shi'is continue to struggle for acceptance by wider segments of the Muslim community. In this context, the goal of Shi'i publishing remains the ratification of Shi'ism as a valid Islamic *madhhab* by the religious authorities. Having demonstrated its extensive influence, we can conclude that publishing is clearly the most effective communicative weapon of struggle for the Shi'is in Indonesia.

In the concluding two chapters we turn to a consideration of the arena of religious politics in Indonesia and strategies adopted by the organisation IJABI.

---

91   Eickelman and Anderson (1997:52).

7. The Mass Organisation Ijabi

Over the course of time, the number of followers of Shi'ism in Indonesia and the number of Shi'i institutions of *da'wa*, education and publishing has continued to increase. Up to the end of Suharto's New Order, the Shi'is in Indonesia were a minority religious group, scattered throughout Indonesia but on the whole confined to urban areas. More importantly, they were not unified under a single socio-religious body. Then efforts emerged to establish a mass national organisation that would bring together all the geographically diverse Shi'i communities. This chapter aims to describe this national Shi'i organisation and reactions to it. We begin with the historical process of the establishment of IJABI *Ikatan Jama'ah Ahlul Bait Indonesia* (Indonesian Council of Ahli Bait Associations), followed by a section dealing with the ideology of IJABI in order to understand the nature of this organisation. In the third section, we survey its on-going development, in particular during the first period of leadership (2000-2004). Finally, a description of opposition to IJABI and the emergence of a Shi'i 'non-IJABI' group is provided.

A. The Foundation of IJABI

After the fall of the New Order in 1998, prominent Shi'i leaders in Indonesia, including Jalaluddin Rakhmat, Husein Shahab, Umar Shahab and Ahmad Baragbah agreed on the importance of establishing a socio-religious organisation that could unite the Shi'i community.[1] Serious attempts to set up such a body had begun in earnest in the early 1990s, with senior Shi'i leaders holding a number of meetings, formal and informal, to discuss the urgent need for, and the possibility of, a Shi'i organisation to bring together all the adherents of Shi'ism in Indonesia.

The first organisation to be set up was MAHDI, an abbreviation of *Majlis Ahlulbait di Indonesia* (Council of the *Ahli Bait* in Indonesia) founded in Jakarta in the early 1990s. It was headed by Ahmad Baragbah, Head of *Pesantren Al-Hadi* in Pekalongan, with Furqon Bukhari as the Secretary. In addition to its executive leadership, the organisation had an advisory board (*pembina*) of 14 members, which included Jalaluddin Rakhmat, Umar Shahab and other prominent Shi'i figures. However, MAHDI did not function well and almost all of its programmes soon failed. The fact that it had no legal status as a socio-religious organisation and was not recognised by the Department of Home Affairs clearly contributed to its problems. It only ever achieved recognition

---

1 Umar Shahab, interview, (9/1/2003).

as a foundation, *Yayasan MAHDI*. The key figures were Ahmad Baragbah, Zainal Abidin al-Muhdar of the Al-Hakim Foundation in Lampung and Zulfan Lindan, a political activist of the Indonesian Democratic Party for Struggle. Eventually, Jalaluddin Rakhmat and his associates withdrew from MAHDI, leaving Ahmad Baragbah and his supporters to continue until the organisation ceased activities.[2] Another factor in MAHDI's downfall appears to have been the fact that the majority of the Muslim community in Indonesia was simply unaware of its existence. Most significantly however, it failed in its primary aim to unite the followers of Shi'ism in the country and to co-ordinate all the Shi'i foundations under its umbrella.

The failure of this association to operate in Indonesia during the New Order era (1966-1998) can be attributed to two reasons: first, there was no agreement among the various groups or factions within the Shi'i community itself on how the organisation should be run and what its ideology should be. Differences of opinion developed between Jalaluddin Rakhmat and his associates with Ahmad Baragbah and other *ustadhs,* particularly regarding the legal status of MAHDI as a Shi'i organisation. Rakhmat and his supporters believed the procedures for managing and running the organisation should be under the control of the advisory board, while Baragbah's group was much more focussed on defining MAHDI's vision and activities, preferring that it become an Islamic foundation rather than an organisation. A second reason for MAHDI's failure can be found in the socio-political situation in Indonesia during the New Order era, which permitted very little space for minority religious groups to express their identity and religiosity. In this regard, the Shi'i *ustadhs* and intellectuals saw that the organisation and its members would face difficulties and even threats, not only from members of the majority Sunni community but also from the New Order regime itself. For example, any request for MAHDI to be granted legal status as a Shi'i association would almost certainly have been denied by the government, since the state was (and still is) heavily dominated by the ideology of Sunni Islam. In 1997, when asked whether Shi'is in Indonesia would establish a mass organisation, Rakhmat, at the time a declared member of the modernist Sunni organisation Muhammadiyah, responded "Because I do not want to become dependent on anyone, I will not join. But to moderate the atmosphere so as not to lead to continuous misunderstanding, I will state my disagreement if the Shi'is in Indonesia establish a social-religious organisation."[3] For most of the prominent Shi'i figures, such an application of *taqiyya* is regarded as an essential method for dealing with any socio-political situation not conducive to the existence or development of the minority group. In sum, a series of complex and interrelated factors - internal and external, religious and socio-political

---

2   Furqon Bukhari, interview, (10/9/2002), Umar Shahab, interview, (9/1/2003).
3   Jalaluddin Rakhmat, interview, by Irwan Natsir, (*Hikmah* 1/11/1997:15).

– led to the failure of Indonesia's first national Shi'i association. And in fact, over the years, the majority of Shi'is in Indonesia seem to have forgotten the existence of MAHDI and its planned role within their community.

After the fall of the New Order, there arose fresh encouragement for, and even insistence on, the need to have a national organisation to unite the Indonesian followers of Shi'ism. These calls elicited a significant response from prominent Shi'i leaders and in turn gained support from the Islamic Republic of Iran. A series of important meetings took place. Four prominent Shi'i *ustadhs* and intellectuals, Jalaluddin Rakhmat, Ahmad Baragbah, Zahir Yahya and Umar Shahab, together with a representative from Iran held a meeting to discuss the possibility of founding a Shi'i organisation in Indonesia. The first meeting resulted in an agreement to found a national organisation but initially failed to form a committee to oversee the process. Eventually Jalaluddin Rakhmat and other intellectuals formed the necessary committee to establish the organisation and define its ideological foundation and principles. The committee also agreed on a name, proposed by Rakhmat, for the organisation - IJABI, an abbreviation of *Ikatan Jamaah Ahlul Bait Indonesia*, or the Indonesian Council of Ahli Bait Associations. Reportedly, Rakhmat originally planned to officially declare the association open at the commemoration of *'Ashura* in 1999 without waiting for agreement from renowned Shi'i *ustadhs*. However, this would have meant that from the outset IJABI could not claim to represent all Shi'i groups in Indonesia. Rakhmat subsequently agreed to postpone its inauguration. He also agreed to hold meetings with other prominent *ustadhs*, mainly Qum alumni, in order that IJABI could be recognised by all Shi'i groups. The meetings were instrumental in establishing the concept of a mass organisation to the wider Shi'i community in Indonesia and were intended to recruit Shi'i *ustadhs* into the process.[4]

One of the most important meetings, conducted in ICC of Al-Huda in Jakarta, brought together Shi'i figures who had previously clashed during their involvement with MAHDI: Jalaluddin Rakhmat, Zainal Abidin al-Muhdar, Husein Shahab, Umar Shahab and Ahmad Baragbah. This meeting produced a general agreement among all the participants to support Rakhmat's proposal to found a Shi'i organisation in Indonesia, to be named IJABI.[5] However, it was not long before old disputes reared their heads and misunderstandings and disagreements between the *ustadhs* and intellectuals impacted upon the process of establishment and development of IJABI. Some reports suggest that these disagreements were not just characterised by differences of ideological opinion but also by personal matters and stereotyping of and by certain groups.

---

4   Umar Shahab, interview, (9/1/2003).
5   Jalaluddin Rakhmat, interview, (2/1/2003).

Despite the disagreements Rakhmat, the architect of IJABI decided to go ahead with the organisation's inauguration on 1 July 2000. He visited Iran to inform Shi'i leaders there of this important strategic plan for the community in Indonesia and to gain the support of the *wali faqih*, Ayatollah 'Ali Khamene'i. The inauguration of IJABI was followed, the very next day, by its first national congress. This historical double event was reported by more than ten national and local newspapers in Bandung and Jakarta. Figures suggest that approximately 2000 Shi'is, from 20 provinces in Indonesia, as well as from Singapore and Iran participated in IJABI's opening ceremony, which took place in Gedung Merdeka, Bandung, where the historic 1955 Asia-Africa Conference had also been held. The choice of this location was to symbolise to the public the significance of the new organisation in the social and religious life of Indonesian society.

A number of Muslim scholars – both Sunni and Shi'i - from home and abroad were invited to speak at the seminars following the inauguration. Some of the most high-profile of the Shi'i teachers and scholars were Shaykh Ja'far Hadi from Iran, Ayatollah Ibrahim Kazerooni from London and Muhammad Baqir and Rusli, both from Singapore. The presence of such dignitaries demonstrated the international support for the establishment of IJABI, Iran's solidarity being the most crucial to its success. However, prominent Indonesian Muslim intellectuals, including Nurcholish Madjid and leaders of Muslim organisations such as Ahmad Syafi'i Ma'arif of Muhammadiyyah and Hasyim Muzadi of NU, who were originally expected to speak at the meeting were notably absent from IJABI's inauguration. These absences called into question the approval of key elements of the Muslim community of Indonesia, namely the Sunni Muslim intellectuals, modernists and traditionalists alike.

It is widely accepted that IJABI"'s inauguration was possible due largely to the democratic atmosphere in Indonesia at that time, fostered by the liberal, moderate President Abdurrahman Wahid. Reporting on the inauguration, the magazine *Gatra* carried the headline "*Mumpung Gus Dur Jadi Presiden*" ('Taking Advantage while Gus Dur is President').[6] As this suggests, the socio-political situation in Indonesia after the fall of Suharto's New Order regime gave freedom and opportunity to the adherents of minority religious groups to express their beliefs and religiosity. It is generally acknowledged that Abdurrahman Wahid was a man of openness and pluralism and that his presidency was marked by the emergence of popular social and religious movements. Such movements developed not out of a desire to take part in the development of the Indonesian state and society, but rather to demonstrate their own identity and existence, something which had not been possible during the New Order period. These new-found freedoms of expression occurred in an environment often described as the euphoria of reformation, *'Reformasi'*. Rakhmat and his associates capitalised

---

6   *Gatra* (15/7/2000).

on the changed social and political situation under Abdurrahman Wahid's government. In fact, Rakhmat admitted that the IJABI inauguration and national congress were held in haste, without sufficient preparation, simply because he and his associates wanted to seize the moment, anxious about the possibility of the fall of President Abdurrahman Wahid. There were rumours that the annual meeting of the People's Consultative Assembly (*Majlis Permusyawaratan Rakyat*, MPR) scheduled for August 2000 would start impeachment proceedings against Wahid, so Rakhmat was anxious to win official recognition for IJABI while he was still in office.[7]

President Abdurrahman Wahid had been invited to attend IJABI's inauguration and to formally open its first national congress; however, he cancelled due to another pressing state duty in Jakarta. Instead, he asked the State Secretary, Djohan Effendy to deputise for him. Effendy did not attend either. In the end, it was the Chief of the Directorate of Social and Political Affairs of West Java, Edy Moelyono, acting on behalf of the Governor of West Java who formally opened and delivered a speech at this historical event. The opening ceremony was marked by all participants standing and chanting a *salawat*, an invocation to the Prophet Muhammad and his Household. While the inauguration went well, inevitably, the absence of Abdurrahman Wahid and other representatives of central government came as a blow to the architects of IJABI and to Jalaluddin Rakhmat in particular. He expressed his disappointment that the president had not sent a representative from Jakarta, which would have sent the clear message that the government supported the organisation. Nevertheless, he went on to tell of the full support offered by President Abdurrahman Wahid to the organisation several days before its declaration, and even long before he became president. Abdurrahman Wahid, claimed Rakhmat, would have mobilised members of the mass organisation NU (of which he had been head) if the Shi'i community had been attacked, or if the Indonesian government had prohibited the Shi'is from practising in the country.[8]

As chief of the steering committee for IJABI's inauguration, Jalaluddin Rakhmat gave an important speech at the event entitled '*IJABI: Menyerukan Suara Serak Sejarah*' (IJABI: Calling Out History's Husky Voice).[9] The speech cited important socio-historical reasons for the establishment of IJABI in the reformation era, a time when the country was entering the new millennium with a strong will to establish an open and democratic Indonesia, free from tyranny and arrogance and allowing its citizens to live according to their beliefs

---

7   *Gatra* (15/7/2000).
8   *Pikiran Rakyat* (2/7/2000), *Metro* (2/7/2000).
9   *Al-Tanwir* (16/7/2000).

Reformation has given us the opportunity to express ourselves without fear or any sense of guilt. We all are important parts of this nation and must make valuable contributions to its prosperity. We view Abdurrahman Wahid's government as the representation of the victory of the Muslim community on the political stage. Long hidden on the historical path was a group of Indonesian Muslims who wanted to demonstrate their religiosity on the basis of a loving devotion to God, His Messenger (Peace be Upon Him) and his Household. In the past, their voices, once in while, were heard from small *surau* (prayer rooms) in villages when they pronounced a supplication: *li khamsatun utfi biha har al-waba' al-hatima, al-mustafa wa al-murtada wa ibnahuma wa Fatima* [I have five (persons) with whom I extinguish the 'heat' of crushing disease: al-Mustafa (the Prophet), al-Murtada ('Ali), his two sons (Hasan and Husayn) and Fatima].[10] Now, in the era of an *'ulama*'s government, they leap out from that darkened path and try to stand in a well-lit place.[11]

Furthermore, Rakhmat's speech defined the general characteristics of IJABI as a new socio-religious organisation. He emphasised that IJABI's intention was not to follow Julius Caesar's victorious statement *Veni, Vidi, Vici*, but rather to sit modestly among existing Muslim organisations and society in Indonesia, while at the same time propagating and implementing the teachings which defend the *mustad'afin* (the oppressed). Rakhmat went on to state that at a time when many Islamic organisations were joining forces with political parties, his community had established a social organisation *without* political affiliations. IJABI was expected to take on the role of assisting people to solve their various difficulties and to face a variety of challenges in order to gain salvation - like the ship of salvation spoken of by the Prophet in the famous Hadith of *Al-Safina*: "the *ahl al-bayt* are like Noah's ark; whoever boards the ark will be safe and whoever leaves it will be sunken". Rakhmat stated that the position of IJABI was becoming the more important when Indonesia faced many economic, social and political crises. He appealed to Muslims in Indonesia to join the ship of IJABI, because IJABI would not be involved in political activities: "This ship is not a political vehicle to achieve important positions in either legislative or executive institutions."[12] The speech was a clear affirmation of the non-political stance of IJABI.

---

10 This supplication is pronounced widely among the followers of traditionalist Islam in Java. It is commonly uttered by the congregation in the mosque prior to the performance of the daily obligatory prayers (Machasin, interview, 22/2/2005). On the strength of this practice, the NU leader Abdurrahman Wahid has suggested that NU is culturally Shi'i.
11 *Al-Tanwir* (16/7/2000:4).
12 *Al-Tanwir* (16/7/2000:4).

Jalaluddin Rakhmat's position has been crucial to the development of IJABI. He even describes himself as "a pregnant mother who then gave birth", saying, "So, I must sacrifice (myself) to be pregnant and now to give birth."[13] This statement contains two important points concerning his position as a Shi'i figure. First, it can be interpreted as meaning that before the reformation era Rakhmat concealed the existence of the Shi'i community in Indonesia. During this time he experienced various difficulties and threats, arising from the fact that the Shi'is were seen as being synonymous with hardliners, militants or revolutionaries. Secondly, his statement can be understood as a declaration that the existence of Shi'is and their organisation in the Sunni-dominated country was thanks to Reformasi.[14] However, Dimitri Mahayana, an engineer and lecturer at ITB who headed the organising committee of IJABI's inauguration, rejects this interpretation. He states that the official declaration of IJABI was not a proclamation of the presence of Shi'is in Indonesia, but rather it was a proclamation of the spirit of Muslim unity, on the basis of loving devotion to the Qur'an and the *ahl al-bayt* of the Prophet as trustees of the traditions of the Prophet.[15]

During the first national congress, participants discussed and laid down the Statute of IJABI, its rules of organisation, its programmes, as well as electing its chiefs and organisers. The congress elected Jalaluddin Rakhmat Chairman of the Advisory Council and Dimitri Mahayana Chief of the Executive of IJABI. The Advisory Council consisted of 12 members nominated by prominent Shi'i *ustadhs* and intellectuals from various areas of Indonesia. Notably, some of these members were actually recognised figures of the Sunni community. (The number 'twelve' may symbolise the twelve Imams within Twelver *Imamiyya* Shi'ism.) The Advisory Council members were: Sayyid Segaf al-Jufri, Sayyid Dr. O. Hashem, K.H. Muchtar Adam, K.H. Djamaluddin Asmawi, Sayyid Muhammad Taufiq Yahya, Sayyid Othman Omar Shihab, Lc., Ust. Hasan Rahmat, Sayyid Ir. Haidar Baqir, MA, Prof. Dr. Ridwan Suhud, Prof. Dr. Sipon Muladi, Sayyid Drs. Ayik Ali Idrus and Sayyid Ja'far Ali Alqadri.

An examination of the position of these members of the Advisory Council of IJABI, as figures prominent in Indonesian society, helps us to understand the influence of IJABI in this Sunni majority country. It is important to note that seven of the twelve members are Sayyids. These seven Sayyids are influential not only in the Shi'i community but also in Indonesian society at large. First, Sayyid Segaf al-Jufri is one of the most respected Shi'i *ustadhs* in Indonesia. He lives in Solo, Central Java and a number of Shi'is in the area have studied under him. Even Jalaluddin Rakhmat regards al-Jufri as his teacher. Second,

---

13 *Pikiran Rakyat* (2/7/2000).
14 *Metro* (2/7/2000).
15 *Pikiran Rakyat* (10/7/2000).

O. Hashem of the al-Saqqaf clan is a Shi'i intellectual and co-founder of YAPI, known for his controversial and polemical works. Third, Muhammad Taufik Yahya, one of the late Husein Al-Habsyi's sons-in-law, lives in Jakarta and is a Shi'i *ustadh* engaged in the field of *da'wa*. Fourth, Othman Omar Shihab is a famous *ustadh* in Jakarta who often appears on Islamic television programmes, although the majority of Muslims in Indonesia are not aware of his adherence to Shi'ism. Haidar Bagir is a famous intellectual-businessman, who founded and the Mizan Publishing Company, well-known for publishing Shi'i books. The two last names are local leaders: Ayik Ali Idrus is a Muslim scholar in Palembang, South Sumatra, who has held several social positions, including the chairmanship of MUI of Palembang. Idrus is not known among the local Muslim community as a Shi'i. Ja'far Ali Alqadri is a Shi'i leader in Pontianak, West Kalimantan.

The non-Sayyids are also influential Shi'i leaders in various parts of the country. Some are religious teachers at Islamic foundations or *pesantren*, while others are university professors. Muchtar Adam is the head of Babussalam, a *pesantren* located in Bandung. He is also a former member of the National People's Representative Council (DPR) of the National Mandate Party (PAN) led by Amien Rais, the former chairman of People's Consultative Assembly (MPR). Adam is engaged in *da'wa* and educational activities in Indonesia. As a Muslim scholar, he has written several books and he is known to have a close relationship with Jalaluddin Rakhmat. Another famous Shi'i teacher in Bandung, also closely related to the chairman of the Advisory Council of IJABI is Hasan Rahmat, who leads a Shi'i *pesantren* in Bandung named *Al-Mukarramah*. Jamaluddin Asmawi is a famous Shi'i figure who has played an important role in the spread of Shi'ism in East Java. He taught Shi'ism at his Islamic foundation in Jember, East Java and is engaged in other *da'wa* activities. He too had a close relationship with Jalaluddin Rakhmat and the late Husein Al-Habsyi of Bangil. Ridwan Suhud is a professor at a university in Bandung and Sipon Muladi is a professor in Samarinda, East Kalimantan. Ridwan Suhud of ITB is known to have converted to Shi'ism long before the victory of the Iranian revolution.[16] In sum, all those who became members of IJABI's Advisory Council are prominent Shi'i *ustadhs* and scholars in Indonesia and respected by adherents of the *madhhab*.

As in other socio-religious organisations, the executive board of IJABI consists of a chairman, general secretary, treasury, and several departments. The leading positions are occupied by Shi'i intellectuals: Dimitri Mahayana became the national chairman and Hadi Suwastio became its general secretary. It is important to point out that three influential figures in key positions of the IJABI leadership structure have close relationships with one another. Both Dimitri Mahayana and

---

16   Wisananingrum (2001:67-68).

Hadi Suwastio studied religion from Jalaluddin Rakhmat while still students at ITB. Both are known as prominent young Muslim intellectuals who have played a role in the development of Shi'ism in the country.

Soon after its declaration, national congress and the inauguration of its leaders and organisers, IJABI requested legal status from the Department of Home Affairs in Jakarta. In early August 2000, a formal letter, supplemented by the organisation's statute, rules of association, national guidelines for the programmes and leadership structure was signed by Dimitri Mahayana, the Chairman of the Executive Board and Hadi Suwastio, the General Secretary, and brought to Jakarta. In response, the Department of Home Affairs granted IJABI formal legal status as a societal organisation on 11 August 2000. The quick processing of IJABI's application and the fact that a Shi'i association was legally recognised can be put down to the positive conditions of Reformasi. Legal recognition means that IJABI officially becomes a national Shi'i organisation in Indonesia, an important event within the Islamic history of the country. Such recognition is crucial symbolic capital in the continuing struggle of the Shi'is in Indonesia.

B. The Ideological Foundations of IJABI

The nature of IJABI ideology can be seen from its Statute, which was formulated and ratified at the first national congress on 2 July 2000. The preamble to the Statute clearly states that the establishment of IJABI is based on the principal doctrines of the Shi'i *madhhab,* even though IJABI itself is declared open to all Muslims, whether Shi'i or Sunni. The Statute goes on to state that devotion to the Prophet's *ahl al-bayt* is the axis that unites Muslims, regardless of *madhhab.* It is agreed that a loving devotion to God can only be achieved through a loving devotion to his Prophet and in turn, a loving devotion to the Prophet can only be achieved through a loving devotion to his Household.

By using the term '*ahl al-bayt*' the organisation indicates its Shi'i nature (although devotion to the Prophet's *ahl al-bayt* is also recognised in Sunnism). Imam Shafi'i, the founder of the Shafi'i school of jurisprudence followed by the majority of Muslims in Indonesia, once wrote "If the Shi'i loves the Household of the Prophet Muhammad, witness, oh Genies (*Jinn*) and Mankind, that I am a Shi'i."[17] The Statute also states that for centuries Indonesian Muslims have attempted to preserve and develop a loving devotion to the *ahl al-bayt* and that the establishment of IJABI is an attempt to continue the struggle of previous *'ulama* and Muslim leaders in this respect.

---

17   Rakhmat (1998:244).

The Statute itself does not provide a definition of *ahl al-bayt*. However, Jalaluddin Rakhmat suggests that the term carries a broad meaning. He interprets the term 'lovers of the *ahl al-bayt*' as not only Shi'is, or those with their own genealogical lines to the Prophet, but all followers of any *madhhab* in Islam who love his Household.[18] By adopting this very broad definition of *ahl al-bayt*, IJABI intended to attract a larger number of followers; however, the reality is that only Shi'is join and participate in the association. The reasons for this are examined below.

Despite its policy of openness and inclusivity, IJABI is clearly Shi'i in nature. This is illustrated in its belief in the five articles of faith (*usul al-din*) as stated in the introduction to its Statute: "the lovers of *ahl al-bayt* in Indonesia are willing to unite and strengthen fronts by establishing a social organisation based on the beliefs in the Oneness of God (*tawhid*), Prophecy (*nubuwwa*), the imamate (*imama*), justice (*'adala*) and the return of servants to their Lord, the Most Merciful and the Beneficent". Unlike the six pillars of faith of Sunnism, these five are specific to Shi'ism. Moreover, as Jalaluddin Rakhmat declared on at least one occasion, the lovers of *ahl al-bayt* mean adherents of Shi'ism.[19]

The preamble to the Statute of IJABI cites the famous Hadith of *Al-Safina* regarding *ahl al-bayt*, namely: "the *ahl al-bayt* is like Noah's ark (in typhoon and floods). Whoever embarks on the ship is safe; whoever leaves it is swung and flung about." This is used as the textual proof for the establishment of IJABI, likened to the ship of salvation that protects its members, helping them to gain salvation both in this world and in the hereafter. In addition, there is an explicit expression of the belief in the twelfth Imam - Imam Mahdi - and recognition of his leadership within Shi'ism. This is followed by a call for his blessing in the establishment and running of the organisation. The Statute also states the position of IJABI as a part of a worldwide movement of Shi'i organisations. In the last paragraph of its introduction, the Statute says:

"By saying *bi ism Allah majraha wa mursaha* [in the name of Allah, whether we sail or not] and with the emission of enlightening radiation of the stars of the Prophet's *ahl al-bayt*, we sail the ship of IJABI which will protect all lovers of the *ahl al-bayt* from their enemies, advance their thought spiritually, intellectually and morally and let all believers prosper, physically and spiritually. Finally, we would like to join this ship together with other ships in the whole world under the blessing and leadership of the Lord of the Age, Imam Mahdi, the Awaited, *'ajjala Allah farajah al-sharif* [May God speed his noble appearance]."

IJABI's ideology is also reflected in its logo, which is an image of Noah's ship. IJABI expects the followers of *ahl al-bayt* in Indonesia to embark on this ship:

---

18   *Pikiran Rakhmat* (2/7/2000).
19   Rakhmat (1998:240-242).

"Aboard they will be transported to the eternal realm of Divine love and directed by the infallible Imams". The ship is also a well-known symbol in Indonesia, an archipelago whose geography stretches along the equator, between Asia and Australia and between the Indian and Pacific oceans. Historically, Indonesians explored the wide oceans in order to sustain life and to learn. The use of the ship logo reflects IJABI's connection to the nation, something not necessarily evident in other Shi'i organisations.

The IJABI logo depicts twin spread sails, which represent *Al-Thaqalayn* (the "Two Weighty Matters"), the Qur'an and the purified *ahl al-bayt* of the Prophet (*'itra*) as mentioned in the Hadith familiar to the followers of Shi'ism. This Hadith contradicts the one well known among Sunnis, which claims the Qur'an and Sunna of the Prophet as constituting the fundamental Sunni legal sources.[20] IJABI believes that all its programmes should be in accordance with the *Thaqalayn* of the Qur'an and the *ahl al-bayt* and the missionary goal to propagate Islamic teachings narrated through the *ahl al-bayt*.

In the logo, a blood-red colour around the ship's sails represents bravery while a white symbolises the purity, holiness and cleanliness of the innermost essence of human beings. Furthermore, the red used in the outlines and the white space within refer to *jamal* (beauty) and *jalal* (strength) among the Attributes of Divinity.

The ship itself is drawn with spiral lines indicating the arms of the *ahl al-bayt* always ready to convey divine blessing. The logo includes five lines that describe the *Ahl al-Kisa* (the People of Cloak, the *ahl al-bayt*) and below these the ship is sailing on nine waves, each representing one of the Imams who lead and guide the whole universe. These 14 waves and lines together refer to the fourteen Infallibles, which include the twelve Imams, the Prophet Muhammad and his daughter Fatima. The text *Ikatan Jamaah Ahlulbait Indonesia*, the name of the organisation, encircles the ship. The twin spread sails, combined with a circle appearing as a beacon, symbolise the light of the universe. The ship is moving from the East, that is, the sunrise and source of illumination. The ship sails across the ocean, bringing with it the light that rends the veils of darkness in the world of non-existence.[21]

It is important to remember that the term *Ahl al-Kisa* (People of Cloak) refers to the five addressed in the Qur'anic verse[22] known within Shi'ism as the *tathir*, or 'purification' verse. This verse (and the event in which the Prophet gathered his immediate household under his cloak before the people of Medina) supplies the principal designation for the immunity of the *ahl al-bayt* and is memorised

---

20 The complete version of the Hadith can be seen p.85 fn.7.
21 http://www.ijabi.or.id/bspweb/maknalogoing.htm.
22 QS (33:33).

by every Shi'i. It states that God wished to remove all abomination from them. Thus the first meaning of *ahl al-bayt* within Shi'ism refers to the five purified people, the Prophet, 'Ali bin Abi Talib, Fatima, Hasan and Husayn. The second meaning of the term also includes nine Imams who are considered infallible as well.

The Statute of IJABI states that the foundation of this socio-religious organisation is Islam and the loving devotion to the Prophet's *ahl al-bayt* (Article 3). Its identity is the Qur'an, the Prophetic Traditions and loving devotion of the purified Household of the Prophet (Article 4). Thereafter, IJABI has five goals:

1. To teach people to live in accordance with the principles of co-existence and the imamate.

2. To introduce and propagate the Islamic teachings narrated through the Prophet's *ahl al-bayt* (Peace Be Upon Him).

3. To empower low economic communities and the oppressed, *al-mustad'afin*.

4. To advance spiritual and intellectual studies.

5. To maintain good relations with all Islamic organisations (article 5).

These goals are to be achieved by undertaking actions as mentioned in Article 6 below:

1. To establish and develop educational (*ta'dib*), economic, social and *da'wa* institutions.

2. To establish and develop Islamic libraries.

3. To conduct Islamic studies and research.

4. To publish bulletins, books, magazines and newspapers.

5. To establish approaches to other Islamic organisations and to create Islamic brotherhood among fellow Muslim communities.

The first and second goals indicate the Shi'i character of IJABI. The first goal is to establish a community of adherents to Shi'ism in Indonesia and IJABI wants to unite them under the umbrella of its organisation. This corresponds to the function of IJABI as a mass organisation to assemble the community of *ahl al-bayt* in Indonesia (Article 9). Related to this is the necessity of the community not only to believe in *imamate* but also to practice all the teachings of Islam, particularly those of the Imams. This goal indicates the internal orientation of IJABI's mission, in so far as it focuses first and foremost on the development and progress of its members and of all Shi'is in Indonesia. The second goal is external, implying that the true teachings of Shi 'ism have not yet spread or been understood among the majority of Indonesian Muslims. It is the duty of IJABI to introduce them to these ideas and to teach them about Shi'ism. Both these goals can be categorised as the religious dimension of IJABI.

The third goal reflects the social character of the organisation, which is to support the oppressed. This is one of the most important aspects of Shi'ism and one frequently emphasised in Shi'i writings. The need to side with those less fortunate perhaps originates from the experiences of the Shi'is themselves as a minority religious group. In the context of Sunni-Shi'i relations, the Shi'is have generally been the oppressed party. For these reasons, IJABI aims to undertake programmes designed to raise up the poor and the oppressed.

The fourth goal of IJABI demonstrates the intellectual and scientific character of the organisation. IJABI states its interest and involvement in studies and research in scientific fields and believes that this will advance spiritual development. IJABI's belief in a unified system of both intellectual and spiritual dimensions is a further reflection of its Shi'i nature.

Just as the first four goals correspond to the first four actions of Article 6, the fifth goal correlates to the fifth action. Regarding this last goal, as a new Muslim organisation, IJABI attempts to forge good relations, not only with existing Muslim associations in Indonesia, such as NU, Muhammadiyah and Persis, but also with other international Muslim - both Sunni and Shi'i - organisations as well as non-Muslim associations. As a recognised socio-religious association, IJABI takes its duty seriously to participate in the development of Indonesian society as a whole.

According to its Statute, IJABI is independent and non-sectarian (Article 7). It is not affiliated to any political party or to the state. Jalaluddin Rakhmat has said that IJABI is not a means for anyone to gain an executive or legislative position. This is affirmed by the fact that those who are active in a political party cannot also join the executive committee. Its non-sectarian character means that followers of any *madhhab* may join IJABI, provided they are adult Muslims and willing to obey the Statutes of the organisation (Article 11). Article 11 is formulated specifically for the purpose of attracting large numbers of members to the organisation. Recognising the need for a broad membership, Rakhmat tried to deny the specific Shi'i nature of IJABI:

> IJABI is not a social organisation that provides an umbrella for Shi'i adherents alone, but it is a social organisation open to all *madhhab* and Muslim groups in Indonesia. Within IJABI at the present time, there are indeed many people coming from a variety of *madhhabs* and groups. They are united in order to love God, His messenger and his *ahl al-bayt*.[23]

IJABI has formulated its own vision: "to present an intellectual movement which enlightens Islamic thought and to empower the oppressed (*mustad'afin*)" and its mission is "to assemble all lovers of the *ahl al-bayt,* from any *madhhab.*"[24] Dimitri Mahayana, the first Chairman of IJABI's Executive Council elaborated on the various kinds of oppression, including socio-economic oppression and oppression against self-expression. He reiterated that socio-economic oppression is the result of global capitalism and the subsequent gap between North and South - the developed and the developing countries - which in turn has led to a new form of imperialism. Oppression in the field of religious expression is the consequence of a lack of tolerance and mutual respect.[25] Similarly, Jalaluddin Rakhmat has emphasised that IJABI is an umbrella organisation for a community which has been marginalised throughout history, pointing out that IJABI does not represent any political elite, but takes the side of the common man and the oppressed. The statements by Mahayana and Rakhmat underscore IJABI's goal to empower those sections of society which have been neglected by many other groups and organisations in the country.[26]

IJABI expects to play a role in the realisation of a just and civilised civil society, *masyarakat madani* (Article 10) and for establishing a just Muslim community in Indonesia as a whole. Dimitri Mahayana also outlined two arenas of empowerment for IJABI's membership: the material and the intellectual. Material empowerment means generating a variety of business and economic opportunities. Thus, IJABI attempts to establish business networks which tie in with existing international Muslim business networks and through which the organisation can improve the economic conditions of its members and of the Muslim community in Indonesia in general. With regard to intellectual empowerment, Mahayana suggests that real empowerment comes from the spiritual depth of human beings, both individually and socially. IJABI hopes to undertake activities that will set in motion a transformation process to produce dynamic thought and a world-view based on the principle of *tawhid* (the Oneness of God) and the ideal of Divine love applied in daily life.[27]

This leads us to another important aspect of the ideology of IJABI, the paradigm of love. Dimitri Mahayana points to an historical example of this 'love paradigm', as practiced by Imam 'Ali bin Abi Talib, the first Imam, who is said to have frequently bathed with the lepers living in surrounding suburban areas of Medina.[28] Leaders of IJABI regard this 'love paradigm' as a unique feature of their new organisation. Many works by Jalaluddin Rakhmat, for example,

---

24 http://www.ijabi.or.id/deforganisasi.htm.
25 *Pikiran Rakyat* (10/7/2000).
26 *Pikiran Rakyat* (2/7/2000).
27 *Pikiran Rakyat* (10/7/2000).
28 *Pikiran Rakyat* (10/7/2000).

promote the importance of love in social and religious life. He once stated that the *Madhhab Alawi* (the *madhhab* of 'Ali, or Shi'ism) is the *madhhab* of love, as it is represented in the life story of 'Ali bin Abi Talib.[29]

We have now established that IJABI was founded on the principal doctrines of Shi'ism. The next step is to scrutinise its organisational principles, and in particular the structure of its leadership. In this respect, IJABI resembles NU, the largest traditionalist Muslim organisation in Indonesia. Its national leadership consists of a Religious Advisory Council, *Dewan Syuro* and an Executive Council, *Tanfidziyah*. This structure was chosen in order to confer status on the *'ulama*, although they do not hold the highest authority. IJABI's Religious Advisory Council is a collective consultative leadership and is positioned at the top of the organisation. The Executive Council is responsible for the implementation of all decisions by the organisation's congress. As is stated in the Statutes, Article 14, each section of the leadership is headed by a general chairman, *ra'is 'am*. The highest authority in IJABI is not in the hands of the Religious Advisory Council, instead it is held by a congress, *muktamar* - either national or extraordinary - at the national level and by regional or district conferences, *musyawarah* at the regional or district levels (Article 12). The Rules of Organisation state that "congress holds the highest authority" (Article 10.2). From this we are to deduce that the authority structure of IJABI is based on the democratic principle that anyone can participate in making organisational decisions through either a congress or a conference.

At the apex of the organisation, the Religious Advisory Council advises and supervises the Executive Council regarding the implementation of all congress decisions. It has no authority over that of the Executive Council. Any final report of the Executive Council regarding the implementation of congress decisions is evaluated by the next session of congress, not by the Religious Advisory Council. The relationship between the Religious Advisory Council and the Executive Council is purely consultative. However, it should be noted that the Rules of Organisation (Article 20.3) state that the members of the Religious Advisory Council consist of *'ulama*, *ustadhs* and intellectuals who "understand the Islamic and the modern sciences, understand the Indonesian social and political context, guard their own self-esteem, do not follow their passions and attempt to safeguard Islamic teachings." These qualifications reflect the high status of the Religious Advisory Council within the organisation.

IJABI's decision to make congress, not the Religious Advisory Council the highest authority is similar to situations in other social and religious organisations in Indonesia. IJABI does not imitate the Shi'i leadership model of *wilayat al-faqih,* which gives the highest authority to the *'ulama'*. Consequently, the majority of

---

29   Rakhmat (1999:294-295).

Qum alumni *ustadhs* view IJABI as an organisation that does not rightly reflect the leadership principles of Shi'ism and this is a reason for their rejection of IJABI. For the leaders of IJABI, the rule is simply a manifestation of democratic organisation, honouring the participation of its members.

C. The Development of IJABI

Although it is too early to evaluate the development of this new socio-religious organisation, let alone predict its future, it is relevant to describe its early growth and the implementation of its programmes. The public attendance at IJABI's inauguration and first national congress in Bandung in July 2000 illustrates the enthusiasm among Indonesian Shi'is for its coming into being. According to media reports, the number of participants reached more than 2,000, with people coming from 20 provinces throughout Indonesia. At the time of the inauguration Jalaluddin Rakhmat claimed that IJABI had about three million followers from a variety of backgrounds, including one ex-dissident Muslim group (which he called a 'traditionalist element'), Muslim intellectuals and even poor people, the *mustadh'afin*. According to Rakhmat's analysis, the majority of the 'traditionalist element' hailed from Makassar, South Sulawesi and West Java. He said that the social basis of IJABI was comparable to that of the Darul Islam separatist movement most active in those areas. It is certainly true that some members of IJABI are ex-members of the now banned Darul Islam (DI/NII). The second group of participants, the intellectuals are the university students and campus groups who were introduced to the religious and intellectual discourses developed by IJABI leaders. The third element, the poor, generally come from West Java and who, in accordance with Shi'i ideology, have been raised up and educated by the same figures who founded or joined IJABI.[30] However, just as with other socio-religious organisations such as NU and Muhammadiyah which also claim millions of followers, these figures cannot be proved. In fact, IJABI meetings and gatherings of late seem to have attracted fewer participants than were at the first national congress.

The Executive Council of IJABI has tried to implement both long-term and short-term programmes, as outlined in the National Guidelines for Programmes (2000-2004). Both programmes have internal and external elements. The IJABI executive structure comprises six departments, each with its own programme, namely: organisation, empowerment of the Muslim community, intellectual development and *da`wa*, education, media and information technology and international relations. As a new organisation, IJABI appears to give priority to raising the profile of the organisation throughout the country by establishing

---

30   *Tekad* (10-11/7/2000).

more and more branches, including regional/provincial leadership councils (*Dewan Pimpinan Wilayah*, DPW), district leadership councils (*Dewan Pimpinan Daerah*, DPD) and sub-district leadership councils (*Dewan Piminan Cabang*, DPC). Some months after its foundation, the national Executive Council initiated various programmes, while Shi'i leaders in several provinces began organise regional conferences. Often these regional conferences were combined with a seminar to which the Chairman of the Religious Advisory Council, Jalaluddin Rakhmat, was invited, along with other Shi'i intellectuals and local Muslim intellectuals and leaders. The regional branch of South Sumatra, for instance, was officially inaugurated on 17 September 2000 and held a conference on the same day. The guests included Jalaluddin Rakhmat, Sri Adyanti Rachmadi and Muslim intellectuals from the capital city of Palembang - Prof. Jalaluddin, the then Rector of IAIN Raden Fatah and Mal An Abdullah, the General Chairman of the provincial branch of NU – who were asked to speak on "Inter-religious Tolerance."[31] Such activities show the early growth of IJABI as a vigorous.

By February 2004, IJABI had 14 provincial, 48 district and 25 sub-district branches. The regional or provincial branches include South Sumatra, West Java, South Sulawesi, JABODEBEK[32] (Jakarta, Bogor, Depok, Bekasi), Yogyakarta, Lampung, North Sumatra, Central Java, East Java, West Nusa Tenggara, Bangka Belitung and Central Sulawesi. Additionally, there are so-called 'regional coordinators' for provinces where a regional branch of IJABI has yet to be established, including Aceh, Riau, Bengkulu, Banten, West Kalimantan, East Kalimantan, Bali and East Nusa Tenggara. IJABI has also established autonomous institutions such as the *Ikatan Pelajar Ahlul Bait Indonesia* (Association of Indonesian *Ahl al-Bayt* Students), *Badan Advokasi dan Pengembangan Hukum dan Hak Azazi Manusia* (Board for Advocacy and the Development of Law and Human Rights) and Fatimiyyah (the *Ahl al-Bayt* Women's League). IJABI has also established a branch in Qum, Iran. Some regional or district branches have already embarked upon their programmes, while others - possibly most others - have not yet been active in implementing programmes for the development of Shi'ism in their areas.

The departments of the national Executive Council of IJABI have drawn up a number of long-term programmes (although these have been less successful than the short-term programmes) including the establishment of provincial and district branches, as outlined in the guidelines. It appears that IJABI relies heavily on the Division of *Imdad Mustad'afin* at the Muthahhari Foundation, to execute its programmes of relief to the poor in the Muslim community. This division has considerable experience in assistance to poor children and orphans; for example, on 2 July 2000 it carried out a mass circumcision programme on

31   *Al-Tanwir* (17/9/2000).
32   This is different from the popular acronym JABOTABEK (Jakarta, Bogor, Tangerang and Bekasi).

the occasion of the celebration of the Prophet's birthday and the inauguration of IJABI.[33] Several other regular programmes of this division involve the participation of students from the Muthahhari Senior High School. Such close co-operation between the two institutions is explained by the fact that the head of the division of *Imdad Mustad'afin*, Sayyid Abu Ali Al-Aydrus is also the head of the Division of the Oppressed within IJABI's Department of Empowerment of the Muslim Community. This joint programme has been relatively successful.

IJABI's Department of the Empowerment of the Muslim Community has also organised a business training programme aimed at providing participants with 'financial intelligence', so that they might go on to create business opportunities for their own personal and organisational benefit. This programme was carried out in co-operation with the McDonald's Company in Indonesia, owned by Bambang Rachmadi, and attracted many participants from a number of regional and district branches of IJABI.

Another relatively active department is that of intellectual development and *da'wa*. This department is responsible for celebrating the holy days of the Shi'i tradition such as the Prophet's birthday, the Imams' and Sayyida Fatima's birthday, *'Ashura*, and *Arba'in*. Additionally, the department has organised training in fields such as philosophy, Islamic law, *akhlaq* (character and morality) and Sufism. Discussions and seminars, national and local, on various topics have been held. Like the Empowerment of the Muslim Community programme, these activities are usually carried out in co-operation with the Muthahhari Foundation and sometimes with the Sehati or Tazkiya Sejati Foundations, headed by Sri Adyanti Rachmadi, wife of the aforementioned Bambang Rachmadi. Furthermore, IJABI has already sent several students to pursue their education in Iran and this annual programme is expected to run well. IJABI is also looking into the possibility of sending students to other countries such as England, America, Australia and Syria.

One of the most important *da'wa* activities conducted by IJABI is a *muballigh* course known as the *Pengkaderan Muballigh* (Preacher Cadre Training). This is important not only for Shi'i *da'wa* (as described in Chapter Four) but also for the consolidation of IJABI members and leaders throughout the country. The training is aimed at providing the cadres of IJABI with the capability to defend the *madhhab* of the *ahl al-bayt*, to enlighten the Muslim *umma* and to defend Islam in the context of global political developments. It deals not only with topics of Shi'ism and *da'wa* technique but also addresses a number of problems confronting the members. The participants are expected to be able make a defense against ideas that are contrary to the Statutes and principles of IJABI.

---

33   *Al-Tanwir* (2/7/2000).

The early development of IJABI has, without question, depended on its central figures, Jalaluddin Rakhmat, Dimitri Mahayana, and Hadi Suwastio and other related institutions, especially the Muthahhari Foundation and Tazkiya Sejati. Support from rich patrons such as Sri Adyanti Sudharmono has also contributed significantly to its early growth. However, in April 2003, a breakdown in relations between Rakhmat and Sri Adyanti and her brother, Tantyo Sudharmono resulted in internal dissension within IJABI. Following this upset, Rakhmat resigned from his position as the director of the Tazkiya Sejati Foundation, which he had occupied since 1997. Tantyo Sudharmono was removed from his position as the chairman of the JABODEBEK branch of IJABI, to be replaced by Budiono.[34] This recent and dramatic episode has clearly affected the later development of IJABI.

The exact reasons behind the discord remain unclear. Jalaluddin Rakhmat and his IJABI associates hint at slanderous remarks towards him during his time at Tazkya Sejati. This resulted in him issuing a circular containing statements cursing his opponents. The circular was sent out to all of the provincial and district branches of IJABI and was received with both positive and negative reactions from IJABI members and members of the Shi'i community at large. Later, Rakhmat justified his cursing through his own publications, *Al-Tanwir*[35] and *Bahtera*.[36] In an article entitled 'The Command for Cursing in the Qur'an and *Sunna*' he states "There are some ignorant people among the followers of *ahl al-bayt* who do not bother to curse those who should be cursed." He goes on to cite verses of the Qur'an and sayings of the Prophet and the Imams which permit the cursing of sinful people, including slanderers. Rakhmat was trying to make use of the point that no religious textual or rational proofs reject the permissibility of cursing.

Dissention has also occurred in local branches of IJABI, including South Sumatra, Central Java and Yogyakarta. Internal conflicts in Palembang, South Sumatra, for instance, contributed to the withdrawal of renowned Shi'i figures such as Jailani and his wife Mariatul Fadilah from IJABI and as a result, IJABI programmes in the area have not run smoothly. The former chairman of the Central Java branch of IJABI was dismissed from his position because of his involvement in the *Yaum al-Quds* demonstration in 2003. This is an annual demonstration, held on the Friday of the first week of Ramadan, prescribed by Ayatollah Khomeini. Shi'i *ustadhs* in Indonesia organised this event to demonstrate their adherence and loyalty to the leader of the Iranian revolution. Given that IJABI promotes itself as a non-political organisation, it forbids its members to be involved in any

---

34   Budiono is a Shi'i figure in Jakarta. Besides leading Shi'i foundations, in 1998 he founded a *nasyid* group called K'PAS (*Kelompok Pencinta Aktif Shalawat*, the Active Lover Group of Singing Invocations) which has been invited to perform at numerous religious events in Jakarta and West Java.

35   *Al-Tanwir* (3/5/2003:1-5).

36   *Bahtera* (October 2003:66-71).

political activities which may threaten its legal status. Consequently, a number of IJABI's executive members who were active in political parties have resigned. This has further reduced the social base of the organisation.

In response to internal discord, IJABI tried harder to strengthen its position. It drew up a list of ten undesirable attributes of non-IJABI behaviour: racism, intolerance, *tarekatism* (following certain Sufi orders and confessing to high spiritual achievement through them), *mahdism* (confessing a capability to communicate with the Imam Mahdi), promotion of a state based on Islamic *shari'a* (such as the Darul Islam/NII movement mentioned above), *salafism* (Wahhabism), *fiqh*-orientation, politics, utilising IJABI for personal gain, and disloyalty. Each of these ten negative attributes was believed to have been present among members of IJABI, threatening its existence and unity and decreasing the efficiency of its programmes. In formulating this list, IJABI hoped its members would dissociate themselves from these ten attributes, rendering IJABI an ideal social-religious organisation.

The problems outlined above resulted in a decrease in both the membership and leadership of IJABI. Its second national congress, held in Jakarta on 27-29 February 2004 was marked by a lack of support by prominent Shi'i figures and Iranian personalities in Indonesia. There was no representative from Iran or ICC of Al-Huda, for example. Other dignitaries who had attended the inauguration and first national congress were mainly absent. Nonetheless, hundreds of participants did attend the seminar, which followed the congress on the topic "Building a Paradigm of Ethics in the Life of Society and the Nation" in which Nurcholish Madjid, Jalaluddin Rakhmat and Juanda from the Indonesian Navy were speakers. Representatives of provincial and district branches of IJABI from throughout the country attended. Although they acknowledged the problems and weaknesses of IJABI's leaders, the participants of the congress unanimously accepted reports presented by Rakhmat as Chairman of the Religious Advisory Council and Dimitri Mahayana as Chairman of the Executive Council. They also agreed to re-appoint Rakhmat to his position in the Religious Council and to elect Furqon Bukhari as the new Chairman and Khalid al-Walid as the new Secretary-General of the Executive Council.

D. Responses to IJABI

During the process of establishing IJABI there had been consensus among followers of Shi'ism in Indonesia and the intellectuals, scholars and *ustadhs* as its leaders about the importance of a national organisation and the approval of its name. This consensus was demonstrated at meetings held in the Al-Huda Islamic Centre in Jakarta. Clearly, at this point in time, Indonesia's Shi'is were united by a common purpose. However, as we saw above, this unity was short-lived and tainted by disputes and misunderstandings among the proponents of IJABI – on the one side Jalaluddin Rakhmat and his associates and on the other, the Shi'i *ustadhs,* who were mainly Qum alumni. This is why the majority of *ustadhs* and scholars had been absent from IJABI's inauguration and its first national congress in Bandung.

Disputes and misunderstandings between the two groups continue to this day. Such discord at the elite level has become widespread among members of the Shi'i community. Public criticism of opponents and the use of *da'wa* activities to defend certain points of view have become commonplace. It is not unusual, for example, for leaders to criticise opponents during *pengajian,* or religious discussions in the hope of gaining support. In short, there is a split in the Shi'i community in Indonesia between the supporters of IJABI and their opponents; between 'IJABIs' and 'non-IJABIs'.

However, it would be an oversight to neglect a third category, the Shi'is who refuse to join either of these camps. Members of this 'neutral' group are clearly troubled by the fact that the establishment of IJABI, instead of promoting unity within the Shi'i community in Indonesia, has exaggerated existing fractures. This group includes a number of well-known Shi'i figures who have tried to bridge the divide. For example, Sayyid Seggaf al-Jufri has made efforts to organise Islamic rituals and commemorations that bring together the IJABI and non-IJABI groups in Solo, Central Java. Another prominent Shi'i intellectual, known for his harmonious relationship with all Shi'i groups, is Haidar Bagir, head of the Mizan Publishing Company. Despite the fact that he was once listed on IJABI's Religious Advisory Council, Bagir has never participated in any IJABI activities. He refuses to take sides with either of the opposing groups, preferring to offer his moral and material support to all Shi'i activities.

And Haidar Bagir is not alone. In fact, the majority of Shi'i scholars who are officially listed as members of IJABI's Religious Advisory Council do not publicly show support for IJABI, nor for its programmes. Some even go so far as to reject the organisation outright. This extraordinary situation is exacerbated by the fact that a number of people listed as members of IJABI's central board or of its regional or district branches rarely participate in IJABI programmes, let alone lead or organise any activity. Furthermore, a number have even acted to destabilise the organisation and its influence. Inevitably, this serious lack of support has led to IJABI's programmes being severely compromised and more often than not unable to achieve their desired results.

As previously mentioned, the proponents of IJABI include ex-dissident elements of the Darul Islam movement and grassroots members who had relations with IJABI's leaders long before the organisation was established. They are brought together through *da'wa* and educational activities held at Shi'i foundations located in various regions. Such activities usually involve eminent Shi'i intellectuals being invited to deliver religious lectures. The supporters of IJABI also maintain their ties through the publication of books and periodicals, in which prominent intellectuals write about Shi'i teachings and ideology. On the whole, the leading figures among IJABI supporters are intellectuals who have considerable influence over the other elements of this group. The majority have graduated from secular universities and have later committed themselves to the Shi'i *madhhab*. Only a small number have graduated from the *hawza 'ilmiyya* in Qum.

In terms of religious thought, it is widely known that IJABI places more emphasis on the importance of *akhlaq,* or personal morality and Sufism than on formal jurisprudence. Moreover, IJABI leaders are openly critical of those who uphold what they call the '*fiqh* paradigm' - a controversial term coined by Jalaluddin Rakhmat - in their religious life and *da'wa* activities. In his Sunday gatherings, Rakhmat continues to present Islamic teachings derived from the Sufi tradition and the traditions of the Imams. These beliefs are also reflected in his numerous written works. For Rakhmat and his associates, Sufism and Shi'ism are inseparable and integral teachings of Islam. As we saw in Chapter Two, he even recommends ignoring some aspects of jurisprudence for the sake of Islamic fraternity and in accordance with the teaching of *taqiyya*.

In contrast, the opponents of IJABI are mainly the learned Shi'i *ustadhs*. Most graduated from the *hawza 'ilmiyya* of Qum, and a few from other Islamic educational institutions in Indonesia or abroad. The majority are Sayyids. They have a significant number of followers who support their institutions and activities. Before the establishment of IJABI, a number of leading figures in this group had headed the *Yayasan Mahdi* that had been set up as a mass Shi'i organisation (refer to the first section above). Like the IJABI group, they have also established Shi'i foundations and *pesantren* which claim to follow the *hawza 'ilmiyya* system of Islamic education in Qum. As we saw in the previous chapter, a few of the Shi'i *ustadhs* have written Islamic books published by Shi'i publishers. Some of their foundations also produce Islamic periodicals. Like the IJABI group, the opponents of IJABI use these activities to maintain their contacts and their relationships.

Unlike the proponents of IJABI, however, the *ustadhs* pay great attention to the entire teachings of Shi'ism, including Ja'fari jurisprudence. It is for this reason that IJABI supporters view them as '*fiqh*-oriented'. For this group, being Shi'i means leaving behind all the non-Shi'i elements of Islam, and instead upholding all the teachings and traditions of Shi'ism, commonly called *tashayyu'* (which literally means 'Shi'ism'). This is necessary, they believe, in order for Shi'is to become true believers and so that the Shi'i community in Indonesia does not become isolated from other Shi'i communities worldwide.[37]

The divide between the two groups in terms of social and educational background and religious orientation leads to intricate conflict and competition with regard to the accumulation of social, cultural and economic capital. The explanation below illustrates the complex factors at play. Competition and conflict originate in the differences in social background among the Shi'i community of Indonesia: those of Arab descent versus the campus group, as well as *ustadhs* versus intellectuals. These divisions are sustained by interrelated personal, religious, political and economic factors. Each group has its own identity which they tend to preserve and strengthen. Each group propagates its own religious ideology, trying to attract as many followers as possible, as well as trying to exert influence among the wider Shi'i population. Whenever possible, these groups attempt to set up an organisation, providing a place for their followers to gather, with a view to becoming the dominant force within the community. This act of establishing a socio-religious organisation can be seen as a political one, even though the organisation itself may be apolitical. Political interests are also evident in the strategies used by members of these groups to gain positions within the new organisation and even influence the formulation of its statutes and rules. The valuable social capital thus obtained can in turn be converted into economic capital, as a statement made by Bahruddin Fanani, speaking for all Shi'is who choose not to join either of the competing groups, affirms. Fanani points out that the main sources of conflict between IJABIs and non-IJABIs are social position and economic resources.[38] In the context of accumulating capital the different groups compete, rather than co-operate, with one another.

There are further issues, some major, some minor and some related to the above-mentioned differences, giving the *ustadhs* cause to reject IJABI. Ahmad Baragbah suggests three reasons for the rejection. The first concerns the name of the organisation. Now, the name of an organisation reflects its identity. The *ustadhs* had originally proposed that the appropriate name for a Shi'i organisation was *Ahlulbait (ahl al-bayt)*. Not only was it succinct and easy to remember, but the term is very important to and is frequently used by the Shi'i community. Some may view this as a minor problem. The second, perhaps more important matter concerns the position of *wilayat al-faqih* in relation to the organisation. This is a political concept, implemented in the Islamic Republic of Iran and gives the *faqih, or* learned man of religion the highest authority over other sections of society. The *faqih* is designated as a leader of the Shi'i community, not just in Iran but worldwide, and the Shi'is in Indonesia are expected to recognise his

---

37   Al-Kaff (2001:2).
38   Bahruddin Fanani, interview, (16/10/2002).

political-religious leadership. Indonesia's Shi'i *ustadhs* believe that the concept *wilayat al-faqih* should be mentioned explicitly in IJABI's Statute, demonstrating the Shi'i nature of the organisation and its deference to the leadership of *wali faqih* in the Shi'i world. In fact, the term is absent from the Statutes of IJABI. This, then, is the main reason for the *ustadhs* to reject and even to oppose IJABI's existence: the *ustadh* group regards IJABI as an opponent of *wilayat al-faqih*. A third factor, also related to the Statute and Rules of Organisation, concerns internal authority. The IJABI Statute and Rules of Organisation state that the highest authority is the national congress. The *ustadhs* argue that this power, like the appointment of the chairman of the Executive Council, should be in the hands of the Religious Advisory Council (*Dewan Syuro*) and not be based on a ballot in the national congress. In support of this argument, they point to experiences at the first national congress, which they believe was not well prepared, something even the organiser, Jalaluddin Rakhmat, also admits.[39]

The *ustadh* group considers IJABI, by not supporting *wilayat al-faqih*, to be *raushan fikr* ('reformed' intellectuals). In Iran these *raushan fikr* have a different political orientation from that of the *'ulama* who have led the country since the Islamic Revolution of 1979. Indonesia's *ustadhs* believe IJABI supporters resemble the *raushan fikr* in Iran in the fact that they emphasise the importance of the intellectuals, rather than the *'ulama* in social and political fields and various other aspects of Muslim life. The attitude of the Shi'i *ustadhs* is supported by a statement by Khomeini: "Islam will not be protected by the *raushanfikr*. It is the *raushanfikr* who dupe the clear verses of the Qur'an."[40]

There is a further issue which is a source of conflict between the IJABI and non-IJABI groups, and that is Jalaluddin Rakhmat's attitude towards the Arab Sayyids. Some Sayyids recognise Rakhmat as anti-Sayyid, although he himself rejects the accusation. They point to statements made by him in an interview on national television which, they say, indicate this prejudice. (Some respondents in my interviews offered a recording of Rakhmat's programme and quoted reports by witnesses to the same effect.) Consequently, many Sayyids are extremely annoyed with him. This is evident in a discussion of M. Hasyim Assegaf's (M. Hashem's) book, *Derita Putri-Putri Nabi: Studi Historis Kafa'ah Syarifah* (the Anguish of the Daughters of the Prophet: A Historical Study of the Kafa'a Sharifa). The book was published by Rosda in Bandung on the occasion of the celebration of Fatima's birthday held by IJABI, in cooperation with Rosda and the Sehati Foundation, in Jakarta in September 2000. One of the main themes of the book is that *kafa'a*, or the principle of equality of birth in marriage partners is the product of Arab culture, is legitimised by the Sunni schools of jurisprudence, and by Shafi'i in particular. *Kafa'a* in marriage is not

---

39   Ahmad Baragbah, interview, (21/10/2002).
40   Alison (2000:28).

recognised in Ja'fari jurisprudence. This book was perceived to be a criticism of the widely held view among the Arab community in Indonesia that a Sharifa - the title given to female descendants of the Prophet - may only marry a Sayyid.[41] (This is the principle of *kafa'a sharifa*). Assegaf makes the point that the Imams strongly reject such discrimination. In Shi'ism, ancestry is not permitted to be the basis for the legality of marriage. Even Imam Khomeini's daughter married a non-Sayyid man.[42] Assegaf goes on to state that the obligation of Sharifas to marry only Sayyids is also contrary to the principles of human rights.[43] Assegaf - himself a Sayyid - and Jalaluddin Rakhmat and Maria Ulfa Anshar were speakers at the same event in Jakarta. In the audience were many Sayyids and Sharifas. During the discussions, a number of criticisms and impolite statements were addressed solely to Jalaluddin Rakhmat, rather than to Assegaf or Anshar. In her anger, one Sharifa shouted out that "even dogs look for good partner."[44]

It is important to point out that the question of Sayyid descent is a classical and sensitive matter which, in the early 20th century, divided the Arab community in the Dutch East Indies into pro- and anti-Sayyid factions.[45] The conflict between these groups even attracted the attention of the colonial government, which made attempts to solve the problem. The mere fact that IJABI would organise a discussion of this topic could be seen as provocative. Before the event, Zein Al-Hadi, a Shi'i teacher in Jakarta sent Rakhmat a letter, warning him that such an activity would be very unpopular.[46] Rakhmat ignored this advice, considering it to be an important intellectual activity and an opportunity to implement one of IJABI's programmes. It is clear that the central problem was not the content of M. Hashem's book *per se*, but rather the deliberate raising of the sensitive issue of the social status of Sayyid versus non-Sayyid.

The Sayyid-non-Sayyid divide is generally recognised within the Shi'i community in Indonesia. Some Shi'i leaders suggest that it corresponds to the divide between non-IJABI and IJABI; others disagree. However, it is a fact that both Sayyids and non-Sayyids have used their organisations and religious gatherings as vehicles to defend and strengthen their own positions, while at the same time attacking the weaknesses of their opponents.[47]

Some Sayyids have tried to understand Jalaluddin Rakhmat's negative attitude towards them. Some suggest that it is a result of a bad experience in his personal

---

41 Sayyid Usman, for instance, strongly rejected marriages between a Sharifa and a non-Sayyid man - either Arab or non-Arab – even if her *wali*, or legal guardian agreed to it. Sayyid Usman maintained that if a marriage of this kind occurs, it should be nullified, and if necessary by force (Azra 1995:12).
42 Assagaf (2000:272).
43 Assagaf (2000:301-302).
44 Ahmad Muhajir al-Muhdar, interview, (29/8/2002).
45 Mobini Kesheh (1999:92-107).
46 Ahmad Muhajir al-Muhdar, interview, (29/8/2002).
47 Bahruddin, interview, (4/9/2002).

relations with Sayyids in the past. One Sayyid informant suggested that Rakhmat had failed in an attempt to marry his son off to a Sharifa in Lampung because the girl's father had opposed the union.[48]

Whether this anecdote is true or not, there is no question that a number of Sayyids have a disharmonious relationship with Jalaluddin Rakhmat and so reject the existence of IJABI as a national Shi'i organisation in Indonesia, refusing to participate in its activities. One well-known Sayyid leader, Zainal Abidin al-Muhdar actually became embroiled in a public spat with Rakhmat. The two squabbled about the Sayyid issue at the Iranian embassy in Jakarta and again at the ICC of Al-Huda in Jakarta. Even though they were seen to apologise publicly to each other at ICC of Al-Huda, their disharmonious relations continue to this day.[49]

Jalaluddin Rakhmat and other IJABI leaders strenuously deny that they harbour any prejudice against the Sayyids. They may well have a point: seven out of twelve members of the IJABI Religious Advisory Council are Sayyids and other Sayyids occupy positions on its Executive Board, including Rakhmat's confidant, Sayyid Abu Ali Al-Idrus. (Abu Ali has headed the division of *Imdad Mustad'afin* at the Muthahhari Foundation and the division of *Mustad'afin* at IJABI). Rakhmat himself insists that he is not at all anti-Sayyid, even though he is reported to have expressed some ethnic stereotypes[50] when referring to Arabs in Indonesia. For example, he quoted a professor of anthropology, Michael Gilsenan, who in a meeting with Rakhmat referred to the uniqueness of the Arabs in Indonesia, saying that they have a racist attitude against the native population, despite being a small minority in the country.[51]

In their own defense, Jalaluddin Rakhmat and his supporters insist that the *ustadhs* had actually agreed to the establishment of IJABI, but that during the process - before the inauguration and national congress - the *ustadhs,* the Arabs and the Qum alumni in particular decided that they should become the dominant leaders of the organisation.[52] Rakhmat stuck to his belief that every decision has to be decided through congress.[53] He once claimed that he was forced to fight against the Arabs for the sake of democracy.[54] As explained above, the *ustadhs* implacably disagreed with congress as the highest authority in the organisation.

---

48   Ahmad Muhajir al-Muhdar, interview, (29/8/2002).
49   Ahmad Muhajir al-Muhdar, interview, (29/8/2002).
50   Stereotype means "a set of ideas based on distortion, exaggeration, and oversimplification that is applied to all members of a group" (Shepard 1981:216).
51   Jalaluddin Rakhmat, interview, (2/1/2003).
52   *Gatra* (6/12/2003:62).
53   Jalaluddin Rakhmat, interview, (2/1/2003).
54   *Gatra* (6/12/2003:62).

In addition to the issues mentioned above, the rejection of IJABI can also be attributed to misunderstandings which occurred during the series of meetings in the process of its establishment. The disharmony reached its peak following a statement by Jalaluddin Rakhmat and Dimitri Mahayana suggesting that a number of the *ustadhs* who were striving to become leaders of the Shi'i community in Indonesia, including IJABI, were incapable of such a role. In response, the *ustadhs* demanded a written apology from Rakhmat. He did write a letter of apology, but his opponents saw its contents as cynical. When he was asked to come to the last meeting to explain himself, three days before the IJABI inauguration, Rakhmat did not attend. As a result, most of the *ustadhs* took the decision not only to boycott IJABI's inauguration and national congress but also to reject IJABI outright as an organisation.[55]

Among the non-IJABI group, Jalaluddin Rakhmat's personality is frequently cited as a source of tension. For example, after the spat and subsequent apologies between Rakhmat and Zainal Abidin al-Muhdar at the ICC of Al-Huda, Rakhmat is reported to have told the evening religious gathering at Tazkiya Sejati that he had been attacked by overwhelming numbers of Sayyids. At other times he is said to have humiliated a number of Shi'i *ustadhs*, and in particular those without a university education. He never invites them to deliver religious lectures at the Tazkiya Sejati Foundation or to attend the religious gatherings held by Sri Adyanti Sudharmono.[56] It is widely acknowledged that teaching at religious gatherings such as those at Paramadina and Tazkiya Sejati, which attract a mainly middle class audience, brings significant remuneration. In addition, Rakhmat's statements in religious gatherings and to the national media discrediting the *ustadhs* are a significant source of disharmony between IJABI and non-IJABI supporters.[57]

Among the initial reactions to the establishment of IJABI, one came from a meeting of a number of Qum alumni *ustadhs* at the Al-Jawad Foundation on 18 June 2000, before IJABI's inauguration. The *ustadhs* at this meeting included Ahmad Baragbah, Zahir Yahya, Muhsin Labib, Husein Al-Kaff, Abdullah Husein al-Aydrus and Muhammad Sueb. The meeting produced two conclusions, which were signed and sent to Jalaluddin Rakhmat: first, a recommendation to cancel the inauguration ceremony and put the establishment of IJABI on hold because it was ill-prepared; second, a rejection of the ideological foundations of IJABI, including its refusal to accept the principle of *wilayat al-faqih* within the structure of the organisation.[58]

---

55   Umar Shahab, interview, (9/1/2003).
56   Ahmad Muhajir al-Muhdar, interview, (29/8/2002).
57   Haidar Bagir, interview, (5/4/2004).
58   Ali (2002:413-414).

Other subsequent attempts have been made to reject the existence and development of IJABI. One of them included a letter stating their rejection of the organisation, signed by 36 prominent Shi'i *ustadhs* and intellectuals and sent to the international Shi'i leader, the *wali faqih* in Iran, Ayatollah 'Ali Khamene'i. This was one of the most important anti-IJABI strategies employed, because from a religious perspective the Shi'i community in Indonesia is an integral part of the Shi'i world under the headship of the *wali faqih*. There have, however, been a number of proponents of IJABI who studied in Iran who have come out in defence of the organisation. Khalid Al-Walid, the then chairman of the Iranian branch of IJABI and current secretary-general of IJABI visited the Rahbar's office to make a number of clarifications regarding the disputes between the proponents and the opponents of IJABI.[59] Despite recurring efforts by IJABI's enemies to convince the centre of Shi'i leadership that the organisation should be rejected, it is clear that IJABI, as a national Shi'i organisation in Sunni-dominated Indonesia and as a part of the worldwide group of Shi'i organisations, still has the formal recognition by the office of the international Shi'i leader in Iran.

A group of Indonesian students in Qum, affiliated to the Association of Indonesian Students (*Himpunan Pelajar Indonesia*, HPI) also publicly rejected the existence of IJABI in a letter dated 22 March 2001 and signed by its presidium, Ibrahim Al-Habsyi (Husein Al-Habsyi's son), Abdullah Beik and Muchtar Luthfi, all of whom have close connections to prominent Qum alumni *ustadhs* in Indonesia. Their rejection was based on the ideological foundations of IJABI and its refusal to accept the principle of *wilayat al-faqih*. The letter emphasised that an organisation designed to bring together all Shi'is in Indonesia must obey the leadership of *wali faqih* absolutely during the occultation of Imam Mahdi, because the *wali faqih* is the representative of the Imam.[60] The letter states

> In the view of HPI, 'to hold *wilaya*' [spiritual investiture] cannot be just jargon. There are several derivations from the principles that are required by the organisation. Therefore, the principles must be implemented in a systematic, not technical, matter.

> Systematically, the establishment of an organisation may not use the principle of 'absolute democracy' (where the highest authority is determined totally on the basis of the quantity of votes) because the Western version of absolute democracy in the view of the *wilayat al-faqih* system is 'rubbish' and has already a long time ago been thrown

---

59   Khalid Al-Walid, interview, (3/7/2002).
60   Ali (2002:417-418).

out by this pure system. From this perspective, HPI cannot accept a Shi'i organisation that claims 'to hold *wilaya*' in the system of establishing leadership, using ways contrary to the principles of *wilaya*.

Technically, the procedure of the organisation may not be contrary to clear and agreed *shari'a* laws and there is no contextual reason to renounce them (with a reason of *taqiyya*, for instance). HPI cannot accept an organisation acting on behalf of Shi'i community but which in fact neglects matters that become precisely the symbol and identity of the Shi'i *madhhab*.[61]

Another important strategic attempt to repudiate IJABI came from a cooperative of leaders of other Shi'i foundations in Indonesia. Following a series of meetings, they agreed to reject IJABI and all of its programmes. One of these meetings was called a 'workshop of the *Ahl al-Bayt* Foundations of all Indonesia' and was held in Jakarta, 7–8 June 2001. It was organised by ICC of Al-Huda to mark the celebration of *Mawlid,* the Birth of the Prophet. It was attended by a number of guests from Iran, including Ayatollah Shaykh Akhtari. This is a clear indication of the lack of support for IJABI from ICC of Al-Huda. Just before the workshop was to take place, IJABI issued a circular, signed by Dimitri Mahayana, the chairman of Executive Board and Hadi Suwastio, the general secretary, on 31 May 2001. The circular listed a number of reasons for declaring the workshop invalid: first, IJABI remains the umbrella organisation for all Shi'i foundations and congregations in Indonesia and so no other organisation is required; second, the establishment of another organisation, if this was the aim of the workshop, would threaten the success of any programmes run by IJABI and the new organisation both; third, the workshop was designed to create disunity within the Islamic community and lead to confusion among the followers of Shi'ism. The opponents of IJABI refuted the IJABI circular by issuing a 'Declaration of the Attitude of Indonesian Ahl al-Bayt Foundations to IJABI' on 8 June 2001 in Jakarta. This declaration rejects the position of IJABI as the umbrella organisation for Shi'i foundations in Indonesia. The main part of the declaration says

Considering and seeing several points below:

- The claim that IJABI is an umbrella organisation for Indonesian all *ahl al-bayt* foundations and congregations is not true
- As a *fait accompli* among the Indonesian *ahl al-bayt* community, the existence of IJABI has resulted in various continuing disputes, dissensions and controversies

---

61   Ali (2002:418).

- The demeanour of some IJABI personnel, both at the centre and in the branches, has made them slanderers who endanger the existence of a number of foundations as well as individuals related to them
- The unclear IJABI vision and mission has resulted in the separation of IJABI from other Indonesian *ahl al-bayt* foundations

Herewith, we, on behalf of the undersigned foundations state the following. We

1. Take no responsibility for any IJABI activities or any related foundations or individuals

2. Reject to being under the organisational umbrella of IJABI

3. Call for the unity of all foundations and communities of the lovers of the *ahl al-bayt* in Indonesia under the shade of the Master of Affair of Muslims, the Grand Ayatollah Sayyid 'Ali Khamene'i.

Twenty-seven Shi'i foundations and one local association from all over Indonesia signed the declaration, including such major institutions as Fatimah and Madinatul Ilmi of Jakarta, IPABI of Bogor, Al-Jawad of Bandung and Al-Hadi of Pekalongan.[62] The majority of the signatories were the chiefs of the foundations, while others were staff members, including the staff of ICC of Al-Huda of Jakarta, an Iran-sponsored foundation in Indonesia. This represents a significant rejection of IJABI by the country's Shi'i foundations.

Another significant development by opponents of IJABI was the setting up of three local Shi'i associations in Java: KIBLAT (*Komunitas Ahlul Bait Jawa Barat*, West Java *Ahl al-Bayt* Community), WASIAT in Central Java and FAJAR (*Forum Jamaah Ahlul Bait Jawa Timur*, Forum of East Java *Ahl al-Bayt* Congregations) in East Java. In contrast to IJABI, these three organisations only function to coordinate the existing Shi'i foundations within their own areas. Proponents of these organisations accuse IJABI's provincial and district branches of usurping the position and function of Shi'i foundations in the regions. They say this has led not only to opposition from the leaders of the Shi'i foundations but also to inactivity at the branches of IJABI, who are failing to implement their own programmes. They believe that both the existing Shi'i foundations and the regional and district branches of IJABI are likely to have the similar programmes, leading to a duplication of efforts.

---

62 Other foundations include AMALI (Medan), Al-Baqir (Bangil), Al-Hujjah (Jember), Al-Kazim (Cirebon), Al-Mujtaba (Purwakarta), CIS (Jakarta), Darul Taqrib (Jepara), Al-Batul (Jakarta), FAHMI (Depok), ICC of Al-Huda (Jakarta), Pelita Hidayah (Malang), Al-Kautsar (Malang), Al-Hakim (Lampung), Safinatun Najah (Wonosobo), Al-Muhibbin (Probolinggo), Al-Aqilah (Tangerang), Al-Wahdah (Solo), Al-Mawaddah (Kendal), Al-Muntazar (Samarinda), Al-Huda (Sumenep), Miftahul Huda (Tangerang), and As-Sajjad (Jakarta). The local organisation was FAJAR (Forum Jamaah Ahlul Bait Jawa Timur).

The leaders of these coordinating organisations are prominent Shi'i teachers who are also Qum alumni. Husein Al-Kaff and Abdullah Assegaf became the founders and leaders of KIBLAT, while Ahmad Baragbah and Miqdad are the founders and leaders of WASIAT. The influential leaders of FAJAR are Zahir Yahya and Muhsin Labib. All of these men graduated from Qum and have become prominent Shi'i teachers and leaders in Indonesia. They have close connections with one another based on their shared ideology and their common aim to propagate Shi'ism in Indonesia.

KIBLAT is an assembly of six Shi'i foundations located in several cities and towns in West Java, including Al-Jawad of Bandung, As-Syifa of Garut, Al-Kazhim of Cirebon, Al-Kautsar of Bandung, Al-Mujtaba of Purwakarta and IPABI of Bogor. KIBLAT's first congress was held in August 2001. WASIAT in Central Java was officially declared at the end of 2002 and has yet to make significant progress. FAJAR, centred in Malang in East Java (home to a large Shi'i community) was officially inaugurated on 21 April 2000, although it had been initiated in 1998. FAJAR used to have significant influence on the Shi'i community in East Java; however, this has since decreased, partly due to its leaders, Zahir Yahya and Muhsin Labib moving to Australia and Jakarta respectively for study. Of the three associations, KIBLAT has been, and continues to be, active in its role as coordinator of the six Shi'i foundations, as well as organising training and education programmes and the celebration of Shi'i holy days. Its activity may be seen as an attempt to compete with IJABI, partly because of its geographical location, close to the national centre of IJABI in Bandung. As for the development of the local associations, WASIAT does not run particularly well. Moreover, these three local coordinating associations are not recognised nationally or legally by the Indonesian government.

A marked difference between these local associations and IJABI can be seen in their incorporation of the concept of *wilayat al-faqih* in their statutes and organisations. Their goal is to establish a community based on the principle of *wilaya,* so that the Shi'i community in Indonesia completely accepts and lives under the umbrella of *wilayat al-faqih*. As an imitation of *wilayat al-faqih*, the structure of these local associations places the so-called *mustashar,* or adviser, a position occupied by prominent local *ustadhs* and Qum alumni, as the highest authority in such crucial matters as formulating ideological, conceptual and strategic policies of the association, and even giving it the power to dissolve the association. As the position of *mustashar* is connected to the *wali faqih*, it is considered to have legitimacy in the *shari'a*.[63] Thus, unlike IJABI, these local associations implement a top-down leadership, giving authority to local *ustadhs* rather than making decisions through a congress.

---

63   Ali (2002:431-432).

There is a desire among proponents of these local Shi'i organisations to found another national Shi'i organisation, different from IJABI in terms of religious and organisational principles and using their local Shi'i associations as its model. This was seen in 2003 when an *ustadh* group in Jakarta established *Forum Al-Husainy*, which aims to assemble and unite nearly all renowned *ustadhs* and activists in the capital city of Indonesia. With the involvement of key figures such as Husein Shahab and Hasan Daliel Al-Aydrus, this forum did succeed in its aims. It attempted to organise various *da'wa* activities using, what they call spiritual, intellectual and social approaches. The spiritual approach, for example, includes holding a monthly *dhikr* congregation in the Al-Bina Mosque in Jakarta. In terms of the intellectual approach, several series of *da'wa* training courses have been organised. In addition, *da'wa* activities have been undertaken using a social approach.[64] This forum, however, differs from the three local institutions, not least because of its emphasis on *da'wa* programmes rather than on the formulation of statutes or other organisational apparatuses. While IJABI is only supported by a small number of Shi'is in Indonesia, the majority of the country's *ustadhs* and activists agree on the necessity of having a single national organisation that is recognised by all groups within the community. Husein Shahab makes the point that that there is always an aspiration among Shi'i leaders to have a single umbrella organisation to ensure programmes of *da'wa*, education and culture achieve maximum results.[65]

To sum up, it is IJABI which has achieved legal recognition from the government, resulting in the accumulation of symbolic capital, and it exercises power in terms of its existence and activities. IJABI is based on the principal doctrines of Shi'ism; however, it operates in accordance with the principles of democracy, placing the highest authority in the hands of a national congress. Despite its legal status, IJABI lacks support from the internal Shi'i community, and the *ustadhs* in particular, who actively reject its nationally recognised position by employing a variety of strategies. Consequently opponents have established local associations that may ultimately manifest themselves within another national Shi'i organisation.

---

64 *Suara Umma* (1/1/2004:55-57).
65 Husein Shahab, interview, (2/4/2004).

8. Sunni Responses to Shi'ism

As we have seen so far, there are influential individuals and institutions within the Shi'i community in Indonesia which have, despite their small numbers, created opportunities through which to propagate the teachings of their *madhhab*. However, there remain a number of obstacles to the growth and development of the community, the most significant being the reactions to this growth from the Sunni Muslim majority. They are complex and range from the extremely negative to the moderate. This chapter deals with those responses to Shi'ism and its development in Indonesia during the period after the Iranian revolution of 1979.

These responses to Shi'ism are a direct result of the nature of Islam in Indonesian society and the state. The majority Muslim population is Sunni, but within this group there are reformist and traditionalist factions with their several related organisations. The chapter begins with an examination of the attitude of such organisations towards Shi'ism. Secondly, it deals with a *fatwa* by Indonesian *'ulama* on Shi'ism. Thirdly, the chapter considers the response of the Indonesian government's Department of Religious Affairs (DEPAG). Fourthly, it deals with the ways in which anti-Shi'i propagation is executed and examines the tensions between Shi'i and Sunni denominations. Finally, it examines the moderate attitude of Muslim intellectuals which has recently allowed room for the further spread of Shi'ism.

A. The General Attitude of Islamic Organisations

By and large, Indonesian Islam is characterised by the strong resistance of Muslim individuals, organisations and institutions to Shi'ism and the Shi'is. The most active and negative response to the development of Shi'ism comes from the reformist Muslim groups, such as Persis and Al-Irsyad and the individuals and institutions linked to them.

Persis was established in 1923 and claims to follow the *ahl al-sunna wa al-jama'a*, even though the intellectual works of its leading figures, including Ahmad Hassan (1887-1958) make little explicit mention of this. The main purpose of Persis is to implement, through propagation and instruction, the 'pure' teachings of Islam, based on the Qur'an and *Sunna* of the Prophet, in all aspects of Muslim life.[1] Persis emphasises the need to abolish all beliefs and

---

1   Federspiel (2001:87).

practices which it considers contrary to these two principal sources. The history of this reformist Islamic organisation is littered with its fierce attacks on the customs of the traditionalists who constitute the majority of the Indonesian Muslim population. Since its establishment, Persis has been "straightforward in its expression, and unrelenting and [has] denounced or condemned others quite readily."[2]

There is no mention of Shi'ism to be found in any Persis publications before Iranian revolution. This can be attributed first to a widespread ignorance about the existence of Shi'is in Indonesia at that time and second to Persis' focus on its battles with traditionalist beliefs and practices, the developing ideologies of the state and with Christianity. However, within a matter of months after the victory of the Iranian revolution, we see Persis publications carrying articles related to Shi'ism. One of the initial responses to events was the inclusion of an article on *mut'a*[3] or temporary marriage, in *Al-Muslimun*, the Persis magazine in Bangil. The article presents the classical arguments between the Sunni and Shi'i views on this topic and reiterates the validity of the Sunni perspective, which rejects the practice. More importantly, however, this article indicates the emerging awareness among Persis members of the spread of Shi'ism in the country. Over the years, Persis has induced intense resistance to Shi'ism and Shi'is in Indonesia, using a variety of methods. Quite simply, Persis believes that Shi'ism is a heretical sect and it sees itself as the frontline in the fight to protect Sunni Muslims.[4] This resistance is most evident when we take into account Persis's close links to the *Dewan Dakwah Islamiyah Indonesia* (Indonesian Islamic Missionary Council), commonly known as DDII.

DDII is closely associated with the reformist Muslim movement in Indonesia, and is well-known for its very negative response to the development of Shi'ism. The organisation's co-founder and first leader was Mohammad Natsir (1908-1993), who had been a student of Ahmad Hassan, the leader of Persis and had been a former leader of the Masyumi party. Since its establishment on 26 February 1967 DDII has been one of the most, if not the most, active and progressive institution in the field of *da'wa* in Indonesia. It claims to be a rallying point for the *umma* and calls for cooperation among existing missionary institutions. DDII urges its missionaries to avoid *khilafiya,* or disputed matters, and instead to promote the basic principles of Islam which are common to all Muslim factions, reformist and traditionalist. It believes this will prevent confusion among the

---

2   Noer (1973:95).

3   The title is *Kawin Mut'ah di Negeri Iran* (Mut'a in Iran) written by Sulhawi Rubba (July 1979).

4   Abduh and Abu Huzaifah (1998: xiv-xviii). A. Ghozy, the head of *Pesantren* Persis in Bangil affirmed that only Persis has declared Shi'is to be unbelievers (A. Ghozy, interview, 4/10/2002). Shi'ism has become a sensitive issue for Persis members. This is illustrated by my experiences during an interview with A. Ghozy. Eight other members of Persis attended, misunderstanding the purpose of the interview. They had expected a debate on Shi'ism and seemed disappointed when I explained I was only gathering data on Persis' official opinion of Shi'ism.

laity and reduce the burdens of the missionaries themselves.[5] DDII's anti-Shi'i propagation is a manifestation of the concept of *difa'* or self-defence, which is directed towards Christianisation (seen as an external threat) and *'paham-paham dan aliran-aliran sesat'*, heterodox ideological currents and religious views such as secularism, *Islam Jamaah* (LDII), the *Ahmadiya* and Shi'ism (which are seen as an internal threat).[6] DDII deems Shi'ism a heterodox sect even though the term *ahl al-sunna wa al-jama'a* is absent in its statutes. It is widely accepted that DDII, along with its leaders and institutions, is one of the great opponents to the propagation of the Shi'i teachings in Indonesia.

DDII established connections with Saudi Arabia and specifically the Muslim World League, *Rabitat al-'Alam al-Islami*,[7] one of the vice-leaders of which was Natsir. From an international perspective, it is clear that the anti-Shi'i movement in Indonesia receives strong support from Middle Eastern countries, Saudi Arabia in particular, whilst the Shi'i movement is supported by Iran. In this context, competition and conflict between Sunnis and Shi'is in Indonesia is fuelled by competition and tension over Muslim primacy between the two big powers. The relationship between these two countries was at its lowest ebb during the period of Khomeini's leadership, in the first decade following the establishment of the Islamic Republic of Iran. Iran successfully established an Islamic state and claims to be the sole authority and representative of 'genuine' Islam. This, along with its attempts to propagate these beliefs to the whole Muslim world, was a direct challenge to the Saudi kingdom and its hold on Muslim primacy. Iran's revolutionary message opposes the Saudi regime, which Khomeini depicts "as oppressive and the ally of other oppressive Muslim governments".[8] The strict Saudi brand of Islam, Wahhabism, is seen by many as a false sect which aims "to create factionalism and division between the world's Muslims" and "to eliminate the history of Islam".[9] Aware of the growing influence of the Iranian revolutionary spirit, the Saudis responded by promoting the message that Iran is an exporter of terrorism and imperialism, determined to destabilise the Gulf States.[10]

The dissemination of Saudi Wahhabism by the Muslim World League is a particular source of tension. The promotion of Wahhabism has direct connections to a worldwide anti-Shi'i movement which is also active in Indonesia. The Muslim World League owns periodicals, publishing houses and agencies and

---

5   Husin (1998:142).
6   Husin (1998:139-140).
7   This organisation was founded in Mecca in 1962.
8   Goldberg (1990:156).
9   Goldberg (1990:156).
10   Goldberg (1990:163).

has missionaries scattered all over the world. It has organised meetings and financed Islamic centres, education, publications and missionary activities in Indonesia.[11]

The second Muslim reformist organisation known for its anti-Shi'i stance is *Al-Irsyad*, a non-Sayyid Arab organisation which was founded in 1914. Its anti-Shi'i attitude appears to run parallel to its anti-Sayyid activities, carried out through *Jami'at Khair,* to which Ahmad Surkati was affiliated. A simple explanation is that Al-Irsyad's anti-Shi'i sentiments are to be expected, given that a large number of Sayyids, the organisation's long-standing enemies, adhere to Shi'i Islam. However, this explanation calls for refinement. Theological reasons also inform the anti-Shi'i attitudes of Al-Irsyad, coupled with its strong ties to anti-Shi'i groups in the Middle East. Its reformist religious doctrines have been influenced by Wahhabism and there are other historical and psychological factors which contribute to its prominent role in Indonesia's anti-Shi'i movement. It came as no surprise, then, that during Al-Irsyad's 36th National Conference, held in Pekalongan, Central Java on 23-26 October 1996, the organisation appealed to the government to prohibit the spread of Shi'ism in Indonesia.[12] The motion urged DEPAG and other government institutions to adopt a firmer attitude:

> To prohibit Shi'ism and other streams contrary to the teachings of the Qur'an and Hadith of the Prophet (May God Grant Him Peace and Salvation) in the whole *de jure* region of Indonesia and also all their activities in any form, either ritual, printing or publication etc. because in the long term it is feared that these will result in conflict among the Muslims in Indonesia as adherents of the teachings of *ahl al-sunna wa al-jama'a.*[13]

In contrast, the largest reformist Muslim organisation in Indonesia, Muhammadiyah appears to take a neutral stance to Shi'ism. It does not involve itself in promoting anti-Shi'i views to its members or to Muslims at large. This is particularly true of the central board of Muhammadiyah, although there is some evidence that local branches and members do conduct anti-Shi'i activities. Like the above-mentioned reformist associations, Muhammadiyah claims to follow the *ahl al-sunna wa al-jama'a;* however, its main concern, since its establishment in 1912, appears to have been with promoting the necessity of Islamic renewal in Indonesia.[14] As Noer has pointed out, although the ideology of Muhammadiyah is similar to that of Persis, Muhammadiyah demonstrates a more patient attitude and shows more understanding towards others.[15] Since

---

11 Goldberg (1990:164).
12 Abduh and Abu Huzaifah (1998:xxi).
13 Pimpinan Pusat Al-Irsyad Al-Islamiyyah (1996:32).
14 Saleh (2001:75).
15 Noer (1973:94-95).

Muhammadiyah holds an influential position within Indonesian society, the fact that it refrains from participation in anti-Shi'i propagation is an interesting phenomenon. Even during the most well-attended anti-Shi'i seminar of 1997 (see Section below) the Muhammadiyah representative was notably absent among the speakers. Yet this should not be taken as meaning that there are no Muhammadiyah scholars willing to enter into discussions about Shi'ism. One possible explanation is that the main priorities of Muhammadiyah are its social, educational and *da'wa* activities, rather than theological debates. In a foreword to a book of papers from this 1997 seminar[16] the Muhammadiyah leader, Amien Rais avoids mentioning the conclusions and recommendations of the seminar. Rather, the foreword emphasises that differences are unavoidable within the dynamics of Muslim society and that the Shi'is constitute a valid section of the Muslim *umma*. Instead of judging Shi'ism a false sect, as other reformist organisations might do, this important modernist organisation sympathetically calls on all Muslims to study Shi'ism critically, using the Qur'an and Hadith as the standard. Muhammadiyah is likely to maintain this moderate attitude towards Shi'ism, given that its current chairman, Muhammad Din Syamsuddin, also has close relations with Shi'i figures in Indonesia.

The largest traditionalist Islamic organisation in Indonesia, Nahdatul Ulama or NU displays conflicting attitudes towards Shi'ism. Unlike the majority of the country's reformist organisations, NU tends not to be involved in anti-Shi'i activities, despite its claim to be an ardent follower and upholder of the *ahl al-sunna wa al-jama'a*. NU holds to the principle that while Shi'ism differs from Sunnism, it is still a part of the realm of Islam. Its priority is to strengthen the teachings of Sunnism among its members and the Indonesian Muslim population at large. However, there has been a noticeable split in the attitudes of NU leaders towards Shi'ism. On the one side there is an extremely negative attitude taken by several *'ulama* who take part in anti-Shi'i activities. On the other side, there is the moderate attitude of those such as Abdurrahman Wahid and Said Agiel Siradj. A number of anti-Shi'i leaders and scholars point to these views, which they consider promote Shi'i teachings to members of NU.[17] The contrast between those holding very negative views of Shi'ism and those with a more moderate opinion has led NU to abstain institutionally from opposing Shi'i propagation in Indonesia. However, the complexities of this issue deepen further, given the fact that some anti-Shi'i *'ulama* belonging to NU are opponents of Abdurrahman Wahid's faction within the organisation. This group of *'ulama* has made Shi'ism

---

16 Abduh and Abu Huzaifah (1998:xii).

17 For Abdurrahman Wahid's response to Shi'ism, see the last section of this chapter. Regarding Said Agiel Siradj, polemics concerning his alleged adherence to Shi'ism have appeared in a number of Indonesian national media. These polemics started when Said Agiel criticized the concept of Aswaja (*ahl al-sunna wa al-jamaá*) as formulated by the founder of the NU, Hasyim Asyari. Several local NU *'ulama* considered him a heretic and as a result he was dismissed from his position as Vice-Secretary of the Religious Advisory Council on the national board of NU.

a weapon in their opposition to Abdurrahman Wahid's leadership. Also relevant is NU's view of religious tradition. Like the Shi'is, NU opposes Saudi Arabia's Wahhabist stance, which wants to abolish all traditionalist Islamic practices. And since its establishment in 1926, NU has come to see the Wahhabism promoted by Saudi Arabia, along with reformist organisations such as Persis and Al-Irsyad, as the 'great enemies' of traditionalist Muslims.

The above description only takes into account the general attitude of the central boards of these Muslim organisations. It appears that at the local level, branches of both NU and Muhammadiyah, and actually nearly all local offices of Muslim organisations, tend to hold a negative attitude towards Shi'ism. This can usually be explained by external factors such as local interest, when anti-Shi'i groups join forces to fight the spread of Shi'ism in their area. In East Java, for instance, some *'ulama* of NU, Muhammadiyah and Persis, in collaboration with the provincial branch of MUI, met in 1992 under the framework of preventing the dissemination of Shi'ism in the region.

B. The Response of MUI

Majlis Ulama Indonesia (Indonesian Council of 'Ulama), commonly known as MUI, was established in 1975 on the initiative of President Suharto. The government regards it as an authoritative religious institution, particularly in respect of religious sects and variants other than the *ahl al-sunna wa al-jama'a*. As implied, the government depends heavily on the *fatwa* or legal opinions issued by MUI. Any analysis of the response of the Indonesian *'ulama* to Shi'ism should also consider the *fatwa* of MUI related to this matter, "because the *fatwa* is an important instrument through which the *'ulama* express their authority".[18]

The position of Shi'ism in Indonesia is complicated by a number of intertwined political and religious factors. On 8 March 1984, MUI held an annual national meeting in which, among other things, the position of Shi'ism was discussed. The result of the meeting was a recommendation or *tawsiya* which reads as follows:

> Shi'ism as a stream existing in the Islamic world has principal differences from the Sunni *madhhab* (*ahl al-sunna wa al-jama'a*) adhered to by Indonesian Muslims. The differences, among others, are
>
> 1. Shi'ism rejects the *Hadith* not narrated by the *ahl al-bayt* whereas the *ahl al-sunna wa al-jama'a* do not differentiate between them,

---

18   Kaptein (2004:116).

provided they fulfil the requirements [recommended by] the sciences of *Hadith*.

2. Shi'ism views that the Imams are infallible, whilst the *ahl al-sunna wa al-Jama'a* views them as ordinary men who are not free from mistakes.

3. Shi'ism does not recognise *ijma'* without the role of the imams whereas the *ahl al-sunna wa al-jama'a* recognise it without requiring the participation of imams.

4. Shi'ism views the establishment of leadership/government (the imamate) as a pillar of religion whereas the Sunnis (*ahl al-sunna wa al-jama'a*) view it as public welfare, with the goal of the imamate being to guarantee and protect *da'wa* and the interest of the *umma*.

5. Shi'ism in general does not recognise the caliphate of Abu Bakr al-Siddiq, 'Umar bin Khattab and 'Uthman bin 'Affan while the *ahl al-sunna wa al-jama'a* recognise the four Rightly Guided Caliphs (Abu Bakr, 'Umar, 'Uthman and 'Ali ibn Abi Talib).

Considering the principal differences between Shi'ism and the *ahl al-sunna wa al-jama'a* as mentioned above, especially regarding the difference on imamate (government), MUI appeals to the Indonesian Muslims who uphold *ahl al-sunna wa al-jama'a* to increase awareness of the possibility of the coming of streams based on the teachings of Shi'ism.[19]

Even though its general content resembles that of the circular previously issued by DEPAG, a major point of interest in this recommendation is that it neither deals with the legal status of Shi'ism in Islam nor defines the legal consequences for those who adhere to it and practice its teachings. Besides reiterating the usual arguments which illustrate the contrasts between the Sunni and Shi'i doctrines, the text only goes so far as to recommend that Sunni Muslims in Indonesia should not follow the teachings of Shi'i Islam. This issuance of a recommendation, not a *fatwa,* is unique and interesting. It is also of significance for Indonesia's Shi'is, because it does not judge Shi'ism to be a false brand of Islam whose teachings deviate from orthodoxy. By implication then, existing Shi'is can, *de jure,* practice their beliefs and carry out their activities. Furthermore, the recommendation means that no individual, group or institution can forbid the missionary efforts of Shi'ism in the country.

Scrutinising the various recommendations issued by MUI from 1975 to 1988, Mudzhar suggests that the recommendation on the Shi'i movement was

---

19   Adlani et al. (1997:90).

issued in support of New Order government policies.[20] One may question why it was necessary for MUI to give a recommendation on Shi'ism at that time. Mudzhar tried to explain the rationale behind it by examining socio-political developments during the early 1980s

> We know that 1979 was the year of the Iranian revolution, which toppled the secular government of the Shah and replaced it with an Islamic one. Apparently the echo of that resounded beyond Iranian territories and reached Indonesia. It was rumoured that some Muslim youths were to be targeted for the exportation of the ideas of the Iranian Islamic revolution. It was in this context that the government saw it necessary to take precautionary steps to prevent such Islamic revolutionary ideas from developing in the country, and it was also in this context that the MUI made its contribution to efforts to preserve the establishment by issuing the *fatwa*. Thus, while the arguments of the *fatwa* were classical and theological in nature, the goals were contemporary and political. It is too obvious to ignore the fact that the actual concern of the *fatwa* was with the doctrine of the *imama* and nothing else.[21]

So the recommendation by MUI was designed to support government policy regarding its response to the export of revolutionary ideas. This is affirmed in a speech in 1984 given by the Minister of Religious Affairs, which reminded the *'ulama* of a growing interest in Shi'ism in the country and of Iran's efforts to spread its revolutionary ideas. At the same meeting, the Coordinating Minister for Politics and Security Affairs also emphasised these tendencies.[22] However, to deny the religious goal of the recommendation completely is misleading. At that time, *'ulama* in Indonesia were aware of, or at least had heard of, a growing number of converts to Shi'i Islam among the Muslim youth, a growing distribution and publication of Shi'i works and an increasing number of students studying in Iran.[23] The *'ulama* were motivated to formulate the *fatwa* in their concern with the situation. In other words, the recommendation by MUI served a dual purpose.

This significant recommendation was a catalyst for controversy regarding Shi'ism in Indonesia. Both positive and negative reactions followed. The positive response was also the pragmatic response: the recommendation reflected the reality in the country following the success of the Iranian revolution. The step taken by MUI was considered important and appropriate. The more radical and indeed negative elements believed MUI's recommendation to be ineffective, since it had no legal effect. The negative responses include regret that the recommendation

---

20   Mudzhar (1993:114).
21   Mudzhar (1993:115).
22   *Tempo* (17/3/1984:66).
23   Natsir (1984:9-10).

was ever issued, the argument being that in fact it has achieved the opposite of what was intended, actually making Shi'ism more popular, because a growing number of people are now eager to learn about it.[24]

Reformist groups within Indonesia continue to urge MUI to issue a *fatwa* on the falsity of Shi'ism, even though MUI has so far resisted these calls. At the national meeting of 1996, for instance, there were fresh appeals to reaffirm the 1984 recommendation.[25] For MUI, however, the 1984 recommendation remains its final and only statement on the matter. The position maintained by MUI's council, as K.H. Ali Yafie affirms, is simply to stress the principal differences between Sunnism and Shi'ism, as outlined in the recommendation.[26]

A second religious judgement made by MUI concerns the practice of *mut'a*, or temporary marriage, which is permitted in Shi'ism (refer to Chapter Three). On 11 October 1996 sent a letter to MUI with regard to the importance of issuing a *fatwa* on *mut'a*. The request was connected to the fear of *mut'a* spreading among the Muslims, particularly a controversial case of one Ali Hasan reported in the national mass media. MUI did not deliver the requested *fatwa* until the following year. On 25 October 1997, the *fatwa* commission of MUI held a meeting regarding the issue of the prohibition of *mut'a*. This followed a letter from the Secretary General of DEPAG on 11 October 1996 requesting a *fatwa* and a letter and decision from the chairman of the Muslim association, Ittihadul Muballighin (*Ittihad al-muballighin*, Union of Missionaries) on the prohibition of this type of marriage. The subsequent *fatwa* issued by MUI includes the classical arguments against *mut'a* and re-affirms the marriage laws of Indonesia. The *fatwa* goes on to state that first, *mut'a* is proscribed and second, any person engaged in *mut'a* must be brought before the courts, in accordance with the prevailing rule of law.[27]

MUI's issuance of the *fatwa* cannot be dissociated from the course of the development of Shi'ism in Indonesia. First, MUI stated that the *fatwa* was a response to what it considered to be a growth in the practice of *mut'a* among Muslims in Indonesia, and in particular among youths and students. Second, according to MUI, there had been anxiety among parents, *'ulama*, leaders, educators and the wider Muslim community, that the practice of *mut'a* was being used as a means of Shi'i propagation in Indonesia. Third, MUI affirmed that the majority of Muslims in Indonesia were Sunnis who reject Shi'ism

---

24   Natsir (1984:9-10).
25   *Media Dakwah* (November 1997:41).
26   *Media Indonesia* (5/10/1997).
27   Adlani et. al (1997:125).

in general and its teaching of *mut'a* in particular.[28] This clearly shows a link between the *fatwa* and the controversial seminar on the falsity of Shi'ism of 1997 described above.

Unlike the seminar, the *fatwa* issued by MUI did not attract a significant response from the Muslim community. There were a number of reasons: first, MUI's judgement of the widespread practice of *mut'a* is questionable because some *'ulama*, including K.H. Ali Yafie doubt the relevance of the *fatwa*. The matter was already sufficiently dealt with in the Islamic law of the majority of Muslims in the country. In fact, moderate Muslim intellectuals, such as Abdurrahman Wahid and Nurcholish Madjid seemed to ignore both the practice of *mut'a* and the issuance of the *fatwa*. The question of *mut'a* also emerged at the National conference of NU in November 1997, about one month after the *fatwa*. Although the conference concluded that *mut'a* was forbidden, inauthentic and to be rejected, interestingly, as Barton and Feilard have shown, the Shi'i permissibility of *mut'a* "did not in itself provoke a major outcry at this national gathering... [and] did not seem to represent automatic grounds for its rejection."[29] Secondly, the focus on and rejection of *mut'a* may be regarded as a part of the anti-Shi'i movement promoted by certain circles of the reformist groups. Some of those active during the meeting of Ittihadul Muballighin suggested that MUI members are speakers for and proponents of the anti-Shi'i movement in general. Thus we see the issue of *mut'a* being used as a weapon to oppose the spread of Shi'ism in Indonesia.

The local branches of MUI also provided responses to Shi'ism; however, they were essentially in line with the views of the central institution. On 2 August 1993, for instance, MUI in East Java held a meeting in Surabaya, which invited *'ulama* from various Muslim organisations, including NU, Muhammadiyah and Persis, as well as the Al-Bayyinat Foundation (an anti-Shi'i organisation). The meeting was led by a well-known anti-Shi'i figure, K.H. Misbach, chairman of the provincial board of MUI and head of the DDII branch of East Java.[30] Originally, the purpose of the meeting was to discuss a question relating to the Court of East Java and Husein Al-Habsyi's book of Qur'anic commentary, in English, *Did the Prophet Frown?* The meeting developed into a forum for a judgement of Shi'ism.

At the meeting some of the participants presented their views on Shi'ism from theological perspectives, while others described the development of the *madhhab* in East Java and in particular in Bangil, where Husein Al-Habsyi lived and headed his famous *pesantren*. It is evident from the discussion at the

---

28   Adlani et. al (1997:123).
29   Barton and Feilard (1999:26).
30   Amsyari (1994:155).

meeting that the most negative views were expressed figures from Al-Bayyinat and Muhammadiyah. Muhammad Baabdullah of Al-Bayyinat of Bangil, for instance, stated that Shi'i doctrines are more dangerous than Zionism and that Shi'is do not have the right to live in Indonesia, a country whose state ideology is based on *Pancasila* (the Five National Principles). Similarly, Muammal Hamidy of Muhammadiyah was of the opinion that all Shi'i activities should be outlawed as they were causing uneasiness within the community. Hamidy also proposed that the provincial branch of MUI should establish a team to scrutinise the characteristics of this false religion. K.H. Rochim Noer, the head of Muhammadiyah in East Java shared Baabdullah's opinion that the Shi'is were unbelievers, at the same time backing Hamidy's proposal to form a team to them and the reasons for their going astray. The meeting approved this motion.[31]

Various responses to the MUI meeting followed. The editor of *Aula*, an NU magazine in East Java criticised the results of the meeting as non-progressive, given that on 9 January 1992 MUI in East Java had already reproduced and distributed the 1984 recommendation on Shi'ism. The editor of *Aula* argued that rather than establish a team to scrutinise the perceived threat of Shi'ism in the region, the provincial MUI should produce a plan of action because the national MUI had already formulated a clear recommendation on the matter.[32]

The issuance of the interrelated recommendation and *fatwa* showed a tolerance by the central board of MUI for the expression of religious sentiment in Indonesia. Its attitude reflects not only the different elements - reformist and traditionalist *'ulama* - within the council but also the different and contradictory responses of Islamic organisations and individuals to Shi'ism. Generally speaking, the 1984 recommendation is a much clearer expression of MUI's moderate attitude than the *fatwa* on the prohibition of *mut'a*, which can be seen as accommodating the reformist elements of the organisation. It is pertinent to note that another controversial *fatwa* was issued by MUI in 2005, also dealing with *mut'a*. However, this *fatwa* explicitly avoided any reference to Shi'ism, most likely because of the influence of moderates within MUI.

C. The Response of DEPAG

The position of DEPAG, the Ministry of Religious Affairs, as an Indonesian government body is important to our analysis. In general, DEPAG carries out research and investigation into controversial religious groups and subsequently produces a formal report or opinion. DEPAG is also responsible for maintaining harmony in Indonesian society and it does so by implementing the concept of the

---

31   *Aula* (September 1993:24-28).
32   *Aula* (October 1993:55).

'trilogy of religious harmony' pioneered by the former Minister Alamsjah Ratu Perwiranegara in the period of his ministry, 1978-1983. This concept promotes harmony between the adherents of different religions, harmony between adherents of the same religion and harmony between religious adherents and the government.[33] It should follow then, that DEPAG should also view Shi'ism from the perspective of the trilogy of religious harmony. However, since the majority of Indonesian Muslims are Sunni, DEPAG is predominantly Sunni, with almost all its ministers, officials and staff adhering to Sunnism. Consequently, DEPAG categorises the presence of Shi'ism in Indonesia as a threat to religious harmony and a religious problem that needs to be solved. The matter is further complicated by the fact that Shi'ism is frequently associated with Iranian revolutionary ideology. Like many Muslim countries in the world, the attitude of the Indonesian government towards the Shi'is, particularly in 1980s, was interspersed with a fear of the export of revolutionary ideas.

There are a number of cases regarding Shi'ism that have attracted the attention and energies of DEPAG. However, two of them in particular warrant further examination. The first case from the year 1982, was that of Abdul Qadir Bafaqih, a Shi'i teacher in Bangsri, Central Java. Following reports that Bafaqih was a Shi'i *ustadh* propagating Shi'ism in the area, on 10 November 1982 DEPAG's Body of Research and Development investigated and presented its findings to the Minister. The report detailed findings about the *ustadh*, his Shi'i teachings and missionary activities, as well as the reactions of local Islamic leaders. It also provided the Minister with advice regarding action to be taken. The report made three important recommendations which are crucial to our understanding of the attitude of the Indonesian government towards Shi'ism. First, from a religious point of view, Shi'ism could not be forbidden because it is widely recognised in the Islamic world. Second, action should be taken to withdraw and forbid further distribution of recordings of Bafaqih's religious preaching among the followers of Sunnism. Third, the Provincial Office of Religious Affairs was advised to approach and guide members of this new Islamic group in order that they might adapt themselves to the religious life of the majority Sunni community.

The Inspectorate General of the same ministry was entrusted with the task of investigating the case further. In its report to the Minister on 27 December 1982 a similar description of Abdul Qadir Bafaqih's religious teachings and activities was provided, however this time there was more emphasis on the social and political aspects of the case. First, there was no evidence of political inclination in the activities of the *ustadh* or the possibility for a 'third party' (Iran) to use them for its own political interest. Second, the report describes how the activities of the *ustadh* created tension between him and local *'ulama*, even

---

33   Ratu Prawiranegara (1982:27).

though there was no evidence of this provoking a public reaction. However, the Inspectorate concluded that the situation had the potential to worsen and so it urged that special guidance, provided by the apparatus of the DEPAG, be carried out for the students of the *ustadh*, with a view to them being brought to live in harmony with other members of the Muslim community.

These two formal reports provide us with important information. First, religious opinion is avoided in the reports; in other words, they demonstrate a neutral attitude towards the newly emerged Islamic group. No judgement is made about whether Shi'ism is a true Islamic school. Second, they illustrate the primary concern of the authority - religious harmony among different Islamic groups in the country. The third point is emphasis in the reports on the possible political implications of this case, namely that somehow there was a connection between Shi'ism and the export of Islamic revolutionary ideas from Iran.

The second case is a textual study on *Yaumul Quds*, a magazine put out by the Iranian Embassy. During the mid-1980's, at the request of the Attorney General, DEPAG's Body of Research and Development conducted scrutiny of and provided a recommendation on the contents of this magazine. After a long summary of the magazine, the Body pointed out that only one article, on *wilayat* or sovereignty, had the potential to create problems in the religious life of Indonesian society and the state and it recommended that the article in question should be censored. In a formal letter to the Attorney General, on 15 January 1986, the Body gave more detailed reasons for its recommendation: first, that the article contained inappropriate terms; second, that it interpreted Qur'anic verses out of context, without connecting them to the *asbab al-nuzul* or known occasions of revelation; third, that its interpretation of these Qur'anic verses was at odds with the religious comprehension of majority of Indonesian Muslims; fourth, that the article was meant to spread the teachings of Shi'ism in Indonesia and therefore presented a risk of creating disorder in religious life and had the potential to become the religious basis for political activity; fifth, that the publication of the article in the Indonesian language could be seen as an attempt to disseminate Iranian revolutionary ideas in the country.[34]

These two cases demonstrate a clear concern by DEPAG for social order within Indonesian society and with the political implications of the spread of Shi'ism in the country. For DEPAG, the fact that the magazine was published by the Iranian Embassy which was well known for its desire to propagate its revolutionary ideas to other countries, served as confirmation that their judgement was correct.

Providing solutions to religious problems is not the only duty of DEPAG. As we will see below, the Department also took on a preventative role with regard to

---

34 *Pusat Penelitian dan Pengembangan Kehidupan Beragama* (1985/1986:81-82, 1986/1987:65-66).

the spread of Shi'ism in Indonesia. This is demonstrated by the issuance of a specific *Surat Edaran* (Circular) reflecting of DEPAG's official views on Shi'ism. The circular, entitled *Hal Ihwal Mengenai Golongan Syi'ah* (Particulars on the Shi'i Groups) was issued on 5 December 1983 by the Director General of Community Guidance and Hajj Affairs, with the approval of the Minister, Munawir Sjadzali (1925-2004). It was intended for internal departmental distribution only. It stated that the department needed to provide its civil servants with information about Shi'ism and its differences with Sunnism. The subtext was that the department wanted to protect all its civil servants from the influence of Shi'ism. The circular, which was sent to all sections within the department, was meant to be a manual for civil servants in carrying out their duties. Moreover, there was a political rationale for issuing the circular, namely "in the framework of warding off every irresponsible negative effort through religious strife that might be able to upset national stability and steadfastness...."[35]

In order to fully understand the official view of DEPAG it is necessary to examine the contents of this circular in further depth. Its introduction provides an historical description of the emergence of three groups within the Muslim *umma* following the death of the Prophet Muhammad, namely the majority Sunnis, the Shi'is and the *khawarij* or seceders from the ranks of the partisans of Ali. It then provides an explanation of the four main divisions within Shi'ism, namely the *Zaydiyya* (said to be the most moderate of the Shi'i sects and the closest to Sunnism), the *Isma'iliyya* (*Sab'iyya* or 'Seveners'), the *Imamiyya* and the *Ghulat* - the 'extremists' who deviate from the true teachings of Islam.

We need to pay particular attention to the DEPAG description of *Imamiyya* Shi'ism, which is followed in Indonesia, Iran and by the majority of Shi'is in the world. DEPAG suggest that this sect has several characteristics: first, its followers believe that Abu Bakr and 'Umar usurped 'Ali's right to the caliphate, consequently *Imamiyya* Shi'is frequently denounce these two caliphs in their religious teachings. Second, they place 'Ali in a higher position than human beings in general, as a mediator between man and God. Third, some followers of this sect even believe that 'Ali and other Imams have divine attributes. Fourth, they believe that the Imams are infallible in both major and minor sins. Fifth, they do not recognise the consensus of opinion among the *'ulama* (*ijma'*) as a principle of Islamic law unless in a matter approved by the Imams; as a result, neither *ijtihad* nor the use of rational opinion is applied in their interpretation of Islamic law. Sixth, they permit the practice of *mut'a* or temporary marriage. Seventh, they believe that the dead Imams will return to this world before Judgement Day to wipe out all evil and punish all of their opponents.

---

35   Surat Edaran (5/12/1983).

The explanation indicates a poor understanding of the principal doctrines of
Imamiyya Shi'ism. Such misleading views may well contribute to a negative
attitude among the civil servants of the department towards Shi'ism and the
Shi'is. The circular goes on to state:

> All those [mentioned above] are not in accord with and even contrary
> to the true teachings of Islam. In the teachings of Imamiyya Shi'ism
> thought cannot develop, *ijtihad* is not permitted. All has to wait for and
> depends upon the Imam. Between the common people and the Imam
> there is a wide, gaping gap or distance, which becomes a fertile place for
> all kinds of *khurafat* [superstition] and *takhayul* [heresy] to deviate from
> the teachings of Islam.

There are two serious mistakes in the above explanation in so far as it contradicts
the historical reality of the Shi'is. First, it is generally accepted that Islamic
thought in the Shi'i world, particularly its philosophical dimension, continues
to develop and in fact can be said to be more developed than Islamic thought
in the Sunni world. Second, *ijtihad* is always open in Shi'i Islam. As we have
seen in the preceding chapters, there is a need for the continued existence of
a *mujtahid,* the religious scholar who has achieved the level of competence
necessary to practise *ijtihad*. It is also a given that the laity must follow a living
marja' al-taqlid - a *mujtahid* - recognised as the source of emulation in matters of
religious law. This has resulted in close ties between the *'ulama* and lay people
in the Shi'i world. All the misconceptions found in the circular clearly originate
from a failure to understand the key concept of the imamate in Shi'ism and from
an ignorance of the historical reality of the Shi'is.

The most significant part of DEPAG's circular, however, is its statement that
Muslims in Indonesia are recognised as the followers of *ahl al-sunna wa al-
jama'a* whose views differ from those of the Shi`is. In the context of the response
to the Shi'is in Indonesia, the link between DEPAG's circular and the previously
described recommendation from MUI, issued some months after the circular,
cannot be ignored.[36]

---

36 Despite the official anti-Shi'i view of the department, Ministers of Religious Affairs have been accused
by anti-Shi'i groups of having paved the way for the development of Shi'ism in Indonesia. The late Munawir
Sjadzali, who was the Minister for two terms (1983-1993) is said to have shocked the religious authorities
through his 're-actualisation' of Islamic law project. Anti-Shi'i groups saw the spread of Shi'ism as a side
effect of Munawir Sjadzali's 're-actualisation' of Islam, as the following quote shows: "In the mean time the
'needle' of Shi'ism slowly but surely is stabbed into the bodies of our youth with the enticement of *mut'a*
that is allowed, whereas in all time this type of fornication under the label of religion was not known" (*Media
Dakwah* November 1997:41). For the re-actualisation of Islam in Indonesia, see Van Dijk (1991). A different
accusation was directed towards M. Quraish Shihab. When he became the Minister of Religious Affairs for
some months at the end of Suharto's presidency in early 1998, Shihab was accused of being a Shi'i and was
considered to have played a role in influencing MUI's attitude to Shi'ism (Jaiz 2002:114). LPPI has distributed
a brochure entitled *Syiah dan Quraish Shihab* (Shi'ism and Quraish Shihab) which includes a statement by a
friend of Shihab in Cairo that he often defended Shi'ism. This became a controversial issue in the Indonesian

We should bear in mind that DEPAG is not an institution of *'ulama* and so it cannot produce *fatwas* or religious judgements binding to the community. The department carries out its duties by providing solutions to existing religious problems and in its prevention of the possible emergence of new religious problems in Indonesian society and the nation. DEPAG can only request that MUI make recommendations on Shi'ism and issue a *fatwa* on *mut'a*, for example. These requests must be based on considerations of the religious life of Muslim society and with a view to resolving problems between Sunnis and Shi'is in order to promote religious harmony in the country.

D. Anti-Shi'i Propagation

A large number of activities have been undertaken by anti-Shi'i groups for the purpose of preventing or reducing the spread of the teachings of Shi'ism in Indonesia. These activities include seminars, discussions, appeals to government authorities and preaching. They are chiefly carried out by the reformist Muslim movement, in particular by DDII and its missionaries and related institutions. The publication of anti-Shi'i writings has also been of major importance. Coser affirms that, like its opponent, the anti Shi'i group realises the great importance of books as "carriers and disseminators of ideas."[37] The publication of books in the vernacular is meant to provide Indonesian Muslims with Sunni views on Shi'ism in the hope that they will be less susceptible to the teachings of Shi'ism and thus less likely to convert to its *madhhab*. These publications are also intended to compete with the growing number of Shi'i works in the market place, particularly those translated from Arabic, English and Persian originals. Mohammad Natsir and other Muslim leaders in the country were truly aware of the growing phenomenon of Shi'i publishing. Natsir once wrote "… meanwhile, the publication of books and brochures on Shi'ism in Indonesian has begun. Some are original works, others are translations from Arabic and English books. They are published in West Java, Central Java, and East Java etc. and find a wide market of readers, particularly among our youth."[38]

---

media, requiring the chairman of MUI, Hasan Basri, to clarify that Quraish Shihab was not a Shi'i but refused to regard the Shi'is as infidels (*Jawa Pos; Republika; Media Indonesia; Terbit* 27/3/1998). The head of LPPI, M. Amin Djamaluddin showed me another document which was to be published in the event that Quraish Shihab had been reappointed in President Habibie's cabinet (1998-1999). Shihab's denials that he was a Shi'i can be found, for instance, in *Terbit* (17/3/1998). A large number of opinions followed in the media (e.g. *Terbit* 20/3/1998, 26/3/1998, 31/3/1998, *Media Indonesia* 12/4/1998) including a long article entitled "*MUI, Quraish Shihab dan Seputar Isu Syi'ah*" (MUI, Quraish Shihab and On the Subject of Shi'i Issue) by Tontowy Djauhari Hamzah (*Terbit* 18/4/1998). All the writers ask him to prove his opposition to Shi'ism. NU however supports Shihab. It is stated in the NU organ, *Aula* that the issue was raised through the political interests of certain individuals or groups (*Aula* April 1998:66).

37   Coser (1982:362).

38   Natsir (1984:9).

Anti-Shi'i literature offered a strong rejection of Shi'ism and its teachings and drew upon both textual and rational proofs. However, it relied heavily on translations of famous Arabic originals works because no Indonesian *'ulama* were able to produce such works themselves. Through the international network established by the reformist leaders, the choice was made for the popular anti-Shi'i works in the Middle East written by Muhibb al-Din al-Khatib (1886-1969) and Ihsan Ilahi Zahir (d. 1987). Al-Khatib was born in Damascus and from 1920 took up permanent residence in Cairo, where he became one of the most resolute advocates of Wahhabism. This was a direct result of the influence of the writings of Ibn Taymiyya (d. 1323) during his education. Al-Khatib was a journalist, commentator, editor and publisher of his own periodicals, *al-Zahra* (1924-1929) and *al-Fath* (1926-1948). He also produced editions of classical Arabic books and Wahhabi writings. He took a fiercely negative stance towards Shi'ism and strongly opposed any attempts to reach rapprochement and conciliation between Sunnism and Shi'ism.[39]

Zahir has been described as "the most prolific Sunni polemicist in recent years."[40] He was the editor of the Islamic journal *Tarjuman al-Hadith* (Hadith Interpretations) published in Lahore and the Secretary-General of *Jam'iyyat ahl al-hadith* (Society of People of the Hadith), a Wahhabi movement. When a bomb exploded during a rally by that movement in Lahore on March 1987 he was fatally wounded and died a few days later in Riyadh. He was buried in Medina.[41] Regarding the translation and publication of his books, on March 1986 Zahir visited Indonesia, including Surabaya, where he became acquainted with the translator of his books, Bey Arifin and the director of Bina Ilmu Publishers, which published his works in Indonesian. Like his predecessor, Muhibb al-Din al-Khatib, Zahir was strongly anti-Shi'i and an opponent of all Sunni sympathisers who promoted ideas of rapprochement, in particular the *Jam'iyyat al-taqrib bayn al-madhahib al-islamiyya* (the Society of Rapprochement between Islamic Denominations), established in Cairo in 1947.[42]

The most influential of the anti-Shi'i works translated into Indonesian are those by Zahir. His books include *Salah Faham Sunnah Syi'ah* ('Sunni Shi'i Misunderstanding', 1983), *Syiah dan Sunnah*[43] (Shi'ism and Sunnism, 1984) and *Syi'ah Berbohong atas nama Ahlul Bait* (The Shi'is Lie in the Name of Ahl al-Bayt, 1987). These are followed in popularity by al-Khatib's *al-Khutut al-Arida* (The Broad Outlines) which was translated into Indonesian under the title *Mengenal Pokok-pokok Ajaran Syiah Al-Imamiyah dan Perbedaannya dengan*

---

39   Brunner (2004:255-256).
40   Ende (1990:226).
41   Ende (1990:226).
42   Ende (1990:226).
43   The English version, *The Shi'ites and the Sunna*, was printed at Lahore in 1984.

Ahlussunnah[44] ('Introducing the Principal Teachings of Imamiyya Shi'ism and their Differences from Sunnism', 1985). The foreword of this book was written by Muhammad Nasif, the then Secretary General of the Muslim World League. It is important to note that al-Khatib regards Shi'ism as a religion outside Islam rather than a *madhhab* within it. These books are distributed widely in Islamic institutions, organisations and libraries throughout Indonesia and this has made them widely read among large segments of Indonesian Muslim society. Their popularity is indicated by the fact that they are frequently, if not always, referred to when Sunni Muslims in the country discuss Shi'ism. The front cover of Zahir's *Syiah dan Sunnah* states: *"Buku ini Dibagikan dengan Cuma-Cuma Tidak Untuk Diperjualbelikan"* (This Book is Distributed Free of Charge, Not for Sale) indicating an absence of commercial interest in its publication. In fact, an introductory note by the translator Bey Arifin to his book *Shi'ism and Sunnism* (1984) announces that the Muslim World League, which is a Saudi-based organisation, promoted and financed the translation and publication of such books "The Muslim World League Centre in Mecca al-Mukarrama with its letter no.1/6/16 on 23 Safar 1404H through the Muslim World League Office in Jakarta with its letter no.133/VII/1404 on 8 December 1983 requested me to translate the book *al-Shi'a wa al-Sunna* into Indonesian."[45]

Even though there is as yet no quantitative data on the Indonesian versions of Arabic anti-Shi'i works, we can assume that the number has increased since the 1980s. (Yet they are still no equal to the plethora of Shi'i works on offer.) To mention but a few of the most popular in Indonesia: Muhammad Malullah's *Syiah dan Pemalsuan Al-Qur'an* ('Shi'ism and Falsification of the Qur'an') published in 1982 by Pustaka Mantik in Jakarta, Muhammad al-Tunsawi's *Beberapa Kekeliruan Akidah Syi'ah* ('Several Mistakes of Shi'i Doctrine') and Abu al-Hasan al-Nadwi's *Dua Wajah Saling Menentang antara Ahlu Sunnah dan Syi'ah* ('Two Opposing Faces between Sunnism and Shi'ism'), both published by Bina Ilmu, Surabaya in 1984 and 1987 respectively. The tendency continues today with different types of publications, ranging from pamphlets to voluminous works, and with tones from provocative to more moderate. The most important of these might be As-Salus's *Ensiklopedi Sunnah-Syiah* ('Sunni-Shi'i Encyclopaedia') originally consisting of four volumes in Arabic. This encyclopaedia was praised in an introductory note by Muhammad Hidayat Nurwahid, the current spokesman of the Indonesian People's Consultative Assembly and prominent

---

44   Its English translation is entitled *Al-Khutoot Al-'Areedah: Exposition and Refutation of the Sources upon which the Shiite Religion is Based*, printed by the Islam Information Centre, South Netherlands, 1983. This indicates a spread of anti-Shi'i propagation in Europe. Takim also notes intense anti-Shi'i propagation via publications in America (Takim 2000:470).
45   Arifin (1984:11).

leader of PKS. Nurwahid, who is known to have a negative attitude towards Shi'ism, claims that it is a "serious and scientific work, which can amplify the scarcity of authoritative literature on Shi'ism."[46]

A recently translated work, Al-Buhairi's *Gen Syi'ah* (The Genie of Shi'ism, 2001) is probably the most provocative of the anti-Shi'i works published in Indonesia.[47] The author, who is motivated by his strong anti-Shi'i attitude, came to Indonesia from Mecca looking for a translator for his work.[48] Al-Buhairi has good connections with the reformist organisation Al-Irsyad.[49] Furthermore, as he admits, his motivation for writing the book arose from his personal experience among Shi'is in India and Indonesia.[50] Al-Buhairi invites, or even challenges Sunni scholars to engage in dialogue or debate with their Shi'i counterparts and he has even offered to cover any expenses that such an event might incur.[51] Significantly, the translation of Al-Buhairi's book is the only publication to have been criticised by Indonesian Shi'is; for example, on the website of the Fatimah Foundation.[52] Thus its contents warrant further review. The contents are summarised by the translator in his introductory note as follows

> Shi'ism was bred by Jews, raised by Zoroastrians, supported by Christians and Hindus, contributed to by Romans and Greeks and financed by colonisers. It is led by liars and ignoramuses. Metaphorically, Shi'ism is the name of a cake of which the ingredients consist of Islam, Judaism, Christianity, Hinduism, Zoroastrianism and Roman and Greek religion.

> Another finding is that Shi'ism and lies are inseparable like twins. Lying is compulsory for Shi'is, paradise can only be gained by lies whilst hell is gained by a frank, just and honest attitude.

> The Shi'is are a collection of stupid people, seen from the spectacles of the Qur'an and Traditions of the Messenger of God (May God grant him peace and salvation). They, says Ustadh Mamduh, are *Baqarun bila Qurun* (cows without horns) meaning a man's head but a cow's brain.[53]

None of such works contain positive or even moderate views on Shi'ism. Two general, but related, points can be drawn from their contents. Firstly, emphasis is placed on controversies between the two *madhhabs*, but with no intention

---

46   Nurwahid (2001:xii).
47   Its full title is *Gen Syi'ah: Sebuah Tinjauan Sejarah, Penyimpangan Aqidah dan Konspirasi Yahudi* (The Genie of Shi'ism: an Historical Overview, Deviation from Faith and the Jewish Conspiracy) published by Darul Falah in Jakarta. Its original is Arabic *al-Shi'a, minhum 'alayhim* (The Shi'is: From Them on Them).
48   Bashari (2001:vii).
49   Al-Buhairi (2001:300).
50   Al-Buhairi (2001:xi-xii).
51   Al-Buhairi (2001:299-300).
52   See www.fatimah.org.
53   Bashari (2001:ix).

of providing rapprochement. Secondly, the main issues of these controversies remain the same as those of past disputes. Ende has correctly summarised the interrelated topics on which Sunni interpretations disagree with Shi'ism: 1) the Qur'an, Shi'i interpretations and alleged distortion (*tahrif*) of its text, 2) the authenticity and Shi'i view of Hadith, 3) the Shi'i view of the Prophet's companions, 4) the history and Shi'i concept of the imamate, 5) Shi'i legal norms, in particular regarding *mut'a*, 6) the Shi'i teaching of *taqiyya* and 7) certain Shi'i religious rituals.[54] The same points of controversy have also coloured books by Indonesian anti-Shi'i authors, whose interpretations rely heavily on the Sunni polemical works in Arabic.

The reformist Muslim groups not only publish translated works but also produce their own anti-Shi'i writings. Apart from being greatly influenced by the above-mentioned works, these writings too can be considered superficial. By and large, they are articles published in the reformist periodicals and booklets. A large number of articles are to be found in *Al-Muslimun* of Bangil; from September 1979 to January 1998 there were 32 titles of anti-Shi'i articles published in this reformist magazine, which is the largest number to appear in the existing Islamic periodicals. In addition, polemical works in the national media indicate a dynamic opposition to the Shi'is in the country.

The works can be classified into two sections: a general category, covering the rejection of Shi'ism as a valid *madhhab* by Islamic orthodoxy and a specific category, dealing with particular aspects of Sunni-Shi'i controversies. Indonesian anti-Shi'i publications began to appear in 1984, the same year in which DDII put out two booklets, the institution's *Soal Syi'ah* (On Shi'ism) and M. Rasjidi's *Apa Itu Syi'ah* (What is Shi'ism?) both of which claim to point out the false teachings of Shi'ism. It should be noted that Rasjidi, a former Minister of Religious Affairs (12 March 1946 - 2 October 1946), Professor of Islamic law at the University of Indonesia, Muhammadiyah activist, Masyumi figure and a Vice-Chairman of DDII is one of Indonesia's Muslim leaders most concerned with the propagation of anti-Shi'i material. To borrow Azra's words, Rasjidi was also a guardian of the faith of the *umma* against Christianity and heterodox currents.[55] In the years following the Iranian revolution, he became an active speaker at Sunni-Shi'i discussions held around the country and produced several polemical works on the subject. Rasjidi's booklet, which carries the circular by DEPAG as its appendix, generally deals with those topics which are sources of past Sunni-Shi'i controversies, so it is not necessary to describe the content here. However, his conclusion is of importance as it directly relates to Islam in its Indonesian social context. Rasjidi writes:

---

54 Ende (1990:221-222).
55 Azra (1994).

We the Indonesians are given great blessings and true guidance with Islam by God, the Creator of the sky. We thank God that the Islam we adhere to is Sunni Islam, which is based on the existing, and the only Qur'an and the Hadith which have been scrutinised, selected and specified in detail by Hadith scholars from Bukhari [d.870], Muslim [d.815], Abu Daud [d.889], Nasa'i [d.915], Turmudhi [d.892] until Ibn Majah [d.886].[56]

The late M. Rasjidi, was a polemicist, educated in Cairo, at the Sorbonne and in Canada. During the 1970s he became involved in polemics with Nurcholish Madjid on the question of secularisation. Following the MUI 1984 recommendation on Shi'ism, Rasjidi wrote a short article entitled "a mere contribution on Shi'ism", which was published in *Tempo*[57] and in a slightly different version in *Al-Muslimun*.[58] It was intended to expand on Ahmad Ghazali's criticism of the MUI recommendation.[59] In it Rasjidi restated the classical Sunni descriptions of Shi'ism, chiefly based on Zahir's polemical works, and stressed the influence of Persian political culture on the religious doctrines of Shi'ism. Rasjidi - reflecting the attitudes of DDII and of Sunni Muslims in general - confused the topics of Shi'ism and war in the article, blaming Iran for the Iran-Iraq conflict. He concluded: "This is what I want to contribute to Indonesian Muslims. We do not hate the Shi'is but we do not accept their doctrine that is contrary to the pure Islamic doctrine, the Sunni doctrine."[60]

Criticism from Shi'is, many anonymously, followed. One of the fiercest attacks on Rasjidi came from Agus Abubakar Arsal Al-Habsyi, who offered arguments to suggest that Rasjidi made a number of fatal mistakes in his analysis of Shi'i doctrines, teachings and history. Let me take one example

In paragraph seven it is written: "Imam in Shi'ism means political leader ..." and so on. In all the Shi'i literature that I have read, never once did I find such a definition. Or maybe Mr. Rasjidi has other references. In the Imamiyya Shi'i understanding, an Imam has the task of carrying out the same duty as a prophet. Like prophets, Imams are the people chosen by God through His Prophet's appointment. The only difference is that prophets receive revelation and Imams, through a special gift, receive the prophets' commands. Thus a prophet is God's messenger and an Imam is prophet's messenger.[61]

---

56 Rasjidi (1984:45). These scholars produced the classical Hadith collections, *al-Sahih, al-Sahih, al-Sunan, al-Sunan, al-Jami' al-Sahih,* and *al-Sunan* respectively. They are commonly called *al-kutub al-sitta* (the Six Books).
57 *Tempo* (12/5/1984).
58 *Al-Muslimun* (July 1984).
59 *Tempo* (14/4/1984:7).
60 Rasjidi (1984a:50).
61 *Tempo* (26/5/1984:7).

Other critics include Ali Muchsin and Ibrahim Abdullah Assegaf, who use their writings to demonstrate a number of errors and misconceptions by Rasjidi[62] (although their arguments are perhaps not as compelling as Al-Habsyi's). Interestingly, Rasjidi only refuted the writings of Ali Muchsin and Ibrahim Assegaf, ignoring Al-Habsyi's arguments. In his refutation, published in *Al-Muslimun*, Rasjidi suggests that Ali Muchsin has in fact made mistakes. Reiterating a common misunderstanding on certain teachings of Shi'ism, Rasjidi claims that both Assegaf and Muchsin appear not to comprehend the principal differences between Shi'ism and Sunnism. However, Rasjidi agrees with his critics on the importance of Islamic brotherhood. He concludes by accusing the Iranian Embassy of propagating Shi'i teachings to the Muslim youth of Indonesia in an unacceptable way.[63]

The second writer of polemical anti-Shi'i works is A. Latief Muchtar (1931-1997) the General Chairman of Persis for 14 years (1983-1997) who, like other reformist Muslim leaders, took a very negative stance on Shi'ism. He had his primary and secondary education in Persis schools. He completed his undergraduate degree in Islamic Studies in Cairo and gained both a Masters degree and a doctorate in the same field from the IAIN of Jakarta. Muchtar had a reputation as a well-qualified reformist scholar. His anti-Shi'i stance is indicated by his membership of DDII and the Muslim World League. In 1986, responding to the development of Shi'ism in Indonesia, Muchtar - under the penname Abu Irfan (his first son being Irfan Setiawan) - wrote a controversial article, provocatively titled "*Awas Akidah Syiah*" (Beware of Shi'i Doctrine) which was published in *Risalah*, the Persis magazine in Bandung.[64] (Between 1986-1987 *Risalah* published a dialogue on Shi'ism between its proponents and opponents). Muchtar admitted that his writing was intentionally provocative because he wanted Indonesian Muslims to be aware of the spread of Shi'ism in their country. He emphasised that his writing should be understood in the framework of Islamic *da'wa* - that is, to 'enjoin to do good and to desist from evil' (*amr ma'ruf, nahy munkar*). Muchtar began his polemic by mentioning the triumph of Iranian revolution and its impact on the Shi'is in other places in the world, such as Lebanon, as well as on Indonesia's Sunnis. He writes: "the extreme and radical Shi'i movement has attracted some of the Muslim youth in Indonesia with its concept of the imamate...."[65] He goes on to explain the origin of Shi'ism as a consequence of political matters

---

62   The titles are "*Syi'ah: Aliran yang Mana*" (Shi'ism: Which Stream?) and "*Syi'ah: Kekeliruan Prof. Rasjidi*" (Shi'ism: the Mistakes of Prof. Rasjidi) respectively (*Tempo* 9/6/1984). Al-Habsyi's criticism is entitled "*Syi'ah: Koreksi terhadap Rasjidi*" (Shi'ism: A Correction of Rasjidi) (*Tempo* 26/5/1984).
63   Rasjidi (1984b:9-10).
64   The article and its response are added as an appendix to the collection of Muchtar's writings, *Gerakan Kembali ke Islam: Warisan Terakhir A. Latief Muchtar, Ketua Umum Persis 1983-1997* (The Movement of Return to Islam: the Last Legacy of A. Latief Muchtar, General Chairman of Persis 1983-1997) published in 1998 by Rosda in Bandung. It is interesting to note that Jalaluddin Rakhmat wrote an introductory note to the book, even though he was one of the polemicists writing in *Risalah*.
65   Muchtar (1998:324).

following the death of the Prophet Muhammad and then describes the divisions within Shi'ism itself. His sources were the (aforementioned) Indonesian versions of books by al-Khatib (published in 1985), Zahir (published in 1984) and al-Tunsawi's (published in 1984), as well as Rasjidi's booklet (published in 1984). Muchtar reiterates the common issues and arguments which reject what he considers to be Shi'i doctrines, including the imamate, the infallibility of the Imams, *mahdism*, *raj'a* (return) and *taqiyya*. However, I believe his uncritical method of reading the sources meant that the mistakes and misunderstandings about Shi'ism which litter his work were inevitable. One of his critics, Abdi Mahaestyo Soeherman, in a no less provocatively titled article, "*Syiah bukan Sampar*" (Shi'ism is not a Contagious Disease) published in the same magazine, identifies the weaknesses and misconceptions contained in Muchtar's article and his sources. Soeherman then provides a version of Shi'i teachings and history mainly based on contemporary Shi'i sources. We do not have personal information on Soehermand, but his writing and sources suggest that he is a Shi'i. To refute this criticism, Muchtar produced yet another long article, praising al-Khatib and Zahir and their works and re-iterating the need to fight against the Shi'i doctrine.[66]

The polemics continued. Saeful Abdullah, M. Syaifullah and Muhammad Khalid were among those who lined up to advise Muchtar to check his sources, to discuss his thoughts with Shi'i *'ulama* or to read Shi'i sources. Ikhwatu Iman and Ika Tanumaja, criticising the critics, offered their support to Muchtar. Jalaluddin Rakhmat also became embroiled in the controversy by delivering an Indonesian translation of Mahmud Shaltut's famous *fatwa* and of the view of Muhammad al-Ghazali (the leader of Egypt's *Ikhwan al-Muslimun*) on the validity of observing Islamic worship according to the Twelver Shi'ism.[67] Rakhmat was clearly seeking authoritative legal religious recognition from international Sunni scholars, including Shaltut, who was the first to recognise Shi'ism as a completely equal denomination. Rakhmat responded to Muchtar's opinions on Shi'ism in his introductory note to the publication of the collected works of Muchtar (1998). One of the most important elements in the controversy was the involvement of the Iranian Embassy in Jakarta, which issued an official statement signed by Alireza Motevali Alamoti, the Embassy's Second Secretary. The essential part of the text reads

66   The title is "*Sekali Lagi, Awas Akidah Syiah*" (Once More, Beware of Shi'i Doctrine) (Muchtar 1998:359-399).
67   Rakhmat (1998:400:413). Mahmud Shaltut's *fatwa* is frequently used by Shi'is to support their opinions in Sunni-Shi'i dialogues. The main part of the *fatwa* (I follow Brunner's translation [2004:289-290]) reads: "1. Islam does not oblige any of its adherents to be affiliated with a specific *madhhab*. Rather, we say: every Muslim has the right to follow any of the legal schools that have been properly handed down and whose rules in their specific (legal) effects are laid down in writing. A person who follows one of these schools is entitled to turn to any other without being subjected to reproach. 2. In the sense of the religious law of Islam (*shar'ah*), it is permitted to perform the divine service (*ta'abbud*) in accordance with the rite of the Ja'fariyya, which is known as *Shi'a imamiyya*, in the same way as in accordance with all schools of the Sunnis."

> Abu Irfan's description of Shi'ism is his own personal belief and ideas which have completely no relevance to the reality of Shi'ism.
>
> We believe that his description of Shi'ism mentioned above is based only on his imagination; it even appears that he has no information or basic knowledge about the broad and deep Shi'i ideology.[68]

Included in the general category of works rejecting the validity of Shi'ism is a compilation of papers originating from an LPPI seminar in 1997. The book, *Mengapa Kita Menolak Syi'ah* (Why We Reject Shi'ism) contains a collection of the seminar papers, a conclusion and a recommendation, clippings from the media and several forewords from Islamic organisations and institutions.[69] The fact that the book is endorsed by the MUI, Muhammadiyah, NU, Persis, Al-Irsyad, Al-Khairat of Palu, DDII, Ikatan Masjid Indonesia (the Association of Indonesian Mosques) and Al-Bayyinat of Surabaya illustrates its widespread support by Islamic organisations - with certain exceptions - for the prevention of the spread of Shi'ism in Indonesia.

In addition, two booklets, written by M.O. Baabdullah[70] and Fuad M. Fakhruddin are worthy of mention.[71] Baabdullah's bi-lingual booklet iin Indonesian and Arabic regarding the *fatwa* and the stance of Sunni *'ulama* on Shi'i doctrine is probably the more important of the two, not least because of its harsh contents regarding the Shi'is as infidels. The late Baabdullah was a famous anti-Shi'i figure in East Java. He lived in Bangil and was affiliated to the Manarul Islam Mosque of Bangil, Al-Irsyad and also had strong ties with Saudi Arabia. Baabdullah was known to be a harsh opponent of the late Husein Al-Habsyi. Both he and Al-Habsyi were of Arab descent, but Al-Habsyi was a Sayyid and M.O. Baabdullah non-Sayyid. Baabdullah believed that Shi'is were *kafirs*, even though they pronounce the confession of faith ("There is no God but Allah and Muhammad is His messenger"). He based his views on the *fatwa* and opinions of great Sunni *'ulama* such as Imam Malik (d. 795), Ahmad bin Hanbal (d. 855), Bukhari (d. 870), Imam Abu Hamid al-Ghazali (d. 1111), Ibn Taymiyya (d. 1328) and Muhammad bin 'Abd al-Wahhab (d. 1787). Baabdullah emphasised that the infidelity of the Shi'is was demonstrated in their thoughts, which run contrary to the true teachings of the Prophet Muhammad. His booklet examines the recent development of the Shi'is, and in this regard makes two important points to support his view that Shi'ism is a religious sect outside Islam: first, he writes that the Shi'i theological distortions of the Qur'an and a number of other false

---

68   Muchtar (1998:403).
69   Abduh and Abu Huzaifah (1998).
70   Baabdullah (1990).
71   Fakhruddin (1990).

doctrines show that the Shi'is of today are more evil than their predecessors. Second, he writes that the contemporary Shi'is have let in various evil and dangerous currents and follow a polytheistic way of life.[72]

In the category of books dealing with specific issues in the Sunni-Shi'i controversies, there are a number of pamphlets which should be mentioned: There are at least two dealing with the prohibition of *mut'a*, one by the previously mentioned Fakhruddin[73] and the other by Muhammad Sufyan Raji Abdullah.[74] *Mut'a* appears to be the most popular topic of discussion, with at least five articles on the subject in Persis' *Al-Muslimun*. Aside from religious texts quoted and used to reject the Shi'i permissibility of *mut'a*, the writings frequently warn of dangerous consequences of the practice, including the high rate of babies born without paternal acknowledgement and the spread of sexually transmitted diseases, such as HIV-Aids. In addition, there are other pamphlets concerning the imamate, the history of the Prophet's companions, *tafsir* or Qur'anic commentary and Hadith. Most of these anti-Shi'i tracts criticise the growing number of works by Indonesian Shi'i intellectuals. In the field of Islamic history, Saleh Nahdi criticises Hashem's *Saqifah*, re-iterating the Sunni idea that the event of *saqifa* - the designation of Abu Bakr as the first caliph succeeding the Prophet Muhammad - was the origin of unity in the *umma*, not its disunity. In the field of *tafsir*, Ja'far Umar Thalib[75] criticises Husein Al-Habsyi[76] re-assertion that the Prophet did frown; and in the field of Hadith, Husnan responds to a chapter of Jalaluddin Rakhmat's *Islam Aktual*. A number of articles published in *Al-Muslimun* carried responses to the works of the Shi'i writers: Abu Hanifah's critique of Hashem's *Saqifah*,[77] Ibnu Mursyid's critique of Husein Al-Habsyi's *tafsir*[78] and Hasyim Manan's criticique of Rakhmat's *Islam Aktual*.[79] In general, these polemical writings all use the same arguments on the falsity of the teachings of Shi'ism, while citing textual and rational proofs from Middle Eastern anti-Shi'i works. Once more, we should reiterate that publishing is a popular way for anti-Shi'i groups to defend their religious ideology and to demonstrate what they believe to be the falsity of Shi'ism.

The second way in which anti-Shi'i propagation takes place is through the holding of seminars, discussions and debates concerning Shi'ism and Sunni-Shi'i relations. These activities are carried out in a framework of Islamic *da'wa* rather

---

72   Baabdullah (1990:83-84).
73   Fakhruddin (1992).
74   The titles include *Kawin Mut'ah dalam Pandangan Islam* (Mut'a in the View of Islam) published in 1992 by Pedoman Ilmu Jaya, Jakarta and *Mengapa Aku Menolak Dikawin Kontrak* (Why I Reject being Married 'in Contract') published in 2000 by Pustaka AlRiyadl, Jakarta.
75   Thalib (1993).
76   Al-Habsyi (1991a).
77   *Al-Muslimun* (December 1987, January-December 1988).
78   *Al-Muslimun* (1992:67-74).
79   *Al-Muslimun* (1992:47-57).

than intellectual discussion. It is no exaggeration to say that Sunni-Shi'i seminars and similar activities regarding Islamic doctrine, history and development have become the hottest and most controversial events in Indonesia. It is perhaps unsurprising, then, that some of the seminars - such as that organised in 1994 in the *Pesantren* Darunnajah, Jakarta, in which M. Rasjidi and Jalaluddin Rakhmat were speakers - descended into chaos because of the high tension between the opposed groups of participants.

Two of the most popular seminars should be examined in detail: one of the first of its kind in Indonesia, and which attracted considerable media interest, was the "Seminar on Islamic Doctrine" organised in Jakarta's Hotel Indonesia on 14 January 1988 by the Middle East Alumni of Jakarta. It can be seen as a counter-action to a similar activity held in Jakarta about a month earlier, on 8 December 1987, at which all the speakers were famous liberal thinkers and 'enemies' of the reformist groups and of DDII in particular. The speakers event included Harun Nasution, Nurcholish Madjid, and Abdurrahman Wahid.[80] In the eyes of the anti-Shi'i group, this seminar was intended to contribute to the spread of Shi'ism in the country.[81] The controversial anti-Shi'i seminar in question involved three main speakers, M. Rasjidi, Ibrahim Hosen and Fuad M. Fakhruddin,[82] who all agreed that Shi'ism was the main cause of the Iran-Iraq war. They also agreed on the danger of Shi'ism for the Indonesian nation. The goal of the seminar was to confirm Shi'ism as a heterodox sect, and in the framework of *da'wa* the participants were each given four anti-Shi'i books, consisting of Indonesian translations of Middle Eastern works by Said Hawa, al-Tunsawi, al-Khatib and Zahir.[83] Abdul Malik M. Aliun, Chairman of the seminar's organising committee said that "the Middle East alumni think it necessary to correct Islamic doctrine from false streams, one of which is Shi'ism, and we the Muslim *umma* need to know Shi'ism in order not to be plunged into sin."[84]

His opinion provoked angry reactions from the more moderate participants at the seminar, including Muslim intellectuals such as Nurcholish Madjid and Alwi Shihab. Following the seminar, no less than six critics wrote articles that were published in the national magazine, *Tempo* responding in particular to

---

80 The seminar was organised in Jakarta by the West Java branch of KOMPPAQ (*Korps Mahasiswa Penghafal dan Pengkaji Al-Qur'an*).

81 One of the critics was Muhammad Hidayat Nur Wahid, who was at the time a student in Saudi Arabia. In *Tempo* (23/1/1988:14-15), he fiercely criticised Madjid's opinion on the fictive figure of Abdullah bin Saba'.

82 Rasjidi's paper is without a title, whilst the papers of Fakhruddin and Hosen are "*Hakikat Syiah dalam Segala Pandangan Hidupnya*" (The Nature of Shi'ism and its all Worldviews) and "*Syi'ah Sebagai Gerakan Yang Membahayakan Eksistensi Islam*" (Shi'ism as a Movement Dangerous to the Existence of Islam) respectively. Hosen's was published in *Mimbar Ulama* (126/XII/1988).

83 They include, respectively, *Khomenisme* (Khomeniism), *Beberapa Kekeliruan Akidah Syiah* (Several Mistakes of Shi'i Doctrine), *Mengenal Pokok-pokok Ajaran Syiah al-Imamiyah dan Perbedaannya dengan Ahlussunnah* (Introducing Principal teachings of Imamiyya Shi'ism and their Differences from Sunnism) and *Syiah dan Sunnah* (Shi'ism and Sunnism) (*Tempo* 23/1/1988).

84 *Tempo* (6/2/1988).

Fakhruddin's statement that "'Ali bin Abi Talib tried to satisfy his personal ambition for the caliphate and therefore he was not Islamic". These critics, including Alwi Shihab, could see that this would be provocative to both Sunnis and Shi'is because of the undoubted personal quality of 'Ali and the prohibition on discrediting one of the four rightly guided caliphs.[85] In his response to Alwi Shihab, Fakhruddin maintained his stand.

The most impressive anti-Shi'i seminar took place in the hall of the Istiqlal Mosque in Jakarta on 21 September 1997. It was organised by LPPI (*Lembaga Penelitian dan Pengkajian Islam*, Institute of Islamic Studies and Research) in collaboration with *Gema*, a bulletin of the reformist Al-Irsyad. LPPI is led by Amin Djamaluddin, who claims to have been a student of Natsir. As a DDII activist receiving a monthly allowance from that organisation, Djamaluddin has a vested interest in blocking the development of religious currents considered false. It also demonstrates the link between LPPI and DDII and their collaboration in the organisation of *da'wa* activities.[86] The importance of this 1997 anti-Shi'i seminar lies in its success, not only in having as its speakers several Muslim leaders representing great Islamic organisations and institutions in the country. Among them was K.H. Hasan Basri (1920-1998) the then General Chairman of MUI, who delivered the opening speech to the seminar. The large number of participants included state officials, military personnel, 'ulama, Muslim leaders, leaders of Islamic organisations and 'ordinary' people. The seminar was widely reported and became the source of a long-running controversy in the Indonesian media.

Amin Djamaluddin, chief of the seminar's organising committee, stated that the seminar was conducted so that authoritative Islamic scholars could provide an explanation of the nature of Shi'ism to the government, security authorities and other related groups, in order that they may "formulate steps to stop the action of the Shi'i people working the land of the Sunnis in Indonesia."[87] The speakers invited were known anti-Shi'i figures, including Moh. Dawam Anwar (a Secretary of the Religious Advisory Council of NU), Irfan Zidny (Head of the Astronomy Board of NU), Thohir Al-Kaff (Al-Bayyinat Foundation of Surabaya), A. Latief Muchtar (the then General Chairman of Persis), Nabhan Husein (the Chairman of Jakarta DDII), Muhammad Hidayat Nurwahid (the Head of Al-Haramain Foundation of Jakarta and later *Partai Keadilan Sejahtera*) and Syu'bah Asa (Vice-Editor of *Panji Masyarakat*). None of the speakers voiced a positive view on Shi'ism. Insofar as we understand the contents of the papers presented, no new interpretations or arguments regarding the sources of Sunni-

---

85   They were Chehab Rukni Hilmy, Zulkifli (*Tempo* 6/2/1988), Doni Darmawan (13/2/1988), Alwi Shihab (20/2/1988), Abdul Kadir and Bismar Siregar (27/2/1988). The organiser of the seminar has clarified the missionary goal of the seminar (*Tempo* 6/2/1988). Fakhruddin's response was published in the same magazine (20/2/1988).
86   Husin (1998:285).
87   Abduh and Abu Huzaifah (1998:xxv-xxvi).

Shi'i controversies were presented. It is evident however that all the speakers had an interest in efforts to prohibit the growth of Shi'ism in Indonesia. For example, K.H. Irfan Zidny expressed his regret over the number of Indonesian Muslim students and intellectuals supporting or even adhering to the teachings of Shi'ism, in spite of the fact that they had only learned these teachings in a short period of time and from Indonesian Shi'i figures who do not have a thorough knowledge of Islam. Zidny suggested that it was the duty of the *'ulama* and leaders of Islamic organisations and institutions to cooperate with state authorities and address the phenomenon of Shi'ism, which he believed to be dangerous to the unity of *umma*.[88]

Ten of the twelve points formulated by the committee at the conclusion of the seminar repeated the well-worn arguments of the Sunni polemical works, including the Shi'i view that the Qur'an was corrupted by the companions of the Prophet, the acceptance of Hadith only through the *ahl al-bayt* of the Prophet, the rejection of the caliphate of Abu Bakr, 'Umar and 'Uthman, the practice of *taqiya* and *mut'a* and the belief in Imams and their infallibility.[89] But two particularly significant points that were made in the conclusion need to be noted: The first is a statement that reads "Indonesian Muslims have the responsibility and obligation to prevent various efforts of falsification and destruction of Sunni doctrines adhered to by Muslims in Indonesia."[90] This invitation was formulated to meet the goal of the seminar to defend the Sunni land from the presence and spread of Shi'ism. The second and highly provocative point made was that throughout history Shi'is have proved to be criminals, traitors and terrorists.[91] This could be considered as a libellous accusation, unless, of course, the committee could prove it.

Regardless of the teachings and the reality of the Shi'is in Indonesia, the conclusion supports the ten points of recommendation drawn up by the seminar's committee. The recommendation read as follows

> Based on the conclusions and to protect the stability, safety and the unity of society, the Indonesian nation and state, this seminar makes the recommendation:
>
> 1. To urge the Indonesian government, in this case the Indonesian Attorney General to immediately prohibit Shi'ism in the whole of Indonesia because, besides having caused uneasiness in society, [it] is a source of destabilisation of the life of the Indonesian nation and state because it is impossible that the Shi'i have a loyal attitude to

---

88   Abduh and Abu Huzaifah (1998:24-25).
89   Abduh and Abu Huzaifah (1998:158-160).
90   Abduh and Abu Huzaifah (1998:158).
91   Abduh and Abu Huzaifah (1998:160).

the Indonesian government. In their teachings of Islam there is no concept of consensus but only the absolute decision of the Imam.

2. To request the Indonesian Attorney General and all related government institutions to cooperate with the MUI and the Board of Research and Development of the Department of Religious Affairs to scrutinise books containing Shi'i views and to prohibit their distribution throughout Indonesia.

3. To urge the government, cq the Minister of Justice to withdraw the licenses of all Shi'i foundations or those spreading the teachings of Shi'ism in Indonesia, such as Muthahhari in Bandung, Al-Muntazar in Jakarta, Al-Jawad in Bandung, Mulla Sadra in Bogor, YAPI in Bangil, Al-Muhibbin in Probolinggo, and Al-Hadi in Pekalongan.

4. To request the government, in this case the Minister of Information to require all publishers to report and deposit examples of all their published books to the MUI to be scrutinised.

5. To remind all Islamic organisations and educational institutions (school, *pesantren* and university) throughout Indonesia to remain on guard against Shi'ism that can influence their members and students.

6. To invite the whole of Indonesian Muslim society to be alert to Shi'ism because Shi'ism is an infidel, false and falsifying sect.

7. To appeal to all women to avoid entering *mut'a* ('contract marriage') that is practised and propagated by the followers of Shi'ism.

8. To appeal to all mass media (print, electronic and audio-visual) and book publishers not to spread Shi'ism in Indonesia.

9. To appeal to the Indonesian government to prohibit the activities of spreading Shi'ism by the Iranian Embassy.

10. Specifically, to expect that LPPI immediately cooperate with MUI and the Department of Religious Affairs to publish a short manual on the falsity of Shi'ism and its principal differences from Sunnism.[92]

There were huge responses - both positive and negative - to this anti-Shi'i seminar and its conclusion and recommendations. Many can be found in the letters to the editors of national newspapers and magazines. Those reacting positively to the seminar, and thus negatively to Shi'ism, expressed their appreciation of the seminar, with its emphasis on the impossibility of unity between Sunnis and Shi'is and doubts about the capability of Shi'is to prove the

---

92   Abduh and Abu Huzaifah (1998:160-162).

truth of their madhhab.[93] In contrast, those reacting negatively to the seminar offer various opinions, including that the seminar discussed questions of Shi'ism while ignoring the contribution made by the Shi'is to Islam. They also point to the inaccuracy of seminar's decision, its non-proportionality and even its non-scientific character.[94] One Shi'i, *ustadh* Alwi Husein al-Muhdar, an alumnus of Al-Azhar University, provided the readers with views of contemporary Middle Eastern *'ulama*, including Sayyid Tantawy and Yusuf Qardawi, who suggest that there are only minor differences between Sunnism and Shi'ism.[95] Several more serious articles were published in the Indonesian media in response to the seminar. The writers, generally proponents of the Islamic Brotherhood, include Muhammad Amin Sadik, Islah Gusmian, Masyhuri and Sihbudi. They wrote articles questioning the relevance of the seminar, suggesting it made a subjective judgement on Shi'ism, regarded as an in absentia judgement.[96] It should not automatically be assumed that all the proponents of this view are Shi'is, although clearly some of them are, including Alwi Husein. The negative responses to the seminar can be subsumed into two categories: first, those stating the irrelevance of the Seminar's decision because it did not involve prominent Muslim intellectuals in the country, such as Nurcholish Madjid, Abdurrahman Wahid and Amien Rais. Second, those propagating the idea of unity or rapprochement between Sunnis and Shi'is, believing there to be only minor, surmountable differences between the two *madhhabs*.

Among the Shi'is themselves, O. Hashem gave the most comprehensive and emotional response to the seminar in his article "*Jawaban Lengkap...*" which was then extended to become the book entitled *Syi'ah Ditolak Syi'ah Dicari* (Shi'ism is Rejected, Shi'ism is Sought).[97] In his response, Hashem declared his strong

---

93 Among others, the writings include "*Terimakasih Adanya Berita Seminar Syi'ah*" (Thanks for News on Shi'i Seminar) by Abdullah Ali (*Pelita* 7/10/1997), "*Syi'ah dan Suni Tidak Mungkin Bisa Bersatu*" (Shi'ism and Sunnism Cannot be United) by Unang D. Mintareja (*Pelita* 31/10/1997) and "*Buktikan Bahwa Syiah Tidak Sesat*" (Prove that Shi'ism is not False) by Tontowy Djauhari Hamzah (*Panji Masyarakat* 17/11/1997).

94 Among others, the views are included in such writings as Saefudin's "*Mengapa Syi'ah Dipersoalkan?*" (Why is Shi'ism Questioned?) (*Pelita* 3/10/1997), Sobar Awanto Habsyi's "*Seminar Syiah: Sebuah Keputusan Yang Menyesatkan*" (Seminar on Shi'ism: A Misleading Decision) (*Republika* 28/9/1997), Achmad Al-Attas's "*Seminar Soal Syiah Yang Tidak Proporsional*" (An Unproportional Seminar concerning Shi'ism) (*Panji Masyarakat* 20/10/1997), Abdullah Husin's "*Seminar Tentang Syiah Tidak Ilmiah*" (Seminar on Shi'ism is Unscientific) (*Panji Masyarakat* 20/10/1997), and B.I. Yakup's "*Mengapa Syiah Ditolak?*" (Why is Shi'ism Rejected?) (*Tiras* 20/10/1997).

95 *Tiras* (24/11/1997).

96 The articles are entitled "*Seminar atau Pengadilan In Absentia*" (Seminar or Sentencing In Absentia) (*Pelita* 10/10/1997), "*Mengadili Syi'ah, Tak Relevan*" (Judging Shi'ism, Irrelevant) (*Media Indonesia* 14/11/1997), "*Titik Temu Sunni-Syiah dan Kerukunan Umat Beragama*" (the Sunni-Shi'i Meeting Point and Religious Harmony) (*Pelita* 17/10/1997), and "*Polemik Suni-Syiah*" (Sunni-Shi'i Polemics) (*Tiras* 17/11/1997), respectively.

97 The full title is "*Jawaban Lengkap terhadap Seminar Nasional Sehari tentang Syi'ah 21 September 1997 di Masjid Istiqlal Jakarta*" (A Complete Answer to One day National Seminar on Shi'ism 21 September 1997 in Istiqlal Mosque, Jakarta), which was republished under another title "*Mengapa Kami Bela Syi'ah*" (Why we Defend Shi'ism). The book *Syi'ah Ditolak Syi'ah Dicari* (Shi'ism is Rejected, Shi'ism is Sought) is published by ICC of Al-Huda, Jakarta, firstly in 2000 and reprinted in 2002.

opposition to the seminar, its conclusion and recommendations and restated Shi'i views on classical topics that are the sources of Sunni-Shi'i controversy. One of O. Hashem's statements is particularly interesting: "Do not think that the Minister of Religious Affairs will join the crazy [action] to prohibit Shi'ism. Our Minister of Religious Affairs is not a stupid person… "[98] In response to Hashem, Djamaluddin and Hidayat Nurwahid wrote to demonstrate from the Sunni perspective what they saw as the weakness of Hashem's arguments. Djamaluddin wrote: "… according to us, it is not that the person who prohibits Shi'ism is crazy but it is exactly the person who defends Shi'ism who is crazy."[99] Djamaluddin ends by emphasising that "Shi'ism is false, falsifying and a sect of infidels."[100]

Once again it is significant to note the involvement of the Iranian Embassy in Jakarta in the discussions of the anti-Shi'i seminar. The Embassy issued a statement through its Social Relations Division making the point that the accusations were not based on the truth about Shi'ism.[101] Of nine points the Embassy then presented, three need mentioning: first, it states that it was the intention of the committee and speakers at the seminar to destroy national stability and unity, as well as the international image of Indonesia as a pluralistic and tolerant society. Second, regarding a point in the seminar's conclusion which states that "the Constitution of Iran decides that the official religion of Iran is Islam which is the *Ja'fari Ithna 'ashariyya* school of Islam…." the Embassy points out "the choice of ideology is a legal right of each nation. For us, such a statement has the same meaning as interference in internal affairs of other nations". Third, the Embassy statement deals with the accusation that Shi'is are terrorists and criminals (Point 12 of the seminar's conclusion). The Embassy suggests that this is simply repeating the propaganda of Zionists and certain arrogant countries.[102]

Amin Djamaluddin was not afraid to speak out. As the chief organiser of the seminar and head of LPPI, he gave both emphasis and explanation in his refutation to the Iranian Embassy's statement.[103] He affirmed that the seminar was offered as Islamic *da'wa* to Indonesian Muslims, and that involving Iran in any discussions and/or a move to prohibit the presence of Shi'is in Indonesia was unavoidable simply because the majority of Iranians are Shi'is. He denied that this amounted to interference in Iran's internal affairs. What is more, he even accused Iran, through its Embassy, of interfering in the pluralistic religious

---

98   Cited in Djamaluddin (n.d:40). These sentences are omitted in Hashem (2002).
99   Djamaluddin (1998:40).
100   Djamaluddin (1998:41).
101   The title is *"Tudingan Soal Syiah Tidak Berdasar"* (Accusations Concerning Shi'ism have no Base) published in *Panji Masyarakat* (3/11/1997).
102   *Panji Masyarakat* (3/11/1997:8).
103   The title is *"Manuver Politik Kedubes Iran"* (Political Manoeuvres of the Iranian Embassy) published in *Panji Masyarakat* (8/12/1997).

life of the Indonesian nationwhich was "to be destroyed through the Shi'i religion, strategically and systematically". Some of Djamaluddin's explanations simply restate hackneyed topics and should not be reproduced here. The public controversy was never solved, but did eventually die down over time. Suffice it to say that seminar was used as a vehicle of anti-Shi'i propagation in Indonesia.

The third method of anti-Shi'i propagation is to make an appeal to the Indonesian government. A clear-cut example is the anti-Shi'i group's approach to the government, asking for the activation of the LPPI seminar recommendations. About a month after the seminar had taken place, LPPI wrote a letter, signed on 17 October 1997, requesting that the government - in this case the Attorney General, the Minister of Justice, the Minister of Education and Culture and the Minister of Religious Affairs - forbid the existence of Shi'ism in Indonesia. The group also called a press conference, after which 15 Islamic leaders, including the LPPI director, Amin Djamaluddin and speakers from the seminar went to the office of the Attorney General and the Department of Religious Affairs to present the same request.[104] In the previous year, LPPI had also sent the Minister of Religious Affairs, the Attorney General and the Chairman of MUI a similar appeal for the prohibition of Shi'i Islam in the country. The Indonesian government failed to respond to either request.[105] As previously mentioned, Al-Irsyad had also made a similar approach to government in 1996.

The campaign for the banning of Shi'ism in Indonesia continued. It became particularly strong following MUI's issuance of the *fatwa* prohibiting the practice of *mut'a*. Working towards its goal of ridding Indonesia of Shi'ism, LPPI distributed a leaflet,[106] and urged MUI to issue a *fatwa,* on the falsity of Shi'ism and to endorse the prohibition of its spread in the country.[107] Despite this request, MUI did not issue a *fatwa*, stating that its 1984 recommendation had been sufficient.

Similar actions took place in other parts of the country, particularly in the areas where major Shi'i institutions are located. The Association of Middle East Alumni of Madura copied the steps of LPPI in its own attempts to prohibit Shi'ism. In 1992, in Pekalongan, Central Java, where the *Pesantren* Al-Hadi is situated, Sunni groups made a resolution on Shi'ism containing four demands: first, for the *Pesantren* Al-Hadi to cease all activities; second, to bring Ahmad Baragbah, the leader of Al-Hadi, before the court as he had organised unlawful marriages; third, to keep a watch on and to prohibit all Shi'i activities in Pekalongan; fourth, to call on the central government to declare, via its GBHN

---

104   *Pelita* (28/10/1997).
105   *Panji Masyarakat* (3/1/1997:74-75).
106   "The Principles of the Falsity of Shi'ism" is published by LPPI in accordance with the recommendations of the mentioned seminar.
107   *Pelita* (1/4/1998).

(*Garis-garis Besar Haluan Negara*, Broad Outlines of the Nation's Direction) that the only form of Islam recognised by the state was *ahl al-sunna wa al-jama'a*. The resolution was delivered to the mayor of Pekalongan and the district People's Representative Council.[108]

The fourth method used by the anti-Shi'i movement to protect Indonesian Muslims from the influence of Shi'ism is conventional preaching, *tabligh* in religious gatherings, *pengajian*. In this regard, we find, or we are told, that anti-Shi'i figures throughout the country include the charge of the falsity of Shi'ism as a topic in their sermons at mosques and other venues. Wisananingrum reported her experience in 1991, when she witnessed a leader of MUI give a sermon on the falsity of Shi'ism at the Al-Muslimun Mosque in Bandung. She believes such actions to be a part of the anti-Shi'i propagation aimed at persuading the Sunni Muslim community to reject the teachings of Shi'ism.[109] A number of anti-Shi'i sermons were also delivered at the DDII mosque in Jakarta. Furthermore, similar sermons were broadcast though radio stations such as At-Thohiriyah FM in Jakarta, which produced a programme about 'false currents'. These were presented by the journalist, Hartono Ahmad Jaiz, who is also an activist for DDII and LPPI.[110] There are many other examples, too numerous to mention. However, a Sunni religious gathering in Bangil in 1993 is worthy of note. This is also an important case in so far as it reveals the high religious tensions running between Sunni and Shi'i groups in Indonesia. It was called the gathering of *Ahl al-Sunna* and combined elements of NU, Persis, Muhammadiyah and the Al-Bayyinat Foundation. Hundreds of participants attended. In this forum, the audience not only learned the teachings of Sunnism but also criticised the teachings of Shi'ism. The gathering was undertaken as a response to the gathering of *Ahl al-Bayt*, which was headed by Zahir Yahya (Husein Al-Habsyi's son-in-law) and Ali Al-Habsyi (his son).[111] It is important for us to bear in mind that religious preaching is the most common and widespread means of propagating anti-Shi'i sentiment in the country.

All four of the abovementioned ways of anti-Shi'i propagation are directed at all segments of the community and state, the laity and the elite. They include both cultural and structural approaches. In the eyes of the anti-Shi'i movement, not only are the Sunni community members to be protected from the influence of Shi'i teachings, but the Indonesian government is expected to take a decision on the prohibition of Shi'ism in the country. So far it has not been possible to

---

108 Zainuddin et.al (2000:113-114).
109 Wisananingrum (2001:92-93).
110 A compilation of his journalistic reports is published as a book entitled *Aliran dan Paham Sesat di Indonesia* (False Streams and Teachings in Indonesia) in which he includes "*Gerakan Syiah di Indonesia*" (the Shi'i Movement in Indonesia) (Jaiz 2002:114-144), mainly derived from his report to *Media Dakwah* (October and November 1997).
111 *Aula* (September 1993:12-13).

examine the effectiveness of anti-Shi'i propagation by means of publications, seminars or religious preaching, but clearly the structural approach to the government has so far failed. There is one notable exception: the city of Mataram in West Nusa Tenggara. In June 2003, the mayor of Mataram issued an instruction for the prohibition of Shi'ism in the city. The instruction stated that Shi'ism could not be distributed to Sunni groups.[112] This prohibition led not only to disappointment from the Shi'is in Mataram but also negative reactions from some members of Mataram's society.[113]

The attempts by the Sunni reformist group to protect their community from the influence of Shi'ism and to prohibit the *madhhab* has inevitably led to high tension between the two groupings. Shi'i figures in Indonesia recount many bitter experiences from negative reactions from the anti-Shi'i group. These reactions were directed not only to individuals but also to institutions and they varied in their severity. One example of an individual experience occurred in 1996. Ali Hasan, a teacher at a junior high school and a religious teacher working from his own house in Sragen, Central Java was imprisoned for three and a half years after being accused of having illegal sexual relations with three girls. The relations were said to have been based on *mut'a*.[114] Ali, supported by a number of his students, denied the accusations and stated that his trial had been 'a farce', '*dagelan*'. He believed that his arrest had been simply a way stop the religious gatherings he held at his house, which had become increasingly popular.[115]

There are also examples of more destructive anti-Shi'i actions, which have badly coloured Sunni-Shi'i relations. The burning down of the branch of *Pesantren Al-Hadi* in Batang, Central Java, in April 2000 is an extreme case in point. It is said that the building and facilities of the *pesantren* were set fire to and destroyed by a large number of people intent on putting a stop to its activities. In fact, before the tragedy occurred the Regent of Batang and the apparatus of the District Attorney had issued instructions to stop the teaching activities at the *pesantren*. In the eyes of the *pesantren*, this was a result of efforts by the anti-Shi'i group to influence the authorities. The *pesantren* had plans to bring the case to the court, but during the judicial process the tragedy took place.[116] This case is evidence that anti-Shi'i action in response to the spread of Shi'ism has also involved the destruction of Shi'i institutions in the name of religious belief and Islamic *da'wa*.

---

112   *Koran Tempo* (4/6/2003).
113   *Koran Tempo* (5/6/2003). The report on the prohibition of Shi'ism issued by the Mayor of Mataram, Moh. Ruslan and the controversies was also covered by *Lombok Post* (3-9/6/2003).
114   *Gatra* (25/5/1996).
115   Ali Hasan, interview, (11/9/2002).
116   *An-Nashr* (18/2000:57-59), *Tempo* (http://www.tempointeraktif.com/majalah/arsip/thn03/edisi07/per-1.htm accessed 17/4/2002).

E. The Moderate Response by Muslim Intellectuals

Amidst the growing efforts of the anti-Shi'i movement in Indonesia, the Shi'is in the country can count on a number of leading Muslim intellectuals inclined to protect them as a minority religious group. They include Nurcholish Madjid, Abdurrahman Wahid and Amien Rais, all of whom are known for their moderate or sympathetic views towards Shi'ism and its adherents. They have been criticised by the anti-Shi'i faction, who accuse them of providing a space for Shi'is to propagate their teachings and at least indirectly contributing to the development of Shi'ism in Indonesia. This idea that the intellectuals have made an indirect contribution is perhaps correct. They are also accused of creating the many barriers that are faced by the anti-Shi'i group in their struggle to prohibit Shi'ism in the country. Given these suggestions, it is important to try to pinpoint the alleged attempts by prominent Muslim intellectuals to provide a space for the Shi'is and Shi'ism in the country.

It is not without reason that a number of Muslim intellectuals were invited to become discussants at a seminar on the religious and political thought of Jalaluddin Rakhmat on 30 October 1997. This event was held in conjunction with the distribution of Jalaluddin Rakhmat's collection of essays, *Catatan Kang Jalal: Visi Media, Politik, dan Pendidikan (Kang Jalal's Notes: Vision of Media, Politics and Education)*. The seminar is interesting in the context of Sunni-Shi'i relations because many people saw it as a counter-seminar, based on the fact that Jalaluddin Rakhmat is a prominent Shi'i leader in Indonesia. The speakers were the above-mentioned prominent intellectuals, Nurcholish Madjid, Amien Rais and Said Agiel Siradj, who substituted for Abdurrahman Wahid. Discussions on Sunni-Shi'i relations did arise during the seminar and Rais, for one, suggested that followers of both Sunnism and Shi'ism should respect and cooperate with one another.[117]

Amien Rais, the former Chairman of Muhammadiyah, does not currently express any extensive views on Shi'ism in his writings or public comments, but rather his general attitude likely corresponds to his positive attitude towards the Iranian revolution. When questioned about his opinion on the LPPI seminar, he was apprehensive. He suggested that the Sunnis should avoid cynicism when discussing Shi'ism, and vice versa, and that both parties should show mutual respect.[118] He seems to avoid giving his opinions about Shi'ism; as a result, neither the Shi'i nor the anti-Shi'i groups can claim that Rais is among their supporters or, indeed, a supporter of the other. That said, Rais strongly rejects Shi'ism on

---

117   *Ummat* (10/11/1997:21).
118   *Kompas* (31/10/1997:15).

the question of doctrine, in particular the immunity of the Imams and Mahdism. It appears to be the worldly political aspects of Shi'ism, particularly the Iranian revolution, that have attracted Rais's sympathy. Iran's strong opposition to the West meets with his approval. His moderate stance on Shi'ism has, in a way, to be understood in the framework of his political attitudes. This stance is also explained by his links to the Muhammadiyah, an organisation more concerned with its educational, social and missionary programmes than theological debate.

Amien Rais's contribution to the development of Shi'ism in the country could be counted from his translation of one of Iranian Ali Shari'ati's books into Indonesian, although it should be noted that he denies any intention to promote Shi'i thought in Indonesia or to expose the classical political conflict between the Sunnis and Shi'is. In his introduction to Shari'ati's work, Tugas Cendekiawan Muslim (The Duties of the Muslim Intellectual, Yogyakarta, Shalahuddin Press, 1984) Rais writes:

> Dr. Ali Shari'ati is a Shi'i whereas the translator is a Sunni Muslim. The motif to translate this book is not to offer fragments of Shi'i thought in Indonesia. For the translator, the Sunni-Shi'i difference is an old-fashioned historical legacy that has resulted in the weakness of Islamic *umma* as a whole. What we need to do is not to expose past political conflicts that will clearly be of no use.[119]

Amien Rais's sympathetic and moderate attitude to Shi'ism has provoked challenges, particularly from the reformist Muslim group. When Rais proposed the levying of the portion of one fifth of income as the religious alms of professionals, or *zakat profesi*,[120] he was seen to have been influenced by the Shi'i teaching of *khums*, 'the fifth'. He was judged by many to be an unbeliever. In response, Jalaluddin Rakhmat, with whom Rais shares a very close relationship, defended him from a Shi'i perspective.[121] Another criticism of Rais, this time by Mudzakkir Husein, has been directed at his frequent praise of Iran while disparaging other Muslim countries such as Saudi Arabia.[122]

Rais's attitude can also be viewed in the context of his close relations with Muslim intellectuals and students, some of whom happen to be adherents of Shi'ism. What is more, many prominent Shi'i figures in Indonesia have close relations with Rais and when he established his political party, the National Mandate Party, he instantly gained support from this segment of Muslim

---

119   Rais (1984:ix).
120   Rais (1988).
121   Rakhmat (1991:145-153, 1998:81-85).
122   *Al-Muslimun* (266/1992:6-7).

society. A number of his party members successfully fought for membership of the national or regional People's Representative Council. From this perspective, then, Rais's attitude to Shi'ism can be seen as socially and politically motivated.

Another of the most persistent defenders of Shi'ism is the intellectual Nurcholish Madjid,[123] who had once advised a gathering of youth at the Al-Azhar Mosque in Jakarta to learn about Shi'ism - an act that is said to have created unease with the mosque's organisers.[124] In the above-mentioned seminar of 1988, when Ibrahim Hosen claimed that the Shi'is have their own Qur'an, Nurcholish Madjid produced a Qur'an printed in Iran, containing an introductory note by the Ayatollah Khomeini, showing it to the audience and stating that it was no different from the Sunni one. He emphasised that an objective and scientific attitude is required when looking at Shi'ism.[125] In one of his articles, Madjid affirmed that by reading the Qur'ans published by the Shi'is, the opinion, or even accusation that theirs was different from that of the Sunnis was invalidated.[126] Commenting further on the seminar, he said he had been upset when the three main speakers denounced the Shi'is, creating dissension rather than peace within Muslim society. Madjid also strongly rejected the view of the speakers at the event that Shi'ism was the main factor in the Iran-Iraq war, adding that the Sunni-Shi'i divide has existed since the early history of Islam.[127]

Madjid's moderate view of Shi'ism can be identified in the paper that he presented.[128] In Madjid's view, the existence of Shi'ism should not be considered as a religious or political problem but instead as a reality which enriches Islamic history and society.[129] According to Madjid, the Sunnis will gain great benefits if their intellectual interaction with Shi'ism is open and receptive. One example is to be found in the field of philosophy, because the philosophical tradition of Shi'ism continues to develop, while in Sunnism it has tended to stagnate. Madjid emphasises that Shi'ism appears to be better than Sunnism in inheriting and advancing its philosophical and intellectual tradition.[130]

On Sunni-Shi'i relations, Madjid points out that each should have a mutual understanding and respect of the other. Each should learn to recognise the other's existence in the framework of equality and fraternity. He writes

---

123 He died in August 2005.
124 *Media Dakwah* (November 1997:47).
125 *Tempo* (23/1/1988).
126 Madjid (1989:15).
127 *Tempo* (23/1/1988:85-86).
128 Madjid's paper entitled *"Sekilas Tinjauan Historis tentang Paham-paham Sunnah-Syi'ah"* (A Glance at a Historical Review of Sunnism-Shi'ism) was then published as an introduction to the Indonesian translation of Jafri's book, *The Origins and Early Development of Shi'a Islam* (Qum: Ansariyan Publications, 1989).
129 Madjid (1989:6).
130 Madjid (1989:15-16).

So once again, the division of human being into groups, like Sunni and Shi'i, is genuine, natural and unavoidable because [it] is a product of a historical process that may not be erased. What is not natural, not genuine and not in accordance with basic human character, *fitra* is when someone or a group claims their own as absolute truth, then immediately forces his or her will and view on others. This is *shirk*, polytheism, which is unforgivable to God.[131]

Madjid also reiterates his view on the need to develop a non-sectarian attitude, one of the basic teachings given by the Prophet Muhammad. A non-sectarian spirit is in accordance with the Qur'anic concept of *hanif*, referring to Abraham's monotheistic religion[132] as the *hanif* religion.[133] Thus, Madjid's moderate attitude towards Shi'ism has a strong theological basis in Islamic tradition. The fact that he provides theological legitimacy for the need for a pluralistic attitude is an important religious and intellectual advancement and has contributed to the religious life and development of Indonesia, a contribution that has not been equalled by Rais or Wahid.

It is not surprising that Madjid's moderate stance has been criticised by anti-Shi'i activists such as Syu'bah Asa, who accuses him of contributing to the spread of Shi'ism in Indonesia. Madjid too had close relations with a number of Shi'i figures, including Jalaluddin Rakhmat. Rakhmat was given the opportunity to present Shi'i teachings during a religious course in Madjid's foundation, Paramadina. Asa cynically describes how Rakhmat's religious lecture was well prepared in terms of fulfilling Madjid's ideals of offering his audience views different from those held by the majority in the country. "With all pleasure he spread doubt about all established Islamic teachings and historical interpretationa, grew *su' al-zan* (the specific character of the Shi'is) in order to divide the *umma's* image of the Prophet's companions perceived by the Muslims (Sunni) as an integrated totality...."[134] The presence of Jalaluddin Rakhmat was said to have resulted in an anti-Shi'i element of the foundation withdrawing its support. In addition, ICAS (the Islamic College for Advanced Studies), the Jakarta branch of a London-based Shi'i institution of higher learning organised a Masters programme in the field of Islamic philosophy and Sufism in cooperation with the Paramadina University.

Former Indonesian President, Abdurrahman Wahid's moderate attitude towards Shi'ism was integral to his tolerance of all minority groups in the country. He used many ways to protect the position of the Shi'is, who were opposed by the majority of Muslim leaders, including some of his own organisation, NU.

---

131   Madjid (1989:19).
132   QS (6:161).
133   Madjid (1995:687-688).
134   Asa (1998:147).

Wahid focused more on the sustainability of the Sunni community itself than on the accusations and attacks on the Shi'i community. In July 1993, for instance, Wahid gave a speech at a thanksgiving of the Tijaniyya Sufi Order, mentioning and praising the last two Sufi saints of the 20th century, Muhammad Alawi al-Jaza'iri and Ayatollah Ruhullah Khomeini. This provoked harsh reactions from certain members of the participants who opposed Wahid's views and was followed by a dialogue between two representatives of the Al-Bayyinat Foundation, a famous anti-Shi'i institution, and Abdurrahman Wahid. In the dialogue Wahid answered questions related to Sunni-Shi'i controversies and responded to rumours that he was Shi'i and propagated Shi'ism in Indonesia. Wahid advised the Al-Bayyinat representative to adopt an objective attitude and engage in dialogue with Shi'i leaders such as Jalaluddin Rakhmat. In turn, Al-Bayyinat told him of their concerns about the spread of Shi'ism in particular areas of East Java and about the tensions between Sunni and Shi'i groups there. The Al-Bayyinat representative said "there is going to be a war between the Shi'i and the Sunni."[135] Al-Bayyinat also requested Wahid's support for its action against the propagation of Shi'ism by Husein Al-Habsyi in Bangil, East Java. The following transcript shows how Wahid coped with the not insignificant pressure (even threats) applied to support their cause:

> AB:[136] Indeed, we have already reacted in a positive manner. But they (Ustadz Husein and his son-in law) do not care for our call [not to spread Shi'ism]. Therefore, there still are religious gatherings of *ahl al-bayt* and *ahl al-sunna wa al-jama'a*. We have even cooperated with the military authorities. We have given them the data on them. We obtained the data because we smuggled our people into their places. They pretended to study there. We cooperated with the military in order that they (the Shi'is) might be afraid.

> (Listening to this explanation Gus Dur looked sad and shed tears.)

> GD: *Abki akhi, abki akhi, abki akhi!* (I weep, my brother; I weep, my brother; I weep, my brother). To solve religious problems, why did you cooperate with the military authorities? You have even given the data to the authorities. This is the same as if you want to kill our own brothers. It is like in the Dutch colonial era when many *'ulama* died because of actions by their own brothers.

> AB: Well, what else can we do? Once [faced] with the military authorities they will be afraid.

---

135   *Aula* (September 1993:18).
136   AB is an abbreviation of Al-Bayyinat and GD is Gus Dur, the popular nickname for Abdurrahman Wahid.

GD: Do you think that using the military authorities will solve the problem? Solve it well, internally. I think it can [be solved]. As well, we can, for example, publish books. We can list the teachings of Shi'ism that we consider deviating. Then, below, we write the true teachings. And in writing this down a scientific and simple language should be used.

AB: If just through writings it cannot [work], Abuna [our father]...

GD: Who says so? In the era of Imam al-Ghazali the development of Shi'ism was even greater but with only one book the Shi'is were confounded. Coping with Shi'ism in your way is like killing cockroaches by bombardment. It will not reach the target. Therefore, it needs a good strategy.[137]

Abdurrahman Wahid, in his attempt to protect the Shi'is, believes that some cultural aspects of Shi'ism are actually already practiced by NU. For example, referring to a prayer of adoration widely practiced among NU members, he pointed out that NU shows loving devotion to the *ahl al-bayt* comprising the five people: the Prophet Muhammad, 'Ali, Fatima, Hassan and Husayn. This is similar to the concept among the Shi'is. The supplication reads *li khamsatun utfi biha har al-waba' al-hatima, al-Mustafa wa al-Murtada wa ibnahuma wa Fatima* (I have five persons with whom I extinguish the 'heat' of crushing disease, the Prophet, 'Ali, Hasan, Husayn, and Fatima). For Wahid, it is not unnatural to take on this Shi'i view, just as the Shi'is have also adopted many aspects of Sunni tradition.[138] However, it is important to make it clear that NU does not take on Shi'i doctrine.[139]

Another indication of Abdurrahman Wahid's sympathetic attitude towards Shi'ism is his providing the opportunity for Shi'i representatives to present their views before NU figures. Jalaluddin Rakhmat, for instance, became one of the speakers in a training programme for young *'ulama*, the Programme for the Development of 'Ulama Vision (*Program Pengembangan Wawasan Keulamaan*, abbreviated to PPWK) which lasted for one year (1995-1996). Moreover, in 1993 he not only allowed the Shi'i group, *Forum Silaturrahmi Ahlul Bait*, to commemorate the ritual of *'Ashura* in the Al-Munawwarah Mosque in Ciganjur next to his house but also delivered the opening speech at the commemoration.[140] He stated that "Frankly, the Sunni has even to learn much from brothers from the Shi'i *madhhab*. Why? Because the Shi'i *madhhab* has never been interrupted

---

137   *Aula* (September 1993:18-19).
138   An example is the adoption of the consensus (*ijma'*) of Muslim jurists as an authoritative argument in the Shi'i legal theory (Stewart 1998:57).
139   Wahid (1999:185-186).
140   The full transcription of the speech is published in *Aula* (October 1993:40-49).

in its philosophical tradition."[141] Consequently, Wahid has been accused of promoting Shi'ism. In response to his critics, Wahid reiterates that the Shi'is should not be regarded as an enemy.[142] Greg Barton gives four reasons for Abdurrahman Wahid's support of the Shi'is: first, by nature Wahid tends to help wronged and oppressed minorities; second, he opposes anything that impinges upon the freedom of faith and principle; third, for Wahid, all Muslim intellectuals can profit from delving into Shi'i scholarship and its ongoing tradition of *ijtihad* and metaphysical philosophy; fourth, he argues that many NU rituals and approaches to Sufism are actually historically rooted in Persian Shi'ism, and therefore NU scholars are advised to understand Shi'i Islam in order that they can understand the nature of Sunni Indonesian traditionalism.[143]

The moderate attitude of the Muslim intellectuals can also be seen in their criticism of the anti-Shi'i seminar of 1997. Abdurrahman Wahid regarded the seminar as '*kurang kerjaan*' ('not enough preparation, peremptory'). He said that it produced subjective judgements without intellectual honesty, judging Shi'ism in absentia. He called for Muslims to unite in order to solve crucial problems. He went on "The Shi'is are Muslims as well. They have the right to live. If the government prohibits [Shi'ism] I will demonstrate."[144] This was a powerful statement and one through which the Shi'is become more aware of Abdurrahman Wahid's protection. In this regard, even though Wahid did not have the same close relations with Shi'i figures as Rais and Madjid, his position as a charismatic leader of the largest Islamic organisation is considered strategically important for the existence and development of the Shi'is in Indonesia.

The most significant impact of Abdurrahman Wahid's moderate attitude with respect to the struggle of the Shi'is came in 2000, during his presidency, in the form of the government's recognition of the national Shi'i organisation, IJABI. The Shi'i leaders recognised and exploited this moment in history as the best opportunity for them to strive for national recognition. Legal recognition is extremely important for the existence of the Shi'is, allowing them to better carry out their social, educational, and missionary activities under the auspices of IJABI. Not only Wahid but also Rais and Madjid supported the establishment of the national Shi'i organisation, and Madjid was a speaker at the second national conference of IJABI on 27-29 February 2004, before an audience of hundreds of Shi'is from all over Indonesia.

---

141   *Aula* (October 1993:47).
142   Mastuki (1999:63-64).
143   Barton (2002:174).
144   *Media Indonesia* (5/10/1997).

9. Conclusion

This study has shown the multi-faceted realities faced by Shi'is living amidst an overwhelming Sunni majority in Indonesia. It has described the chief tenets of the *madhhab* of the *ahl al-bayt,* revealed the different elements within this community, introduced their leaders and the methods they employ and strategies appropriate to the existing social, religious and political context. It is the single great hope of the Shi'is to gain recognition in their Sunni-dominated country.

We have considered the three main social groupings that constitute the Shi'i community in Indonesia, each arising from its own historical context. The first, oldest and most eminent are the people of Arab descent, chiefly the Sayyids who trace their family lines back to the Prophet Muhammad and who became the founders of the Shi'i community. In the latter part of the 19th century, Shi'ism attracted further followers among Arabs in the Indonesian archipelago, due to increasingly extensive contact between the Hadhramaut and the Malay-Indonesian world. This group quietly maintained their adherence to Shi'ism until the victory of the Iranian revolution in 1978-1979.

The second group consists of graduates from the *hawza 'ilmiyya,* the Shi'i institutions of learning in Qum, Iran. Although a number of Indonesians had studied in Qum prior to the outbreak of the Iranian revolution, this number increased significantly following the establishment of the Islamic Republic of Iran and with an intensification of interaction between the Iranian government and Indonesian Shi'i *'ulama.*

The third is the campus group, mainly graduates from secular universities who engaged in Islamic gatherings at campus mosques and other religious venues. This group emerged in response to the victory of the Iranian revolution and can be seen as part of an 'Islamic cultural revival' which began on the campuses during the New Order's de-politicisation of Muslim society.

These three main groups are interconnected and use various methods to spread Shi'i teachings and to attract followers to their *madhhab*. An 'internal conversion' of Muslims from Sunnism to Shi'ism has occurred slowly through a variety of ways, including education, links of kinship and friendship and the use of print publications.

Social divisions during the formation of the Shi'i community have contributed to a lack of a single leader to be recognised by all groups. Sociologically, the Shi'i leaders may be classified into *ustadhs* and intellectuals. The *ustadhs* have been educated in the fields of religious knowledge gained in Islamic educational institutions, while the intellectuals have been formally trained in the secular sciences and possess a non-formal religious training.

Until 1994, the most influential Shi'i *ustadh* was Sayid Husein AL-Habsyi, a member of the traditional Arab Shi'i group. Al-Habsyi played an important role in the spread of Shi'i teachings in Indonesia through *da'wa*, education and his writings. Today, however, the position of Shi'i *ustadh* is more often filled by an alumnus of Qum. One of these prominent *ustadhs* is Husein Shahab, who devotes himself to the field of *da'wa*, takes part in the establishment of Shi'i foundations and produces scholarly works.

The most prominent intellectual is Jalaluddin Rakhmat who, besides lecturing at universities, has established and now heads an Islamic foundation, engages in *da'wa* activities and writes books. Important determinants of leadership in the Shi'i community in Indonesia are educational background and religious accomplishment, engagement in the field of *da'wa*, education and publication and close connections with Shi'i *'ulama* in Iran.

Turning to religious aspects of the Shi'i community, among the fundamental beliefs that set *Ithna 'Ashari*, or 'Twelver' Shi'ism apart from Sunnism is that of the imamate, which colours all Shi'i teachings. This is the belief in the twelve Imams succeeding the Prophet Muhammad, from 'Ali ibn Abi Talib, the first, to the Mahdi, the twelfth and current Imam, who went into occultation and whose open return is awaited by believers. The imams are regarded as secondary to the Prophet Muhammad, but also infallible nevertheless.

Shi'i belief is practised according to Ja'fari jurisprudence, which embraces codes of conduct concerning *'ibadat,* or religious duties and *mu'amalat,* or social relations. Additionally, there are rituals and ceremonies which form important components of Shi'i piety, such as the observance of 'Ashura in commemoration of the martyrdom of Husein.

For Shi'is living in a hostile Sunni environment, another unique aspect of their teachings is *taqiyya,* which is the doctrinal basis for stigmatised Shi'is to implement strategies of dissimulating personal and social identity in their interaction with the Sunni majority. While their system of belief cannot be negotiated upon, its expression in terms of practice, particularly of *fiqh,* or jurisprudence may be performed according to the school upheld by the Sunni majority. *Taqiyya* is instrumental in the carrying out of Shi'i *da'wa*, education, publishing and the running of organizations.

In order to gain recognition of their *madhhab* and their identity the Shi'is of Indonesia have utilised varied strategies - individually, institutionally and organisationally. This study has revealed the ways in which they hope to achieve the ultimate goal of official recognition.

Shi'ism has to be spread by means of *da'wa,* or outreach in the broadest sense of the term. The missionary character of Shi'ism is as inherent as it is in Islam in general. *Da'wa* can be carried out at both an individual and institutional level and are closely interrelated. Every Shi'i has the obligation to undertake *da'wa* activities, and the prominent Shi'i figures portrayed in this thesis have played an important role as a *da'i,* or practitioners of *da'wa.*

Da'wa becomes more intensive and carefully programmed through Shi'i institutions, which are scattered throughout Indonesia. The institutions (a few are big, but most are small) are mainly centred in towns where sizeable Shi'i communities reside. The name of Shi'ism is never mentioned in their publicly stated aims, owing to its negative connotations among the Sunni majority. The neutral and generally recognised term of *ahl al-bayt* is preferred. As far as their ideals are concerned, the Shi'i institutions share a common missionary objective, namely to realise an Islamic society.

The established Shi'i institutions generally possess these components: a leader, usually an *ustadh,* the *jama'a,* or the body of students and followers, educational activity and a physical centre of activity. *Da'wa* includes *tabligh,* or preaching, *ta'lim,* or teaching, and social work. *Da'wa* training is also carried out for the purpose of enhancing the knowledge and skills of the *da'is,* as well as motivating and affirming their missionary zeal.

In addition to *da'wa,* education is an important area of struggle towards the recognition of Shi'ism in Indonesia. Differing from *da'wa,* education is directed towards the training of children of school age to become the next qualified Shi'i generation. The Shi'is run a number of educational institutions; these can be divided under the traditional *pesantren* system and the modern school system. Renowned *pesantren* include YAPI in Bangil, East Java and Al-Hadi in Pekalongan, Central Java, while the currently most famous school is SMU Muthahhari in Bandung, West Java. Each institution has its own system of education, discussed in Chapter Five. With regard to religious orientation, each establishment may implement either direct or indirect strategies in the promulgation of the *madhhab.*

Al-Hadi is known for its direct strategy, affirming its Shi'i character in the curriculum, books and in the daily life of teachers and students. Al-Hadi expects to inculcate in all its students the knowledge of the teachings of Shi'ism and its traditions. Students are expected to have a comprehensive understanding of the Shi'i teachings and to put them into practice in their daily lives.

The other two educational institutions, however, apply an indirect strategy, in the sense that they follow the national school curriculum supplemented with basic branches of Islamic knowledge. Their students come from both Sunni and Shi'i families. It is through the Islamic subjects that certain aspects of Shi'i teachings, in comparison with Sunni teachings, are introduced.

The dissemination of Shi'i teachings and traditions is also carried out through print publishing, which has been instrumental in the growth and development of the *madhhab* in the country. Besides a number of Shi'i-owned publishing houses participating in the production of Shi'i books, many Shi'i institutions operate in the field of cultural production in addition to their activities in the field of *da'wa* and education. Regardless of differences in their institutional character, they publish Indonesian translations of foreign Shi'i works written by prominent Shi'i *'ulama* and intellectuals, mainly from Iran, Iraq and Lebanon. These translated works encompass all fields of Islamic knowledge and all aspects of Shi'i Islam and they continue to enjoy a significant position in meeting the demands of the religious and intellectual dimensions of the Shi'i individual, group and community alike.

The works of Indonesian Shi'i *ustadhs* and intellectuals, covering various branches of Islamic knowledge have also been published. Periodicals, scientific journals, magazines and bulletins are all produced by Shi'i institutions. Unlike *da'wa* and education, such publications may have an extensive impact through their potential to reach an unlimited audience, be it Shi'i or Sunni. This impact may also be greater in the lack of a single religious authority in Indonesia, a country which encourages religious pluralism and a situation from which Shi'ism has been able to benefit.

Shi'ism and its adherents have gained recognition in the eyes of moderate Muslims in Indonesia; however, the Shi'is continue to struggle for recognition from wider segments of society.

An attempt to gain official government recognition was undertaken through the establishment of the mass organisation IJABI, or the Indonesian Council of Ahli Bait Associations. IJABI, as the national organisation of Shi'is in Indonesia has achieved legal recognition from the state. This achievement results from three strategic factors: the utilisation of the term *ahl al-bayt* to hide Shi'i identity; the use of the opportunity to establish a national organisation in the *Reformasi* era since 1998 (a time marked by the emergence of popular movements - social, religious or ethnic) and thirdly, the political regime under the moderate President

Abdurrahman Wahid, a man known for his belief in openness and pluralism. Recognition means that IJABI accumulates symbolic capital so that it can carry out its programmes to achieve its vision and mission.

However, despite its legal recognition, IJABI has lacked support from the internal Shi'i community, mainly the *ustadhs*, for a variety of reasons, ideological, political and even personal. Several efforts have also been made to reject the position of IJABI as the single national Shi'i organisation. As a result, IJABI has not managed to exert an extensive influence in the life of the Shi'i community.

With regard to Sunni response to Shi'ism, complex reactions, ranging from extremely negative to moderate are revealed in the discussion in Chapter Eight. Negative responses come from reformist groups, in particular from Persis, Al-Irsyad and individuals and institutions linked to them. The reformist movement strives to abolish all beliefs and practices considered contrary to the two principal sources of Islam, the Qur'an and Sunnah. However, this is not always the case if moderate leaders within the reformist movement, such as those of Muhammadiyah, have good relations with Shi'i figures.

Traditionalist Muslim groups, such as the organisation NU, tend to be accommodative and moderate and more involved in efforts to strengthen the practice of Sunnism among their own members than participating in anti-Shi'i activity. MUI, the Indonesian Council of 'Ulama, is regarded as an authoritative institution by the government. It generally never issues *fatwas* on Shi'ism, but in 1984 it put forth a recommendation to protect Sunni Muslims from the influence of Shi'i teachings.

In terms of outright negative responses to Shi'ism, a large number of activities have been carried out to prevent or reduce its spread. These include the publication of anti-Shi'i works, the holding of seminars and discussions, appeals to the government for action, and general preaching. This has led to high tensions between Shi'is and anti-Shi'i individuals, tensions which spilled over in April 2000 with the burning down of the Batang branch of *Pesantren* Al-Hadi in Central Java.

In spite of these activities, a number of leading Muslim public intellectuals have adopted a moderate stance towards Shi'ism. Among them are Nurcholish Madjid, Abdurrahman Wahid and M. Amien Rais, all of whom are considered to have made room for the development of Shi'ism in Indonesia. The government's official and legal recognition of the national Shi'i organisation, IJABI in 2000 can be seen as a direct result of Abdurrahman Wahid's moderate attitude.

In their relations with the Sunni majority the stigmatised Shi'is apply strategies appropriate to the social, religious and political conditions under which they find themselves. In this, they uphold the teaching of *taqiyya*, which has sound textual and rational bases. Comparing Goffman's sociological view,[1] we see that common strategies include information management and adaptation, implemented through *da'wa*, education, publication, organisation and even in the ritual life of the community. Information management deals with the concealment of personal and social identity, institutions and Shi'i terminology, signs and symbols from the Sunnis. The concealment of real goals and interests are inherent in these strategies.

Information management is also implemented in their interaction with Sunnis: in formal contacts, such as seminars, discussions and interviews and in informal daily encounters. Ambiguous answers to questions regarding Shi'i identity, using religious terms generally recognised by the Sunni majority and prioritising textual reasons from Sunni sources are common techniques implemented by the Shi'is in most of their *da'wa*, education, publishing and organisational life, particularly during those activities in which members of the Sunni majority also participate.

Adaptation is another way in which the Shi'is adjust to the norms and rules of the Sunni majority. They may perform religious rituals according to the Shafi'i *fiqh* of the majority in Indonesia, particularly when in public congregation. This practice is even seen as significant to the maintenance of Islamic fraternity - an Islamic value that is promoted at all times and places. In this way, Shi'i identity often remains hidden from the majority, which is crucial to the preservation and consolidation of their position in the Sunni-dominated country.

The strategies implemented can be seen within a framework of reconversion and reproduction. Reconversion strategies are the transferring of accumulated capital into another type of capital, the most sought after being symbolic capital. By implementing information management and adaptation, the Shi'i *ustadhs*, intellectuals and lay adherents may accumulate a particular type of capital and transform it into another type. For example, the cultural and social capital gained from the prestige of the *ustadhs* and intellectuals may be transformed into economic capital, enabling them to gain higher social and economic positions in society.

Reproduction strategies are "sets of practices designed (and mediated) to maintain and improve (one's) position."[2] The ultimate aim of the Shi'i struggle in Indonesia is to obtain recognition of Shi'ism and its followers by the Sunni majority, both the laity and the religious class. The legal recognition of IJABI by the government boosts the position of Shi'ism and its adherents. This is only one aspect of recognition and the struggle for the social and religious recognition of Shi'ism is a continuing process.

---

1 Goffman (1986).
2 Mahar (1990: 18).

In short, the Shi'is in Indonesia, as a stigmatised group, have implemented various strategies depending on existing political, social and religious situations, in order to gain recognition and to occupy a legitimate position and to exercise legitimate power in society. Throughout their entire history they have struggled for recognition - that fundamental dimension of social life - the achievement of which is an unending duty.

Bibliography

Abaza, Mona 2004 "Markets of Faith: Jakartan Da'wa and Islamic Gentrification" *Archipel* 67: 173-202

Abbas, Siradjuddin 1969 *I'itiqad Ahlussunnah Wal-Jama'ah*. Jakarta: Pustaka Tarbiyah

Abdillah, Masykuri 1997 *Responses of Indonesian Muslim Intellectuals to the Concept of Democracy (1966-1993)*. Hamburg: Abera Verlag Meyer & Co.

Abduh, Umar and Abu Huzaifah (eds) 1998 *Mengapa Kita Menolak Syi'ah: Kumpulan Makalah Seminar Nasional tentang Syi'ah di Aula Masjid Istiqlal Jakarta 21 September 1997*. Jakarta: Lembaga Penelitian dan Pengkajian Islam

Abduh, Umar 2001 *Pesantren al-Zaytun Sesat: Investasi Mega Proyek dalam Gerakan NII*. Jakarta: Darul Falah

Abdul Baary, Hafid 1987 *Khomaini: Revolusi Islam ataukah Provokasi terhadap Islam*. Yogayakarta: LSI

Abdullah, Taufik 1996 "The Formation of A New Paradigm? A Sketch on contemporary Islamic Discourse" in Mark R. Woodward (ed) *Toward A New Paradigm: Recent Developments in Indonesia Islamic Thought*. Tempe, Arizona: Arizona State University Program for Southeast Asian Studies, 47-88

Abu Ammar, Hasan 2000 *Imam Mahdi Menurut Ahlussunnah waljama'ah*. Jakarta: Yayasan Mulla Shadra

-------- 2002 *Akidah Syi'ah, Seri Tauhid: Rasionalisme dan alam Pemikiran Filsafat dalam Islam*. Jakarta: Yayasan Mulla Shadra

Abu Batoul 1998 "Messianisme" *An-Nashr* 14: 65-68

Abu Qurba 2003 *Taqlid dalam Ajaran Syiah Imamiyah*. Fathu Makkah

Abu-Rabi', Ibrahim 1996 *Intellectual Origins of Islamic Resurgence in the Modern Arab World*. New York: State University of New York Press

Adam, Muchtar 2003 *Perbandingan Mazhab dalam Islam*. Bandung: Penerbit Babussalam

Adlani, A. Nazri *et al.* (eds) 1997 *Himpunan Fatwa Majelis Ulama Indonesia*. Jakarta: Majelis Ulama Indonesia

Afif, H.M. 1989 "Gerakan Kelompok Islam Isa Bugis" in Abdul Aziz *et al.* (eds) *Gerakan Islam Kontemporer di Indonesia.* Jakarta: Pustaka Firdaus, 75-140

Akhavi, Shahrough 1980 *Religion and Politics in Contemporary Iran: Clergy-State Relations in the Pahlavi Period.* Albany: State University of New York Press

Alatas, Alireza 2002 *Biarkan Syiah Menjawab 1.* Magelang: Bahtera

-------- 2003 *Biarkan Syiah Menjawab 2.* Magelang: Bahtera

-------- 1977 *Aliran Syi'ah di Nusantara.* Jakarta: Islamic Research Institute

-------- 1985 *Sekitar Masuknya Islam ke Indonesia.* 4th edition. Solo: Ramadhani

Ali, Abdullah Yusuf 1991 *The Meaning of the Holy Qur'an.* New Edition with Revised Translation and Commentary. Brentwood, Maryland: Amana Corporation

Ali, Fachry and Bachtiar Effendy 1986 *Merambah Jalan Baru Islam: Rekonstruksi Pemikiran Islam Masa Orde Baru.* Bandung: Mizan

Ali, Syamsuri 2002 *Alumni Hawzah Ilmiah Qum: Pewacanaan Intellectualitas dan Relasi Socialnya dalam Transmisi Syiah di Indonesia,* PhD Dissertation, Program Pascasarjana UIN Syarif Hidayatullah Jakarta

Amansyah, A. Makarausu 1969, 1970 "Mazhab Syi'ah di Tjikoang" *Bingkisan* 2, (1969) 11:27-39; 3 (1969) 1-2:25-45; 3 (1979), 5-6:2-6

Al-Amin, Muhsin 1986 *A'yan al-Shi'a,* vol. 2 and 8. Beirut: Dar al-Ta'aruf li al-Matbu'at

Amsyari, Fuad 1993 *Masa Depan Umat Islam Indonesia: Peluang dan Tantangan.* Bandung: Al-Bayan

-------- 1994 "Yang Saya Kenal, KH. Misbach" in Herry Mohammad and Akbar Muzakki (eds) *80 Tahun K.H. Misbach, Ulama Pejuang Pejuang Ulama: Dari Guru Ngaji, Masyumi sampai MUI.* Surabaya: Bina Ilmu, 154-157

Anam, Fahrul 1998 "Pandangan Jalaluddin Rakhmat tentang Halalnya Pernikahan Mut'ah." Skripsi Sarjana, Fakultas Syariah IAIN Sunan Gunung Djati, Bandung

Anis, Muhammad "Konsep Imamah Islam dan Imam Ma'sum" (http://www.fatimah.org/artikel/masum.htm accessed 6/7/2005)

Anwar, Zainah 1987 *Islamic Revivalism in Malaysia: Dakwah among the Students.* Petaling Jaya: Pelanduk Publications

Anwar, Marzani 1989 "Gerakan Islam Jama'ah" in Abdul Aziz *et al.* (eds) *Gerakan Islam Kontemporer di Indonesia*. Jakarta: Pustaka Firdaus, 21-73

Anwar, Muhammad Syafi'i 1995 *Pemikiran dan Aksi Islam Indonesia: Sebuah Kajian Politik tentang Cendekiawan Muslim Orde Baru*. Jakarta: Penerbit Paramadina

Anwar, Zaiful 1982 *Tabut dan Peranannya dalam Masyarakat*. Padang: Proyek Pengembangan Permuseuman Sumatera Barat

Bin Aqil, Muhammad 1907 *al-Nasa'ih al-Kafiya li man Yatawalla Mu'awiya*. Singapore

Arifin, Bey 1984 "Sepatah Kata dari Penerjemah" in Ihsan Ilahi Zahir *Syi'ah dan Sunnah*. Translated by Bey Arifin. Surabaya: Bina Ilmu, 11-12

Asa, Syu'bah 1998 "Prospek Hubungan Islam Ahlus Sunnah dan Syi'ah" in Umar Abduh dan Abu Hudzaifah (ed) *Mengapa Kita Menolak Syi'ah: Kumpulan Makalah Seminar Nasional tentang Syi'ah di Aula Masjid Istiqlal Jakarta 21 September 1997*. Jakarta: Lembaga Penelitian dan Pengkajian Islam, 122-156

Assagaf, M. Hasyim 2000 *Derita Puteri-puteri Nabi: Studi Historis Kafaah Syarifah*. Bandung: Remaja Rosda Karya

Al-Attas, Syed Farid 1985 "Notes on Various Theories Regarding the Islamization of the Malay Archipelago" *Muslim World* 75 (3-4): 162-175

-------- 1997 "Hadhramaut and the Hadhrami Diaspora: Problems in Theoretical History" Ultrike Freitag and William G. Clarence-Smith (eds) *Hadhrami Traders, Scholars and Statemen in the Indian Ocean 1750s-1960s*. Leiden: Brill, 19-38

-------- 1999 "The Tariqat al-'Alawiyya and the Emergence of the Shi'i School in Indonesia and Malaysia" *Oriente Moderno* 18 (2): 323-339

Atiyeh, George N. 1995 *The Book in Islamic World: the Written World and Communication in the Middle East*. Albany, New York: SUNY

-------- 1995 "Introduction" in George N. Atiyeh (ed) *The Book in the Islamic World: The Written Word and Communication in the Middle East*. Albany: State University of New York Press, viii-xviii

Atjeh, Aboebakar 1965 *Perbandingan Mazhab, Sji'ah: Rasionalisme dalam Islam*. Jakarta: Jajasan Lembaga Penjelidikan Islam

Azmi, Wan Hussein "Islam di Aceh: Masuk dan Berkembangnya hingga abad XVI" A. Hasjmy (ed) *Sejarah Masuk dan Berkembangnya Islam di Indonesia*. Bandung: Al-Ma`arif: 174-218

Azra, Azyumardi 1992 *The Transmission of Islamic Modernism to Indonesia: Networks of Middle Eastern and Malay-Indonesian `Ulama in the Seventeenth and Eighteenth*. Ann Arbour: UMI

-------- 1993 "Tradisionalisme Nasr: Eksposisi dan Refleksi, Laporan dari Seminar Seyyed Hossein Nasr" *Ulumul Qur'an: Jurnal Ilmu dan kebudayaan* 4(4): 106-111

-------- 1994 "Guarding the Faith of the Ummah: the Religio-Intellectual Journey of Mohammad Rasjidi" *Studia Islamika: Indonesian Journal for Islamic Studies* 1 (2): 87-113

-------- 1995 "Syi'ah di Indonesia: Antara Mitos dan Realitas" *Ulumul Quran: Jurnal Ilmu dan kebudayaan* 6 (4): 4-19

-------- 1995a "Hadhrami Scholars in the Malay-Indonesian Diaspora: A preliminary Study of Sayyid 'Uthman" *Studia Islamika: Indonesian Journal for Islamic Studies* 2 (2): 1-33

-------- 1997 "A Hadhrami Religious Scholar in Indonesia: Sayyid 'Uthman" in Ulrike Freitag and William Clarence-Smith (eds) *Hadhrami Traders, Scholars, and Statesmen in the Indian Ocean, 1750s-1960s*. Leiden: Brill, 249-263

-------- 1999 "Perbukuan Islam: Merambah Intelektualisme Baru" in *Islam Reformis: Dinamika Intelektual dan Gerakan*. Jakarta: Rajawali, 215-228

-------- 1999a "Akar-akar Ideologi Revolusi Iran: Fislafat Pergerakan Ali Syari'ati" in M.Deden Ridwan (ed) *Melawan Hegemoni Barat: Ali Syari'ati dalam Sorotan Cendekiawan Indonesia*. Jakarta: Lentera, 47-75

-------- 2001 "Globalization of Indonesian Muslim Discourse: Contemporary Religio-Intellectual Connections between Indonesia and the Middle East" J.H. Meuleman (ed) *Islam in the Era of Globalization: Muslim attitudes towards Modernity and Identity*. Jakarta: INIS

Baabdullah, M. O. *Fatwa dan Pendirian Ulama Sunni terhadap Aqidah Syi'ah*. Bangil: Penerbit Ma'had 'Aly Ilmu Fiqh dan Da'wah Masjid Manarul Islam

Baabud, Musyayya 2002 *Mengapa Sebaiknya Kita Sujud di atas Tanah?* Jakarta: Pustaka Zahra

Al-Baqir, Muhammad 1983 "Pengantar Penterjemah" in A. Syarafuddin al-Musawi *Dialog Sunnah Syi'ah: Surat Menyurat antara Asy-Syaikh Salim al-Bisyri al-Maliki Rektor al-Azhar di Kairo Mesir, dan as-Sayyid Syarafuddin al-Musawi al-'Amili Seorang Ulama Besar Syi'ah.* Bandung: Mizan, xxi-xxxv

-------- 1986 "Pengantar tentang Kaum Alawiyin" in Allamah Sayid Abdullah Haddad *Thariqah Menuju Kebahagiaan.* Translated by Muhammad al-Baqir. Bandung: Mizan, 11-68

-------- 1999 *Fiqih Praktis Menurut Al-Quran, As-Sunnah dan Pendapat Para Ulama.* Vol I. Bandung: Mizan

Bagir, Haidar 1988 *Murtadha Muthahhari: Sang Mujahid Sang Mujtahid.* Bandung: Mizan

-------- 1989 "Ali Syari'ati: Seorang 'Marxis' yang Antimarxisme dan Seorang Syi'i yang 'Sunni'" in Ali Syari'ati *Ummah dan Imamah: Suatu Tinjauan Sosiologis.* Bandung: Pustaka Hidayah

-------- 1990 "Iftitah: Membangun Sebuah Tradisi" *Al-Hikmah: Jurnal Studi-studi Islam* 2: 2-4

-------- 1995 "Syi'ah versus Sunnah: Biarlah menjadi Sejarah Masa Lampau" *Ulumul Quran: Jurnal Ilmu dan Kebudayaan* 6 (4): 3

-------- 2003 "Mereka-reka 'Mazhab' Mizan: Sebuah Upaya 'Soul Searching'" in Haidar Bagir (ed) *20 Tahun "Mazhab" Mizan.* Bandung: Mizan, 31-46

-------- 2005 *Buku Saku Filsafat Islam.* Jakarta: Arasy

-------- 2005a *Buku Saku Tasawuf.* Jakarta: Arasy

Baharun, Mohammad 2004 *Epistemologi Antagonisme Syi'ah.* Malang: Pustaka Bayan

Baried, Baroroh 1976 "Shi'a Elements in Malay Literature" Sartono Kartodirdjo (ed) *Profiles of Malay Culture: Historiography, Religion and Politics.* Jakarta: Ministry of Education and Culture, Directorate General of Culture, 59-65

Barton, Greg 1995 "Neo-Modernism: a Vital Synthesis of Traditionalism and Modernism in Indonesian Islam" *Studia Islamika: Indonesian Journal for Islamic Studies* 2 (3): 1-75

-------- 1998 "The Origins of Islamic Liberalism in Indonesia and its Contribution to Democratic Reform" Working Paper Series, Centre for Asian and Middle Eastern Studies, Faculty of Arts, Deakin University, Victoria, Australia

-------- 1999 *Gagasan Islam Liberal: Telaah terhadap Tulisan-Tulisan Nurcholish Madjid, Djohan Effendi, Ahmad Wahib and Abdurrahman Wahid*. Jakarta: Paramadina

-------- 2002 *Gus Dur: The Authorized Biography of Abdurrahman Wahid*. Jakarta-Singapore: Equinox Publishing ltd.

Barton, Greg and Andree Feillard 1999 "Nahdlatul Ulama, Abdurrahman Wahid and Reformation: What Does NU's November 1997 National Gathering Tell Us?" *Studia Islamika: Indonesian Journal for Islamic Studies* 6 (1): 1-40

Bashari, Agus Hasan 2001 "Pengantar Penerjemah" in Mamduh Farhan Al-Buhairi *Gen Syi'ah: Sebuah Tinjauan Sejarah, Penyimpangan Aqidah dan Konspirasi Yahudi*. Jakarta: Darul Falah, vii-x

Beik, Abdullah 1997 "Husein Al-Habsyi: Ulama Lintas Mazhab" *Al-Isyraq: Media Pencerahan Umat*. YAPI Bangil, 1 (5): 14-16

Boland, B.J. 1971 *The Struggle of Islam in Modern Indonesia*. Leiden: KITLV

Bourdieu, Pierre 1977 *Outline of a Theory of Practice*. Translated by Richard Nice. Cambridge: Cambridge University Press

------- 1986 "The Forms of Capital" in John G. Richardson (ed) *Handbook of Theory and Research for the Sociology of Education*. New York *et al*: Greenwood Press, 241-258

Brakel, L.F. 1970 "Persian Influence on Malay Literature" *Abn-Nahrain* 9: 1-16

-------- 1975 *The Hikayat Muhammad Hanafiyyah: A Medieval Muslim Malay Romance*.Den Haag: Nijhoff, KITLV Bibliotheca Indonesica 12

------- 1977 *The Story of Muhammad Hanafiyyah: A Medievel Muslim Romance Translated from the Malay*. Den Haag: Nijhoff, KITLV, Bibliotheca Indonesica 16

Van Bruinessen, Martin 1990 "Indonesia's Ulama and Politics: Caught Between Legitimising the Status Quo and Searching for Alternatives" *Prisma: the Indonesian Indicator* 49: 52-69

-------- 2002 "Genealogies of Islamic Radicalism in Post-Suharto Indonesia" *Southeast Asia Research* 10 (2): 117-154

Brunner, Rainer 2004 *Islamic Ecumenism in the 20th Century: The Azhar and Shi'ism between Rapprochement and Restraint*. Leiden and Boston: Brill

Al-Buhairi, Mamduh Farhan 2001 *Gen Syi'ah: Sebuah Tinjauan Sejarah, Penyimpangan Akidah dan Konspirasi Yahudi*. Translated by Agus Hasan Bashari. Jakarta: Darul Falah

Bukhori, M. Imam n.d. "Ustadz Husein Al-Habsyi: Profil Ulama Kontemporer" *KSAF: Untuk Pencerahan Pemikiran dan Kebeningan Hati.* YAPI Bangil: 5-19

Al-Chaidar 2000 *Sepak Terjang KW9 Abu Toto (Syekh A.S. Panji Gumilang) Menyelewengkan NKA-NII Pasca S.M. Kartosoewirjo.* Jakarta: Madani Press

Chittick, William C. 1989 "Translator's Introduction" in Muhammad Husayn Tabataba'i *A Shi'ite Anthology.* Qum: Ansariyan Publications, 15-19

Compton, Boyd R. 1995 "Front Anti Komunis: Sayap Radikal Masyumi" in Anwar Harjono et.al *M. Natsir: Sumbangan dan Pemikirannya untuk Indonesia.* Jakarta: Media Dakwah, 38-48

Coser, Lewis A. *et al.* 1982 *Books: The Culture and Commerce of Publishing.* New York: Basic Books

Cowan, H.K.J. 1940 "A Persian Inscription in North Sumatra" *TBG* 80: 15-21

Damanik, Ali Said 2002 *Fenomena Partai Keadilan: Transformasi 20 tahun Gerakan Tarbiyah di Indonesia.* Jakarta: Penerbit Teraju

Departemen Agama RI 1989 *Al-Quran dan Terjemahnya.* Semarang: CV. Toha Putra

Dhofier, Zamakhsyari 1999 *The Pesantren Tradition: the Role of the Kyai in the Maintenance of Traditional Islam in Java.* Tempe: Arizona Sate University Press

Van Dijk, C. (Kees). 1981 *Rebellion under the Banner of Islam: the Darul Islam in Indonesia.* The Hague: Martinus Nijhoff

-------- 1984 "Islam and Socio-Political Conflict in Indonesian History" *Social Compass* 30 (1): 5-25

-------- 1990 "The Indonesian State: Unity in Diversity" in S.K. Mitra (ed) *The Post-Colonial State in Asia: Dialectics of Politics and Culture.* New York: Harvester Weat Sheaf, 101-129

-------- 1991 "The Re-Actualization of Islam in Indonesia" *Rima* 25 (2):75-83

-------- 1998 "Dakwah and Indigenous Culture, the Dissemination of Islam" *BKI* 154 (2): 218-235

-------- 2001 "The Indonesian Archipelago from 1913 to 2013: Celebrations and Dress Codes between International, Local, and Islamic Culture" in J. H. Meuleman (ed) *Islam in the Era of Globalization: Muslim Attitudes towards Modernity and Identity.* Jakarta: INIS, 51-69

-------- 2001a *A Country in Despair: Indonesia between 1997 and 2000.* Leiden: KITLV Press

Djajadiningrat, P. A. Hoesein 1958 "Islam in Indonesia" in Kenneth W. Morgan (ed) *Islam: The Straight Path.* New York: The Ronald Press Company, 375-402

Djamaluddin, M. Amin 2000 *Catatan Atas Jawaban Lengkap Dr. O. Hashem Terhadap Seminar Nasional Sehari tentang Syi'ah 21 September 1997 di Aula Masjid Istiqlal Jakarta.* Jakarta: LPPI

Effendy, Bahtiar 1994 *Islam and the State: The Transformation of Islamic Political Ideas and Practices in Indonesia.* Ann Arbor: UMI

Eickelman, Dale 1978 "The Art of Memory: Islamic Education and Social Reproduction" *Comparative Studies in Society and History* 20 (4): 485-516

Eickelman, Dale and J. W. Anderson 1997 "Print, Islam, and the Prospects for Civic Pluralism: New Religious Writings and Their Audiences" *Journal of Islamic Studies* 8 (1): 43-62

Elryco, Heru 2002 *Ahlu Bait dan Al-Qur'an: Peninggalan yang Terlupakan.* Bandung: Rosda

Enayat, Hamid 2005 *Modern Islamic Political Thought: The Response of the Shi'i and Sunni Muslims to the Twentieth Century.* New Edition. London: I.B. Tauris

Ende, Werner 1973 "Schiitische Tendenzen bei Sunnitischen Sayyids aus Hadhramaut: Muhammad b. Aqil Al-Alawi (1863-1931)" *Der Islam* 50: 82-97

-------- 1990 "Sunni Polemical Writings on the Shi'a and the Iranian Revolution" in David Menashri (ed) *The Iranian Revolution and the Muslim World.* Boulder, San Francisco, Oxford: Westview Press, 219-232

Esposito, John (ed) 1990 *The Iranian Revolution: Its Global Impact.* Miami: Florida International University Press

Esposito, John 1991 *Islam and Politics.* 3rd edition. New York: Syracuse University Press

Fachruddin, Fuad Mohd. 1992 *Kawin Mut'ah dalam Pandangan Islam.* Jakarta: Pedoman Ilmu Jaya

Fakhruddin, Fuad Muhammad 1990 *Syi'ah: Suatu Pengamatan Kritikal.* Jakarta: Pedoman Ilmu Jaya

Fatimi, S. Q. 1963 *Islam Comes to Malaysia.* Singapore: Malaysian Sociological Research Institute

Federspiel, Howard M. 1970 *Persatuan Islam: Islamic Reform in Twentieth Century Indonesia*. Ithaca, NY: Modern Indonesia Project, Sutheast Asia Program, Cornell University

-------- 1999 "Muslim Intellectuals in Southeast Asia" *Studia Islamika: Indonesian Journal for Islamic Studies* 6 (1): 41-76

-------- 2001 *Islam and Ideology in the emerging Indonesian State: the Persatuan Islam (PERSIS), 1923 to 1957*. Leiden: Brill

Feener, Michael 1999 *Developments of Muslim Jurisprudence in Twentieth Century Indonesia*. Ann Arbor: UMI

-------- 1999a "*Tabut*: Muharram Observances in the History of Bengkulu" *Studia Islamika: Indonesian Journal for Islamic Studies* 6 (2): 87-130

Fischer, Michael M.J. 1980 *Iran: From Religious Dispute to Revolution*. Cambridge, Mass: Harvard University Press

Fischer, Michael M.J. and Mehdi Abedi 1990 *Debating Muslims: Cultural Dialogues in Postmodernity and Tradition*. Madison: University of Wisconsin Press

Fox, J. James 1991 "Ziarah Visits to the Tombs of Wali: The Founders of Islam on Java" in M.C. Ricklefs (ed) *Islam in the Indonesian Social Context*. Clayton, Victoria: Centre for Southeast Asian Studies, Monash University, 19-38

Freitag, Ulrike 1997 "Hadhramis in International Politics" in Ulrike Freitag and William G. Clarence Smith (eds) *Hadhrami Traders, Scholars, and Statesmen in the Indian Ocean, 1750s-1960s*. Leiden, New York, Kolen: Brill

-------- 2003 *Indian Ocean Migrants and State Formation in Hadhramaut: Reforming the Homeland*. Leiden and Boston: Brill

Gade, Anna M. 2004 *Perfection Makes Practice: Learning, Emotion, and the Recited Qur'an in Indonesia*. Honolulu: University of Hawaii Press

Geertz, Clifford 1960 *The Religion of Java*. Glanco-Ill: the Free Press

-------- 1959-60 "The Javanese Kijaji: The Changing Role of a Cultural Broker" *Comparative Studies in Society and History* 2: 228-249

Goffman, Erving 1986 *Stigma: Notes on the Management of Spoiled Identity*. New York: Touchstone Book

Goldberg, Jacob 1990 "Saudi Arabia and the Iranian Revolution: the Religious Dimension" in David Nenashri (ed) *The Iranian Revolution and the Muslim World*. Boulder, San Francisco, Oxford: Westview Press, 154-170

Al-Habsyi, Agus Abubakar 1984 "Syi'ah: Koreksi terhadap Rasjidi" in *Tempo* 25 May 1984, 7

Al-Habsyi, Ali Umar 2002 *Dua Pusaka Nabi Saw: Al-Qur'an and Ahlulbait: Kajian Islam Otentik Pasca Kenabian.* Jakarta: Pustaka Zahra

Al-Habsyi, Husein 1991 *Sunnah Syi'ah dalam Dialog: Antara Mahasiswa UGM dan UII Yogya dengan Ustadz Husein Al-Habsyi.* Solo: Yayasan Ats-Tsaqalain

-------- 1991a *Benarkah Nabi Bermuka Masam: Tafsir Surab Abasa.*Bandung: Al-Jawad

-------- 1992 *Nabi SAWW Bermuka Manis Tidak Bermuka Masam.* Jakarta: Al-Kautsar

-------- 1992a *Sunnah-Syi'ah dalam Ukhuwah Islamiyah: Menjawab "Dua Wajah Saling Menentang" Karya Abul Hasan Ali Nadwi.* 2nd edition. Malang: Yayasan Al-Kautsar

-------- 1993 *Agar Tidak Terjadi Fitnah: Menjawab Kemusykilan-kemusykilan Kitab Syi`ah dan Ajarannya.* Malang: Yayasan Al-Kautsar

Al-Habsyi, Hidayatullah Husein 2002 "Sakralisasi Sebuah Pernikahan (Tambahan dari Penerjemah) in Ja'far Murtadho al-'Amili *Nikah Mut'ah Dalam Islam: Kajian Ilmiah dari Berbagai Madzhab.* Translated by Hidayatullah Husein Al-Habsyi. Solo: Yayasan Abna' Al-Husain, 169-217

Hadimulyo 1985 "Manusia dalam Perspektif Humanisme: Pandangan Ali Syari'ati" in M. Dawam Rahardjo (ed) *Insan Kamil: Konsepsi Manusia Menurut Islam.* Jakarta: Grafiti Press

Haikal, Husain 1984 *Indonesia Arab dalam Pergerakan Kemerdekaan Indonesia.* PhD Thesis Universitas Indonesia Jakarta

Hakim, Bashori A. and Arya Hadiwiyata 1997/1998 "Pengkajian Kerukunan Hidup Beragama di Semarang: Studi Kasus Kelompok Syiah di Bulustalan, Kecamatan Semarang Selatan" in *Pengkajian tentang Kerukunan Hidup Umat Beragama: Studi Kasus-kasus Keagamaan.* Jakarta: Pusat Penelitian dan Pengembangan Kehidupan Beragama, Badan Penelitian dan Pengembangan Agama, Departemen Agama RI

Hamidy, Badrul Munir (ed) 1991/992 *Upacara Traddisional Daerah Bengkulu: Upacara Tabot di Kotamadya Bengkulu.* Bengkulu: Bagian Proyek Inventarisasi dan Pembinaan Nilai-nilai Budaya Daerah Bengkulu, Direktorat Sejarah dan Nilai Tradisional Departemen Pendidikan dan Kebudayaan

Hamka 1974 *Antara Fakta dan Hayal "Tuanku Rao", Bantahan terhadap Tulisan-tulisan Ir. Mangaraja Onggang Parlindungan dalam bukunya "Tuanku Rao".* Jakarta: Bulan Bintang

-------- 1982 *Ayahku: Riwayat Hidup Dr. H. Abdul Karim Amrullah dan Perjuangan kaum Agama di Sumatera.*Jakarta: Penerbit Ummininda

-------- 1983 *Tafsir Al-Azhar.* Vol. 29. Jakarta: Pustaka Panjimas

-------- 1984 *Islam: Revolusi, Ideologi, dan Keadilan Sosial.* Jakarta: PT. Pustaka Panjimas

Hamzah, Abu Bakar 1991 *Al-Imam: Its Role in Malay Society 1906-1908.* Kuala Lumpur: Pustaka Antara

Harun, Lukman n.d. "Dunia Sedang Menyaksikan Kebangkitan Islam" in Rusydi Hamka and Iqbal Emsyarip Arf Saimima (eds) *Kebangkitan Islam dalam Pembahasan.* Jakarta: Yayasan Nurul Islam: 125-136

Hasan, Hadi 1928 "Persian Navigation in Early Muhammadan Times" in *A History of Persian Navigation.* London: Methuen, 95-149

Hashem, M. 1987 *Abdullah bin Saba': Benih Fitnah.* Bandar Lampung: YAPI

-------- 1989 *Abdullah bin Saba' dalam Polemik.* Bandar Lampung: YAPI

Hashem, O. 1987 *Saqifah: Awal Perselisihan Umat.* Bandar Lampung: YAPI

-------- 1994 *Saqifah: Awal Perselisihan Umat.* 3rd edition. Jakarta: Al-Muntazhar

-------- 2002 *Syi'ah Ditolak Syi'ah Dicari.* 4th edition. Jakarta: Al-Huda

Hasjmy, A. 1983 *Syi'ah dan Ahlussunnah: Saling Rebut Pengaruh dan Kekuasaan sejak Awal Sejarah Islam di Kepulauan Nusantara.* Surabaya: PT. Bina Ilmu

Hefner, Robert W. 1993 "Islam, State, and Civil Society: ICMI and the Struggle for Middle Class" *Indonesia* 56:1-35

-------- 1997 "Print Islam: Mass Media and Ideological Rivalries among Indonesian Muslims" *Indonesia* 64: 77-103

Hernowo 1998 "Pengantar Editor" in Jalaluddin Rakhmat *Mejawab Soal-soal Islam Kontemporer.* Bandung: Mizan, xxv-xviii

-------- 2001 *Mengikat Makna: Kiat-kiat Ampuh untuk Melejitkan Kemauan Plus Kemampuan Membaca dan Menulis Buku.* Bandung: Kaifa

-------- 2003 "Sekolah Itu Bernama Mizan: Sekilas 'Sejarah' Mizan" in Haidar Bagir (ed) *20 Tahun "Mazhab" Mizan.* Bandung: Mizan, 9-16

Hidayat, Ahmad 2000 "Iftitah: Menyongsong Fajar Kesadaran Konstruktif" *Al-Huda: Jurnal Kajian Ilmu-ilmu Islam* 1 (1): n.p

Howarth, Toby 2001 *The Pulpit of Tears: Shi'i Muslim Preaching in India*. PhD Thesis, Vrije Universiteit Amsterdam

Humphreys, R. Stephen 1999 *Islamic History: A Framework for Inquiry*. Revised Edition. London: I.B. Tauris

Husain, Syarif Hidayatullah 2001 *Shalat dalam Madzhab Ahlul Bait*. Solo: Yayasan Abna' Al-Husain

Husein, Muhsin 1997 "Ustadz Husein: Antara Gagasan dan Tantangan" *Al-Isyraq: Media Pencerahan Umat* 1 (5): 3-7

Husein, Alwi 1998 *Keluarga yang Disucikan Allah*. Jakarta: Lentera

Husin, Asna 1998 *Philosophical and Sociological Aspects of Da'wah: A Study of Dewan Dakwah Islamiyah Indonesia*. Ann Arbor: UMI

Ibrahim, Umar 2001 *Thariqah 'Alawiyah: Napak Tilas dan Studi Kritis atas Sosok dan Pemikiran Allamah Sayyid Abdullah al-Haddad Tokoh Sufi Abad ke-17*. Bandung: Mizan

Ismail, Engku Ibrahim 1989 "Pengaruh Farsi dalam Sastra Melayu Islam di Nusantara" *Ulumul Qur'an: Jurnal ilmu dan Kebudayaan* 1 (3): 38-44

Jafri, S.H.M. 1988 "Translator's Introduction [to Sahifa al-Sajjadiyya]" (http:// al-islam.org/sahifa/intro.html accessed 13/9/2005)

-------- 1989 *The Origins and Early Development of Shi'a Islam*. Qum: Ansariyan Publications

Jaiz, Hartono, Ahmad 2002 *Aliran dan Paham Sesat di Indonesia*. Jakarta: Pustaka Al-Kautsar

Jamil, M. Yunus 1968 *Tawarikh Raja-raja Kerajaan Aceh*. Banda Aceh: Iskandar Muda quoted in A. Hasjmi 1983 *Syi'ah dan Ahlussunnah Saling Rebut Pengaruh dan Kekuasaan sejak Awal Sejarah Islam di Kepulauan Nusantara*. Surabaya: Bina Ilmu

Jones, Sidney R 1980 "It can't Happen Here: a Post-Khomeini Look at Indonesian Islam" *Asian Survey* 20 (3): 311-323

Jong, Huub de and N.J.G. Kaptein (eds) 2002 *Transcending Borders: Arabs, Politics, Trade, and Islam in Southeast Asia*. Leiden: KITLV Press

Joppke, C. 1986 "The Cultural dimensions of Class Formation and Class Struggle: On the Social Theory of Pierre Bourdieu" *Berkeley Journal of Sociology* 31:53-78

Al-Jufri, Jaffar 2000 *Imam Mahdi: Figur Keadilan*. Jakarta: Lentera

Al-Kaff, Husein Muhammad "Imamah: Bimbingan Ilahi Menuju Kesempurnaan Wujud" (http://aljawad.tripod.com/arsipbuletin/imamah.htm accessed 6/7/2005)

-------- 'Asyura Seberkas Cahaya Ilahi" (http://aljawad.tripod.com/buletinew/edisi_ke_10.htm accessed 14/3/2002)

-------- 2001 "Tradisi Tasyayyu'" *Buletin AlJawad* 6 (10): 1-4

-------- "Ijtihad dan Taqlid" (http://aljawad.tripod.com/artikel/ijtihad.htm accessed 4/8/2005)

-------- 2001 "Tabi'iyyat al-tashayyu' fi Indonesia." *Al-Huda: Jurnal Kajian Ilmu-ilmu Islam* 1 (3): 121-129

Kaptein, N.J.G. 1994 *Perayaan Hari Lahir Nabi Muhammad SAW*. Jakarta: INIS

-------- 1995 "Circumcision in Indonesia: Muslim or Not" in Jan Platvoet and Karel van der Toorn (eds) *Pluralism and Identity: Studies in Ritual Behaviour*. Leiden: E.J. Brill, 285-302

-------- 1997 *The Muhimmat al-Nafais: A Bilingual Meccan Fatwa Collection for Indonesian Muslims from the End of the Nineteenth Century*. Jakarta: INIS

-------- 1998 "The Sayyid and the Queen: Sayyid 'Uthman on Queen Wilhelmina's Inauguration on the Throne of the Netherlands in 1898" *Journal of Islamic Studies*, 9 (2):158-177

-------- 2004 "The Voice of the 'Ulama': Fatwas and Religious Authority in Indonesia" *Archives de Sciences Sociales des Religions* 125: 115-130

Karim, Muhammad Rusli 1997 *HMI MPO dalam Kemelut Modernisasi Politik Indonesia*. Bandung: Mizan

Karim, M. Rusli 1999 *Negara dan Peminggiran Islam Politik: Suatu Kajian Mengenai Implikasi Kebijakan Pembangunan bagi Keberadaan 'Islam Politik' di Indonesia era 1970-an dan 1980-an*. Yogyakarta: Tiara Wacana Yogya

Kartomi, Margaret J. 1986 "Tabut – A Shi'a Ritual Transplanted from India to Sumatera" in David P. Chandler and M.C. Ricklefs (eds.) *Nineteenth and Twentieth Century Indonesia: Essays in honour of Professor J.D. Legge*. Clayton, Victoria: Centre of Southeast Studies Monash University, 141-162

Kasiri, Julizar, Paulus Winarto, dan Nurul Faizah 2000 "Tragedi Karbela: Peringatan Asyura di Era Keterbukaan" *Gamma* 19-25 April 2000:38

-------- 2000 "SMU Plus Mutahhari: Model Inovasi Sistem Pendidikan" *Gamma* 9-15 February 2000:66-67

Kohlberg, Etan 1987 "Western Studies of Shi'a Islam" in Martin Kramer (ed) *Shi'ism, Resistance, and Revolution*. Boulder: Westview Press, 31-44

Kostiner, Joseph 1984 "The Impact of the Hadrami Emigrants in the East Indies on Islamic Modernism and Social Change in the Hadramawt during the 20th Century" in Raphael Israeli and Anthony H. Johns (eds) *Islam in Asia Volume II Southeast and East Asia*. Jerusalem: The Magnes Press, The Hebrew University, 207-237

Kramer, Martin (ed) 1987 *Shi'ism, Resistance, and Revolution*. Boulder: Westview Press

Labib, Muhsin 2003 "Hawzah Ilmiah Qum: Ladang Peternakan Filosof Benua Lain" in *Al-Huda: Jurnal Kajian Ilmu-ilmu Islam* 3(2): 147-164

------- 2004 *Husain: Sang Ksatria Langit: Roman Sejarah Islam*. Jakarta: Penerbit Lentera

LPPI n.d. *Pokok-Pokok Kesesatan Syi'ah*. Jakarta: LPPI

-------- n.d. *Syi'ah dan Quraish Shihab*. Jakarta: LPPI

Madjid, Nurcholish 1987 *Islam, Kemodernan dan Keindonesiaan*. Bandung: Mizan

-------- 1989 "Kata Pengantar: Sekilas Tinjauan Historis tentang Paham-paham Sunnah-Syi'ah" in S. Husain M. Jafri *Awal dan Sejarah Perkembangan Islam Syi'ah: dari Saqifah sampai Imamah*. Jakarta: Pustaka Hidayah, 5-19

-------- 1995 Skisme dalam Islam: Tinjauan Singkat Secara Kritis-Historis Proses Dini Perpecahan Sosial Keagamaan Islam" in Budhy Munawar-Rachman (ed) *Kontektualisasi Doktrin Islam dalam Sejarah*. Jakarta: Paramadina, 668-691

Madrid, Robin 2001 *Fundamentalist and Democracy: The Political Culture of Indonesian Islamist Student*. Michigan, Ann Arbor: UMI

Mahar, Cheleen *et al.* 1990 "The Basic Theoretical Position" in Richard Harker *et al.* (eds) *An Introduction to the Work of Pierre Bourdieu: The Practice of Theory*. Hampshire and London: The Macmillan Press ltd, 1-25

Mahayana, Dimitri 2003 "Sebuah Makna di Balik Syahadah Agung" in *Syi'ar* March 2003: 8-10

Malik, Dedy Djamaluddin and Idi Subandi Ibrahim 1998 *Zaman Baru Islam Indonesia: Pemikiran dan Aksi Politik Abdurrahman Wahid, M. Amin Rais, Nurcholish Madjid, Jalaluddin Rakhmat*. Bandung: Zaman Wacana Mulia

Mallat, Chibli 1993 *The Renewal of Islamic Law; Muhammad Baqer as-Sadr, Najaf, the Shi'i international*. London: Cambridge University Press

Al-Mandari, Safinuddin 2003 *Demi Cita-Cita HMI: Catatan Ringkas Perlawanan Kader dan alumni HMI Terhadap Rezim Orde Baru*. Jakarta: Karya Multi Sarana

-------- 2003a *HMI dan Wacana Revolusi Sosial*. Makassar: Pusat Studi Paradigma Islam

Marrison, G.E. 1955 "Persian Influences in Malay Life: 1280-1650" *Journal of the Malayan Branch of the Royal Asiatic Society* 28:52-69

Martin, Richard C. and Mark R. Woodward with Dwi S. Atmaja 1997 *Defenders of Reason in Islam: Mu'tazilism from Medieval School to Modern Symbol*. Oxford: Oneworld

Martin, Vanessa 2000 *Creating an Islamic State: Khomeini and the Making of a New Iran*. London and New York: I.B. Tauris

Mastuki HS (ed) 1999 *Kiai Menggugat: Mengadili Pemikiran Kang Said*. Jakarta: Pustaka Ciganjur

Maulana, Pudji 1998 "Sekilas Marja'iyah" *An-Nashr* 14: 30-32

McVey, Ruth 1983 "Faith as the Outsider: Islam in Indonesian Politics" in James P. Piscatori (ed) *Islam in the Political Process*. Cambridge et.al: Cambridge University Press, 199-225

Von der Mehden, Fred R. 1993 *Two Worlds of Islam: Interaction between Southeast Asia and the Middle East*. Miami: University Press of Florida

Menashri, David (ed) 1990 *The Iranian Revolution and the Muslim World*. Boulder: Westview Press

Meuleman, Johan n.d. "Modern Trends in Islamic Translation" Provisional Version of A Contribution for the History of Translation in Indonesian and Malaya Project, Association Archipel, Paris 2-4 April 2002

Minhaji, Akh. 2001 *Ahmad Hassan and Islamic Legal Reform in Indonesia (1887-1958)*. Yogyakarta: Kurnia Kalam Semesta Press

Misdi, Muhammad 1993 "Syiah Hendaknya Mawas Diri" *Aula*, December 1993: 79-84

Mobini-Kesheh, Natalie 1999 *The Hadrami Awakening: Community and Identity in the Netherlands East Indies, 1900-1942*. Ithaca, New York: Southeast Asia Program Publications Cornell University

Momen, Moojan 1985 *An Introduction to Shi'i Islam: the History and Doctrines of Twelver Shi'ism*. New Haven and London: Yale University Press

Muchtar, A. Latief 1998 *Gerakan Kembali ke Islam: Warisan Terakhir A. Latief Muchtar, Ketua Umum Persis 1983-1997*. Bandung: Rosda Karya

Mudzhar, Muhammad Atho 1993 *Fatwa-fatwa Majelis Ulama Indonesia: Sebuah Studi tentang Pemikiran Hukum Islam di Indonesia, 1975-1988*. Jakarta: INIS

-------- 2003 *Islam and Islamic Law in Indonesia: A Socio-Historical Approach*. Jakarta: Office of Religious Research and Development, and Training, Department of Religious Affairs

Mughniyya, Muhammad Jawad 1973 *al-Shi'a fi al-Mizan*. Beirut: Dar al-Ta'aruf li al-Matbu'at

Muhaimin, Abdul Ghoffir 1995 *The Islamic Traditions of Cirebon: Ibadat and Adat among Javanese Muslims*. PhD Thesis Department of Anthropology, Australian National University, Canberra

-------- 1999 "The Morphology of *Adat*: The Celebration of Islamic Holy Days in North coast Java" *Studia Islamika: Indonesian Journal for Islamic Studies* 6 (3): 101-130

Al-Muhdhar, Khadijah Sundus Husein 1998 *Doa Kumayl, Thaif, Keselamatan, Tawassul, Ziarah*. Jakarta: Yayasan Fatimah

Mulyadi, Arif "Mahdiisme: Pandangan Masa Depan" (http://aljawad.tripod.com/arsipbuletin/mahdiisme.htm accessed 6/7/2005)

Munir, Muh. 1993 "Syiah Sesat dan Menyesatkan: Sebuah Tanggapan" *Aula*, November 1993: 56-59

Mursyid, Ibnu 1992 "Nabi Pernah Bermuka Masam: Koreksi atas Tafsir Ustadz Husein al-Habsyi" *Al-Muslimun* 262: 67-74

Muzaffar, Chandra 1987 *Islamic Resurgence in Malaysia*. Petaling Jaya, Selangor: Penerbit Fajar Bakti Sdn.Bhd.

Muzani, Saiful 1994 "Mu'tazilah Theology and the Modernisation of the Indonesian Muslim Community: The Intellectual Portrait of Harun Nasution" *Studia Islamika: Indonesian Journal for Islamic Studies* 1 (1): 91-131

Nadwi, Abu al-Hasan Ali 1987 *Dua Wajah Saling Bertentangan antara Ahlu Sunnah dan Syi'ah*. Surabaya: Bina Ilmu

Nagata, Judith 1984 *The Reflowering of Malaysian Islam: Modern Religious Radicals and Their Roots*. Vancouver: University of British Columbia Press

Nakash, Yitzhak 1994 *The Shi'is of Iraq*. Princeton: Princeton University Press

Nasr, Seyyed Hossein 1987 *Traditional Islam in the Modern World*. London: Kegan Paul International

-------- 1988 *Ideals and Realities of Islam*. London: Unwin Hyman Inc.

-------- 1989 "Introduction" in Muhammad Husayn Tabataba'i *A Shi'ite Anthology*. Qum: Ansariyan Publications, 5-11

-------- 1992 "Filsafat Perennial: Perspektif Alternatif untuk Studi Agama" *Ulumul Qur'an: Jurnal Ilmu dan Kebudayaan* 3 (3): 86-95

Nasution, Harun 1987 "Syi'ah, Asal-usul, Ajaran-ajaran dan Perkembangan" in Nico Tampi *Diskusi Buku Agama*. Jakarta: Tempo, 3-16

Natsir, Mohammad 1984 "Kata Berjawab" in Ihsan Ilahi Zahir *Syi'ah dan Sunnah*. Translated by Bey Arifin. Surabaya: Bina Ilmu, 9-10

Noer, Deliar 1973 *The Modernist Muslim Movement in Indonesia, 1900-1042*. Kuala Lumpur: Oxford University Press

Bin Nuh, Abdullah 1965 *Uchuwah Islamyah*. Jakarta: Jajasan Lembaga Penjelidikan Islam

-------- 1401/1981 *Risalah Asyura 10 Muharam*. Bogor: Majlis Al-Ihya

Nurjulianti, Dewi and Arief Subhan 1995 "Lembaga-lembaga Syi'ah di Indonesia" *Ulumul Quran: Jurnal Ilmu dan Kebudayaan* 6 (4): 20-26

Nurmansyah, Dede Azwar 2001 "Merajut Dialog Kreatif dan Bebas Prasangka" *Al-Huda: Jurnal Kajian Ilmu-ilmu Islam* 1 (3): 137-154

Nurwahid, M. Hidayat 1998 "Menyoal Gaya Pembelaan Syi'ah, Jawaban dan Tanggapan untuk O. Hashem" in Umar Abduh and Abu Hudzaifah (ed) *Mengapa Kita Menolak Syi'ah: Kumpulan Makalah Seminar Nasional tentang Syi'ah di Aula Masjid Istiqlal Jakarta 21 September 1997*. Jakarta: Lembaga Penelitian dan Pengkajian Islam, 210-221

-------- 2001 "Kata Pengantar: Mendudukkan Kembali Sunnah Syiah" in Ali Ahmad As-Salus *Ensiklopedi Sunnah-Syiah, Studi Perbandingan Aqidah dan Tafsir*. Jakarta: Pustaka Al-Kautsar, vii-xii

Panitia n.d. "Biografi Al-Marhum Ustadz Husein Al-Habsyi: Pendiri Yayasan Pesantren Islam YAPI Bangil", a Paper read at the 9th Celebration of Husein Al-Habsyi's death (*haul*), 9 September 2002

Parlindungan, Mangaraja Onggang 1964 *Pongkinangolngolan Sinambela Gelar Tuanku Rao: Teror Agama Islam Mazhab Hambali di Tanah Batak 1816-1833*. Jakarta: Penerbit Tanjung Pengharapan

Peeters, Jeroen 1998 "Islamic Book Publishers in Indonesia: A Social Network Analysis" in Paul van der Velde and Alex Mckay (eds) *New Developments in Asian Studies: An Introduction*. Leiden and Amsterdam: Kegan Paul International in association with IIAS, 209-222

Pelras, Christian 1993 "Religion, Tradition, and the Dynamics of Islamization in South Sulawesi" *Indonesia* 57, 133-154

Pengurus Besar Ikatan Jamaah Ahlulbait Indonesia n.d Anggaran Dasar, Anggaran Rumah Tangga, Program Kerja and others

Pimpinan Pusat Al-Irsyad Al-Islamiyyah 1996 *Keputusan-Keputusan Muktamar ke-36 Al-Irsyad Al-Islamiyyah Pekalongan 10-13 Jumadil Akhir 1417/23-26 Oktober 1996*. Jakarta

Poston, Larry 1992 *Islamic Da'wah in the West: Muslim Missionary Activity and the Dynamics of Conversion to Islam*. New York and Oxford: Oxford University Press

Probotinggi, Mochtar 1986 "Tentang Visi, Tradisi, and Hegemoni Bukan-Muslim: Sebuah Analisis" in Mochtar Probotinggi (ed) *Islam Antara Visi, Tradisi, dan Hegemoni Bukan-Muslim*. Jakarta: Yayasan Obor Indonesia, 187-252

Pusat Penelitian dan Pengembangan Kehidupan Beragama 1985/1986 *Studi Kasus-Kasus Keagamaan*. Jakarta: Badan Penelitian dan Pengembangan Agama Departemen Agama RI

-------- 1986/1987 *Mazhab Syi'ah*. Jakarta: Badan Penelitian dan Pengembangan Agama Departemen Agama RI

Rachman, Abd. 1997 *The Pesantren Architects and their Socio-Religious Aspect 1850-1950*. Ann Arbor: UMI

Rahardjo, M. Dawam 1983 "Ali Syariati: Mujahid-Intelektual" in Ali Syari'ati *Kritik Islam atas Marxisme dan Sesat Pikir Barat Lainnya*. Bandung: Mizan, 7-32

-------- 1993 *Intelektual, Inteligensia dan Perilaku Politik Bangsa: Risalah Cendekiawan Muslim*.Bandung: Mizan

Rahimi, Babak 2004 "Ayatollah Ali al-Sistani and the Democratization of Post-Saddam Iraq" *The Middle East Review of International Affairs* 8 (4) (http://meria.idc.ac.il/journal/2004/issue4/jv8no4a2.html accessed 5/10/2005)

Rahmat, Hasan "Imam Mahdi: Suatu Kajian Teks" (http://aljawad.tripod.com/arsipbuletin/imammahdi.htm accessed 6/7/2005)

Rahnema, Ali 2000 *An Islamic Utopian: A Political Biography of Ali Shari'ati*. London: I.B. Tauris

Rais, M. Amin 1985 "International Islamic Movement and their Influence upon the Islamic Movement in Indonesia" *Prisma: The Indonesian Indicator* 35: 27-48

-------- 1987 *Cakrawala Islam: Antara Cita dan Fakta*. Bandung: Mizan

-------- 1984 "Kata Pengantar" in Ali Syariati *Tugas Cendekiawan Muslim*. Yogyakarta: Shalahuddin Press

Rakhmat, Jalaluddin 1984 "Muthahhari: Sebuah Model Buat Para Ulama" in Murtadha Muthahhari *Perspektif Al-Quran tentang Manusia dan Agama*. Bandung: Mizan, 7-37

-------- 1986 *Islam Alternatif: Ceramah-ceramah di Kampus*. Bandung: Mizan

-------- 1986a "Ukhuwah Islamiah: Perspektif Al-Quran dan Sejarah" in Haidar Bagir (ed) *Satu Islam Sebuah Dilema*. Bandung: Mizan, 61-105

-------- 1988 "Epilog: Ijtihad, Sulit Dilakukan Tapi Perlu" in Haidar Bagir and Syafiq Basri (eds) *Ijtihad Dalam Sorotan*. Bandung: Mizan, 173-201

-------- 1990 "Iftitah: Raja yang Filosof" *Al-Hikmah: Jurnal Studi-studi Islam* 1: 2-4

-------- 1991 *Islam Aktual: Refleksi Cendekiawan Muslim*. Bandung: Mizan

-------- 1993 "Pengantar" in *Yayasan Muthahhari Untuk Pencerahan Pemikiran Islam*. Bandung: Yayasan Muthahhari, 5-7

-------- 1994 *Membuka Tirai Kegaiban: Renungan-renungan Sufistik*. Bandung: Mizan

-------- 1995 "Dikotomi Sunni-Syi'ah Tidak Relevan lagi" interview by Arief Subhan and Nasrullah Ali-Fauzi in *Ulumul Quran: Jurnal Ilmu dan Kebudayaan* 6 (4): 92-103

-------- 1997 *Catatan Kang Jalal: Visi Media, Politik, dan Pendidikan*. Bandung: Rosda

-------- 1997a "Dakwah dan Komunikasi Massa: Kooperasi atau Konfrontasi" in Idi Subandy Ibrahim and Dedy Djamaluddin Malik (eds) *Hegemoni Budaya*. Yogyakarta: Bentang, 49-56

-------- 1998 *Jalaluddin Rakhmat Menjawab Soal-soal Islam Kontemporer*. Bandung: Mizan

-------- 1998a *Reformasi Sufistik: 'Halaman Akhir' Fikri Yathir*. Bandung: Pustaka Hidayah

-------- 1999 *Tafsir Sufi al-Fatihah: Muqaddimah*. Bandung: Rosda

-------- 1999a *Rekayasa Sosial: Reformasi atau Revolusi?* Badung: Rosda

-------- 2001 *Rindu Rasul: Meraih Cinta Ilahi Melalui Syafaat Nabi*. Bandung: Rosda

-------- 2002 *Al-Mustafa*. Bandung: Muthahhari Press

-------- 2002a *Dahulukan Akhlak di atas Fikih*. Bandung: Muthahhari Press

-------- 2003 *Psikologi Agama: Sebuah Pengantar*. Bandung: Mizan

Rambo, L.R. 1993 *Understanding Religious Conversion*. New Haven: Yale University Press

Rasjidi, M. 1984 *Apa Itu Syi'ah*. Jakarta: Media Dakwah

Ratu Perwiranegara, Alamsjah 1982 *Pembinaan Kerukunan Hidup Umat Beragama*. Jakarta: Departemen Agama RI

Ricklefs, M.C. 2001 *A History of Modern Indonesia since C.1200*. 3rd edition. Hampshire: Palgrave

Riddell, Peter G. 1997 "Religious Links Between Hadhramaut and the Malay-Indonesian World, c. 1850 to c.1950" in Ulrike Freitag and William Clarence-Smith (eds) *Hadhrami Traders, Scholars, and Statesmen in the Indian Ocean, 1750s-1960s*. Leiden: Brill, 217-230

Ridwan, M. Deden 1999 "Pengantar Editor" in *Melawan Hegemoni Barat: Ali Syari'ati dalam Sorotan Cendekiawan Indonesia*. Jakarta: Lentera, 1-43

Roff, William R. 2002 "Murder as an Aid to social History: the Arabs in Singapore in the Early Twentieth Century" Huub de Jong and Nico Kaptein (eds) *Transcending Borders: Arabs, Politics, Trade and Islam in Southeast Asia*. Leiden: KITLV Press, 91-108

Ropi, Ismatu 1999 "Depicting the Other Faith: A Bibliographical Survey of Indonesian Muslim Polemics on Christianity" *Studia Islamika: Indonesian Journal for Islamic Studies* 6 (1): 77-120

Rosiny, Stephan 1999 *Shia's Publishing in Lebanon with Special Reference to Islamic and Islamist Publications.* Berlin: Verlag Das Arabische Buch

-------- 2001 "The Tragedy of Fatima Al-Zahra in the Debate of Two Shiite Theologians in Lebanon" in Rainer Brunner and Werner Ende (eds) *The Twelver Shia in Modern Times: Religious Culture and Political History.* Leiden, Boston, Koln: Brill, 207-219

Rosyidi 2004 *Dakwah Sufistik Kang Jalal: Menentramkan Jiwa, Mencerahkan Pemikiran.* Jakarta: KPP

Hamka, Rusydi and Iqbal E.A. Saimima (eds) n.d. *Kebangkitan Islam dalam Pembahasan.* Jakarta: Nurul Islam

Al-Samawi, Muhammad Tijani 1993 *Akhirnya Kutemukan Kebenaran.* Translated by Husein Shahab. Bandung: Pelita

Safwan, A. M. "Ikatan Jamaah AhlulBait Indonesia (IJABI) Sebagai Gerakan Sosial Keagamaan," paper presented to Muslim Student Association of Agricultural Technology Department, Gajahmada University of Yogyakarta 21 February 2001 (http://raushanfikr.tripod.com/makatul/sosio-agama.htm accessed 27/1/2003)

Salam, Solichin 1960 *Sekitar Wali Sanga.* Jogjakarta: Menara Kudus

-------- (ed) 1986 *APB Arabian Press Board: Sejarah dan Perjuangannya.* Jakarta: Panitia Sejarah APB, 85-86

-------- 1992 *Ali Ahmad Shahab: Pejuang Yang Terlupakan.* Jakarta: Gema Salam

Saleh, Fauzan 2001 *Modern Trends in Islamic Theological Discourse in 20th Century Indonesia: A Critical Survey.* Leiden, Boston, Koln: Brill

Al-Samarrai, Qassim 1968 *The Theme of Ascension in Mystical Writings: A Study of the Theme in Islamic and non-Islamic Mystical Writings.* Baghdad: the National Printing and Publishing Co.

Schimmel, Annemarie 1995 "Nur Muhammad" in Mircea Eliade (ed) *The Encyclopaedia of Religion*, Vol. 11. London: Simon & Schuster and Prentice Hall International, 23-26

Schwarrz, Adam 1994 *A Nation in Waiting: Indonesia in the 1990s.* Boulder: Westview Press

Bin Shahab, Hasan 1328/1908 *al-Ruqya al-Shafiya min Nafathat Sumum al-Nasa'ih al-Kafiya*. Singapore: Zanbar Printing Office

Shahab, Husein 1986 *Jilbab Menurut Al-Qur'an dan As-Sunnah*. Bandung: Mizan

-------- 2002 *Seni Menata Hati*. Bandung: Hikmah

Shahab, Muhammad Asad 1962 *Al-Shi'a fi Indonesia*. Najaf: Matba'a al-Ghary al-Haditha

-------- 1986 "Al-Tashayyu' fi Indonesia" in Hasan al-Amin *Da'irat al-Ma'arif al-Islamiyya al-Shi'iyya*, vol. 8. Beirut: Dar al-Ta'aruf li al-Matbu'at, 319-324

-------- 1996 *Abu al-Murtada Shahab: Ra'id al-Nahda al-Islahiyya fi Janub Sharq Asia*. Qum: al-Mu'awaniyya al-Thaqafiyya li Majma' al-'alami li Ahl al-Bayt

Shahab, Umar 1999 "Pengantar" in Muhammad Jawad Mughniyah *Fiqih Imam Ja'far Shadiq*. Jakarta: Lentera, ix-xiii

Shahabuddin, Sayyid Abubakar bin Ali 2000 *Rihlatul Asfar: Otobiografi (1287-1363H)*. Translated by Ali Yahya. Jakarta: N.p.

Shils, Edward 1968 "Intellectuals" in David L. Shils (ed) *International Encyclopaedia of the Social Sciences*, vol. 7. New York: the Macmillan Company and the Free Press, 399-424

Shodiq, M. 1998 "Imam Mahdi" *An-Nashr* 14:25-29

Sihbudi, Riza 1996 *Biografi Politik Imam Khomeini*. Jakarta: Gramedia dan ISMES

Sila, M. Adlin n.d. "Model Tasawuf Masyarakat Perkotaan: Kasut Pusat Kajian Tasawuf (PKT) Tazkiyah Sejati," paper presented in a seminar held in the Office of Research and Development, Department of Religious Affairs, Jakarta, 30 November 2000

Sirajuddin, D. A.R. and Iqbal Abdurrauf Saimima 1986 "Yang disini, Syiah Gado-Gado, Pak" *Panji Masyarakat* 513 (August 1986): 20

Soeherman, Abdi Mahaestyo 1998 "Syiah bukan Sampar" in A. Latief Muchtar *Gerakan Kembali ke Islam: Warisan Terakhir A. Latief Muchtar, Ketua Umum Persis 1983-1997*. Bandung: Rosda, 342-358

Shepard, Jon M. 1981 *Sociology*. St. Paul, Minnesota: West Publishing Co.

Shepard, William E. 1987 "Islam and Ideology: Towards a Typology" *International Journal of Middle East Studies* 19:307-336

Snouck-Hurgronje, C. 1906 *The Acehnese.* Vol. I. Translated by A.W.S. O'Sullivan. Leiden: E.J. Brill

Steenbrink, Karel A. 1985 "Dari Ulama ke Intelektual" *Pesantren* 2 (4): 63-72

Stewart, Devin J. 1998 *Islamic Legal Orthodoxy: Twelver Shiite Responses to the Sunni Legal System.* Salt Lake City: the University of Utah Press

Sunyoto, Agus 1987 *Sunan Ampel: Taktik dan Strategi Dakwah Islam di Jawa Abad 14-15.* Surabaya: LPLI Sunan Ampel

Syafi'i, Ahmad 1983/1984 "Profil Ustadz Abdul Qodir Bafaqih: Studi tentang Perkembangan Faham/Aliran Syi'ah di Desa Bangsri Kabupaten Jepara Prop. Jawa Tengah" in *Agama dan Perubahan Sosial di Indonesia.* Vol. II, Jakarta: Proyek Penelitian Keagamaan Badan Penelitian dan Pengembangan Agama Departemen Agama RI

Syamsuddin, M. Sirajuddin 1991 *Religion and Politics in Islam: The Case of Muhammadiyah in Indonesia's New Order.* Ann Arbor: UMI Dissertation Services

Syuaib, Muhammad Bagir 1423/2002 "Tanda-Tanda Kerusakan Zaman" *Buletin al-Jawad* 4 (12): 1-4

Tabatabai, Muhammad Husayn 1995 *Shi'a.* Translated by Seyyed Hossein Nasr. Manila: Al-Hidaya Inc.

Takim, Liyakatali 2000 "Foreign Influence on American Shi'ism" *The Muslim World* 90: 459-477

Tamara, M. Nasir 1980 *Revolusi Iran.* Jakarta: Sinar Harapan

-------- 1982 "Agama dan Revolusi Iran: Peranan Aliran Shi'ah sebagai Ideologi Revolusi" *Prisma* 11 (9): 14-25

--------1986 *Indonesia in the Wake of Islam 1965-1985.* Kuala Lumpur: Institute of Strategic and International Studies

Tampi, Nico J. 1987 *Diskusi Buku Agama: Trend Bacaan 1980-an, Cermin Meningkatnya Telaah Keagamaan.* Jakarta: Tempo

Tapol 1987 *Indonesia: Muslims on Trial.* London: Tapol

Thalib, M. tt. *Imamah dan Ummah: Sebuah Telaah Ilmiah.* Yogyakarta: Pustaka LSI

Thalib, Ja'far Umar 1993 *Nabi SAW Memang Pernah Bermuka Masam: Jawaban terhadap Buku: Benarkah Nabi SWA Bermuka Masam? Tafsir Surat Abasa.* 2nd edition. Jakarta: Pustaka Al-Kautsar

Al-Tihrani, Agha Buzurg 1404/1984 *Tabaqat A'lam al-Shi'a*. vol. 1. 3rd edition. Mashhad: Matba'a Sa'id

Turkan, Miqdad "Khumus: Hukum dan Peranannya" (http://aljawad.tripod. com/arsipbuletin/khumus.htm accessed 4/8/2005)

Uthman, Sayyid 1911 *I'anat al-Mustarshidin 'ala Ijtinab al-Bida' fi al-Din*. Batavia

Wahid, Abdurrahman 2000 *Melawan Melalui Lelucon: Kumpulan Kolom Abdurrahman Wahid di Tempo*. Jakarta: Pusat Data dan Analisa Tempo

Al-Walid, Khalid 2004 "Surat dari Imam Al-Mahdi as." *Bahtera: Pemcerahan dan Pemberdayaan* March 2004: 10-16

Watson, C.W. 2005 "Islamic Books and their Publishers: Notes on the Contemporary Indonesian Scene" *Journal of Islamic Studies* 16(2):177-210

Wieringa, Edwin 1996 "Does Traditional Islamic Malay Literature Contain Shiitic Elements? Ali and Fatimah in Malay Hikayat Literature" *Studia Islamika: Indonesian Journal for Islamic Studies* 3 (4): 93-111

Winstedt, Sir Richard 1969 *A History of Classical Malay Literature*. Kuala Lumpur: Oxford University Press

Wisananingrum, Hafsah 2001 *Syi'ah di Kota Bandung 1979-2000*. BA Thesis, Faculty of the Humanities, Gadjah Mada University, Yogyakarta

Woodberry, J. Dudley 1992 "Conversion in Islam" in H. Newton Malony and Samuel Southard (eds) *Handbook of Religious Conversion*. Birmingham, Alabama: religious Education Press, 22-40

Woodward, Mark R. 1996 "Conversations with Abdurrahman Wahid" *Toward New Paradigm: Recent Developments in Indonesian Islamic Thought*. Tempe, Arizona: Arizona State University, Program for Southeast Asian Studies, 133-154

Yamani 2001 *Wasiat Sufi Ayatullah Khomeini: Aspek Sufistik Ayatullah Khomeini Yang Tak Banyak Diketahui*. Bandung: Mizan

-------- 2002 *Antara Al-Farabi dan Khomeini: Filsafat Politik Islam*. Bandung: Mizan

Yayasan Muthahhari 1993 *Yayasan Muthahhari untuk Pencerahan Pemikiran Islam*. Bandung: Yayasan Muthahhari

Yulina, Reina 1997 *Hubungan antara Latihan Berfikir Kritis dalam Metode Quantum Learning dengan Prestasi Siswa SMU (Plus) Muthahhari*. BA Thesis, Faculty of Communications, Universitas Islam. Bandung

Zainuddin, A. Rahman *et al*. 2000 *Syiah dan Politik di Indonesia: Sebuah Penelitian*. Bandung: Mizan dan PPW-LIPI

Zamzami, Abdul Mukmin 1999. *Konsep Pendidikan oleh Ustadz Husein Al-Habsyi*. Dibagikan dalam Rangka Haul ke 6 Al-Marhum Al-Ustadz Husein Al-Habsyi

Zuhri, Saifuddin 1981 *Sejarah Kebangkitan Islam dan Perkembangannya di Indonesia*. 3rd Edition. Bandung: Al-Ma'arif

Zulkifli 2004 "Being a Shi'ite among the Sunni Majority in Indonesia: A Preliminary Study of Ustadz Husein Al-Habsyi (1921-1994)" *Studia Islamika: Indonesian Journal for Islamic Studies* 11 (2): 275-308

-------- 2005 "Seeking Knowledge Unto Qum: The Education of Indonesian Shi'i Ustadhs" *IIAS Newsletter* 38: 30

Magazines, Newspapers, Websites

Aula

Bahtera

Dialog Jumat Republika

Forum Keadilan

Gatra

Hikmah

Islamuna

Al-Isyraq

Al-Jawad

Jawa Pos

Kompas

Koran Tempo

Lombok Post

Media Dakwah

Media Indonesia

Metro

Al-Muslimun

An-Nashr

Pamphlet YAPI

Panji Masyarakat

Pelita

Pembina

Pikiran Rakyat

Republika

Risalah

Suara Ummah

Syi'ar

Al-Tanwir

Tekad

Tempo

Tempo Interaktif

Terbit

Tiras

Ummat

http://www.ijabi.or.id

http://www.fatimah.or.id

http://www.majelisulama.com

http://www.icc-jakarta.com